THE MAKING OF THE MOVIE

By Jonathan Smith

Volume One

RAISE THE TITANIC THE MAKING OF THE MOVIE

© 2022 By Jonathan Smith

All Rights Reserved.

No portion of this publication may be reproduced, stored, and/or copied electronically (except for academic use as a source), nor transmitted in any form or by any means without the prior written permission of the publisher and/or author.

Published in the United States of America by:

BearManor Media
1317 Edgewater Dr #110
Orlando FL 32804
bearmanormedia.com

Printed in the United States.

All photos used with permission.

Typesetting and layout by DataSmith Solutions

Cover by DataSmith Solutions and Jonathan Smith

ISBN — 978-1-62933-871-2

About the Author

Jonathan Smith is a British *Titanic* historian with over 40 years of experience in the field of *Titanic* research and collecting. Over the years he has worked alongside world renown *Titanic* authors, historians and archives. His previously published articles and research papers on the subject of *Titanic* cover varying topics from technical research on the building of the ship to the tragic night the liner went down. He was one of the technical consultants for the acclaimed British television series *Titanic: The Mission* for Channel 4 and National Geographic and has appeared in several documentaries. For the 100th anniversary of the disaster he was one of the advisors and historians on the award-winning live show *Titanic: Minute by Minute* on the BBC. He has also provided material for the BBC collectors series *Flog It!* Other notable works include advisor, technical consultant and interviewee on the documentaries *Titanic: Ready for Launch*, the documentary *A Day to Remember* that covered the historic replica build of *Titanic's* largest anchor and the Working Horses film which included a chapter on *Titanic's* anchors and how they were transported by horse and dray in 1911. More recently he was one of the technical consultants to the model kit manufacturer Trumpeter Models and the release of the world's largest *Titanic* model kit. In 2007 and 2015 he supplied the Special Features section and inner sleeve notes for the UK Network DVD and Blu-ray release of the movie *Raise the Titanic*. In 2021 he became the technical consultant and advisor for the film studio preparing to preserve and restore the remains of the original 55ft Raise the *Titanic* film model. RAISE THE TITANIC: *The Making of the Movie* is his first book on the *Titanic* subject that has been over a decade in the making. He lives with his wife Toni Ann and their English springer spaniel Bella in their home near to the city of Wolverhampton, England.

Acknowledgements

In the preparation of this book I have had the extreme pleasure of assistance from many sources from *Titanic* enthusiasts to those in the film industry. Without their help and support this book would not have come to its full fruition. For that I am eternally indebted to them.

Special gratitude goes to: actor David Selby who was always there to answer my questions and for taking the time to write the foreword for this book; FX legend John Richardson who was an email or phone call away to share his production adventures, tricks of the trade, support for my little book project and for the writing of the shared foreword; to Jeff Herne for his time in assisting with the editing; Jean Pierre Borg for his continued support and who is always there to help; Narcy Calamatta for his many tales from the production time in Malta; Ken Marschall for sharing his fascinating insights of working on the movie mod- el in California and for allowing many of his photographs to be reproduced here for the first time; artists Cyril Codus and Lionel Codus for their exceptional work and who are always there to assist come rain or shine. Geoffrey Mackrill for sharing his collection and stories of working on the production. And to my loving wife Toni Ann for putting up with my *Titanic* obsession and supporting me every step of the way.

I would also like to thank those who came forward to share their own collections, their own stories and their own memories. I apologise in advance if I have left anyone out. In no particular order: Jerry Jameson (director); John DeCuir. Jr (art director); David Harris (special effects); ITV Studios; Walter Winterburn; Simon Mills; Drew Struzan; Rob Burman (Burmans Studio); Doug Llewelyn (Doug Llewelyn Productions); Eugene Nesmeyanov; Stuart Williamson; Nick Stathopoulos; Geoff Leonard; Jon Burlingham; the late Robert Gibbons (*Titanic* historian); Sue Connelly; Gabriel Christopher- Cawood Waters; John Fry; Colin Cook; Steve Hall; Joe Sciberras; Mike Jones; Alan Quale; William Barney; Garth Thomas; Jim Olson; Dan Cherry; Jonathan Scott; the gravediggers of Southby graveyard; Peter Lewis; Elang Erlangga; Andy Tree; Angela Catherine; Tom Haight; Bill Thomas; Capt. Lawrence Dali; Ged Jones; Commodore Ronald Warwick; Mario Hristovski; Teresa Trower; Faye Taylor; Henry Brayshaw; Alan J. Adler; Kellen Butler (President and Director of *Friends of the Hunley, Inc.*); Mike Seares; Patrick Walsh; Selim San; Philip Kiel (President of *Photo-Sonics, Inc.*); Shane Strat- on; Leo Walker; Tom Wedge; Peter Lewis: William Van Dorp; *Marine Photos & Publishing Co*; the late Lawrence Suid; Tony Holt; Tommy Bernard; Kento Gebo (special FX artist); David Harris (special FX artist); the team at Network on Air; James Perkin; the late Steve Rigby (*Titanic* historian); Les Walker; William Brower; David Ashely Bubb; Adam Lively; Terry Moore; Charles Pellegrino; Walter Nones; Mike Branigan; Colten Vanosdale; Sandy Saling; Greg Nicholls; Delinda Peterson; David B. Reeves Cicero; Glen Barker; Alex McDonald; IMDb; Jim Scoular; Senthil Kumar and Ben and the team at BearManor Media for their hard work in bringing to life my dream.

I wish to dedicate this book to my mother and to my late father who was taken from me at such an early period of my life and age. As a child he pushed me to pursue my fascination with *Titanic* that soon became an obsession. Thank you for the childhood memories; the love and the reassurance that life, no matter the challenges, can be rewarding.

And lastly, the late Wayne Velero; fellow *Raise the Titanic* enthusiast, author and founder of the *Clive Cussler Collector's* Society. Wayne's energetic enthusiasm for collecting was second to none and I am proud to personally own some of his collection. I will always be grateful for his support for my book project from the offset. Thank you, Wayne, for everything you did and the memories you have left behind.

Foreword

So much has been written about the *Titanic*, and about many of the people who lost their lives when the great ship hit an iceberg and sank. I was quite young when I first read about the tragedy and about some of those lost lives. It was very emotional. So, when I received a call in 1979 about meeting with a producer for a film called *Raise the Titanic*, I was intrigued but also somewhat perplexed. Did they really intend to raise the *Titanic*? And why? Why disturb the final resting place for so many? Was this a treasure hunt? Whatever, I was pleased that day to receive an offer to do the film. My friend, the wonderful Jason Robards, encouraged me to do the film. "They are going to take us around the world." Perhaps not the best reason to commit to something but I was all for it. I had not seen a script but if Jason was involved, that was all I needed.

It all happened very fast. Before I knew it, I was trying to fall asleep in my bunk bed on board a huge Navy ship out in the Pacific Ocean. Early that morning, I had my first helicopter ride. We took off from the ship's deck, made a few circles and then re-landed. It was my character's arrival. Soon after I watched fellow actor, J.D. Cannon being put, several stories below deck, into a small dingy, dangling in the sea along-side our enormous ship. It seemed J.D. was stranded in the tiny dingy and, after a while, nobody blamed him for making a mild complaint. Before I knew it, I was holding on in an inflatable boat emerging from the well of the ship. It was manned by two terrific members of the Navy Seals. They told me not to worry... "We won't let anything happen to you!"

Out at sea, I was instructed to climb into a two-man submersible about to dive down into the Pacific Ocean. The hatch was closed and down we went for a nice ride. When we resurfaced, the hatch was opened and I started to climb out of my cramped space, but was greeted by a helicopter whirling loud overhead, it's spinning blades stirring up the ocean so that it was quite difficult to climb out and jump back into the inflatable boat. Apparently, the camera crew was also surprised by the force of the whirling helicopter's blades and was unable to get the shot. So, back into the submersible and down we went. That take was successful. The Navy seals took very good care of this actor, as indeed did the producers, director, and crew.

The film had gotten off to a rough start when the original director quit, but Jerry Jameson was hired and he pulled together a great team including Matt Leonetti, the director of photography. With Jerry at the helm, the production was off and running. The challenges were great, but the spirit and commitment remained high to the end of filming. Months later, we even welcomed a return trip to Cornwall to refilm the cemetery scene where some passengers of the *Titanic* are buried. It is a beautiful site, but the fate of those and the other victims of the *Titanic* were always with the cast and crew. When I finally got to see the finished film, I found the scene where the *Titanic* is raised to the surface accompanied by John Barry's wonderful music to be extremely moving, and a fitting tribute to those who lost their lives. I also have been quite moved by Jonathan's life-long passion and devotion to the *Titanic* story and of the resulting film, *Raise the Titanic*, which captured a young man's imagination culminating in the book you are about to read.

David Selby

Jonathan first contacted me some years ago to talk about my involvement in the film *Raise the Titanic*. Talking to him about the filming brought back many memories for me not just about the hard and challenging task of filming underwater and raising a 55' long model that weighed 10 tons up from the depths of our 36' deep filming tank but also the extravagant and often needless costs that surrounded the movie. It also did not take long for Jonathan's infectious obsession to rub off on me. I know that he was introduced to tales about the *Titanic* when he was very young by his father and a neighbour who had been a diver in the Royal Navy. Their discussions over the garden fence often touched on a wish to find the wreck and maybe even salvage it.

Jonathan was taken to see the film when it was first released and it firmly embedded itself in his imagination probably mostly due to the raising sequence and the wonderful theme music written by the great John Barry. Jonathan's father sadly passed away when he was only 12, but before he passed, he convinced him that he should always follow his passion regardless of other people and to ignore his school friends who mocked him for his "morbid" interest. This passion has lasted for many years, following the eventual discovery of the great ship and the trips that Jim Cameron the film director made filming underwater in 3D. Jonathan has amassed a vast collection of newspaper and magazine articles along with stories from those of us who worked on the film. One thing that has impressed me the most is Jonathan's appreciation of the way that we filmed the picture all those years ago. The reality of shooting with real models in a real underwater environment has given the film a quality that as Jonathan's says is far better than one would attain with CGI, which as good as it is it cannot match the nuances of filming in camera.

Jonathan's book really is a lifetime's work and I cannot wait to read it myself; I know that it will be the definitive work on the film and how it was made and interestingly it will cover why the film was not well received at the box office. It will also, I am sure, be an homage to his father who first instilled in him an interest in a wonderful ship which was a marvel of its time and the great interest and following it has had over the years covering the search and the eventual discovery of the wreck over 12,000 feet down in the Atlantic Ocean.

John Richardson

Introduction

Why Raise the Titanic? That question has been put my way more times for as long as I care to remember. The subject of *Titanic* is that of a global phenomenon captivating much of the public's imagination long before James Cameron's multi award-winning film hit cinema screens during the winter of late 1997. To bring the story of *Titanic*'s tragic demise to the masses in a new way was a rarity and one such author had the foresight to do just that in a unique and compelling way. In 1976 American adventure writer Clive Cussler took hold of *Titanic*'s enduring legacy and created a completely bold new story, a fictional one, that oozed future possibilities of realism on the efforts to not only find the wreck of the doomed liner but also to bring her rusting hulk back to sunlight. *Raise the Titanic* was an international success for Cussler and the intriguing story not only ceased the imagination of the public but also the attention of the film makers. As a young boy growing up in the landlocked West Midlands in the United Kingdom, I became familiar with my region's connection to the sea and of course *Titanic* from the history of manufactures who supplied to these historic ships. But it was the story of *Titanic* that intrigued me from the very start. Why a ship claimed to be "unsinkable" by her owners would founder with such a great loss of life after striking an iceberg was something that even Lieutenant Columbo would find hard to explain. This mystery alone was enough to keep my young mind busy for the decades to follow.

In the latter part of the 1970s I read in the press that a popular British television mogul, Sir Lew Grade, was to bring Clive Cussler's novel to the big screen in an epic multi-million-dollar movie adaptation. I was instantly curious to know how this would be done. What would *Titanic* look like after all those years on the bottom of the ocean? How were they going to raise her? My late father, knowing of my interest in *Titanic*, would collect various cuttings from newspapers and magazines and hand them onto me so to build up my collection in a large scrapbook. *Raise the Titanic* was already being lapped up by the media who delighted in publishing varying news articles on the movie, the actors, the lavish cost of the production and of course the star of the film; the *Titanic*.

The film was scheduled for a release during the summer of 1980 and with this in mind the media brought together another *Titanic* story as it followed the preparations by Texas oil tycoon Jack Grimm who had announced to the world that he had selected a team of experts who were planning on sailing out to *Titanic*'s last known reported location in search of the actual wreckage with the idea of showing to the world the photographs and video evidence of the liners final resting place. *Titanic* fever had now gripped the world once again and for me as a child this was like all my birthdays coming together at once. The year of 1980 was shaping up to be, as the media would label it, "The Year of the Titanic", and was becoming an extremely memorable part of my young life and one I would never forget. Summer came and went and so did the hopes of Jack Grimm who failed to find the wreck. Mother nature was not on his side and neither were the press who turned their attention to criticizing his expedition failure while mocking his previous other equally failed dreams to find mythical entities such as the Loch Ness monster, Bigfoot and the fabled remains of Noah's Ark. And with the film *Raise the Titanic* now running well over budget and behind schedule the subject of *Titanic* began to turn with much negativity courtesy of the press. While it showed that *Titanic* was beginning to fall out of favour with the media, would this be the case with the general public? By August 1980 the movie had hit the theatre screens in the

United States and the critic's verdict on the movie was not good. But I did not care. Then in December my turn came to watch the film.

More than forty years have now passed since *Raise the Titanic* hit the cinema screens and I still remember to this very day the shear excitement I had waiting in line with my parents to go in, to sit down and watch that film in awe. December 1980 still seems like only yesterday for me and my passion for the film has never waned. I still watch the movie on a regular basis as I not only still enjoy it for what it is but more importantly for the nostalgic trip back in time to when I was ten years of age sitting in that seat at the cinema and looking up at the huge screen and seeing *Titanic*, rusty, covered in mud and sand, bursting up out of the water to the beautiful score by John Barry. In real life the wreck of the *Titanic* sits over two miles down beneath the cold bleak waters of the North Atlantic, broken, twisted and collapsing. And there she will remain for all eternity. But it was through the startling imagination of fiction penned by one man combined by the world of movie magic where fact and fiction clashed in a visual feast on celluloid for the big screen. *Raise the Titanic* shares a special place in my heart for many reasons. It was my first big screen outing of a *Titanic* movie. It also takes me back to my childhood of innocent times and those times before I lost my father to cancer when I was 12 years old. But *Raise the Titanic* became more than just a film for me. It became a collective memory consisting of good times, of the sad times, but essentially a way for me to remember a time in my life I will never see again but can remember with such detail because of this film, much like a song can connect you to the past or to a certain part of your life. And since 1979 that scrapbook has blossomed into a collection of newspaper cuttings, magazines articles, press kits, countless publicity and behind the scenes photographs, props, storyboards and endless stories of which some will be found amidst the pages of this very book.

I come back to that question once again. *Why Raise the Titanic?* The film is generally looked upon as a production failure and that of a symbol on how *not* to create a movie both by critics and moviegoers alike. But are their refutations justified? Hopefully this book will not only be beneficial for fans who want to learn more about their favourite movie but answer some of the questions for those who were critical towards the production and those new to the film. And further more I hope my book will not only reveal many new stories but will also offer new and exciting insights and lay to rest many of the myths that have built up over the years. This making of book is an accumulation of decades of work on a film that is largely ignored and brought together as a complete volume outlining the movies conception right through to how the impossible was made possible making this work not only the first of its kind but also the most definitive making of collective on the movie *Raise the Titanic*. Closing this introduction, I would like to quote from the movies original poster tagline which I feel is appropriate and acquaint the reader on the journey they are about to follow.

First, they said God himself couldn't sink her.
Then they said no man on earth could reach her.
Now - you will be there as we…

Contents

About the Author V
Acknowledgements VII
Foreword IX
Introduction XI

Volume 1

Chapter 1	Cinematic *Titanic*	1
Chapter 2	Mr Entertainment	49
Chapter 3	The Grandmaster of Adventure	63
Chapter 4	Two Directors	87
Chapter 5	Preproduction Begins	105
Chapter 6	The Building of a Legend	125
Chapter 7	Salvage Fleet	175
Chapter 8	Mediterranean Film Facility	227
Chapter 9	Casting the Characters	287
Chapter 10	Rewriting History	305
Chapter 11	Doomed from the Start	311
Chapter 12	Cold War Interference	363
Chapter 13	The Mediterranean Caper	377
Chapter 14	The Other *Titanic*	409

Bibliography 491

CHAPTER 1

Cinematic *Titanic*

"I name this ship Titanic. May God bless her and all who sail in her."

A Night to Remember

What else could possibly be written about the night the *Titanic* went down? In the annals of history, there have been many specific historic dates that are now set in stone such as the end of World War Two, the fall of the Berlin Wall, or the terrifying events of 11 September 2001. The sinking of the *Titanic* in the early hours of Monday, April 15, 1912, is just one such key event that left a significant mark on history and changed the course of marine laws for the better. The list of written works on *Titanic* is staggering beyond belief. Her tragic demise has captured the public's imagination since the news broke of her sinking and confirmed in the press the loss of nearly 1,500 souls. In modern times *Titanic* is well known to the next generation of enthusiasts following on from the release of James Cameron's blockbuster *'Titanic'* in December 1997. At the time no one, not even James Cameron, could have predicted just how successful his movie would become. Although *Titanic* has been given the big-screen treatment many times before, James Cameron had the perfect ingredient to add into the *Titanic* folklore with a love story with the ship acting as the backdrop. And while tens of millions around the world flocked to watch a film with a story everyone knew the outcome of, it did not stop people of all ages from going back to view the movie time and time again.

Once more the subject of *Titanic* had captured the publics imagination as the film went on to win an incredible 11 Academy Awards and to become the largest grossing movie of its time. And yet in the early days of production, the movie did not go without its fair share of criticism as filming issues resulted in delays in the production that began to echo the old days of problems during 1979 and 1980 with *Raise the Titanic*. Many must have thought yet another disaster of a movie was on the cards. The film's box office opening weekend proved otherwise and this disaster epic went on to sail into movie history. *Titanic* has always been the topic for big-screen storytelling and while today both James Cameron's *'Titanic'* and William MacQuitty's 1958 movie adaptation of Walter Lord's best-selling novel *A Night to Remember,* are cherished among *Titanic* enthusiasts as the defining *Titanic* movies, the latter being largely regarded as the definitive retelling of the disaster, the real-life events of April 1912 have appeared on-screen under varying incarnations.

Queen of the Ocean

The Royal Mail Steamship *Titanic* was designed to operate for the White Star Line as part of a trio of passenger liners for the lucrative Southampton to New York trade, via Cherbourg in France and Queenstown in Ireland,. Once completed, *Titanic* would join her older sister *Olympic* and later joined by the third of the Olympic-class fleet, *Britannic,* which was still under construction in Belfast. *Titanic* was built alongside *Olympic* at the world-famous Harland & Wolff shipbuilders located at the Queens Island yards in Belfast, Northern Ireland. Her keel was laid down on slipway No.3 on the 31st of March 1909 as yard build number 401. To ease pressure on the workshops at the yard, both *Olympic* and *Titanic*'s construction had a lapse of six months between them as hull frames, hull plating, and many other hull components were crafted. *Titanic* was designed to represent the finest in shipbuilding technologies of Great Britain during the Edwardian period, leading to financial gain for her owners and the ultimate in luxury for her passengers.

In October 1910, the White Star Line proclaimed in print that both the ships were constructed in such a way, that with the simple flick of a switch, the closure of the hulls watertight door systems would render both vessels unsinkable. This brazen terminology would eventually go on to haunt her owners for years to follow. *Titanic* was made ready for launch on 31 May 1911 as over one-hundred-thousand spectators lined the embankments of the river Lagan. The 24,000-ton hull of *Titanic* took only 62 seconds from the time she started to move from the slipway to coming to a stop assisted by tons of drag chains in the oily waters of the river. Moments later she was pulled to the fitting out quay where she would undergo ten months of interior and power plant installations as she received her boilers, engines, towering masts and funnels, and some of the finest interiors, matching many of the large stately homes and establishments that defined the rich and the privileged of modern-day society.

Titanic was every part the titan. At the time of her entry into service, she was 882ft. 9in (269.1m) in length, 92ft. 6in (28.2m) at her widest beam, 175ft (53.3m) from her keel to the top of her funnels, and 46,328 gross registered tonnage, making her not only the largest passenger liner in 1912 but the world's largest man-made movable object. Her funnels were large enough in diameter to allow passage of a steam locomotive, while her largest anchor weighed an impressive 15.5 tons and took a team of twenty Clydesdale horses with a haulage dray to transport it to the shipyards. At her stern was her gigantic steel rudder that weighed 101 tons and towered 78ft. 8in. in height. Her immense hull could be pushed along at a steady speed of 21 knots with an estimated top speed of 24 knots (27mph). Her 29 boilers, 24 double-ended and 5 single-ended, had a combined total of 159 furnaces where 176 firemen fed the boilers an estimated 650 tons of coal by hand over a 24-hour period. Her outer manganese-bronze, three-bladed propellers had a diameter of 23ft. 5in. (7.2m) and were propelled by a pair of four-cylinder, triple-expansion reciprocating steam engines that had a combined weight of 915 tons and produced a combined 30,000hp. Her solid manganese-bronze centre propeller of 16ft. 6in. (5.1m) was powered by a low-pressure forward-directional only steam turbine producing 16,000 shaft-horse power at 165 revolutions per minute. Her power plants produced an output of 100 volts via four sets of 400-kilowatt dynamos creating 4,000 amps and a total combined capacity of 16,000 amps collectively. Over 2,000 steel plates were used in her construction and a staggering three million wrought iron rivets were driven into her hull, both by hand and, where required, with the use of hydraulic rivet machines,hher . She was a floating city of steel, wood, and glass. She soon became a symbol of modern engineering and that of the greatest of the works of man.

Titanic was as beautiful inside as she was externally. Her luxurious interiors offered the best that money could buy with sweeping solid oak and wrought iron grand staircases topped off with elegant decorative domes. First Class passengers could dine in style in either the elegant Louis Seize period surroundings of the à la carte restaurant or the Jacobean splendour of the 532-seater Dining Saloon. Rich mahogany and mother-of-pearl inlays were to be found in the Smoking Room while the beautiful Louis Quinze style Lounge was inspired by the Palace at Versailles. For pleasure, passengers could take in the sea air by either strolling along the boat deck or the enclosed 500ft. long A-deck promenades that were screened off towards the bow for comfort or the open section towards the stern for those more eager to enjoy the gentle breeze blowing in off the sea. Beneath the second funnel on the boat deck passengers could gather to socialize or try their hand at the various appliances in the gymnasium by taking to the rowing machines, exercise bicycles, ceiling-mounted punch ball, or the electric horses made to simulate riding a horse.

Out on deck, they could participate in deck games such as shuffleboard, deck quoits, sack races, egg and spoon races, or the set of swings attached to the awning bar on the rear mast. Other luxuries to be had were a plunge in the ship's heated swimming bath, maybe a game or two in the squash court, to end the day being pampered by stewards in the Turkish Bath and Cooling Rooms, or relaxing in a deck chair out on the deck with a book as a steward brings you your favourite hot or cold beverage at your call. Second Class and Third Class were not left out. For Second Class passengers they could browse the books in the Adams-style library or relax in the Louis XVI smoking room and dine in the 17th century period styling of the dining room. Out on deck, they had two areas of spacious promenades from that of the aft end of the boat deck or the enclosed section of the promenade on C-deck. Third Class on *Olympic* and *Titanic* was a great improvement compared to other passenger liners of the time. With ales and stout on tap along with bottled beers, a lively time could be had any time of the day or night as passengers made their own entertainment in the general room or smoking room with music and songs from instruments they brought onboard themselves or take to the upright Steinway piano that graced the room. Third Class had plenty of deck space on offer from the forward and aft well decks to the raised poop deck on the stern that gave an almost uninterrupted view out to sea. When fully accommodated *Titanic* could carry 2,435 passengers and a crew of 892.

Titanic went ahead with her sea trials on Tuesday 2 April 1912 where the liner went through a series of tests and manoeuvres out in Belfast Lough and the open waters off Ireland under the watchful eye of the inspectors from the British Board of Trade. Satisfied with the *Titanic*'s appointments and handling, the Board of Trade passed and certificated her for 12 months from that date making her now ready to be handed over to her owners; the White Star Line. Later that evening she made her way out of Belfast for the trip to Southampton where she arrived on high tide just after midnight on Thursday 4 April where tugs assisted her into berth No.44 of the White Star Line dock. The next six days would see the new liner prepared for the maiden voyage as over 5,000 tons of coal was loaded by hand from coaling barges and dumped down chutes into the coal bunkers below. Vast tons of cargo was loaded into her holds including copious amounts of food, thousands of bottles of wines, beers, ales, and stouts including 63 cases of Champagne, 1,196 bags of potatoes, 300 cases of shelled walnuts, 76 cases of dragon's blood which was a sap extracted from palm trees in the Canary Islands, and, crated up and lowered into her hold, was a brand new and expensive 25hp Renault automobile.

Sailing day was 10 April and the first people to come aboard were crew at 5:18 A.M. later joined by *Titanic*'s builder Thomas Andrews who was head of a team of crew known as the "guarantee group" put on board especially for the liner's maiden voyage so to monitor the operation of the vessel on her first Transatlantic trip. At 7:30 A.M. the 62-year-old Edward John Smith came aboard. His officers having already spent the night on board the ship. Captain Smith was a highly experienced master and earned the nickname as the "Millionaires Captain" largely down to the large vessels he commanded and the clientele who booked passage to say they had sailed with him in charge. By 11:30 A.M. passengers were now making their way on board to be guided to their cabins by the ship's crew. But not all had such luxury as some Second Class and mainly Third Class were left to their own devices to find their accommodations. A short while later at 12:15 P.M. with the Southampton harbour pilot on board, *Titanic* blew her steam whistles as tug boats pulled at the liner to move her away from her berth and out into Southampton Water. With passengers waving down at those on the quayside and the toots and whistles from the little tug boats occasionally drowned out by *Titanic*'s booming call, it marked that her maiden voyage had now begun. Excitement quickly mounted moments later when *Titanic* passed two vessels that were secured to the quayside. Her immense size and close proximity to the two vessels created a suction within the water that pulled the two ships towards *Titanic*. The American Line's S.S. *New York* broke her mooring lines and, caught in the suction, her stern was swung around into the departing path of *Titanic*.

The quick thinking of Captain Smith giving the order to stop saved both *Titanic* and the *New York* from making contact with each other. But for some onboard, those of a more superstitious disposition, this incident was looked upon as a bad omen.

Titanic resumed her voyage to drop the pilot off near Cowes by the Isle of Wight where she headed out into the deeper waters of the English Channel to arrive in the Grande Rade of Cherbourg harbour at 6:30 P.M. where the two White Star Line tenders *Nomadic* and *Traffic* transported passengers and mail from the quayside out to the new ship. Just after 8 P.M. *Titanic* was now steaming away from the French coastline for her overnight journey to Queenstown, renamed as Cobh in 1920, on the south coast of County Cork. *Titanic* arrived in Ireland at 11:30 A.M. on 11 April where she dropped anchor off Roches Point lighthouse. Like Cherbourg, Cork harbour was not deep enough to allow such large liners to come in close to Queenstown. And so, the passengers and mail were ferried from the White Star Line quay by the steamers *America* and *Ireland* and out to the liners in the deeper waters. Following the exchange of mails and disembarking passengers, *Titanic* weighed anchor for the last time and turned her bows away from the Irish coast at 1:40 P.M. and headed out past the headlands and out into the cold waters of the Celtic Sea. Beyond lay the relentless waters of the North Atlantic Ocean. Her final port of call was New York some 2,700 nautical miles away where *Titanic* was due to arrive at the White Star Line Pier 59 during the early morning hours of Wednesday 17 April. Onboard were a total of 2,208 passengers and crew.

The next couple of days at sea were uneventful. Passengers settled down to on-board activities as the crew of *Titanic* built up the miles with the new liner. She was responding remarkably well for a new ship with the exceptions of teething problems such as heating issues in some cabins where passengers commented on how cold they were and, in other cases, to how uncomfortably hot they were. Her first full day at sea on 12 April had *Titanic* average 21.2 knots covering 484 nautical miles in the first 24 hours. On Saturday ,this had increased to 519 nautical miles at an average running speed of 20.91 knots. It was during those dates when the two Marconi operators, John Phillips and Harold Bride, began to receive ice warnings from steamers hundreds of miles ahead of them out in the Atlantic. The warnings were acknowledged as per common practice. It was during the 13th when complications arose with the Marconi radio equipment that resulted in the radio system malfunctioning and going off-air. Normal procedures for the employed operators of the Marconi Company were to not carry out any repairs and to wait until the vessel arrived in port for the fault to be reported and an experienced employee of the Marconi Company came to repair the equipment. However, John Phillips had concluded he knew what the fault was, and, with the assistance of Bride, they disassembled the unit, found the break in the coil causing the issues, and repaired it.

By Sunday morning of April 14, the radio was now up and running as the two operators tried to settle back down into a routine of not only sending out passenger messages but also receiving those which were now delayed. One such message of importance indicated much ice ahead of the *Titanic*. falling sea temperatures, it revealed that the liner would soon be among the ice. As night fell, orders were given to the bridge officers to keep a sharp lookout for potential ice, with the order passed onto the lookouts that were the eyes of the ship high up in the crows nest. By 10:30 P.M. the temperatures had dropped dramatically, forcing many passengers walking the open decks back inside to the warmth of the vessel. After 11 P.M. stewards began turning off lighting in some communal areas to encourage passengers to go to their cabins and turn in for the night.

At 11.40 P.M. and high up in the crow's nest, lookouts Frederick Fleet and Reginald Lee fought the biting cold of the night. They only had twenty more minutes until they were relieved at midnight by the next pair of lookouts. The evening was icy cold. The sky was cloudless and blanketed with stars. That night there was a new moon. The sea was eerily flat as a pond. Suddenly Fleet spots something amiss right ahead of *Titanic*. The sky that was littered with stars was suddenly without them in one particular spot. With no navigational lights seen the object showed no sign of being another vessel. It could only be one thing. Fleet quickly pulled the chord of the crow's nest bell as three heavy clangs pierced the otherwise silent night. He immediately lifted the telephone, which connected him directly to the bridge. Sixth Officer James Moody answered the call with a simple "what do you see?" Fleet called aloud "Iceberg, right ahead!" Moody relayed the call to First Officer William Murdoch who rushed out onto

Titanic's bridge wing. Calculating in such a short space of time, Murdoch gave the order to the Quartermaster to turn *Titanic* to port with the hope of avoiding any impact with the object. But *Titanic* was too close to the iceberg and both made contact. At first, it was thought the hull had cleared the side of the huge wall of ice. But down below, in the forward holds and boiler room No.6, it was a different story as riveted seams ruptured as the mass of ice pushed against the ships steel plates compromising five of the watertight compartments. As water entered in such great volume through the many breached compartments the crew now faced the possibilities of losing the ship.

Upon the request of Captain Smith, Thomas Andrews went below decks to inspect the flooding. He concluded that *Titanic* was doomed and only had sixty to ninety minutes to stay afloat. Crews quickly set to work in uncovering the lifeboats, to fill them with provisions and swing them out level with the boat deck for passengers to be guided into them. With *Titanic*'s apparent safety systems incorporated into her construction, along with her older sister *Olympic,* it was deemed that no serious accident could occur to such a liner like *Titanic* that would result in the lifeboats being used other than to ferry passengers and crew from a stricken vessel over the short distance to the safety of another ship. One other factor of consequences with the lifeboats was that the British Board of Trade's very own regulations on such craft were grossly outdated at the time of the construction of *Titanic,* meaning that the 46,328-ton liner was to enter service with the same lifeboat capacity of a 16,000-ton vessel. As larger vessels were built and their passenger and crew accommodations increased, the rules and regulations regarding lifeboat capacity was never updated to meet the needs of the shipping. During the latter stages of *Titanic*'s construction, the Board of Trade's regulations mandated that only 16 lifeboats were required by maritime law for *Titanic*. White Star Line did not agree with this number, along with the builders Harland & Wolff, who supplied *Titanic* and her sister *Olympic* with lifeboat davits that could work with two lifeboats per davit set. The Board of Trade refused and *Titanic* was approved with just 16 lifeboats. White Star Line formerly went against the decision by having additional four lifeboats of a collapsible type supplied raising the total to that of 20 lifeboats with a new holding capacity of 1,178 persons.

At first, passengers refused to think that anything was wrong with *Titanic*. The idea of being awoken late at night, told to dress warmly and proceed to the boat deck with lifejackets in hand was not entertaining, as many scoffed at the idea that the "unsinkable" *Titanic* was in any danger. But as passengers gathered on deck and the first of the distress rockets exploded in the clear night sky above the ship, the seriousness of the situation soon began to dawn. Some lifeboats were lowered and sent away from the ship's side partially filled. One left with just 13 people on board when it was built to hold 45 persons. But as the gravity of the situation became more evident the lifeboats were being filled with some even leaving the sinking ship and exceeding the required capacity and weight restrictions. Captain Smith realized that help was still hours away and that *Titanic* had just a short space of time left before she slipped beneath the waves. After 2 A.M. the power began to fade and the ship's lights dimmed with an eerie deep orange hue. As survivors in lifeboats watched on in horror, *Titanic* slowly lifted her stern clear of the water to reveal her propellers with a chorus of heavy sustained creaking, loud pops, and deep rumblings.

At 2:16 A.M. *Titanic* sudden downwards plunge as the flooding overtook the vessel. Her bow vanished beneath the cold waters of the Atlantic and a wall of water came rushing up onto the boat deck. A series of loud reports sounded across the water as the cables that stabilised the huge forward funnel gave way. The funnel unseated itself and toppled forwards, smashing down onto the bridge before rolling off to the port side and into the water to sink from sight. A minute later the lights began to flicker, go out, come back on again, then become extinguished for good. *Titanic*, now a huge black silhouette outlined by the stars of the clear sky, groaned and creaked before emitting a thunderous report as the hull collapsed at the base of the third funnel splitting the liner into sections consisting of the bow and stern. As the stern settled back the bow pulled away to vanish beneath the surface. As it did so it pulled the stern back up sending the severed hull section twisting to port, capsizing and ditching everything loose into the sea to then vanish from sight with a series of thuds and booms. Onboard there still remained over 1,000 helpless people. The time was 2:20 A.M. April 15, 1912. A muttered voice from one of the lifeboats broke the sombre night air. "she's gone!

Dotted around the area were the lifeboats and their dazed and frightened occupants. Large quantities of debris that was forced out of the ship as she broke apart littered the water. The air was full of the cries of help from those who had been ditched into the frigid clutches of the North Atlantic. As the minutes passed so did those who succumb to the –2 freezing temperatures. By the time the lifeboats had been mustered together with one freed up to look for survivors, it was all too late as 1,496 men, women and children had perished in the disaster. Just before 4 A.M., a light was seen on the horizon. Hope was coming. Salvation was in the form of the 13,556-ton Cunard Line passenger liner R.M.S. *Carpathia* who had picked up *Titanic*'s radio distress calls and her master, Captain Arthur Rostron, immediately turning his vessel around and raced at full steam the 58 nautical miles to the disaster area. As the liner was greeted by icebergs and much pack ice, the early rays of the Monday morning sun began to reveal a number of lifeboats emerging from the haze, the occupants shouting, the sounds of oars clashing. *Carpathia* must have been an angel with her glaring lights, her hull doors open, teams of crew members huddled around the ship's railings and her lifeboats swung out ready to help. Slowly she came to a stop to reveal crew who had lowered rope ladders down the side of the hull and makeshift slings to help up any of the wounded. Cold, frightened, bewildered and grieving, one by one the survivors made their way up the rope ladders to the safety of the *Carpathia*'s deck and the welcoming arms of her the crew.

Joseph Boxhall, *Titanic*'s surviving Fourth Officer, made his way to the bridge to see Captain Rostron. With much emotion, he confirmed that *Titanic* had gone down at around 2:20 A.M. taking hundreds of people with her. Just after 8 A.M., the *Carpathia* was joined at the scene by the 6,223-ton Leyland Line steamer *Californian* which had stopped during the night after being surrounded by icebergs just over 10 nautical miles from *Titanic*'s position. Her master, Captain Stanley Lord, offered assistance and joined in one last search with the *Carpathia* of the area looking for more survivors. *Carpathia* left the scene of the disaster around 9 A.M. as the last survivors came aboard. As her crew secured several recovered lifeboats down on deck, *Carpathia* turned and steamed back towards America where she would arrive at the Cunard Pier in New York on the rainy evening of Wednesday 17 April carrying just 712 survivors *Titanic* survivors.

A couple of days following the sinking, inquiries into the disaster began to reveal the events leading up to the tragic first and last voyage of the R.M.S. *Titanic*. Her sinking created a turning point in Edwardian society as social divides came under scrutiny. Shipping companies and their owners were forced to update their safety equipment. This also included the British Board of Trade who reviewed their outdated regulations on lifeboats which at the time of the sinking of *Titanic* was nearly five decades out of date. From the loss of *Titanic* also came many changes in safety at sea including more lifeboats with more than enough capacity for every person on board. And a year later in 1913, the International Ice Patrol was conceived to watch over icebergs and ice flows that drift into shipping lanes that could become a threat to shipping. From the seeds of disaster, there grew a remarkable phenomenon as the story of *Titanic* gripped the public's fascination. It was not long until her tragic demise would be put to the big screen as Hollywood gave the disaster a cinematic retelling that was to captivate audiences of all ages for decades to come..

Early Days of *Titanic* on Film

Titanic on celluloid can be dated back to 1909 when during the construction of her older sister, *Olympic*, *Titanic* made a very brief film appearance. Their construction caught the attention of many. Not only were they documented in photographic form for publications such as *The Shipbuilder* and *Engineering* magazines, but those in the film industry to capture on film the workings of shipyards that specified in building these mammoth vessels. So confident was White Star Line with modern shipbuilding that when they published their own pamphlet in October 1910 covering the construction of both *Olympic* and *Titanic*, they boasted, "as far as it is possible to do so, these two wonderful vessels are designed to be unsinkable." As the hull of *Olympic* neared completion on slipway No.2, a film crew from the Kineto company catalogued stages of her construction. On one particular day at the yard during the summer of 1910, they filmed scores of Harland & Wolff platers and riveters as they poured down the gangways on either side of the hull after a full day's work. As the camera is cranked over to the left it stops at slipway No.3 to show the steel framework of *Titanic* rising up from the gantry floor. This all too brief footage would become the very first moving film of *Titanic* until February of 1912 when the liner was again filmed being slowly manoeuvred into the confides of the Thompson Graving Dock in Belfast for her first drydocking during the fitting out process. This and the other clips of the footage, just a matter of seconds in length, are the only known pieces of moving footage to exist of *Titanic*. Traditional to *Titanic* folklore, there are stories that footage exists of the liner being launched on May 31, 1911, along with film captured at the berth 44 of the White Star Line dock in Southampton during her departure at noon on April 10, 1912. While these two cases could be looked upon as being mere rumours, one may be true, that being the launch footage which was thought to have been documented by a German film agency brought over to record the event. But as no copies are known to exist the story remains just that; a story. But maybe one day somewhere a rusty metal canister will be discovered with its contents of a reel of film and upon it the long-lost footage of *Titanic* in all her majesty. Until then we can enjoy the many incarnations of *Titanic*'s enduring legacy that were put to film from the grainy footage of *In Night und Eis*, the only surviving *Titanic* movie from 1912, right up to James Cameron's blockbuster from 1997.

But what about those films that drew in audiences around the world that were released weeks following the sinking? Theatre's seized upon the moment to profiteer from the disaster with newsreels wrongly, and purposely, screening short films showing the disaster in moving images. While audiences flocked to the theatres to view these varying stories of *Titanic* in words and pictures in the form of newsreels, many of them were edited footage of *Olympic* leaving New York in the summer of 1911 for her return maiden voyage trip back to Southampton. But for many theatre owners, the topic of the world's greatest maritime disaster was too good a money-making opportunity to ignore. The first proper film on the *Titanic* disaster was produced by the Éclair Film Company in the U.S.A and was put on 660ft of film reel in May 1912. Titled *Saved from the Titanic,* it was a fictional story written by and starring one of *Titanic*'s actual survivors, actress Dorothy Gibson, who had boarded the liner at Cherbourg to travel First Class. The whereabouts of this film are largely unknown with speculations that a copy may have survived to this day. In 1912 the Continental-Kunstfilm of Berlin produced *In Night und Eis* (*In Night and Ice*) and with a running time of 30-minutes it was considered to be the first proper *Titanic* movie to show to audiences the disaster that befell the great liner. The film was thought to be lost until early 1998 when the German film archivist Horst Lange came forward with a print of the complete film.

The story of *Titanic* was to surface again in 1929 with the production of the British International Pictures *Atlantic* that was also co-released with Süd Film Company of Germany. Regarded as Britain's first talkie movie, *Atlantic* followed the story of a large ocean liner that collides with an iceberg and sinks. While not directly associated with *Titanic*, certainly not by name, the White Star Line thought otherwise and contacted the film studios in Elstree to stop production. The reply received was that filming was now too far advanced. But they did argue their corner claiming that *Atlantic*, while not being directly connected to *Titanic*, was a nod towards the disaster but more importantly based on the play *The Berg*. In 1943 it was Germany's turn again to turn their attention in bringing the loss of *Titanic* to the big screen; albeit in a very controversial way. With war raging across Europe the topic of *Titanic* became a propaganda tool when a film was commissioned by the Nazi Propaganda Minister Joseph Goebbels to not just show off the superior quality of German film making but also to cement the superior quality of Germany's political hold on the world during the onslaught of World War Two. One key aspect of the film was to inflame tensions between countries by using Nazi propaganda to win over the German public by ridiculing both English and American capitalism. While British officers flock to save themselves, it is the German officers who rise to become the heroes of the story. 'Titanic' had its premiere in November 1943 to a Nazi-occupied Paris. But with British retaliation bombing raids being conducted across Germany it forced Goebbels to pull the film for a later screening that never materialised. It was rediscovered in 1949 to be subsequently banned across many western countries. In 1992 a censored version was released to VHS in Germany but in 2005 the film was finally restored and the uncensored version was put to disc through the Kino Video catalogue.

Titanic Sails into Hollywood

With the war over and Hollywood booming, the story of *Titanic* was given the big-budget treatment when Twentieth Century Fox brought to the screen their adaptation of the disaster. Their lavish production of '*Titanic*' had its premiere in Virginia, U.S.A on April 11, 1953. With its all-star cast of Barbara Stanwyck, Robert Wagner and Clifton Webb, who, coincidentally, had sailed on board *Titanic*'s sister *Olympic* during the 1920s, the production was to be the first of two major movies for that decade. While the main point of the movie was focused upon the fictional characters of Richard and Julia Sturges fighting over the custody of their son and daughter, there is no denying that the back drop of the story kick-started the 1950s trend in bringing the doomed liner to a larger audience. The film certainly left a mark with the public as it went on to snap up the Academy Award for Best Writing, Story and Screenplay. With *Titanic* fever now raging, author and long-time shipping enthusiast, Walter Lord, penned his bestselling 1955 novel *A Night to Remember* which retold the night of the sinking based around a number of survivor accounts retold to him. From his completed work a big-screen adaptation was to follow in what would eventually become the most iconic *Titanic* movie of all time. In 1958 the Rank Organisation released the Golden Globe-winning *A Night to Remember* which drew in audiences from around the world. Created in a black and white docu-drama style, *A Night to Remember* is regarded today as the definitive *Titanic* movie and one endorsed by many *Titanic* scholars. The years that followed had *Titanic*'s story retold time and time again through newspapers, magazines and the occasional cameo appearance in a film or television programme.

It was not until September 1979 that she made it to the big screen once more and this time in glorious full colour. Television-film producer Roger Gimbel delivered to the screen his retelling of the disaster with *S.O.S. Titanic*, originally named *Titanic Down*. It featured David Warner as surviving Second Class passenger Lawrence Beesley, Helen Mirren in the role of one of the ship's stewardesses, Harry Andrews as Captain Smith, Ian Holm as Bruce Ismay and David Janssen as millionaire John Jacob Astor. The story followed closely many survivors' accounts of the voyage but the overall film was somewhat of a letdown with the low budget restraints of the production. The film did have a short run at cinemas, but its home was more suited to that of television screens. The warning signs from *S.O.S. Titanic* should have been enough to have alarmed those working on the production of *Raise the Titanic*. But that bell wasn't sounded loud enough to be heard.

The wrecks discovery in 1985 spurned a wealth of major documentaries covering every aspect of *Titanic*'s story from construction, through to disaster, the discovery of the wreck and the salvaging of artefacts from the ocean floor. The discovery of *Titanic* in September 1985 did reveal one intriguing major discovery in that she had broken apart during the final moments of the sinking. By 1996 the public was made aware that a multimillion-dollar film project was in the works to bring to the big screen the most up-to-date retelling of the *Titanic* disaster, by the man who brought the world the *Terminator* and *Aliens*. But not before one more low budget affair to whet people's appetites. Released as a two-part TV-movie the Konigsberg/Sanitsky Company production of '*Titanic*' was pushed out to gain the attention of the public while the James Cameron film was still in its postproduction stages. Starring Catherine Zeta-Jones and Peter Gallagher in fictional roles, the story weaved around the disaster while the odd historical character flits amongst inaccurate sets and some highly questionable looking CGI imagery. While the production lacks much historical accuracy, it does have one redeeming feature in that it was the first film production to portray the liner breaking apart during the sinking.

By early 1997, and with some critics panning James Cameron's forthcoming *Titanic* tale as the next disastrous flop due largely to the film being behind schedule, and, if you were to believe the critics, the spiralling budget costs, '*Titanic*' was on course for an uncertain future. How wrong they were. Cameron's epic love story set on board the ill-fated liner made its first appearance on November 1, 1997, at the Tokyo International Film Festival, followed on November 18 with the world premiere screening in London. The story of *Titanic* had gripped people in a way like never before as two lovers from dividing classes of society meet on the decks of the doomed liner, to then steal people's hearts around the world. Over twenty years have now passed since James Cameron's blockbuster hit theatre screens and yet the fascination with *Titanic* has hardly subsided. With the advancement in today's film technology, the question is often asked if we will see another motion picture covering the events of April 1912. While there is no denying that '*Titanic*' from 1997 is, without doubt, the most recent telling of the story for the big screen and still the most accurate of all the *Titanic* movies released previously, a lot more facts have been unearthed on the real disaster which can shape the story even more and to the point that die-hard fans have asked for an updated big screening outing for *Titanic*, some even suggesting a retelling in a docu-drama style just like that of *A Night to Remember*. One cannot but wonder if any big studio will take the gamble and revisit *Titanic*'s legacy once more or will Lord Lew Grade's 1970s suspicion of "oh no, not again" come back to haunt potential film makers? But then Lew Grade is among that list of people who did bring the story of *Titanic* to the big screen; and he did so in spectacular if somewhat unorthodox style.

The *Olympic-Class* liners of the White Star Line that were designed to cater for the rich and poor in ferrying them across the waters of the North Atlantic. The first of the class was *Olympic* (top) which entered service in June 1911. In April 1912 *Titanic* (centre) left Southampton for her first and last voyage. The third of the fleet was *Britannic* in 1915 (bottom) that was never to see service as a passenger liner. The delays brought about by the loss of *Titanic* pushed the liners build into the early months of WWI where *Britannic* was chosen to serve as a hospital ship. Her loss to a mine in November 1916 was yet another major blow for the shipping company. *(Illustration © Cyril Codus 2019)*

It is the mid-morning of 31 May 1911 and ticket holding spectators make their way among the maze and lattice work of steel towards the visitors stands lining slipway No. 3 of the Queens Island shipbuilding works of Harland & Wolff to witness the launch of the world's largest ocean liner that would surpass all other great man-made objects on earth. *(The Illustrated London News, June 10, 1911 - Author's collection / Mersey Maritime Museum – Photography © Jonathan Smith – Author's collection)*

It is 12:15pm on the 31 May 1911 and the 24,000-ton hull of the unsinkable *Titanic* enters the oily waters of the River Lagan in Belfast. It took just a mere 62 seconds from the time she began to move to the moment she came to a stop on the water. Moments later crews in small craft would appear by her side and detach all the launching cables for the shipyard tugs to pull the hull to the near-by fitting out basin. *(Author's collection)*

The excursion ferry *Viper* that operated between Belfast docks and out across the Irish Sea to the holiday destination of Bangor on the northwest of Wales makes for an interesting contrast between her own sleek features to that of the huge hull of the *Titanic* that is moored up to the quayside of the Belfast fitting-out basin, June 1911. *(Author's collection)*

Titanic's enormous 15.5-ton centre anchor sitting on the W.A. Ree haulage company dray after arriving at Dudley Railway Station from the local anchor and chain manufacturer Noah Hingley & Sons Ltd. Once the dispatch documents had been approved the anchor would be loaded aboard a freight train that would take it to Fleetwood Docks 126 miles away on the west coast of England. From there it was loaded aboard the cargo ship *Duke of Albany* for the journey across the channel to Belfast and the shipyards of Harland & Wolff. *(The Railway News, May 13, 1911 – Author's collection)*

A worker of the Darlington Forge company stands in front of the assembled 101-ton steel rudder of the *Titanic/Olympic*. *(Engineering, October 21, 1910 – Author's collection)*

Built on a nightmarish scale. The huge Scotch Marine Boilers for *Olympic* and *Titanic* are lined up in the assembly sheds at the Harland & Wolff shipyard prior to being loaded onto narrow gauge trolley trucks and pulled to the fitting out basin where each boiler would be lowered down through the boiler casings of the hull and seated within the ships massive engine rooms. *(Engineering, October 21, 1910 – Author's collection)*

Harland & Wolff workers pose beneath the huge overhanging stern of the *Olympic* in early May 1911 and emphasizing the sheer scale of the Olympic-Class liners manganese-bronze propellers. *(Harland & Wolff Ltd - plate H1512)*

One of the funnels makes its journey down the Queens Island Road from the boiler shops at Harland & Wolff to the fitting out basin a short distance away. *(Author's collection)*

TOP: The first week of March 1912 and *Titanic* (right) has been moved out of the dry dock facility so *Olympic* (left) can enter for a port side propeller replacement following losing a blade when the liner struck what was thought to be a waterlogged derelict out at sea. ABOVE: With the *Olympic* now repaired and returned back to service, *Titanic* is moved back into the dry dock facility. *(Period postcard - Authors collection)*

This rare photograph of *Titanic* was taken in the early hours of daylight on the morning of April 2, 1912. In boiler room #6 the pressure is up in her boilers as smoke begins to emerge from the towering forward funnel. The day before should have been her original date for the sea trials. However, heavy winds blowing across Belfast Lough, a detached stern cable having dropped into the water around the propellers and the late arrival from Southampton docks of her master; Captain Edward John Smith, it was decided that the trials would be postponed until the following day. *(Author's collection)*

Titanic's older sister *Olympic*, pictured in Southampton Water in July 1911. Although both ships were built side by side and from the same plans, one of the most defining contrasts between the two liners was the A-Deck promenade with *Olympic* having the entire promenade fully open unlike *Titanic* that underwent last minute changes to have the forward end enclosed off. *(Author's collection)*

April 2, 1912 and *Titanic* displays all her majesty as she is guided through the shallow waters of the Victoria Channel and out towards Belfast Lough where she will begin a full day of sea trials. On board are officials from the Board of Trade keeping account of how the ship performs before the official documents are signed and dated allowing the ship to be handed over to her owners. *(L'Illustration, April 20, 1912 / Harland & Wolff Ltd – Author's collection)*

Amateur photographer Thomas Pearse from Bristol has made the journey to Southampton on the 8 April to capture this view of *Titanic* sitting at Berth 44 of the White Star Line dock. *(Period postcard – Author's collection)*

With the new liner the talk of the town, local newspaper photographers head to the docks to see the world's largest ocean liner and take a snapshot for their tabloids. This April 1912 photograph taken inside the storage sheds of the White Star Line dock in Southampton shows the impressive number of thousands of cased bottles of beer waiting to be hand loaded aboard the *Titanic*. *(Author's collection)*

c1933 aerial image of the former White Star Line dock at Southampton. At this time the dock had been renamed as the Ocean Dock. However, the dock buildings and berth numbers were still the same as in *Titanic's* time. *Olympic* is seen moored along-side berth 46. Opposite at berth 44 (right) is the United States Line S.S. *Leviathan* sitting in the same location that *Titanic* occupied between the dates of 4 - 10 April, 1912. *(Author's collection)*

Titanic photographed on the 9 April; the day before her maiden voyage. *(Period postcard – Author's collection)*

Photographed from the decks of the steamer *Beacon Grange*, *Titanic* is tugged out from the White Star Line dock and into the water of the River Test at the start of her maiden voyage. *(Period postcard – Author's collection)*

Titanic is brought to a sudden stop moments after starting her maiden voyage. As a precaution the tugboat *Vulcan* remains alongside. *(ABC Archive)*

Following dropping off the harbour pilot, *Titanic* begins to pick up speed as she steams past Cowes, Isle of Wight, and bound for the open waters of the English Channel and her first port of call at Cherbourg. *(Beken & Son period postcard – Author's collection)*

It is just before 6:30pm and *Titanic* steams into the French port of Cherbourg. Dropping anchor in the waters of the Grande Rade, she awaits the two White Star Line tenders *Nomadic* (left) and *Traffic* (right) to ferry passengers and mail from the quay side. *(Postcard – Author's collection / Painting © Stuart Williamson / Postcard – Author's collection)*

Just visible behind *Titanic's* stern are the funnels of the S.S. *New York* (black funnels with white banding) that has broken free from her mooring lines and in the process of being moved to safety. *(Author's collection)*

The morning of April 11, 1912 and *Titanic* steams towards Queenstown on the southern coast of Ireland. As passengers are seated for breakfast, the ships officers are busy testing the vessels main compasses by manoeuvring *Titanic* through the channel on a zig-zag course. *(Painting © Elang Erlangga)*

This photograph was taken from one of the two Queenstown tenders approaching *Titanic* as she sits at anchor in the waters off Roches Point lighthouse just after 11:30am. With Queenstown being a shallow water port, all of the large liners were required to stop in the deeper water of the channel where the tenders would travel the 4-mile distance from the quay to the waiting ship. *(Author's collection)*

Guglielmo Marconi, the creator of the Marconi radio system including the unit supplied and used on board the *Titanic*. *(Author's collection)*

Titanic's radio operators John "Jack" Phillips (left) and his junior assistant Harold Bride. Although they worked on board the *Titanic,* they were not employed by the White Star Line but rather the Marconi company. *(Author's collection)*

Lookout Fredrick Fleet who, along with Reginal Lee, spotted the mass of ice ahead of *Titanic*. He is pictured here during the hearings into the disaster. *(Author's collection)*

William McMaster Murdoch, *Titanic*'s First Officer. Murdoch is pictured here in 1911 on the open bridge of *Olympic*. *(Author's collection)*

"Iceberg, right ahead!" Although this 1912 illustration inaccurately depicts the moment steel and ice meet, it does not deviate from the seriousness of the situation. *(April 1912 edition* of La Domenica del Corriere – *Author's collection)*

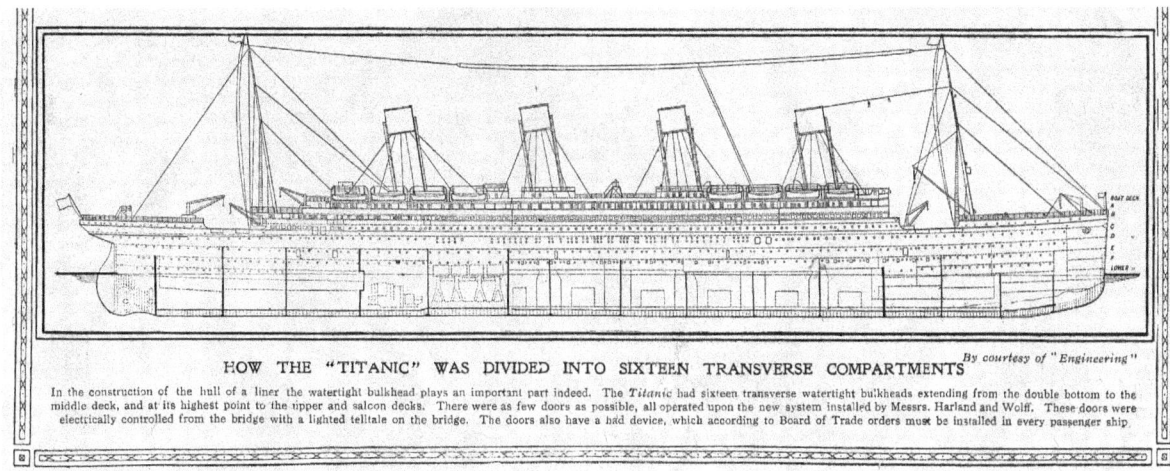

This illustration from May 1912 shows how *Titanic*'s hull was divided by a series of bulkheads that created a total of sixteen watertight compartments. The term watertight is often misinterpreted where *Titanic* is concerned. The bulkheads were built to withstand a certain amount of pressure if the compartment became breached and flooded. A series of pumps built into the floor of the boiler and engine rooms would allow for the incoming water to be pumped out. But the severe nature of the damage sustained to *Titanic*'s hull meant that the pumps could not handle the intake of water from the flooding. As for what exactly was watertight; that was the doors in the bulkhead that could allow crews to pass from one compartment to the next and in which all the doors could be closed electronically or manually. It was perceived by her builders that a compartment would not become flooded enough to overspill the top of each bulkhead. *(Author's collection)*

"Unsinkable"; the term that would come back to haunt the White Star Line. This section comes from a small pamphlet released by White Star in November 1910 boasting about the safety features incorporated into the hulls of *Olympic* and *Titanic*. *(Author's collection)*

Master of the *Titanic*. Edward John Smith was a highly experienced and much loved by both passengers and crew, Smith was a captain's captain earning high praise and repetition. He is pictured here on the morning of the ships sailing from Southampton when the press came aboard for a brief tour of the new liner. Smith, obliging for a photographer from the *Illustrated London News*, is photographed alongside the Officers' Quarters located at the rear of the bridge on the boat deck of *Titanic*. *(Author's collection)*

ABOVE: When *Titanic* was under design, she had originally been envisioned to carry 32 lifeboats that would cater for all onboard. This original Harland & Wolff plan shows how the boats could have been placed on the boat deck with one boat at the edge of the deck and another sat inboard making it two boats per lifeboat davit set. Despite the best efforts of the shipbuilders, the decision was overturned by the Board of Trade. *Titanic* would sail from the builder's yards with a total of 20 lifeboats. on board. TOP: This photograph was taken on board *Titanic* during her brief stop at Queenstown and shows the set of port side lifeboats partially lifted up off the boat deck to allow 2nd class passengers more room on the open deck. As passengers take in the crisp spring air, little did they realise that four days later they would be huddled up in the biting cold of the night hoping for a place in one of these small wooden craft. *(Cork Examiner / Original shipbuilders plan – Mersey Maritime Museum – Photography © Jonathan Smith)*

With the lifeboats uncovered, filled with provisions and swung out level with the boat deck, crews operating under the rule of women and children first began to load the lifeboats. Those first few boats to leave the sinking *Titanic* were woefully under laden. Lifeboat No. 1 left the *Titanic* with just 12 occupants; two being passengers and the other ten being that of crew. The boat was designed to hold 45 persons. *(Publicity photograph for A Night to Remember 1958 – Author's collection)*

The *Titanic* goes down, April 15, 1912 *(La Domenica del Corriere - Author's collection)*

As the liners bows dip beneath the frigid water of the North Atlantic, *Titanic* takes on a slight list to port side throwing the No.1 funnel off its axis. As the sea comes rushing up over the bridge it slams into the funnel, buckling inwards the steel and sending the towering giant crashing down in a shower of soot and sparks onto the hordes of helpless swimmers who had been washed off the deck seconds before. *(The Year 1912 – Author's collection)*

Frightened passengers and crew struggle up the ever-increasing incline of *Titanic*'s stern as the liner goes through her agonising death throws. *(Publicity photograph for* A Night to Remember *1958 – Author's collection)*

Chapter 1 : Cinematic *Titanic* • 31

With an almost deafening roar, *Titanic* rears her stern skywards. Across the water comes the painful cries of those still trapped on board. Their screams become a chorus of pain and grief that suddenly becomes dwarfed by the horrendous sounds coming from the wreck as *Titanic* breaks apart. As the stern pitches over and vanishes beneath the waves, a voice is heard coming from a nearby lifeboat, "She's gone!" The time is 2:20am on the 15 April, 1912. *(Painting © Stuart Williamson)*

For some moments after the *Titanic* had vanished beneath the waves, a deathly silence came over the water. It was as if the world had somehow been paused. Then abruptly the silence was shattered by the throats of hundreds of helpless victims who suddenly arrived at the surface having been dragged down with the wreck. Survivors in lifeboats could do nothing but listen or clasp their hands over their ears at the horrifying sounds all about them. Washed off the deck of the *Titanic* the overturned lifeboat collapsible B had become a refuge for a number of men who had pulled themselves from the sea to sit perched on the overturned hull. They were the lucky ones. Within minutes of being exposed to the harsh conditions of the North Atlantic, hundreds would go on to perish in the freezing waters. *(Publicity photograph for* A Night to Remember *1958 – Author's collection)*

The Cunard liner R.M.S. *Carpathia* which in the early hours of Monday April 15 heard the distress calls of the stricken *Titanic* and raced at full steam to reach the area. She arrived at the scene of the sinking at 4 am to be greeted by a sea covered with icebergs and lifeboats. *(Author's collection)*

Lifeboat No. 14 is photographed from the decks of the *Carpathia* as the sail is taken down by Harold Lowe; *Titanic*'s surviving Fifth Officer. Moments later she is joined by collapsible lifeboat D. *(L'Illustration, May 4, 1912 – Author's collection)*

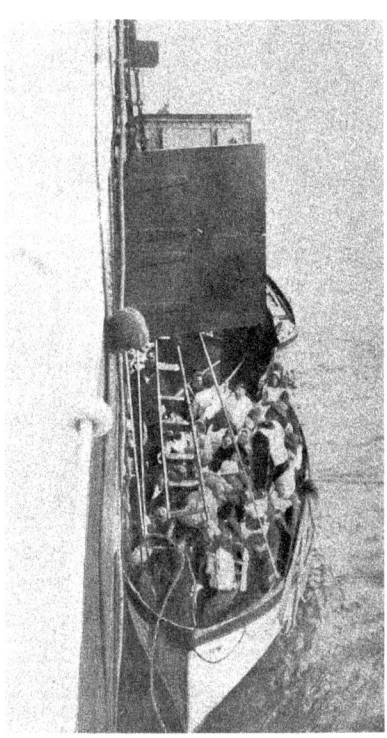

Lifeboat No.11 is pictured secured to the hull side of the *Carpathia* as *Titanic* survivors are offloaded. It would have been a scary experience for the passengers who were not accustomed to exchanging between a small wooden craft to that of a large liner in the middle of the ocean. *(L'Illustration, May 4, 1912 – Author's collection)*

Press photographers brave the harsh New York rains to catch a glimpse of *Titanic* survivors on the decks of *Carpathia*. But before the liner could make her way to the Cunard berth, she stops at the entrance to the White Star Line pier to offload *Titanic*'s rescued lifeboats. *(Author's collection)*

These thirteen small boats are all that is left of the world's largest ocean liner. Secured to the White Star Line pier in New York, dock personnel are seen removing artefacts from the interior of the lifeboats as a prevention from souvenir hunters out to make a buck or two. The question as to what became of these lifeboats is still largely debateable. The lifeboats were no longer of any use. Following being inspected with several craft showing some signs of damage from being brought aboard the *Carpathia*, the boats were put into dry storage in the pier lofts in New York for several months until the insurance claim was settled. As the lifeboats were nothing now but matchwood it is extremely likely that the boats were completely destroyed having served their purpose. And with the new laws that came into practice from the results of the loss of *Titanic*, all shipping lines had to follow in updating their life saving equipment. *(Brown Brothers – Author's collection)*

One of *Titanic's* original lifeboat name plates that was removed when the boats were offloaded in New York. Readers may have spotted the plate has a prefix of "S.S." and not "R.M.S." This is because the S.S. signifies the lifeboat having come from a steam ship. The designated R.M.S. was added in documentation when *Titanic* entered service having on board a Royal Mail postal sorting office giving her the prefix of a Royal Mail Ship. This surviving example is on public display at the Maritime museum in Liverpool. (Photograph © Jonathan Smith)

Newspaper boy Ned Parfett announces to a shocked London the terrible news on *Titanic* while selling copies of the paper outside the Trafalgar Square offices of the White Star Line on April 16, 1912. Ned went on to lead a tragic life when he joined up to fight in WWI. On October 29 while serving with the British Army in France, and just a matter of days before the Armistice of 1918, Ned received his orders to go on leave. As he returned to the bunker to collect his belongings, he was killed by a shell during a German bombardment. *(Author's collection)*

Titanic newspaper billboards line the exterior of the William Scott Stationary & Tobacconist of No. 40 Penny Lane, Liverpool in April 1912. *(Period postcard – Author's collection)*

One of the many memorial postcards that was published within days of the disaster featuring Captain Smith, Marconi operator John Phillips and a view of the *Titanic* in Southampton Water. *(Period postcard – Author's collection)*

This single frame from the Kineto company film covering the construction of *Olympic* is the first piece of footage to show *Titanic*. This view is looking directly at slipway No.3 and shows the timbered scaffolding that is supporting the keel of *Titanic* that is slowly rising upwards to form the knife-edge of the bow. Directly off to the right is slipway No.2 with the hull of *Olympic* in the process of being plated. *(Kineto Co)*

Chapter 1 : Cinematic *Titanic* • 37

Six frames from the Kineto footage showing stages of *Olympic*'s construction at Harland & Wolff. Going clockwise: The double bottom of *Olympic* takes shape on slipway No.2. One of the steel hull plates measuring 30ft x 6ft is lowered into place. The army of riveters at work fixing one of the huge steel hull plates to the liner's internal frames. One of the steam traction engines at work at the foot of *Olympic*'s bow. Interesting view looking over the forecastle on *Olympic*'s bow. The launch of *Olympic* took place just after midday on the 20 October, 1910. As she was the first of the class her hull had been painted white to show off her elegant lines to the scores of photographers lined up around the yard. *(Kinto Co)*

Six frames from footage taken in early February 1912 as *Titanic* is pulled into the Belfast Graving Dock facility. At this stage of her fitting out she is still to have a number of structures finished off including the cabs that overhand the main navigation bridge, installation of her lifeboats and the enclosing of the forward end of the A-Deck promenade which will distinguish the difference between *Titanic* and her older sister *Olympic*. *(Gaumont)*

Six frames from footage taken in the summer of 1911 of a departing *Olympic* from New York. This well-known moving picture was extensively used in theatres from mid-April 1912 to deliver paying audiences an enthralling experience of seeing genuine footage of the doomed *Titanic*; albeit the footage being of her older sister. *(Gaumont)*

Original magazine advertisement for the first moving picture based on the *Titanic* disaster. Filmed just two-weeks after the event, *Saved from the Titanic* had the leading role played by twenty-three year old singer, model and actress Dorothy Gibson who was an actual *Titanic* survivor. *(Author's collection)*

Publicity photograph issued for the 1912 moving picture *In Night und Eis* that is based on the *Titanic* disaster. *(Author's collection)*

The British International Picture's adaptation of *The Berg* that was released to the public in 1929. *(Author's collection)*

The controversial Nazi propaganda film *TITANIC* from 1943 and a still from the movie showing the *Titanic* at sea. *(Author's collection)*

Hollywood takes on the disaster with the release of their first big budget production *TITANIC* from 1953. *(Author's collection)*

Chapter 1: Cinematic *Titanic* • 43

Actor Laurence Naismith in the role of Captain Smith, speaks with Helen Russell-Cooke, the daughter of the real master of the *Titanic* on the bridge set during filming on *A Night to Remember*. *(Rank Organisation – Authors' collection)*

Kenneth More and producer William MacQuitty inspect a scale model of the *Titanic*. *(Rank Organisation – Author's collection)*

Titanic survivor Lawrence Beesley on the set of *A Night to Remember*. *(Rank Organisation – Author's collection)*

Released by the Rank Organisation in 1958, *A Night to Remember* is considered to be one of the definitive disaster movies covering the ill-fated maiden voyage of the *Titanic*. *(Rank Organisation – Author's collection)*

The disaster turns colour with the release of *S.O.S. Titanic* by EMI films in 1979. *(Author's collection)*

74-year-old *Titanic* survivor Eva Hart on the set of *S.O.S. Titanic* during filming at Shepperton Studios *(Author's collection)*

Chapter 1 : Cinematic *Titanic* • 47

Thomas Andrews (Geoffrey Whitehead) delivers the news to Captain Smith (Harry Andrews) that *Titanic* is going to sink as the horrified Bruce Ismay (Ian Holm) looks on. *(EMI Publicity photograph – Author's collection)*

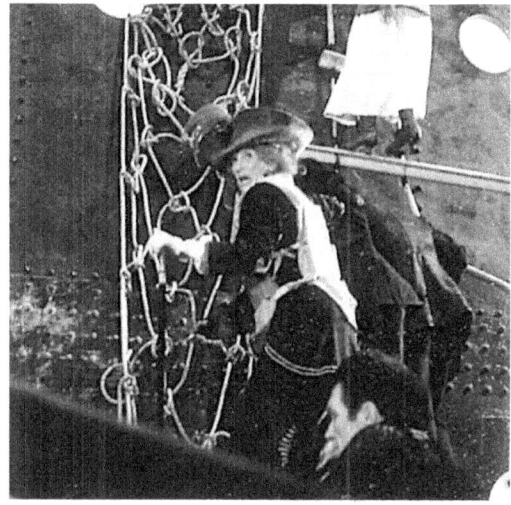

First Class passenger Molly Brown (Cloris Leachman) begins to climb the rope ladder to safety up the towering hull of the rescue ship *Carpathia*. *(EMI Publicity photograph – Author's collection)*

Imagination overload is plentiful in this 1979 Japanese publicity brochure for *S.O.S. Titanic*. The most obvious error being the iceberg gash that is not only far too long but on the wrong side of the ship. *(Author's collection)*

The impressive full-scale exterior set of the *Titanic* for James Cameron's epic take on the events of April 1912. *(Publicity photograph © Twentieth Century Fox 1997 – Author's collection)*

Birds eye view overlooking the huge exterior set for James Cameron's *TITANIC* at the Baja film studios, Rosarito, Mexico. Alongside the replica sits an authentic recreation of the passenger and goods sheds of Southampton docks. These outbuildings would be removed when the time came to film the sinking scenes. With the *Titanic* set partially built on a hydraulic system within the tank, the tank could be flooded and the *Titanic* set angled down at the bow to simulate the sinking. When filming had completed the entire *Titanic* set was broken up and destroyed. *(Jim Scoular collection)*

CHAPTER 2

Mr Entertainment

"Power? It's an ugly word. It's sort of egotism to think one has power. I don't have power over people. I'm doing a job that I enjoy – to promote balanced entertainment."

Lew Grade

If the question was to be asked "who raised the *Titanic*?" to a fellow fan, what would their answer be? Clive Cussler? His fictional character of Dirk Pitt? What about Lord Lew Grade of Elstree? While Grade did not appear in Cussler's novel, Grade was no fictional character. He was for his time one of the United Kingdom's most prominent and leading entertainment moguls who brought to the small screen some of the most iconic television shows of the 1960s and 70s. Lew Grade was born Lovat Winogradsky in the small village of Tokomak in Ukraine on 25 December 1906. His brother Boris (later changed to Bernard) would be born on September 5, 1909. During the early years of his life conflicts were raging across Ukraine with Cossack violence taking hold as hostility and discrimination against the Jews spread like wildfire resulting in fatalities. Writing in his 1987 autobiography *Still Dancing*, Lew recalled his only memories of his home in Tokmak of that of a house standing within its own grounds and overlooked by apple orchards and apples strewn everywhere. While those all too few memories were of innocent times for Lew, little did he know of the battle scars that would become embedded from the anti-Semitism which would see over one million Jews emigrating from Russia between the years of 1897 to 1914. By 1912 the Winogradsky family decided to leave Tokmak for a better life in England and London's East End, more precisely Brick Lane in Bethnal Green that would eventually become their new home.

Their father rented two rooms over a shop until finances improved which would see them move to better accommodation on the Boundary Estate in the North West corner of Bethnal Green. Lew would recall in his autobiography *Still Dancing* that after being born into such a large house surrounded by apple orchards, "London looked extremely depressing". But it was a world away from the troubles in Ukraine. Lew's father had made a living from pressing trousers, something that would come to help his son Lew, when, at the age of 15, he become an agent for the women's clothing company of Tew & Raymond. Unlike his mother and father who found it difficult with communications, English now having to be their third language, to come to England at the age of 6, Lew soon picked up the language far quicker than that of his parents ever could. His mother Golda and father Isaac shared a passion for entertainment. They loved to sing and were known back home in Tokmak to take participate in public held shows. This fascination in entertaining was soon to rub off on the young Lew. His job working for Tew & Raymond on Little Argyll Street in London's West End had him located in an office just a short distance from the London Palladium. His valuable contribution to the company, that of having a very good memory and expertise in arithmetic's, soon had Lew on the promising ladder to the top that by the age of 16 he was earning a healthy £1 per week, a considerable sum of money back then. But Lew had a problem with his bosses, not so much Reymond, but that of Tew, who lacked any sort of humour and who began to run the company into the ground. It was something that Lew took exception to and in what would become a typical Lew Grade characteristic in adult life. Lew changed his career path by leaving the company and setting up business with a man who he knew had no talent for such a business – his father, Isaac. Lew would refer to him as being "An excellent singer, but not a good businessman". And so Winogradsky & Son came into being. The company's speciality was that of embroidery, but while Lew had no expertise in such manufacturing, he did have a head for getting the right equipment at the right prices, and, more importantly, knew who the clients were. And with the company now operating with eight machines it felt more like Son & Winogradsky.

Happy Feet

In his youth, Isaac had been a very keen dancer. His Russian acrobatic mode to entertain, not just for the public but also his family, was keenly watched by his sons Lew, Bernard and the youngest, Leslie. All the fast-flying foot expressions in dance enthralled the young Lew, and his parents were aware of this. By the mid-1920s as the Charleston dance craze that had been imported over from America swept across Great Britain, Lew, aided by his parents, ceased upon the opportunity to embark upon this thrilling new dance routine. While Bernard mastered the ability of chatting up the ladies, Lew was a little more on the shy side. But his dancing skills were what he used to catch the ladies' attention. His prowess led to him entering the Charleston Championship of London, and, spurred on by a healthy £25 championship winnings, the dancing did wonders for Lew's self-esteem, pushing him on further to become super-confident and winning tournaments and more cash prizes. In later life, Lew would recall "it was the *winning* that provided the real pleasure." Abraham Goldmaker, a friend and former dance-floor rival, said of Lew "Being with Lew made you believe life was worthwhile." And then in 1926, Lew, who for the sole purpose of entertainment, decided he could no longer enter competitions under the name of Louis Winogradsky and changed it to Louis Grad. His commitment to the dance tournaments would see him win time and time again and, in the end, he would be crowned Charleston Champion of the World. Following the successful competition, he then spent the next four weeks performing on stage at the Piccadilly Hotel. Not only did the audience love him he also got to dance and earn £50 per week, which for a 19-year-old young man of the time, was a tremendous amount of money. After a short career in dancing in France, Lew returned to England to continue with his passion for entertaining.

Tragedy struck in 1935 when his father died from cancer brought on by complications with Hodgkin's disease. The previous year Lew had started his own talent agency in a period that would make a name for him among the showbiz circles. This new career path would eventually lead him to arrange entertainment for soldiers during WWII. But Lew's time in the British Army was to be short-lived when he was discharged following twenty-four months of service on the grounds of injuries to his legs from all the rigorous dancing he had subjected himself to. This revelation would earn him the nickname of Mr Squeaky Knees while out with his colleagues on parade. The period following the war had Lew travelling back to Paris again on business while his younger brother Leslie continued to make a name for himself in London. The time was now right for the two brothers to form a joint business, Lew & Leslie Grade Ltd, which would take them across the Atlantic to New York and establish a new office in America that began to draw in the attention of many stars of the day. It did not stop there, as the Grade brothers expanded with an additional office in California. Watch out world, the Grade Brothers were coming! By 1951 they had become one of the most prominent agencies in the United States with equally prominent clientele such as Bob Hope, Judy Garland, Cab Calloway, Danny Kaye, Louis Armstrong, Harry Belafonte, Mario Lanza, and a list that just kept growing. Across the pond in London, the Grade brothers became one of the leading agencies for booking stars for the world-famous London Palladium venue. But Lew was not content with just the agency as upon the horizon there would be a door that would open to bigger and greater adventures.

It was during 1954 and following on from a great deal of lobbying in London through parliament on the development of commercial television that Lew's business senses peaked as he turned his sights towards creating quality programmes for British television. The Times newspaper advertisements had caught his attention with their printing of applications for major territories with a minimum figure of £3m of investments. It was this successful bid that would pave the way for what would become the ITV network. With this in mind Lew teamed up with Prince Littler, the British theatre proprietor and impresario, and Val Parnell, the British actor, director, presenter and theatrical impresario, to form the Incorporated Television Company (ITC) on 10 September 1954. The main headquarters would be located in London while its divisional parenting company of Associated Film Distribution (AFD) would set up home in the United States. During that time Lew continued forwards to establish Granada Productions in the United Kingdom. With these new companies, they could reach out with their services to the United States, Germany, France, Australia and more importantly across the length and breadth of Great Britain. What was to follow during the 1960s and 1970s would become one of the leading television networks ever to air to the masses and their showcasing content that is still yet to be matched to this very day. While Lew and Bernard played out their games of family rivalry, Bernard would eventually be left out of his older brother's consortium. But he could hardly complain that his older brother Lew had taken the leap into television. While Bernard used his skills in theatrical management to become the Life President of the annual Royal Variety Performance, the highly acclaimed television live performance in which money was raised for charities; it became a position he was to hold onto for twenty years. He would then become the Chief Executive of the EMI Group Limited in 1978 until his departure two years later. It was during his position working for EMI when in 1978 he withdrew the funding for the highly acclaimed Monty Python film Life of Brian. A move he would profess over uncertainties due to the films impending religious implications. Working for EMI would have him and Lew cross paths once more and, uncannily, the dispute would be over the *Titanic*. But that is another story for another chapter.

Birth of Classic Television

Lew Grade's companies of ITC, ATV and ITV were featuring prominently in television viewings. Being that of commercial networks, they were clocking up viewing figures better than that of the BBC. His rise in the entertainment industry would see Lew knighted in 1969 to become a life peer; Baron Grade of Elstree. Throughout newspapers and magazines, Lew Grade was often prefixed with the name "Mr ATV" with his very name alone becoming to symbolize a quality assurance of great television entertainment. But what of those shows that made him and his network such a household name? Where does one even start? Lew can claim credit for bringing to the small screen the original puppet-master Gerry Anderson as ATV became the broadcasting ground for *Thunderbirds, Stingray, Captain Scarlet and the Mysterons*. There were other well-known productions such as *The Muppet Show, Man in a Suitcase, Peter Gunn, The Prisoner, Danger Man, Charlies Angels, Jason King, The Persuaders, The Saint, Randall and Hopkirk, Space 1999, Joe 90*; to name but a few. And if that wasn't enough there was also *The Julie Andrews Show, The Tom Jones Show, The Dean Martin Show* and of course *Saturday Night at the London Palladium*.

Lights, Camera, Action!

Grade's first outing in movies came in 1969 when he backed the United Artists movie *Crossplot* which featured *The Saint's* Roger Moore in a relatively low budget spy drama set in the sleazy world of a modelling agency in London. Following his support of actress Shirley MacLaine, he went forward in financially backing two films she wanted to make, *Desperate Characters* (1971) that went on to win the Berlin Film Festival award. The following year *The Possession of Joel Delaney* was released. Both films were well received which gave confidence in Grade and his future role as a financier of future movies. Julie Andrews approached Lew to help with two films she wanted to develop with her husband Blake Edwards. While Andrews had already previously been part of the ATV line-up with her television show, Grade ceased upon the opportunity to have the leading star of *Mary Poppins* and *The Sound of Music* present in his movie financial credits. The first of the two was *The Tamarind Seed* in 1974 and the second was to become the movie that secured Lew's name in the film industry. During the Lew and Leslie Grade agency days, Lew had become friends with the ever-comedic Peter Sellers. From that friendship they developed a bungling and always incompetent police character; Inspector Clouseau, for which Sellers would be offered the part for *The Return of the Pink Panther* (1975) and then again for *The Pink Panther Strikes Again* (1976). The film franchise became a success for Lew Grade's ITC company giving an advantage to Lew and his ATV worldwide company in enticing actors in from the United States. One selling tactic of Lew was that he was normally able to recover back sixty percent and more of the filmmaking costs. This became not just a bond from Grade, his assured guarantee, but also a guarantee of good reputation for actors and directors assigned to his movies.

Through the 1970s Grade's film list began to grow with classic productions such as *Farewell My Lovely* (1975), *The Boys from Brazil* (1978), *The Long Good Friday* (1980), Monty Python's *Life of Brian* (1979). But like many productions there will always be those that didn't fare so well with the critics including *Capricorn One* (1977), *The Cassandra Crossing* (1976), *Saturn 3* (1980), *The Legend of the Lone Ranger* (1981) and, of course, *Raise the Titanic*. But nestled among those were critically acclaimed award winners *On Golden Pond* (1981) and *Sophie's Choice* (1982), both receiving Academy Awards, along with Lew's closing film chapter with the success of *The Dark Crystal* (1982). But the costly nature of several of his financed films began to cast a shroud over his companies, resulting in Grade's reputation as that of a film mogul being brought into question. The repercussions of 1982 were to have a severe knock-on effect on Lew Grade as he struggled to keep onto his position as Mr Entertainment. While it was not a total loss for Grade, there was light at the end of the tunnel when American television writer and producer Norman Lear brought in Lew to head the London division of the Embassy Communications International in the distribution of films and television programmes until the Coca-Cola Company purchased the company in June 1985. Grade went on after that to launch the Grade Company to then become vice-president of the Loews Theatre Group that owned a series of cinema chains across America. By the mid-1990s Grade had returned once more to familiar territory as head of ITC until the company ceased trading all together in October 1998.

Goodbye Sir Grade

After an adventurous life, Lew Grade passed away on 13 December 1998 from the results of heart failure at the age of 92. It is without question that the Grade brothers left a mark on the entertainment industry and can be looked upon as being some of the true pioneers of today's television. Leslie Grade died in October 1979 at his residence in France aged 63. Bernard, mostly known in the entertainment industry as Lord Delfont following his knighthood in 1974, passed away at his home in Sussex, England, on January 17, 2008. Of the three brothers, it would be Lew who became the most recognised for his grand adventures. His reign in the entertainment industry was unprecedented for the time and while his television shows went on to become cult classics it was just one film project that would symbolize his adventurous nature, his courage to take on Hollywood as the media mogul who brought the film world a specimen of how *not* to deliver a movie. That film would be known as... *Raise the Titanic*.

Lord Lew Grade channelling another great British icon of the film industry; Alfred Hitchcock. *(Author's collection)*

The slum-like dwellings of Brick Lane in Edwardian London showing the harsh conditions that the Winogradsky family encountered after moving to rented rooms located above a shop. *(Author's collection)*

Lew in 1933 with his dancing partner, Anna Roth. *(TopFoto)*

Regardless of their brotherly rivalry for each other, Lew and his younger brother Bernard (left) were a strong duo in the entertainment business both in the United Kingdom and their ventures of branching out overseas. *(Publicity photograph - Author's collection)*

The London landmark where many stars were born on a *Saturday Night*. *(Period postcard – Author's collection)*

With more and more households tuning in their television sets at home, Lew Grade rapidly became a name you could trust in delivering quality entertainment for all the family. *(ATV publicity photograph – Author's collection)*

Grade in his element in 1973 during a broadcast of *Saturday Night at the London Palladium*. *(Daily Mirror – Author's collection)*

Grade's company that was an embodiment of entertainment and value. *(Author's collection)*

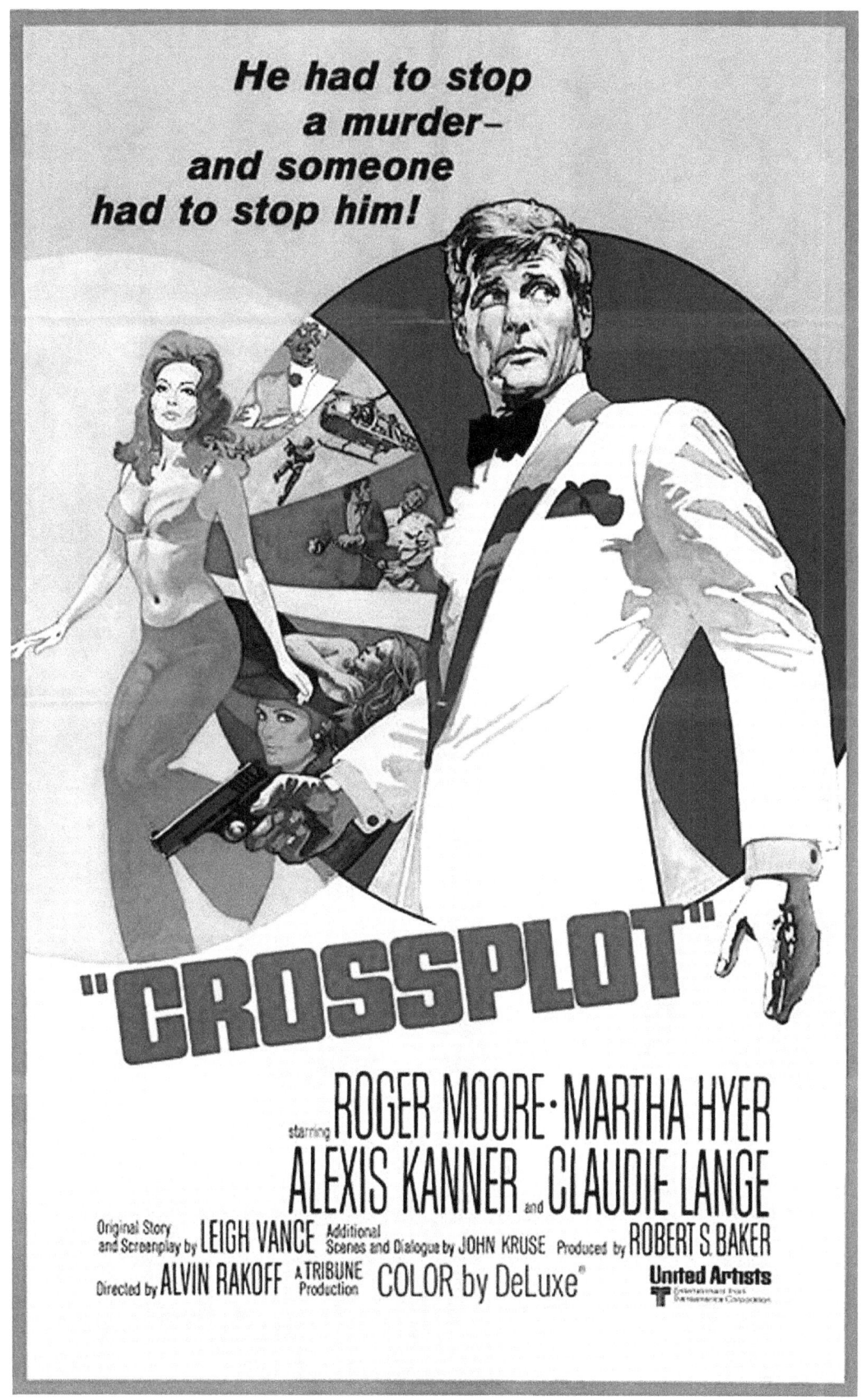

Lew Grade's first financially endorsed film *Crossplot* starring a future James Bond. *(Author's collection)*

(Author's collection)

(Author's collection)

(Author's collection)

Chapter 2: Mr Entertainment • 59

(Author's collection)

As news spreads through newspapers of Lew Grade turning to bigger productions, Grade invested in his own methods of publicity including a number of in-house published material such as the *ITC Magazine* that covered many of the feature films in the works from Grade's companies of ITC, Marble Arch Productions, Pimlico Films and ACC. These two issues from 1979 and 1980 include films such as *Capricorn One*, *The Boys from Brazil*, *The Muppet Movie* and *Raise the Titanic*. *(Author's collection)*

(Author's collection)

(Author's collection)

(Author's collection)

Chapter 2: Mr Entertainment • 61

(Author's collection)

The Dark Crystal was a bitter sweet project for Lew Grade being that it not only was it to become a firm favourite for many fans of science fiction, but it was to be Grade's swan song for his beloved ITC company. *(Author's collection)*

'Who was running the show here up until now?'

On the passing of Lord Grade on the 13 December 1998, British newspapers took to honouring the television mogul in their unique ways including this charming sketch by cartoonist *mac* for the Associated Newspapers Ltd in London. *(Associated Newspapers Ltd – Author's collection)*

A Celebration of the Life of Lord Grade of Elstree
1906 - 1998

Sunday 18th April, 1999, 7pm
The Prince of Wales Theatre
London

He loved fine cigars, the passion of signing up new talent and a keen eye for quality entertainment. Grade may be remembered for a handful of film failures. But he left behind a legacy with some of the most important and best loved television shows ever put to film that rightfully earned him the title of Mr Entertainment. *(Author's collection)*

Memorial booklet printed for the guests invited to a gathering of those from stage and screen to mark a special celebration of the life of Lord Lew Grade. *(Author's collection)*

CHAPTER 3

The Grandmaster of Adventure

"There is a fascinating aura about the sinking of the Titanic *that has gripped thousands of nostalgia freaks, including myself."*

Clive Cussler

It is of no surprise that countless authors have become fascinated by the events of April 15, 1912, when the R.M.S. *Titanic*, the pride of the White Star Line, went to the bottom of the North Atlantic creating an enduring legacy that is still prominent over one hundred years later. *Titanic* in print exceeds that of thousands of works from those that cover the disaster to the technical aspects of the vessel and her factual history reworked by writers of fiction. While many *Titanic* book lovers have such works as Walter Lord's *A Night to Remember* or Robert Ballard's *The Discovery of the Titanic*, many will have had at one point been aware of Clive Cussler's best seller, *Raise the Titanic!*

The idea of finding and raising the wreck can be traced back to 1914 when American architect Charles A. Smith devised a plan of using a custom designed unmanned submarine equipped with electromagnets could attach themselves to the hull of the sunken liner. Upon attachment, it would then release a marker buoy indicating the location of the ship. Once this was achieved, other magnets would do the same thing. His thought was that with enough magnets he could then lift the ship with winch cables attached to a fleet of barges and tow the wreck to shallow waters in a step-by-step formation. Although it sounded like something from the pages of a Jules Verne novel, it was considered plausible. and the story made it into the newspapers of the time. During the 1960s more plans came afoot to find the wreck and possibly raise her. Some of the ideas were considered as serious scientific research such as hundreds of thousands of ping pong balls being delivered to the wreck inside bags to then be attached to her hull. But the idea of ping pong balls descending 12,460ft down into water pressures of three tons per square inch is but laughable as the pressure would simply crush them flat. The idea of salvaging her did not stop, even following her discovery in September 1985, as her discovery raced around the world, it kick started the imagination of those who had thought that the raising of the *Titanic* was still a possibility despite photographic evidence supporting the fact she had broken apart during her sinking. On 8 September 1985 *The Sunday Mirror* newspaper reported that a British underwater salvage engineer had concocted an idea to raise the wreck by using 180,000 tons of Vaseline pumped into polyester fibre bags slung around the hull. Another story published that same day in *The Sunday Times* stated that *Titanic* could be lifted by encasing the hull in a wire and fabric framework which would be pumped full of liquid nitrogen freezing the wreck into a giant block of ice, sending the hull to the surface. And while it all sounds incredibly naïve and funny today, it was considered both possible and even plausible back then.

Once again, the idea of raising the *Titanic* was to remain among the pages of fiction. But things did change a little when during 1987 a French team financed a series of dives to the wreck site to plunder the debris field and to recover hundreds of artefacts. The years to follow would see creation of RMS *Titanic*, Inc who would become the salvers of possession to *Titanic*'s wreck site and fortune. Their expeditions resulted in thousands of additional items recovered from the sea bed, from the smallest of trinkets such as children's marbles. to a huge twenty-ton hull section aptly named The Big Piece. *Titanic*, in many ways, has been raised, if somewhat in fragments, but nonetheless salvaged. Yet despite the nature of the wrecks condition many arc back to Clive Cussler's book with wishful thinking that *Titanic* should have been found in the near-pristine way as portrayed on the pages of his novel. But Cussler was not the only author to raise the fabled liner. In 1990 acclaimed science fiction author, inventor and explorer, Arthur C. Clarke, penned the novel *The Ghost from the Grand Banks* that centred around two groups of salvage teams who set out to raise both sections of *Titanic* in time to mark the one-hundredth anniversary. But it is Clive Cussler's 1976 classic that everyone goes back to. And rightfully so. *Raise the Titanic* would be the third novel by Cussler in his long-running Dirk Pitt adventure series. The first came in 1973 with the novel *The Mediterranean Caper* followed in 1975 with *Iceberg*. The years to follow would see the successful franchise of his fictional Dirk Pitt with the progression to other works including the NUMA files, Oregon files and the latest publications of his Isaac Bell series making Clive Cussler one of the most respected adventure writers of our time.

Clive Cussler and Dirk Pitt *Raise the Titanic*

Clive Eric Cussler was born on 15 July 1931 in the City of Lights known as Aurora, located some forty miles from Chicago. At the tender age of six he became influenced by the sea during a family outing with his mother and father to Huntington Beach at Orange County in Southern California. That dip in the waters of the Pacific Ocean in 1937, running headlong into the surf and spray, was to spark a life-long ambition of adventure tales. The following years would see another passion of Cussler come to light with automobiles and aviation, starting from parts delivery driver and moving to engine construction and maintenance. While working in a managerial role at an Aquatic diving store in Newport Beach during 1968, he would bring into work a portable typewriter that he would turn to during the quiet periods. The time working in the shop also brought him closer to expertise in diving that would later benefit his fulfilment of becoming an author of sea stories and grand tales. Cussler developed a writing style similar to that of Alistair MacLean, a hero of his, of which Cussler acknowledges him being "the master" of the genre in adventure writing. But unlike the ever-changing protagonist of MacLean works, Cussler wanted something different in his action hero that would carry more stories forward. While England had James Bond courtesy of Ian Fleming, Clive Cussler was to give America Dirk Pitt.

Cussler's idea of Pitt came from an encyclopaedia entry for William Pitt the younger, the Prime Minister of Britain who became the youngest Prime Minister at the age of twenty-four in 1783. That surname of Pitt struck a better chord to Cussler than anything previously. But Pitt's forename was already there from the very start with that of Clive's son, Dirk. And so, Dirk Pitt, the rugged muscular six-foot-three trouble-shooter with thick black hair who loves classic automobiles, diving the oceans for their riches, beautiful women and attracting the villains, came into being and who would be loved by millions of readers for decades to follow. Clive Cussler finished his first novel *The Sea Dweller* in 1967. It would re-emerge later when published under the new title of *Pacific Vortex* which introduced the character of Dirk Pitt. To continue forwards Cussler needed a literary agent. He contacted Peter Lampack of the William Morris Agency in New York, forwarding on *The Sea Dweller* and a new work titled *Catch A Teaser by The Fin*. Lampack would later respond to why he signed up Cussler

> "Not only was I intrigued by the idea of an ongoing adventures series, I found Dirk Pitt to be an attractive and compelling protagonist. Clive is a natural storyteller, an extremely important attri-

bute if he hoped to maintain the reader's interest throughout a series. I was pretty sure I could find a publisher for *Catch A Teaser by The Fin*, but I was not impressed with *The Sea Dweller*."

In November 1973 *Catch a Teaser by the Fin*, which had been purchased by Pyramid Books for $5,000, was now published under the new name of *The Mediterranean Caper* to sell at a respectable 32,000 copies. Turning his attention to writing full-time, Clive and his family moved to Estes Park in Colorado where he could work on his third novel, *Iceberg*, later released in September 1975 by Dodd, Mead & Co. It was to be the fourth story that became Cussler's third novel which would assign Clive Cussler's name into the annals of literature. Cussler's *Titanic* has its early roots from some of the ideas envisioned by author Geoffrey Marcus in his 1969 book *The Maiden Voyage* which chronicles the first and last voyage of *Titanic* with a series of survivor accounts, inquiry reports and his personal take on the events leading up to and after the sinking. Marcus' investigative approach into the disaster certainly left an impression on Cussler who accredited *The Maiden Voyage* as an invaluable source during the writing of *Raise the Titanic*. Cussler later expressed that the story of the disaster had fascinated him for many years.

"The *Titanic* was a legend even before she went down. She was the largest, most magnificent, and most sumptuously appointed vessel which had ever put to sea."

Cussler's idea was that due to the depth in which the liner had vanished, there would be very little in the way of marine life. The combination of darkness, low levels of oxygen and the salt in the freezing waters could likely have kept *Titanic* in a remarkable state of preservation. His *Titanic* would be portrayed in the book as being in one piece, sitting over 12,000ft down in the biting cold surroundings of the Atlantic Ocean. Her masts are fallen. Decks almost devoid of fittings. Funnels ripped away from her superstructure while a huge gaping gash in her side from the iceberg appears grotesque and cruel. As the story progressed from Cussler's typewriter that sat upon a makeshift desk created from an unfinished door laid upon two sawhorses and placed in the corner of the basement, the characters and various plots began to weave into unique stories of a suspenseful Cold War setting with *Titanic* as the backdrop. And if *Titanic* alone could not capture the reader's attention then the tension between two of the world's superpowers would.

"My original inspiration was based on fantasy and desire to see the world's most famous ship brought up from the sea bed and towed into New York Harbor, completing her maiden voyage begun three-quarters of a century before. Fortunately, it was a fantasy shared by millions of her devoted fans."

Cussler's *Raise the Titanic!* begins on the night of April 14, 1912. A ragged looking passenger in his cabin on board a liner is awoken from a jarring sensation. Upon realizing the vessel had struck a huge iceberg and is taking on water, he forces a crew member to take him down to the ship's cargo hold where there sits a large vault. The passenger, after opening the steel door, retreats into the steely tomb muttering the words "Thank God for Southby." The crew member makes his way upon deck just as the liner sinks from beneath him. Reaching out he grabs hold of the vessel's flag, ripping it free from the mast as the ship slips beneath the waters. The story then leapfrogs to July 1987 where scientist Dr Gene Seagram, who is heading a top-secret program creating a satellite defence system for the Pentagon, is tasked to track down an extremely rare ore named Byzanium that is required to power the system. He discovers that the last known traces were mined from a Russian island back in 1912. Of those who led that fatal operation, only one makes it out alive to then journey to Southampton with the ore which will be sent by ship to America. The ship it is placed on board is the R.M.S. *Titanic*. Realising that the only known supply of Byzanium is sitting on the bottom of the North Atlantic, Seagram contacts Dirk Pitt of the National Underwater and Marine Agency to lead the task in not only searching for the wreck, but also in successfully raising to it.

The story shifts to the Atlantic Ocean as submersibles search the depths, find the wreck, then raise it. During that time the CIA have pressured the President of the United States to leak the story to the Soviet

Union with the hopes of capturing one of the Soviet's best intelligence officers. But the CIA want the ore for themselves. Once the *Titanic* is raised the situation intensifies when Hurricane Amanda; a name that inspired Cussler and taken from the daughter of the owner of the publisher Viking Press, rips through the area threatening both the wreck and salvage crews. But during the storm, the Russians who have been watching the operations from their own vessel, cease upon the opportunity to take control of the *Titanic* and take American crews' hostage. Events escalate resulting in a gun battle. With the help of U.S. SEALs, the situation is brought under control and the *Titanic* is secured and towed to New York. On board, the full impact of the complications of the operation becomes apparent when crews prise open the vault to discover the Byzanium was never placed on board the ship, but buried in a graveyard in the coastal village of Southby in England. The revelation causes Seagram to have a nervous breakdown. The story ends with the successful testing of The Sicilian Project out in the Pacific Ocean.

In June 1974 Cussler forwarded the manuscript for *Raise the Titanic!* to Peter Lampack. While Lampack found the story great, the publisher Dodd Mead & Co, rejected the novel on the grounds that it was overly long, citing the book to be an expensive print. The story then caught the attention of Viking Press who offered an advance of $7,500 along with limited changes to the manuscript. One interesting note is that during the talks with Viking Press on the cover design for the book, the publisher's sales department suggested that the title *Raise the Titanic!* would accompany the commissioned artwork better than Cussler's original working title. It has often been speculated to what title Cussler was to use for the novel. However, correspondence between the author and Viking Press during February and March 1976 makes it clear that the title was originally to be 'Titanic'. But as large portion of the story focused on the search and recovery of the liner it would make more sense to add to the title and catch the public's imagination.

The manuscript continued to grab the attention of publishing houses including those of Macmillan and Sphere in Great Britain, who offered a healthy $22,000 for the rights. This was the start of a bidding war as Cussler's *Titanic* story spread from publishing house to publishing house. The decision was taken by Lampack to sell the paperback rights in the United States through an auction. This was a clever and wise move that would pay off handsomely. The auction, set for June 1975, attracted many of the big paperback publishing houses including Bantam, Avon and Pocket Books. As Cussler sat at his writing desk, he answered the telephone call from Lampack who delighted in informing Clive that Bantam had successfully pulled through with the winning bid of $840,000. Cussler had the forethought to secure the rights to both *Iceberg* and *The Mediterranean Caper* and with the new deal from Bantam they furthered their commitment to Cussler by paying $40,000 each to keep them from entering the market until Bantam had established their true calibre. And if that wasn't enough an extra $100,000 was then put forward for the Book of the Month Club entry.

In February 1976 at the request of Viking Press, Cussler went about editing the manuscript into a more presentable finished work. The meeting between the publisher and author in their Madison Avenue offices had a profound effect on Cussler that on his return home he penned a letter to the publisher.

> "If anyone had ever told me that sitting elbow to elbow with a sharp-pencilled editor for nine hours at a stretch was a pleasurable experience, I'd have laughed. I'm not laughing now. What can I say about Cork Smith except that he's one hell of a guy? I can honestly state that I absorbed more technique in regards to writing craftsmanship from him in three days than I ever learned with three semesters of University English."

On 10 March Cussler received the confirmation letter from Viking Press that *Raise the Titanic!* was going into print. The publisher began promoting the book around summer sending out cards outlining the forthcoming release of the novel in the Fall of 76. The first run of the novel would amount to 65,000 copies with Viking Press investing $40,000 in nationwide advertising campaigns from bookstore display posters down to newspaper ads for maximum publicity. With the disclosure that *Raise the Titanic!* had sold for a staggering $840,000, it was not long before the media picked up the story and ran with it. As the book went through the printing presses, advanced copies made their way out for review. The first impressions were good. Columnist Barbara Bannon for *Publishers Weekly*, August 1976, referred to the story as "awesome" and "cleverly done". The September 15 *Library Journal* review called the story "spellbinding" and likened it to a "spy-spangled thriller for the Peter Benchley readership."

But not everyone liked the adventure. *The People* had received a copy, read it. and refused to publish a review of any kind as the editor decided he didn't like it. The October 21 issue of *The Christian Science Monitor*, reviewer John Moorhead found it was a "ripping good story" but "the characters strain credulity, the dialogue offends taste." But it was the review in the November issue of *Harper's Magazine* that delivered the most offensive with, "If good books were rewarded with flowers and bad books with skunks, on a scale of one to five, *Raise the Titanic* would deserve four skunks." Evan S. Connell's parting shot of "The only question is whether Hollywood will buy it" may have been the end of the matter for a now disgruntled Clive Cussler. But he was to have the last laugh when the film rights were snagged up back in August. That October, *Raise the Titanic* hit bookstores in hardback format from Viking Press, and by the last week of January 1977 the book had reached the #2 position on the New York Times Best Seller list, continuing to dominate the sales list well into March. That spring, Sphere Books over in London had picked up their side of the publishing deal in releasing the novel in paperback after Michael Joseph Publishers had completed the printing in hardback for UK distribution. Exciting news reached Cussler during summer 1977 that *Raise the Titanic* had been selected for an adaptation for the Best Sellers Showcase comic strip. Illustrated by Frank Bolle the strip ran from 15 August to 9 October and was printed in both colour and black and white formats, totalling 192 individual panels per series; three panels Monday to Saturday and six panels for a Sunday.

Cussler's tour dates in the UK for Sphere was to be a busy time with the author being interviewed at locations from London to Edinburgh between the dates of 24 April to 7 May 1978. However, Cussler made arrangements to travel earlier than originally expected, to attend the National Scottish Diving Conference being staged that April. As he prepared to travel to the UK, Nick Austin, the Editorial Director for Sphere congratulated Cussler on his follow up to *Raise the Titanic!* with the release of *Vixen 03*. In a letter to the author, Austin wrote,

> "Thank you for writing the latest Dirk Pitt tale – I haven't enjoyed a thriller as much since... well, if I can say so without sycophancy, since RAISE THE TITANIC! So it cost us $150,000 – so what? It's worth every cent of the price as far as Sphere's concerned. I don't know by what magic act of the creative imagination you managed to follow TITANIC with something equally as gripping but you sure as hell did."

Cussler's UK tour was a great success. As the Sphere paperback release hit the #1 spot, the author was treated to a day trip, courtesy of the publishing company, to the Beaulieu Motor Museum in Hampshire to view the museum's collection of vintage automobiles; another passion of Cussler who himself was an avid historic car enthusiast. On 3 April Sphere forwarded the list of their current sales of books to Cussler. The news was good as sales of *Raise the Titanic!* in paperback had now exceeded 387,000 copies.

Hollywood Comes Calling

The earliest publicly released news of film rights to *Raise the Titanic* being sold came in August 1976 when Hank Grant of *The Hollywood Reporter* announced that producer Robert Schaffel had bagged the screen rights to the story. This never turned out to be the case, as Peter Lampack had previously contacted several productions company's he thought would show interest in Cussler's *Raise the Titanic!* and the prospect of adapting the book. Of those approached one was Lew Grade's Associated Communications Corporation (ACC) who at first turned the idea down. Lew Grade recalled during an interview in January 1998.

"A great friend called Dick Smith, the head of General Cinemas in America, called me and said I had to read this 800-page manuscript called *Raise the Titanic*. When I saw the title, I said 'Oh my god, no' because the *Titanic* story had been done to death". The manuscript was handed personally to Grade during Richard "Dick" Smith's business trip to London. Handing Grade a box, Smith said, "It's a manuscript and I'd like you to read it." Grade all but responded with "Fine, I'll read it."

Grade's observation on the *Titanic* title clearly had little effect on his judgement of a great storytelling adventure. Putting the manuscript to one side turned out to be a productive turn of events when a few days later curiosity got the better of Grade who picked up the work and started to read through it. This was at ten o'clock at night and four hours later, without having put it down, Grade had finished reading it. What he saw was great potential in expanding the story on the lines similar to the James Bond franchise of films. There and then he wanted the film rights and he was determined to get them, regardless.

The following Friday Grade contacted Cussler's agent Peter Lampack to make the necessary appointment to meet in New York to secure the rights for a movie. The telephone call was to the point, harsh even, as Grade asserted his businessman prowess with Lampack. For *The New York Times* Grade described the conversation.

> "I said, 'I've read The *Titanic*; I want it.' He (Lampack) said: 'I've got several offers.' I said, 'I'm coming to New York Monday, you be at my hotel.' He comes in the afternoon about four o'clock. I said, 'I want to do a deal; you won't leave this room until we do a deal. I don't want bidding. You are either people in a position to do a deal, or else I forget it.' He said, 'I'll have to go back to Clive Cussler.' I said, 'Do it now, or I withdraw my offer, here's the telephone.' And he telephoned Clive, and he said. 'OK, provided I have a walk-on part and one sentence.'"

But there was one slight drawback. Grade had been beaten to the post by *It's a Mad, Mad, Mad, Mad World* producer and director Stanley Kramer who had not only obtained the rights but had already started on preproduction stages. Regardless of this potential dilemma, it was not going to deter Lew Grade from getting what he wanted. Kramer had previously worked as producer and director on the 1977 Gene Hackman film *The Domino Principal* for Grade's entertainment company ITC. A simple conversation between the two men concluded with the rights being secured by Grade while Kramer agreed to lead Grade's *Titanic* movie project as both producer and the director. Grade's entertainment companies of ITC, AFG, AFD and ACC had handed over a combined $450,000 for the exclusive rights to turn Cussler's story into a multi-million-dollar blockbuster while an additional $400,000 went to Stanley Kramer as repurchase rights to prevent any future bidding wars for the role of producer and directorial. The first news on the successful bid was released in several columns on October 13, 1976, when both *The Hollywood Reporter* and *Daily Variety* announced the deal between Cussler and Grade with a view that not only would a director be revealed within a week but that principal photography would begin sometime in 1977.

In February 1977 Aaron L. Michelson wrote for the *Best Sellers* journal that *Raise the Titanic!* was "an exciting and enthralling mixture of science fiction, intrigue and cliff-hanging adventure that will entertain and grip the reader from the first few pages until the final sentence." By the spring of 1978 *Raise the Titanic!* had clocked up an impressive 145,000 copies in book sales while reaching the number two slot in the bestseller lists and holding onto that position for twenty-six consecutive weeks.

The *Sahara* Debacle

Since the release of *Raise the Titanic!* Clive Cussler has gone on to become one of the most influential fiction writers of our time creating an impressive list of adventure stories put into varying categories of multi-book series that include the Dirk Pitt Adventures, NUMA Files, The Oregon Files, Fargo Adventures and the Isaac Bell Adventures. Cussler's book legacy comes in a titanic scale with sales of over one hundred million copies of the Dirk Pitt adventures alone. Cussler's flair for adventure with his protagonists was something that filmmakers could snap up to bring a new type of hero to the screen to rival James Bond. The subject of *Titanic* was already a winner in attracting the attention of the public and with the growing fascination in locating and possibly raising the wreck, *Raise the Titanic!* ticked the boxes in creating entertainment away from the pages of a book. While Cussler was not happy with how his *Raise the Titanic* was adapted for the screen, the book sales the film generated did make up for some of the woes even though Cussler did vow to never have another of his novels fall into the hands of a studio. He did keep to his word for nearly twenty-five years until Paramount Pictures came calling in 2004 with interest in turning his 1992 Dirk Pitt adventure *Sahara* into the first of a franchise of Cussler/Pitt movies. Featuring Matthew McConaughey as Pitt, Steve Zahn as Giordino and William H. Macy as Sandecker, the story follows Pitt as he searches for the long-lost remains of the ironclad *Texas* that vanished in 1865 carrying a cargo of Confederacy treasury gold. As the search intensifies, Pitt and Giordino discover an environmental disaster in the making from contamination leaking from a chemical plant that, once it reaches the sea, would kill ocean life around the world. Despite an army of those out to stop him, Pitt sets out to close down the plant and prevent such a climatic event from ever happening.

With echoes of *Raise the Titanic* from 1980, *Sahara* suffered greatly at the box office grossing just $119m worldwide of the original $221m budget allotted for the film production and marketing. While the film received a mixed public response, the critics were not that sympathetic with the consensus that *Sahara* was "a mindless adventure flick with a preposterous plot." The most scathing comment came from Claudia Eller when *Sahara* ranked as the most expensive film flop of all time in her article for the *Los Angeles Times* in 2014. With another of his novels poorly adapted, Cussler could no longer sit back and remain silent. In February 2005 and before the film's release, Cussler began legal action against the movie's producer Philip Anschutz and his entertainment company Crusader Entertainment LLC, suing them for $100m for failing to consult Cussler during the screenplay writing period. Cussler felt he had been ignored, lied to and deceived from the offset, even though he had been given certain approval rights to the script, actors and directors under the agreement that he had absolute control over the book's adaptation. Anschutz hit back stating that Cussler had an "obstructive presence" which contributed to the film's problems that amounted to a counterclaim of over $20m against the author. With both parties now facing allegations of breach of contract, the ongoing dispute continued right through to 2012 when both parties were summoned into court to face the $20m court fees accumulated over a decade of feuds. It finally came to a close in 2013 when the Second Appellate District for California's Appeals Court concluded that following years of litigation, both sides were to recover nothing – not one dime of damages and no declaratory relief. The *Sahara* fallout did mark the end of any chance of another Cussler novel ever making it to the screen. Maybe third time lucky if any of the novels are adapted for television? Who knows what the future holds?

Cussler's Enduring Legacy

Cussler's interests in *Titanic* did not stop within the pages of a book when during the spring of 2000 Cussler announced that his real-life NUMA team had discovered the final resting place of the former Cunard liner R.M.S. *Carpathia*. Launched in 1902, the 13,500-ton passenger ship entered the history books as the saviour of 712 *Titanic* survivors when her master, Arthur Rostron, raced the vessel at full steam through the night to arrive in the area just before dawn on 15 April 1912. *Carpathia*'s tragic end came when, following a torpedo attack on 17 July 1918, she sank and came to rest came nearly 500ft down in the cold dark waters of the Atlantic some 120 miles off the coast of Ireland. While Cussler was successful in raising the *Titanic* in the realms of fantasy, he did open the door to the salvaging of an important part of American history when his NUMA team, led by diver Ralph Wilbanks and funded by Cussler, positively located and identified the wreck of the *H.L. Hunley*, the Confederate submarine that was lost during the American Civil War in February 1864 claiming the lives of all eight of its crew. The wreckage was located in 27ft of water in the waters off Charleston Harbor, South Carolina, in April 1995 and was discovered buried beneath several feet of river silt and laying on her starboard side in a remarkable state of preservation. For the next five years, the wreck site was closely monitored until an agreement had been finalised to salvage the remains. On the 8 August 2000, the hull of the *Hunley* was successfully lifted from the river bed, dropped down onto a supporting barge and towed to the former Charleston Navy Yard and the Warren Lasch Conservation Center for the first stages of years of preservation in a sodium hydroxide bath that would eventually lead to the wreck being allowed to be exposed to the air.

With the *Sahara* debacle now behind him, Cussler carried on delivering to fans a plethora of fanciful adventure books, even branching out to co-author with other established writers; Graham Brown, Craig Dirgo, Jack Du Brul, Boyd Morrison, Paul Kemprecos, Justin Scott, Grant Blackwood, Thomas Perry, Russell Blake, Robin Burcell and even his son, Dirk Cussler. Nearly five decades have passed since his acclaimed novel on the raising of the unsinkable liner was released to much media attention. And yet after all that time, he refused to close the door on his *Titanic* quest. Cussler fans were enthralled to see the return of their hero Dirk Pitt in 2019 with the release on August 22 of the highly anticipated novel *The Titanic Secret*; an unusual combination of a prequel and sequel coming together and arcing back to the events at Angel Mine, the mining of the precious ore and the journey into the cargo hold of the *Titanic* docked in Southampton.

As we entered a new decade Clive Cussler refused to sit back and relax as he continued to work tirelessly from his literary factory home in Scottsdale, Arizona. delivering to his abundance of fans all over the world startling and gripping adventure stories alongside many notable authors. Cussler's dedication to the world of adventure writing came to an end when on 24 February 2020 he passed away peacefully at his home at the tender age of 88. His passing was like an afterword from one of his adventure books. But now it marks a new chapter in his legacy as a number of his works previously unpublished are destined for book stores over the coming years along with some of the Cussler series being picked up by his son Dirk Cussler and previous writing partners.. They will become a fitting tribute to one of America's most influential masters of adventure. Cussler's passing reminded me of the following passage from *Raise the Titanic*. Cussler had battled the many in life and within the pages of his fictional works in delivering multiple best sellers on demand and time constraints to fulfil those who need his creative genius in their hands. But instead of longing for Southby he will always be in his beloved Colorado.

"*The deed is only a eulogy now, for I am but dead. Praise God, the precious ore we labored so desperately to rape from the bowels of that cursed mountain lies safely in the vault of the ship. Only Vernon will be left to tell the tale, for I depart on the great White Star steamer for New York within the hour. Knowing the ore is secure, I have this journal in the care of James Rodgers, Assistant United States Consul in Southampton, who will see that it reaches the proper authorities in the event I am also killed. God rest the men who have gone before me. How I long to return to Southby.*

Joshua Hays Brewster
April 10, 1912"

* * *

The Works of Clive Cussler

The following is a list of released publications by Clive Cussler starting with his first novel in 1973 right through to the latest release in 2021. The list includes all adventure series, solo and co-authored works, and publications for younger readers and non-fiction works covering his classic car museum collection to wreck hunting.

DIRK PITT

The Mediterranean Caper – *also published as Mayday!* (1973) * Iceberg (1974) * *Raise the Titanic!* (1976) * Vixen 03 (1978) * Night Probe! (1981) * Pacific Vortex (1983) * Deep Six (1984) * Cyclops (1986) * Treasure (1988) * Dragon (1990) * Sahara (1992) * Inca Gold (1994) * Shock Wave (1996) * Flood Tide (1997) * Atlantis Found (1999) * Valhalla Rising (2001) * Trojan Odyssey (2003) * Black Wind *with Dirk Cussler* (2004) * Treasure of Khan *with Dirk Cussler* (2006) * Arctic Drift *with Dirk Cussler* (2008) * Crescent Dawn *with Dirk Cussler* (2010) * Poseidon's Arrow *with Dirk Cussler* (2012) * Havana Storm *with Dirk Cussler* (2014) * Odessa Sea *with Dirk Cussler* (2016) * Celtic Empire *with Dirk Cussler* (2018) * The Devils Sea *with Dirk Cussler* (2021)
Note: Pacific Vortex was Clive Cussler's first ever written novel, pre-dating The Mediterranean Caper. It was not considered for publication until 1983.

NUMA FILES

Serpent *with Paul Kemprecos* (1999) * Blue Gold *with Paul Kemprecos* (2000) * Fire Ice *with Paul Kemprecos* (2002) * White Death *with Paul Kemprecos* (2003) * Lost City *with Paul Kemprecos* (2004) * Polar Shift *with*

Paul Kemprecos (2005) * The Navigator *with Paul Kemprecos* (2007) * Medusa *with Paul Kemprecos* (2009) * Devil's Gate *with Graham Brown* (2011) * The Storm *with Graham Brown* (2012) * Zero Hour *with Graham Brown* (2013) * Ghost Ship *with Graham Brown* (2014) * The Pharaoh's Secret *with Graham Brown* (2015) * Nighthawk *with Graham Brown* (2017) * The Rising Sea *with Graham Brown* (2018) * Sea of Greed *with Graham Brown* (2019) * Journey of the Pharaohs *with Graham Brown* (2020) * Fast Ice *with Graham Brown* (2021)

THE OREGON FILES

Golden Buddha *with Craig Dirgo* (2003) * Sacred Stone *with Craig Dirgo* (2004) * Dark Watch *with Jack Du Brul* (2005) * Skeleton Coast *with Jack Du Brul* (2006) * Plague Ship *with Jack Du Brul* (2008) * Corsair *with Jack Du Brul* (2009) * The Silent Sea *with Jack Du Brul* (2010) * The Jungle *with Jack Du Brul* (2011) * Mirage *with Jack Du Brul* (2013) * Piranha *with Boyd Morrison* (2015) * The Emperor's Revenge *with Boyd Morrison* (2017) * Typhoon Fury *with Boyd Morrison* (2017) * Shadow Tyrants *with Boyd Morrison* (2018) * Final Option *with Boyd Morrison* (2019) * Marauder *with Boyd Morrison* (2020)

ISAAC BELL ADVENTURES

The Chase (2007) * The Wrecker *with Justin Scott* (2009) * The Spy *with Justin Scott* (2010) * The Race *with Justin Scott* (2011) * The Thief *with Justin Scott* (2012) * The Striker *with Justin Scott* (2013) * The Bootlegger *with Justin Scott* (2014) * The Assassin *with Justin Scott* (2015) * The Gangster *with Justin Scott* (2016) * The Cutthroat *with Justin Scott* (2017) * The Titanic Secret *with Jack Du Brul* (2019) * The Saboteurs *with Jack Du Brul* (2021)

FARGO ADVENTURES

Spartan Gold *with Grant Blackwood* (2009) * Lost Empire *with Grant Blackwood* (2010) * The Kingdom *with Grant Blackwood* (2011) * The Tombs *with Thomas Perry* (2012) * The Mayan Secret *with Thomas Perry* (2013) * The Eye of Heaven *with Russell Blake* (2014) * The Solomon Curse *with Russell Blake* (2015) * Pirate *with Robin Burcell* (2016) * The Romanov Ransom *with Robin Burcell* (2017) * The Gray Ghost *with Robin Burcell* (2018) * The Oracle *with Robin Burcell* (2019) * Wrath of Poseidon *with Robin Burcell* (2020)

CHILDREN'S BOOKS

The Adventures of Fin Fiz (2006) * The Adventures of Hotsy Totsy (2010)

THE SEA HUNTERS

The Sea Hunters *with Craig Dirgo* (1994) * The Sea Hunter II *with Craig Dirgo* (2002)

NON-FICTION BOOKS

Clive Cussler and Dirk Pitt Revealed *with Craig Dirgo* (1998) * Built for Adventure: The Classic Automobiles of Clive Cussler and Dirk Pitt (2011) * Built to Thrill (2016)

The American architect Charles A. Smith. *(Missouri Valley Special Collections)*

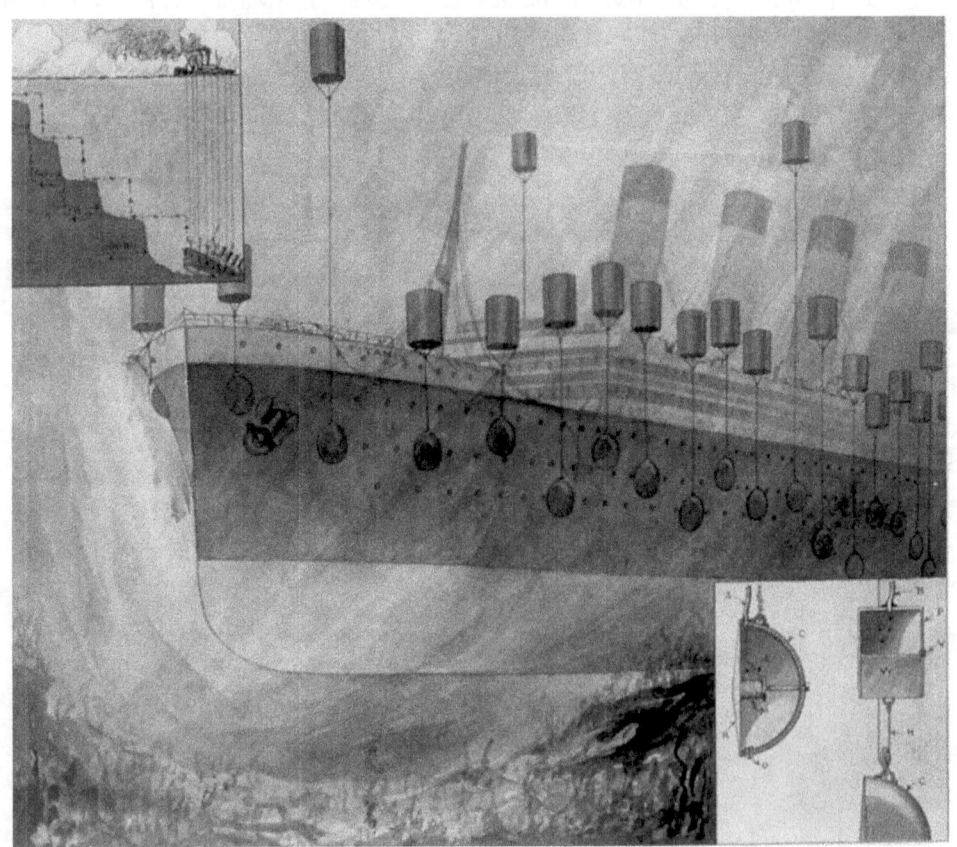

Charles A. Smith's rather flamboyant plan from 1914 on the use of strong magnets to raise the *Titanic*. *(Author's collection)*

Cussler's first published novel released in 1975 that was later reissued under the new title of *Mayday! (Walter Winterburn collection)*

Viking Press publishers publicity photograph of Cussler in the late 1970s. *(Walter Winterburn collection)*

"Thank God for Southby." It is the early morning of 10 April, 1912 and mining engineer, Arthur Brewster and his seven boxes of deadly cargo, await to board the world's largest and most luxurious ocean liner. *(Period photograph edited by Jonathan Smith)*

William Pitt "the younger", the British Prime Minister in 1783. *(Period etching – Author's collection)*

The 1969 first edition of *The Maiden Voyage* by Geoffrey Marcus that left Cussler impressed. *(Author's collection)*

A room with a view. Clive in his home office overlooking the snow-covered landscape of Colorado. Even his scale *Titanic* model makes an appearance. *(Author's collection)*

March 2, 1976

Mr. Thomas H. Buinzberg, President
Viking Press, Inc.
625 Madison Avenue
New York, New York 10022

Dear Mr. Guinzberg:

Thank you for the warm and friendly courtesy extended by you and your firm during my working stay in the Big Apple last week. It was also a great pleasure meeting you, Mr. Guinzberg. Taking time to have lunch with me was a considerate gesture and I truly appreciated it. Sorry you missed the Knicks vs. the Braves. It was a thriller.

If anyone had ever told me that sitting elbow to elbow with a sharp-penciled editor for nine hours at a stretch was a pleasureable experience, I'd have laughed. I'm not laughing now. What can I say about Cork Smith except that he's one hell of a guy. I can honestly state that I absorbed more technique in regards to writing craftsmanship from him in three days than I ever learned with three semesters of University English.

I've finished the rewrites Cork suggested and they should be retyped and in his hands for his final approval by Monday.

I have a gut feeling that TITANIC will come home a winner, and you can count on me to do whatever is necessary to give it a good kick in the stern.

Again, Mr. Guinzberg, thank you for your hospitality.

Yours with compliments,

Clive Cussler

CC:bc

March 5, 1976

Miss Amanda Guinzburg
c/o Thomas H. Guinzburg
Viking Press, Inc.
625 Madison Avenue
New York, New York 10022

Dear Amanda:

I don't suppose you receive many letters from people you have never met. I know I didn't when I was a little boy. The only mail that ever came addressed to me were mostly birthday cards from my grandparents, aunts and uncles, and of course valentine cards from my schoolmates. Is is that way with you too?

The reason I am writing to you, Amanda, is to ask you a big favor. You see, I have written a story entitled "Titanic" which your Daddy is going to make into a book. And, part of the story is about a great ship that is caught in a giant storm known as a hurricane. Now funny as it may seem, hurricanes are given names, girls names as it so happens: Hurricane Suzy, Hurricane Cindy, Hurricane Heidi, to name a few. I guess this is done because everyone knows girls are sugar and spice and everything nice, but they can also become a trifle capricious and restless at times.

So the favor is this, Amanda. Will you allow me the honor of giving my story's hurricane your name? I think it would be great fun if we called it Hurricane Amanda. I think you might find it fun too. If you agree, just tell your Daddy and he will take care of any required details.

I hope you enjoyed receiving this letter as much as I enjoyed writing it, Amanda. Maybe we can meet the next time I climb down from the Rocky Mountains and come to New York.

Always make your parents proud of you.

Your friend,

Clive Cussler

P.S. Please tell your Daddy to forgive me for misspelling his name in my last letter to him.

THE VIKING PRESS INC · PUBLISHERS
625 MADISON AVENUE, NEW YORK, N.Y. 10022
Cable: VIKPRESS *Telex:* 233776 *Telephone:* (212) PLAZA 5-4330

March 10, 1976

Mr. Clive Cussler
7731 West 72nd Place
Arvada, Colorado 80005

Dear Mr. Cussler:

We are delighted that we will be publishing your book, TITANIC.

In order that we may have the latest biographical information and supporting lists to assist us in promoting your book, we would appreciate it if you would complete the enclosed form and send it back to me at your earliest convenience. We will be holding our sales conference shortly and it would be most helpful if we could make the information from the form available to our salespeople at that time.

You will note a request for a recent photograph on the bottom of the last page. I hope that you will be able to send one along also.

We look forward to working on your book during the coming months.

Sincerely,

Julia Diamant,
Assistant to the
Director of Publicity,
Mary Hornby

Cussler's letter dated March 2, 1976 to the publisher Viking Press expressing his beliefs in his *Titanic* tale. This charming letter sent three days later shows the gentle side of the author who named the hurricane in his story after the daughter of the President of Viking Press. That same week Cussler received news his novel was going into print. *(Author's collection)*

```
THE VIKING PRESS INC · PUBLISHERS
625 MADISON AVENUE · NEW YORK · N Y · 10022
Cable: Vikpress   Telephone: (212) PL 5-4330

                                        April 12, 1976

Mr. Clive Cussler
7731 W. 72nd Place
Arvada, Colorado  80005

Dear Clive:

Thanks again for being so prompt in sending me
material. Last week we had a pre-conference on
all books that will be published in the Fall and
Winter. After Alan Williams impassioned presentation
of THE TITANIC I think that everyone at Viking will
soon become a member of The Dirk Pitt Fan Club!
The book really sounds terrific and I look forward
to reading it along with ICEBERG.

                                Sincerely,

                                Julia

                                Julia Diamant
                                Publicity Dept.
```

Welcome to the Dirk Pitt fan club. *(Author's collection)*

"A great adventure thriller capable of riveting readers the same way *The Day of the Jackal* did   Super"
—Barbara Bannon, *Publishers Weekly*

HERE'S THE ACTION ON FALL'S BIGGEST BOOK

 Giant first printing of 65,000 copies

 $40,000 initial budget for national advertising

 Terrific subsidiary rights sales, including Bantam paperback, Playboy Book Club, the Literary Guild, and The Doubleday Book Club

 Major author tour coast to coast—TV, radio, and other personal appearances, with lots of press coverage

 Appearance in 7 major Christmas catalogues

 Four-color poster shipping with books

 Use the post-paid business reply to order this fantastic fall seller (and take the opportunity to sign up for co-op ads in your city)

This rare publisher card promotes the novel outlining the print run of the first edition and promotional duties for the author. *(Author's collection)*

Chapter 3: The Grandmaster of Adventure • 77

Advanced Reading Copy (ARC) of an uncorrected proof for *Raise the Titanic!* These very early printings sent out by the publisher are sought after by collectors for their unique print. *(Author's collection)*

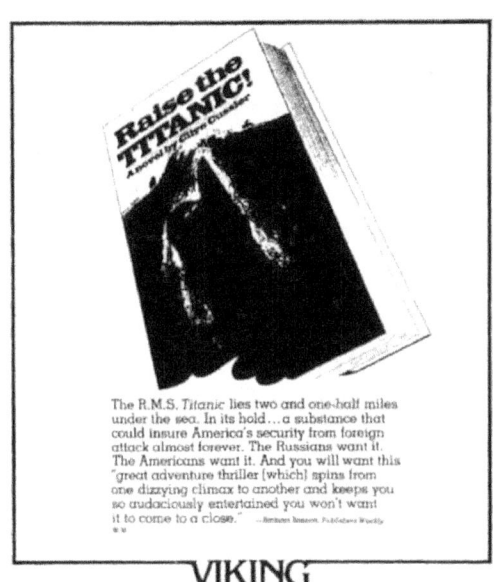

Newspaper advertisement promoting the release of *Raise the Titanic*. *(Author's collection)*

The Viking Press first edition hardback of *Raise the Titanic*! *(Author's collection)*

Cussler's "Get it up!" inscription in signed copies of *Raise the Titanic!* that makes for a desirable collectible among fans. *(Author's collection)*

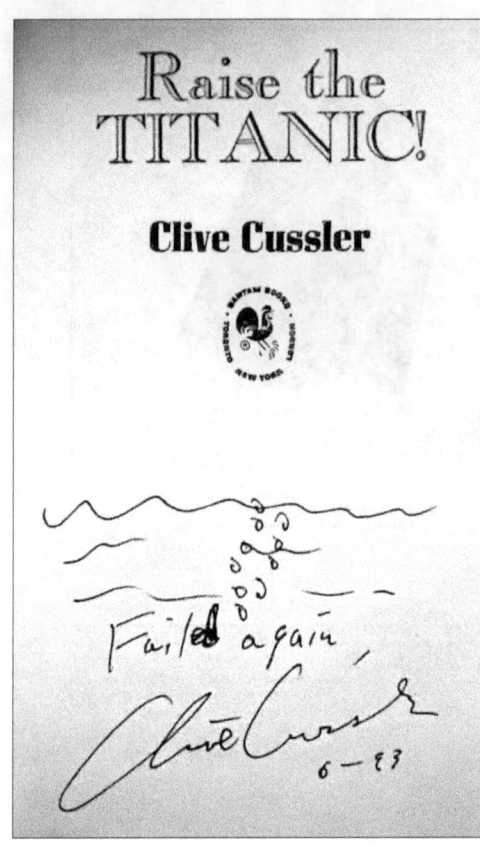

Embroidered patch for NUMA; *National Underwater Marine Agency,* Cussler's fictional marine expedition company that would become a reality in the years to follow. *(Author's collection)*

This is one of the more unusual inscriptions from Cussler with this example taking aim at the failure that Cussler could see with the movie adaptation of his best-selling novel. *(Shane Stratton collection)*

Sphere UK bookstore advertising poster from 1977. *(Author's collection)*

The man who makes James Bond appear amateurish. *(Author's collection)*

Cussler during the promotional touring of his novel. *(Publicity photograph – Author's collection)*

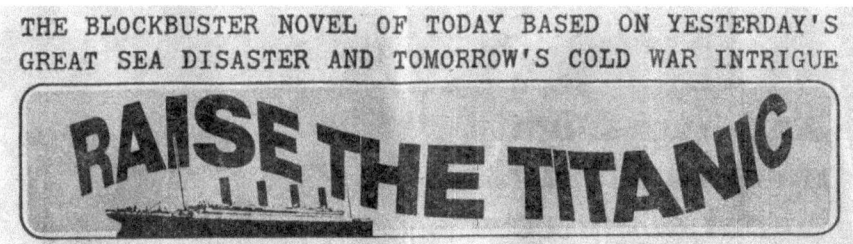

Header for the adaptation of Clive Cussler's *Raise the Titanic!* that was printed in the March 1977 issue of the *Daily Express* newspaper. *(Author's collection)*

Lyft Titanic!... Swedish edition from 1977. *(Author's collection)*

This scarce 1977 Argentinian edition of the novel is a condensed version of the story but is uniquely packed with comic-book style illustrations that make it the only book version of the novel to be fully illustrated. *(Author's collection)*

Titanic braves the hurricane. One of the many illustrations from the condensed version *Rescaten el Titanic* published in 1977. *(Author's collection)*

Selection of the *Best Sellers* series featuring an adaptation of Cussler's *Raise the Titanic!* with artwork by the legendary artist Frank Bolle. *(Author's collection)*

The Bantam Press sampler from July 1977 that features two chapters from the novel to entice new sales in the paperback. This bookmark was another publicity piece from *Bantam Books* advertising their paperback release of the novel. *(Author's collection)*

Chapter 3: The Grandmaster of Adventure • 81

Metal publicity badge produced by *Sphere* books in the UK for book store staff to wear in advertising the release of *Raise the Titanic!* in 1978. *(Author's collection)*

LEFT: Original letter sent from *Sphere* Books to Cussler in April 1979 praising the success of sales for their paperback edition of *Raise the Titanic!* and their newest Cussler release; *Vixen 03*. *(Author's collection)*

Original letter header of the main London offices of ITC in 1979. *(Author's collection)*

LEFT: Entertainment mogul Lord Lew Grade sets his sights on a potential movie blockbuster. *(ITC publicity photograph – Author's collection)*

With *Raise the Titanic* leading the idea of a film franchise to rival MGM Studios James Bond, Grade could see the potential in a series of films based around Cussler's fictional hero Dirk Pitt with Grade setting his sights on *Mayday!* and *Iceberg*. *(Sphere Books Ltd)*

Stanley Kramer; the controversial director. *(Publicity photograph – Author's collection)*

Clive Cussler on the set of *Raise the Titanic* during filming in Washington at the Mayflower Hotel in a cameo role of a press reporter. Part of the deal originally had Cussler directing a question at Admiral Sandecker (Jason Robards) who was addressing the press following the discovery of the *Titanic*. *(Author's collection)*

Chapter 3: The Grandmaster of Adventure • **83**

The 1992 first edition of *Sahara*. *(Author's collection)*

(Author's collection)

Clive Cussler giving evidence during the court hearings in 2007 over the fallout from the movie adaptation of *Sahara*. *(Associated Press)*

The twisted remains of the former Cunard liner *Carpathia*. *(Painting © Stuart Williamson)*

The salvaged hull of the *Hunley*. *(Photography © Jim Woods)*

Cussler in the tank at the propeller end of the hull of the *Hunley*. *(Photograph © Kellen Butler / Friends of the Hunley)*

The Grandmaster of Adventure. *(Photograph © Walter Winterburn collection)*

Special author editions that make for wonderful collectibles. *(Aaron Griffin collection)*

Cussler's wide and varied writings from the period of Dirk Pitt through to the Isaac Bell adventures and Cussler putting fantastical tales together for children with *Vin Fiz*. *(Aaron Griffin collection)*

Chapter 4

Two Directors

"When you see the Titanic emerging above the water it's the most exciting, awesome thing ever filmed. It's a three-minute ballet from the time the ship breaks water until it finally settles down."

Jerry Jameson

At first glance, it would appear that Jerry Jameson was the ideal choice for directing *Raise the Titanic* having previously worked on the 1977 disaster movie *Airport '77* and presenting an action-adventure motion picture with a respectable $6 million budget. As Jameson took to the director's chair on the preproduction of *Raise the Titanic,* he had already worked out who of the crew he wanted to return following on from his *Airport* collaboration. But Jameson was never the first choice for Lew Grade and his monumental task of salvaging the *Titanic*. That accolade went to the multi-award-winning and sometimes controversial producer and director, Stanley Kramer.

Stanley Kramer

Steven Spielberg described him as "one of our great filmmakers, not just for the art and passion he put on screen, but for the impact he has made on the conscience of the world." Stanley Earl Kramer was born in Manhattan on September 29, 1913. It was at the age of 20 when he turned his attention to writing. Following graduation from New York University, he got a degree in business administration, leading him to develop an impetuosity to write for newspaper columns. From this, he enrolled in a paid internship for the writing department for Twentieth Century Fox. The great depression of the 1930s failed to keep him away from motion pictures when he took on odd jobs where possible to keep within the film industry circle, working as a film cutter for Metro-Goldwyn-Mayer and researching and authoring for Columbia Pictures. He developed an exceptional attitude towards editing and understanding with great ability the overall structure of the film he worked upon. During World War II he assisted with training films for the Signal Corps in New York, to then leave the army with the rank of first lieutenant. After the war, he would set up his own independent film company, Screen Plays Inc. His first success came in 1949 with the release of Champion starring the then largely unknown Kirk Douglas. The film was a huge success for Kramer not just the films low budget production but with it going on to win an Academy Award. In 1951 he was offered the opportunity to form a production unit with Columbia Pictures and given free rein over what films he wanted to make. During the period with Columbia, he had a highly successful run of films including *Death of a Salesman* (1951), *High Noon* (1952), *The Wild One* (1953), and *The Caine Mutiny* (1954), which would become his last film with Columbia Pictures.

Kramer returned to his independent company roots to continue with the success of producing and directing, including films that became a symbol of his production skills and those that raised eyebrows due to their controversial tones dealing with issues of racism, greed, nuclear wars, and fascism, the kind of topics that Hollywood studios regarded as taboo. In 1958 Kramer directed *The Defiant Ones*, which saw two of the film's characters, Sidney Poitier and Tony Curtis, shackled together but united in brotherhood. *On the Beach* (1959) for United Artists was Kramer's postapocalyptic science fiction movie which touched on the sensitive subject of nuclear war which has annihilated most of the Northern hemisphere with radioactive dust. His 1961 *Judgement on Nuremberg* was a fictionalized account of the real-life trials following the Nazi defeat in World War II. The film was nominated for eleven Academy Awards with it going on to win two of them. In 1963 Kramer turned his attention, in the light of his previous films, to release *It's a Mad, Mad, Mad, Mad World*, the epic comedy for United Artists. The mid-1960s to the 1970s saw another string of successful films, including more award winners including *Ship of Fools* (1965) and the controversial *Guess Who's Coming to Dinner* (1967). In 1971 and 1973 Kramer produced and directed two films for Columbia Pictures, *Bless the Beasts and Children* followed by *Oklahoma Crude*. In 1977 Kramer had his first outing working for Lew Grade when he produced and directed for ITC *The Domino Principal* starring *The French Connection* and *The Poseidon Adventure* star Gene Hackman. When the film rights for *Raise the Titanic* first came to light Kramer obtained them from Clive Cussler's agent Peter Lampack. Kramer had shown much interest in bringing Cussler's book to the big screen while wanting to do justice to the story. When Lew Grade be- came interested in the film, he repurchased the rights directly from Kramer handing over $400,000 while shaping the deal that Kramer would be onboard as the movie's producer and director. The earliest news to break publicly on Kramer joining Grade for *Raise the Titanic* came on 18 October 1976 in *Variety* magazine. While Kramer continued postproduction work on Grade's *The Domino Principle*, Adam Kennedy had already begun on the first stages of the screenplay for *Raise the Titanic*.

Kramer's *Titanic*

By June 1977 Kramer was now progressing through the preproduction stages of *Raise the Titanic* and had already set his sights on the actor to play the leading role of Dirk Pitt. James Brolin, who had already appeared in Grade's ITC science fiction film *Capricorn One*, seemed the obvious choice for the role with his handsome on-screen presence. With July approaching the opportunity was there to capture footage in New York that will be used in the film's ending chapters as the raised *Titanic*, pulled by tugs, is guided into the Navy dockyards in Brooklyn. For this Kramer needed an occasion that would capture the excitement of *Titanic*'s arrival without the need of calling upon hundreds if not thousands of extras. Kramer's first and only outing to lens *Raise the Titanic* was put into place for the weekend celebrations in New York to mark the cities Son of Op Sail events which would see a huge flotilla of varying craft including ocean liners, sailing vessels, yachts, and countless small watercraft as they take to the waters of the harbour. The itinerary for the festival which was to cover three days, Saturday to a Monday, would see tens of thousands of spectators flocking to the harbour front. This would be the perfect opportunity for Kramer to capture the events. Preparations for the filming began in June with the locations chosen, submitted for approval, and crews along with equipment hired from Harold E. Wellman, A.S.C. Initially nine camera points were selected to film sequences that had now been storyboarded.

Locations picked were the lower end of Johnson Avenue overlooking the river, the water's edge to the Holland Tunnel, and another at Jersey City and one set up at Ellis Island. One was stationed at Liberty Island and a unit positioned at Fort Joy, one on the west bank of the Brooklyn Bridge, another on the junction of Washington and Lafayette, and one located at the World Trade Center. The last remaining unit was further up the Hudson at the water's edge of 43rd Street near to the Lincoln

Tunnel at Weehawken. On 29 June permissions were granted on several of the locations, but not all. Changes were made to cover the celebrations with a move over to the rooftop of the Commercial Trust Bank and a new camera location at the World Trade Center. A 6' x 5' platform was put together and airlifted to the southwest corner of tower two of the World Trade Center. It was positioned with a height of four feet clearance over the electrified rooftop parameter fence, with a view looking directly out towards the East River to capture scenes with boats in the water as they make their way under the Brooklyn and Manhattan bridges. During postproduction stages these scenes would be edited with matte effects showing the *Titanic* and the two tugboats.

Filming the celebrations began on the morning of Friday 1 July with two cameras while Saturday 2nd and Sunday 3rd, six cameras would result in nearly 25,000ft of footage recorded with anamorphic cameras with 50 to 500 zooms. With Kramer's camera units in place, the first day of filming guaranteed many large vessels and smaller craft were in focus giving views of liners such as Cunard Line's *Princess* and *Queen Elizabeth II* along with the *Rotterdam* and *Statendam*. Of the footage filmed by Kramer that weekend several scenes were to be incorporated into the film with two main views matted in with footage shot in the tanks at Malta with the *Titanic* wreck miniature, giving long-distance shots of the derelict surrounded by vessels as she is towed along New York's East River. While those scenes did make it into the movie one sequence was put forward for consideration, the filming of one of *Titanic*'s actual survivors. Robert Gibbons, one of the co-founders of the *Titanic Enthusiasts of America*, later renamed to the *Titanic Historical Society,* recalled the decision,

> "We tried to get them to insert a scene of Edwina MacKenzie into that sequence by just filming her at her house at Hermosa Beach up against the sky, but the production people couldn't spare the $2,500 to go there and film it."

With the New York sequences in the can the production now moved over to California for the meticulous work of recreating the *Titanic* in miniature at the CBS Studio Center. From the offset, Kramer wanted to inject his flare of filmmaking into the movie and to deliver on-screen a lavish spectacle. In an interview with columnist Army Archerd for Variety magazine in September 1977, he commented "It's now a special effects world." But soon after committing to the film Kramer begin to realize what a titanic task bringing Clive Cussler's story to the screen was going to be. At the CBS Studio Center, the plans drawn up for the huge *Titanic* model had been hung up on the wall as Kramer's team from the model department brought *Titanic* from the scaled detailed schematics into reality.

"Creative Differences"

The scale of the build was monumental, from the various miniatures down to the planned sets. As the model work progressed and grew, so did the costs. Disagreements soon arose between Kramer with Kramer pushing for more money if the production was ever to be a success. As Grade began to dig his heels in, this, in turn, frustrated Kramer even more, as if the film itself wasn't challenging enough. Then in November 1977 came the news that American television-movie producer Roger Gimbel was working on his own *Titanic* project retelling the night of the sinking for the then-named *Titanic Down* which later would be released as *S.O.S. Titanic* in 1979. Was this going to become a race to see who could get their *Titanic* film out first? It was looking that way. Kramer must have felt more pressure upon his shoulders with this news while keenly aware that the sinking of *Titanic* has been done before with such films as *A Night to Remember* (1958) and *Titanic* (1953). But little did he realize that the financial backer of Gimbel's *Titanic Down* was non-other than Lord Delfont, Lew Grade's brother Bernard. The brotherly rivalry of the two Grades was soon to rear its ugly head as the production of *Raise the Titanic* continued over at the CBS Studio Center. The movie's original budget of £6m set by Grade was rapidly vanishing as the astronomical costs of the models, tanks and sets increased, consuming great chunks of the budget and forcing Grade to dig deeper and increase the budget to over £12m. While big-budget films of today cost in the region of an estimated $150 million and more, in 1977 the new budget of £12m for *Raise the Titanic* was staggering when compared to the budget that same year for *Star Wars* which was an estimated $11 million.

For the time *Raise the Titanic* was the most expensive film production and with Grade as the financial backer, it was Grade's biggest adventure to date. For Grade to get his money's worth and have delivered a true spectacle of movie magic, only that could be achieved with the help of Stanley Kramer. Yet they still argued and disagreed over the costs. The project could have been handled better if Grade had cut his losses there and then, accepted defeat that it was too big an undertaking for him and his companies, but this is Lew Grade, Mr. Entertainment, and Grade lived by his own rule; "Give me an idea typed on one page and, if I like it, I can make someone a very rich man." And so, Grade pursued his goal to bring *Titanic* onto the big screen. But the growing pressure of the production upon the shoulders of Kramer became too much. After nine months of the project, Stanley Kramer bowed out of being the film's producer and director in December 1977 citing "creative differences" and in a move that could easily have jeopardized the whole film production.

Production manager for ITC Bernard J. Kingham went out to the CBS Studio Center during those calmer times and was given the impression that the *Titanic* miniature was going to be given its water-filming tank within the studio grounds. This never came to light. When crews were brought in to construct the tank and dug into the ground the hole would soon begin to fill with water. The instability of the grounds, the size of the *Titanic* model, and the enormous scale of the tank were never fully appreciated. For Kingham, he knew that the only tank in the world big enough to put the *Titanic* model in was over in Malta but yet that tank while being wide enough was not deep enough to finalize the film's all-important raising scenes. This huge headache played upon Kramer, and with Grade applying pressure to keep within budget while he whittled away at the film's expenses, Kramer's departure begins to make sense. But Kingham's remark to Grade to think about cutting his losses fell upon deaf ears. Too much money had already been put into *Raise the Titanic* and Grade was not going to throw the production away.

Christmas of 1977 had Grade sitting upon his slowly floundering ship. But not all was lost. In January 1978 *The Hollywood Reporter* ran the story of three *Titanic* movies planned, Roger Gimbel's *Titanic Down*, a three-hour production for NBC-TV by *The Outer Limits* producer Lou Morheim who would later drop the project to work on *Titanic Down* and the still in the works ITC movie *Raise the Titanic*. Then the story takes a new step forwards when Lew Grade announces in February 1978 that he, and former president of ABC Entertainment, Martin Starger, have now joined forces to create the new Marble Arch Productions. Grade's role was that of chairman while Starger was made the company chief executive and deputy chief executive of Grade's other companies, ATV and ACC, this giving Jack Gill a managerial role within the company. However, unaware to Grade, back in London, Gill was already part of a three-man directors committee formed to keep a close eye on Grade's extravagant spending of company investments and curb his wild cinematic projects. By early 1978 it was becoming clear that Grade's much-celebrated American distribution networks were now slowly being drawn into a state of collapse while all the while Grade continued to fund *Raise the Titanic*, oblivious to the fact that any future film projects would, essentially, be unable to reap any financial rewards.

It was during February 1978 when Stanley Kramer had not only given Grade's *Raise the Titanic* the cold shoulder but also that of Los Angeles, moving to Seattle and settling his family down while returning to producing, if only for a short period, releasing *The Runner Stumbles* in 1979 as his final production before retiring. From 1980 to 1996 Kramer wrote a column on movies for the *Seattle Times* and hosted a weekly movie show on KCPQ, which was now owned by the Fox Company. In 1997 he went on to author his biography titled *It's a Mad, Mad, Mad, Mad World: A Life in Hollywood* in which he reflects on the times during his most recognized movies. The book has one major omission. *Raise the Titanic* is nowhere to be seen. Stanley Kramer passed away on 9 February 2001 in Los Angeles aged 87 from complications with pneumonia. While Kramer is remembered here as the director that *Raise the Titanic* never had, it would appear that he evacuated the doomed ship in the first lifeboat long before the iceberg came along making him best known as the man who directed a Hollywood legend.

"If I am to be remembered for anything I have done in this profession, I would like it to be for the four films in which I directed Spencer Tracy."

Jerry Jameson

With Stanley Kramer no longer involved with the production, *Raise the Titanic* was without a producer and director. However, Lew Grade still firmly believed in his product. After all, he had invested far more than he wanted to and was never the type of businessman to back out of a deal. He realized that his *Titanic* project was becoming the well-known set phrase of "the show must go on!" In March 1978 Army Archerd1 reported that *Singing in the Rain* director Stanley Donen was currently in talks with Lew Grade to guide *Raise the Titanic* on screen. But yet again the project was dealt another blow as Donen was unable to work due to other film commitments. What was Grade to do? Then at Marble Arch Productions Martin Starger introduced Grade to Jerry Jameson who had recently completed *Airport '77* for Universal Pictures.

Jerry Jameson was born in Los Angeles in November 1934. He began his career as an editor for television serials with his first job working on The Andy Griffith Show in 1964. The years to follow would see Jameson creating a healthy catalogue of television productions working on *I Spy, Ironside, The Six Million Dollar Man, Murder, She Wrote, Magnum, P.I., Dallas, Dynasty, Dr. Quinn Medicine Woman,* and *Walker, Texas Ranger*. Jameson's film debut came in 1974 with the TV movies *Terror on the 40th Floor* followed a year later with *The Secret Night Caller, The Deadly Tower, The Lives of Jenny Dolan,* and *The Call of the Wild* (1976). "My TV background taught me to work quickly and to operate under all kinds of strange conditions. I've been on this project now for about a year and a half. Next time I'll take a somewhat smaller project to do."

His first film directorial came in 1977 with that of the third instalment of the *Airport* disaster series of movies. The March 1977 review of the film in *The New York Times* published an unsympathetic view of the film using Jameson's television productions as an excuse to discredit the look of the movie; "The film was directed by Jerry Jameson, most or whose experience has been in television, but 'Airport '77' looks less like the work of a director and writers than like a corporate decision." If Lew Grade still had any reservations, Starger's recommendation won over the decision and Jameson joined the team in May 1978 as the movie's new director with lensing of actors and model sequences to commence in October. That August *Raise the Titanic* was now back in production with Jerry Jameson at the helm, William Frye as producer, and Martin Starger as executive producer as the three men turned their attention to finding their leading humans stars and those in the industry who can finally achieve the impossible job of bringing the complexity of the screenplay to the big screen.

Treacherous Voyages

Jameson's working relationship on-screen with the United States Navy would deliver the much-needed equipment and personnel to make the audience believe more in the reality of the story's salvage operations. The decision behind the involvement of the navy was easy following their involvement on *Airport '77*. The story played out in the cramped confines of a Boeing 747 that is carrying an elite team of wealthy passengers en route to the lavish resort owned by wealthy philanthropist Philip Stevens, played by Hollywood legend James Stewart. When the aircraft is hijacked for its cargo of priceless art, it is forced to fly below radar resulting in the engines stalling leading to the airliner being brought to crash land on the ocean surface within the Bermuda Triangle. Moments later the plane slides beneath the waves and comes to rest on the sea bed. While the passengers and crew onboard struggle with survival the United States Navy is called upon to save those trapped on board. A plan is put into action in attaching lifting bags to the hull of the aircraft in an attempt to lift it to the surface for a successful rescue mission. The production had a working budget of $6m and despite any fears from frequent flyers, the movie went on to earn an estimated $30m in the box office that year. This was a successful start to Jameson's big-screen directorial debut and Martin Starger could see that Jameson possessed the ability to handle the special effects sequences for *Raise the Titanic* like a field marshall directing a battle.

"I'd been offered other projects while I was in preproduction on TITANIC, but I've stuck with it," said Jameson in an interview in June 1980. "It took us a year just to develop the screenplay. We used up nine writers and, in the end, we went back to the first one and got the script that we could live with. Getting a script was very difficult. Each version was no good." But as the production progressed and complications stacked up, Jameson began to have doubts about the project to the extent that, like Kramer, contemplated walking. "I almost asked to be taken off it," Jameson said to reporter Ralph Kaminsky for *Box Office* magazine. But regardless of all these setbacks, Jameson persevered with the project as *Titanic*'s legacy slowly drew him in. "There's a mystique involved around the thought of the *Titanic*. Just the word catches the imagination. And to make a movie about raising the *Titanic* is such an unusual thing – the kind of filmmaking you never think of doing. When you see the *Titanic* emerging above the water it's the most exciting, awesome thing ever filmed. It's a three-minute ballet from the time the ship breaks water until it finally settles down."

Jameson liked to use cast and crew that he had worked with previously in the industry. *Raise the Titanic* stars Paul Carr, Charles Macaulay, and Michael Pataki who had already been lensed by Jameson in other productions, while cinemaphotographer Matthew F. Leonetti had seven features films under his belt working with Jameson that included several tv-movies produced between 1974/75. Also returning to work with Jameson were three *Airport '77* production crew members; set decorator Mickey S. Michaels, editor J. Terry Williams and producer William Frye.

It was Jameson alternating between his well-established melodramas for television to the occasional theatrical offering which sparked the attention of Martin Starger. Jameson was diverse in his directorial approach to putting a story to screen during the 1970s epidemic of television movies and when families gathered around the tv set in the living room to watch the numerous soaps that dominated the small screen. But before anyone judges Jameson too harshly, thinking that he should have stuck to melodramas for television, Jameson was one of many directors during the 1970s who delivered to the screen the disaster genre of entertainment. Irwin Allen rightfully earned the nickname of The Master of Disaster with his enthralling effects-laden disaster movies such as *The Poseidon Adventure, The Towering Inferno, The Swarm*, and *Beyond the Poseidon Adventure*. They were the defining disaster films of that decade. Jameson took that genre and crafted it into something smaller in budget for the equally smaller screen.

Jameson's first disaster movie came in 1974 with *Heatwave*, a made-for-TV production starring Bonnie Bedelia (*Die Hard*) and Ben Murphy (*Alias Smith and Jones*) as a couple trying to survive a deadly heatwave that falls upon a remote small town causing a total blackout and water shortage for the inhabitants. As the heat continues to rise, so does the hostility of the residents as they begin to turn upon one another. On the heels of *Heatwave* there came another two made-for-television features; *Hurricane* and *Terror on the 40th Floor*. Future *Dallas* star Larry Hagman led the cast of this short film about a storm chaser who gets caught up in a horrific hurricane that touches down over Florida and forcing a tidal wave towards the helpless characters who were adamant about sitting it out. *Terror on the 40th Floor* was Jameson's take on Irwin Allen's disaster epic *The Towering Inferno* as the golden voice of *Charlie's Angels* and *Dynasty*'s Blake Carrington, actor John Forsythe, becomes trapped with several business colleagues on the 40th floor of an office skyscraper during a Christmas party when a fire starts in the building's basement to soon spiral out of control and rages upwards. While the production oozes the flare of Jameson's melodramas, there is no Steve McQueen or Bruce Willis on hand to save the day. His 1978 production of *A Fire in the Sky* was Jameson's take on the earth, or in this case Arizona, coming to an end when an astronomer, played by Richard Crenna (*Rambo*), warns of a comet on a collision course with the planet. But the governor is reluctant to evacuate without any solid proof that Phoenix will be struck. As the comet approaches earth within proximity, the U.S. Air Force tries to intercept the comet and blow it up with the use of nuclear warheads. The plan fails, the townsfolk can only take shelter and pray for survival as the comet enters the atmosphere to strike the town. Two decades later Hollywood would take that concept to release their box office successes; *Deep Impact* and *Armageddon*.

Although these low-budgeted films were typical of the many melodramatic shows that dominated 1970s television networks, it did show that there were producers and directors out there who could deliver some of the spectacles of bigger productions for a minimal budget. What could they do if the budget was increased? Jameson fitted that criteria and the proof of the pudding would be revealed with *Airport '77*. To Starger it made perfect sense to have Jameson leading the production of *Raise the Titanic* and deliver a product without increasing the budget time and time again. As weeks turned into months and *Raise the Titanic* progressed it slowly became apparent that despite the healthy budget the entire feature film was as challenging for the crews as anything they had previously worked on. Jameson's approach to *Raise the Titanic* was adventurous in itself. He had the background in delivering entertainment from the many smaller budget movies he had previously worked on. While those productions were more drama-based for their characters, the budget reflected on the actors chosen to bring the entire production together in Jameson's melodramatic flare. Although the success of *Airport '77* resulted in the door being opened for Jameson's next big motion picture, the execution of the project, which relied upon the large extent of the special effects with the miniatures, was hampered by delays and spiralling costs that despite the constant criticism from the director, the producer, and the studios, still meant that *Raise the Titanic* and the sheer scale of the production was far greater than they had anticipated. This was no tv-movie production that Jameson had become accustomed to. Kramer's exit from the project was a clear sign of the restraints being applied by the studios and despite his best efforts could not work to the set budget. That should have been enough to convince Jameson that the project was troubled. And yet, against all the odds, if the audience were to look past the movie's clunky editing, then one begins to see that Jameson, regardless of the mounting problems, stuck with the film and delivered on his contract even if he at one point had contemplated throwing in the towel.

The forty years which have passed have not been kind on Jameson's connection to *Raise the Titanic* starting at its world premiere in 1980. The critical response was negative on so many levels. In the years before *Raise the Titanic,* Jameson was ingrained in the entertainment industry for his deliverance of smaller budgeted productions. Raising *Titanic* for the big screen was a job that became too problematic for Jameson and despite his best efforts and delivery, it was the critical response the movie received and the relentless public flogging alongside other unsuccessful box office features that unjustifiably put Jameson's name unfairly in the category of churning out a string of "flops" while completely ignoring his extensive career of highly entertaining features outside of the world of *Titanic*. His 2015 feature film *Captive* puts Jameson on top form as director and returns to his roots of suspenseful drama movies. The story, based on true events, focuses on two broken souls who are unwillingly thrown together as Brian (David Oyelowo), a mass murderer on the run, holds captive recovering drug addict Ashley (Kate Mara) and her daughter Paige (Elle Graham) in their home as the authorities carry out a citywide manhunt. *Captive* is full of suspense with the two main actors delivering powerful performances that stay with you long after the credits have rolled.

Four decades have passed since the release of *Raise the Titanic*. And despite Jameson being at a spritely 87 years of age, he is still active in the film industry, directing, producing, and editing with much defiance and passion.

Stanley Kramer *(Author's collection)*

High Noon from 1952 *(IMDb)*

(IMDb)

The Domino Principal from 1977 that was a joint production between Stanley Kramer, Lord Lew Grade and Martin Starger. *(Author's collection)*

Chapter 4: Two Directors • 95

(Author's collection)

Kramer behind the camera during filming on *The Domino Principal*. (Author's collection)

1980s publicity photograph of James Brolin. *(Author's collection)*

View from the viewing platform of the World Trade Center looking out over the East River, the Brooklyn and Manhattan bridges and towards the Naval dockyards. *(Photograph © Jonathan Smith 1989)*

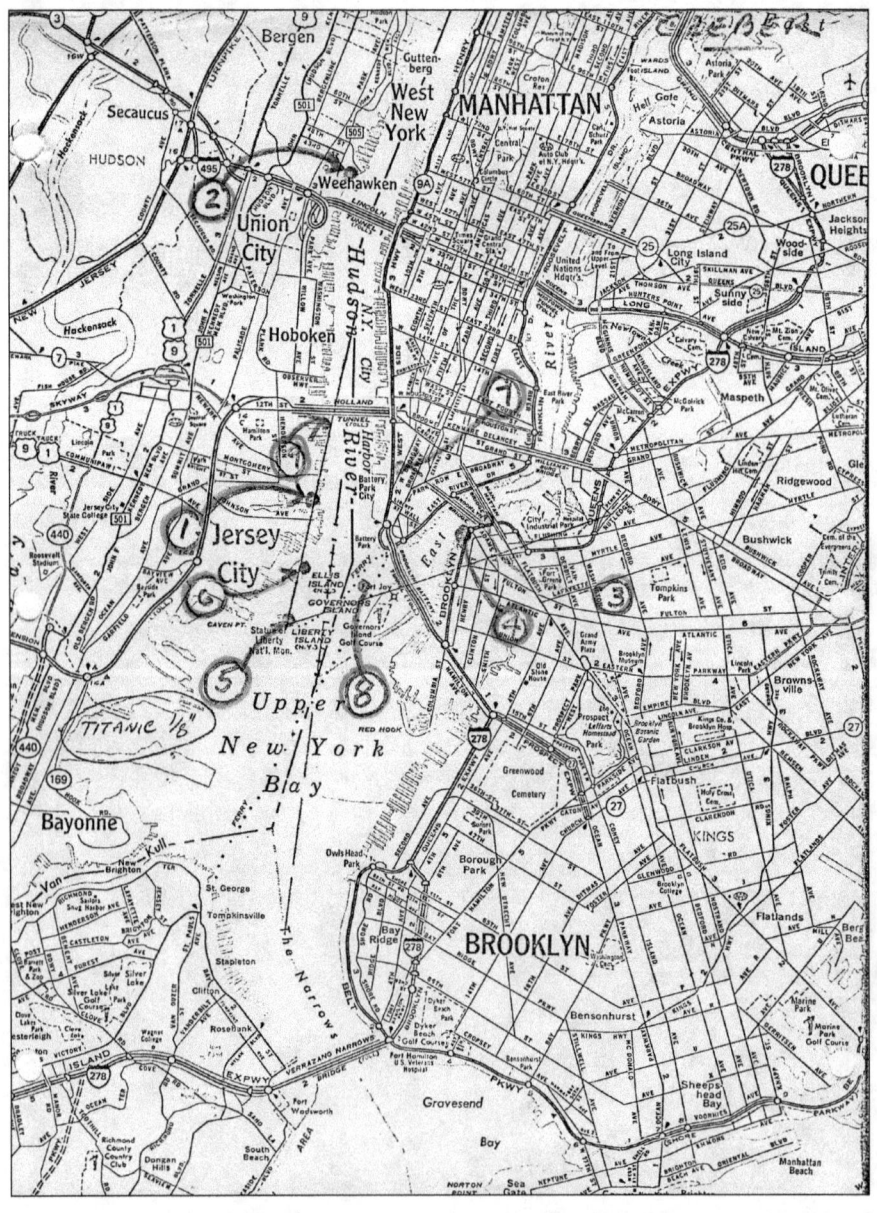

Original camera location map from the production of *Raise the Titanic* that originally belonged to production designer William "Bill" Creber. With a total of nine cameras with crew filming, Kramer felt it was enough to capture footage required for the movie's atmospheric scenes of the raised *Titanic* finally making port in New York. *(Author's collection)*

Chapter 4: Two Directors • 97

Americana of New York

Fly American / Stay Americana

Seventh Ave. at 52nd Street
New York, New York 10019
212 581 1000

THE RAISING OF THE TITANIC

JULY 1, 1977

FRIDAY'S WORK SCHEDULE
2 CAMERAS
6,000 ft of FILM — LOADED
4,000 — CANNED — CHANGING BAG
~~FULL COMPLEMENT of PRIME~~
~~Sepherical LENSES~~
2 SET OF ANAMORPHIC LENSES
including 50 to 500 ZOOMS
If we do not BUILD the PLATFORM —
we will need 2 PARALLEL TOPS —
WEDGES and TIE DOWNS
CAMERA CREWS to OPERATE 2
CAMERAS
GRIPS and Electricians

HAROLD E. WELLMAN, A.S.C.

For Instant Reservations:
In the continental United States
Call 800 228-3278 Toll Free.
In Nebraska Call Collect 401 572-7900

Correspondence from Harold E. Wellman, A.S.C. dated 1 July, 1977 for the equipment requirements loaned to Kramer's crew in capturing footage during Son of Op Sail. What is of interest is the film's title of *The Raising of the Titanic* which is one of several pieces of documentation that uses that same title during the early production stages. *(Author's collection)*

98 • *Raise The Titanic*

The twin towers of the World Trade Center in 1989. *(Photograph © Jonathan Smith)*

Original early concept sketches created for the Kramer shoots in New York. *(Author's collection)*

Passing under the Brooklyn Bridge. In reality the clearance between the underneath of the bridge structure and the surface of the river would not have been enough for the wrecked *Titanic* to pass beneath without striking the bridge. *(Photograph © Jonathan Smith)*

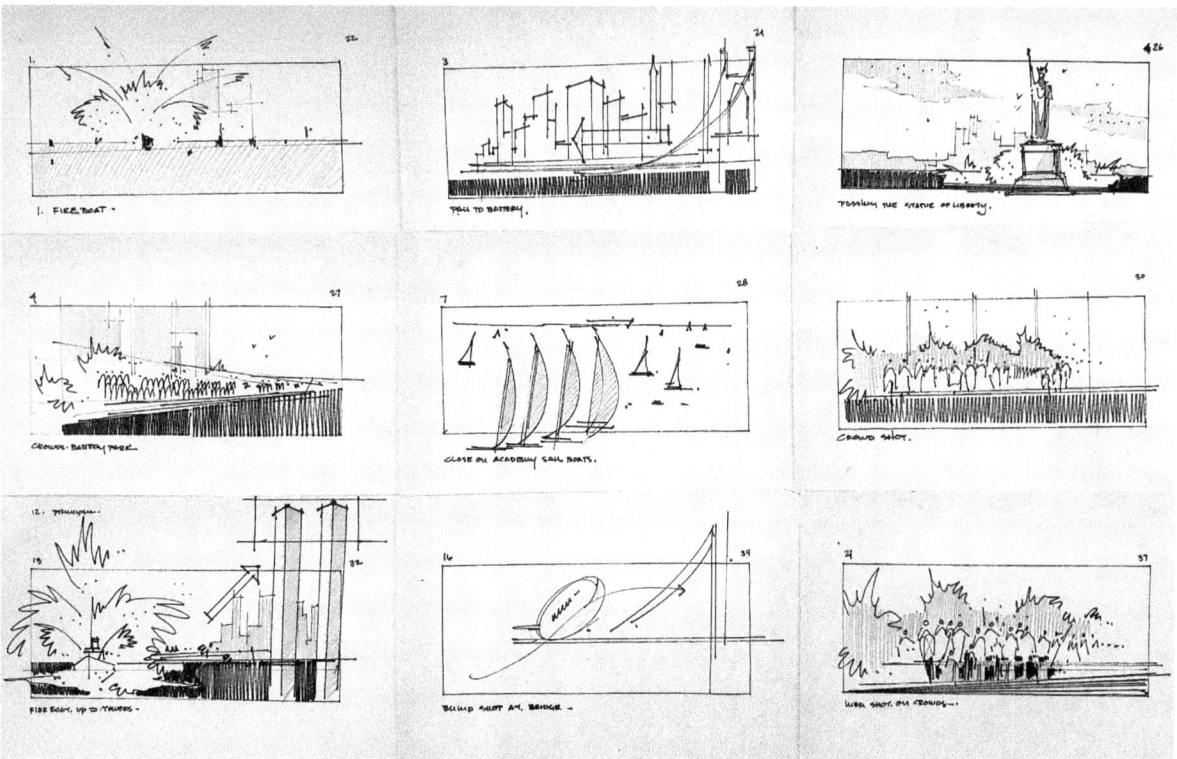

A series of revised storyboards for *Raise the Titanic* that follow the pattern of the sequences to be filmed during the Son Op Sail events. It was from this footage where matte work with the models would be later added that would eventually appear in the film when Jerry Jameson took over. *(Author's collection)*

The main television offices to the CBS Studio Center in Los Angeles that comprises of television, film and set backlots to form Studio City. The movie studio complex would become the workshops of where the *Titanic* and other miniatures for *Raise the Titanic* would be constructed. *(Company advertising postcard – Author's collection)*

Kramer joking around on the set of *Bless the Beasts & Children*. *(IMDb)*

Kramer on set with legendary Spencer Tracy. *(Publicity photograph – Author's collection)*

Chapter 4: Two Directors • 101

Jerry Jameson on the set of *Airport '77*. *(Publicity photograph – Author's collection)*

The third instalment of the *Airport* disaster movie franchise. *(Author's collection)*

Singing in the Rain director Stanley Donen. *(Publicity photograph – Author's collection)*

Raise the Titanic film producer William Frye. *(AFD/ITC – Author's collection)*

Set Decorator Mickey S. Michaels on the set of *Raise the Titanic*. *(Author's collection)*

The Bat People was Jameson's entry into the horror genre in 1974. The film starred three actors who would later have roles in *Raise the Titanic*; Stewart Moss, Michael Pataki and Paul Carr. *(IMDb)*

Jameson's first disaster movie outing with *Heatwave* in 1974. *(Author's collection)*

(Author's collection)

The cast of *Terror on the 40th Floor* with John Forsythe (centre, back row) leading the group to safety as a fire breaks out in their office skyscraper. *(IMDb)*

Chapter 4: Two Directors • 103

Jameson behind the camera during filming at the Mayflower Hotel in Washington for *Raise the Titanic*. *(Millimeter Magazine, June 1980 - Author's collection)*

(IMDb)

(IMDb)

Director Jerry Jameson talks through a scene with actor David Oyelowo on the set of the Paramount Pictures movie Captive from 2015. *(Publicity photograph © Evan Klanfer/ Paramount Pictures – Author's collection)*

It was producer William Frye (second from right) who recommended to Lord Lew Grade to hire friend Jerry Jameson (far left) as the director for *Raise the Titanic*. It was Jameson's directorial role for the disaster movie *Airport '77* and the use of the U.S Navy that became a selling point for Frye in getting Grade to agree. *(Press photograph – Author's collection)*

Chapter 5

Preproduction Begins

"It ends just like you do. I don't understand that kind of thinking. You're both a couple of cynics. You think this is some kind of lousy game. If I felt the way Sandecker does I wouldn't have started the damned project in the first place."

Gene Seagram

To bring Cussler's vision of salvaging *Titanic* from page to the big screen required an extensive workforce from those scouting for locations, to the many advisors and technical consultants. From preproduction artists responsible for extracting a book's sentence and putting it into a visual presentation for storyboards, to the camera crews and sound recordists, screenplay writers and set decorators along with the model makers and make-up artists. It becomes a colossal task for any studio be them big or small. The idea behind putting the story of *Titanic* to the screen was never one of the easiest projects to begin with, even for those committing to films on the sinking of the liner. Until the purchasing of the film rights to *Raise the Titanic* no film had covered such an extravagant story of a team of salvagers going out to find and raise such a large ship. It was almost as if the premise of the story came from the minds of the great science fiction authors. What Clive Cussler had created was a story that was as captivating as the sinking of the legendary liner and one that could become reality if the mind was to let it.

The previsualization of *Raise the Titanic* was of a lavish production that had to work visually on the screen as a movie with elements of documentary-style research that had to convince the audience of the possibilities that deep-water wrecks could be salvaged. From the very start, the production was costly. This was no ordinary adventure film that could be achieved with set-pieces scouted from everyday locations. Brand new sets had to be constructed that, at the wave of the director's hand, could be changed at any given time to present the story according to the screenplay. The model work alone for the adaptation would be colossal and on an unprecedented scale. Building a replica of the *Titanic* was just the beginning as the production also required matching scale navy vessels, submersibles, remote helicopters, lighting systems, lifting tanks, submersible equipment, to scale figurines, artificial icebergs, ships boilers, broken funnels, and a tank big enough to put them all in. Set pieces were needed to represent areas of the *Titanic* from the grand staircase to large portions of the ship's decks, deckhouses, hull sides, and interiors of the submersibles. To then put all that model work onto the screen required a screenplay, storyboards, and the producer and director to visualize the production through concept artworks. Outside the circle, Clive Cussler was questioning the film's budget of £7m that Grade's companies had put forward. The budget was in keeping with the bigger Hollywood studio productions of the time.

Although the sum was large for 1977, Cussler felt it could not justify successfully transferring his story from page to the screen. It did not matter if Cussler had spoken his mind about the budget as the film's first director expressed the need for more money to do the story justice. As the movie entered the early stages of preproduction, Grade was to make sure that his *Titanic* film stayed within budget and delivered on time a British financed motion picture of tremendous proportions that would make Hollywood sit up and take notice.

Early Visions of *Titanic*

Grade's £7m budget soon began to dwindle as the film went into pre-production stages as concept artists, screenwriters, model builders, draftsmen, welders and building contractors with their workforce brought the production slowly together. With *Titanic* as the main character on the screen, her look as a long-lost wreck had to be done right that reflected a combination of the book and real life. Cussler created his *Titanic* as a wreck almost intact, sitting upright on the ocean floor, and preserved in such a way that she was stable enough to be moved and brought up through nearly 12,500ft of water. His *Titanic* was holed by both the iceberg and from the boilers that broke free during her sinking to burst from within the hull. Her masts were now mere stumps, some air vents still present on the decks and except for the fourth funnel laying collapsed across the rear of the boat deck, the other three funnels were completely missing having been carried away during the fall to the sea bed. Cussler opted for a unique approach in having his *Titanic* in such a state of preservation that despite sitting on the ocean floor for 64 years she had very little decay. Even her paint was still prominent after all these years. Cussler's imagining of the wreck of *Titanic* in 1976 was in keeping with the general census of what she may look like according to marine experts of the day. Carrying over that vision to film was dependent on the production's art director and how they wanted the main star to appear on the screen. When Jerry Jameson took over, the decision was to keep the movies 1912 opening sequence intact to show off the *Titanic* replica at the time of her maiden voyage. Once the sinking sequences were done, to work within budget, the model FX unit would then break the miniature down and age it accordingly. The use of plans and photographs to build the *Titanic* replica were readily available from a matter of sources from the original builders of Harland & Wolff in Belfast, down to archival material within shipping historian collections and society archives. To bring all this together required experts in the field of naval, marine salvage, marine biologists, and *Titanic* research.

The artistic look for the movie was envisioned by the Hollywood stalwart; art director and production designer John DeCuir. In 1977 DeCuir had over thirty years of experience under his belt having brought to the screen the visuals of *The King and I*, *South Pacific*, *Cleopatra*, *Hello, Dolly!* and later in 1984 his final production, *Ghostbusters*. The early wreck concepts came together from John DeCuir and his son John DeCuir Jr with contributions from Joe Hurley, B. Bramham, and the world-renowned *Titanic* artist Ken Marschall. Ken was already making waves in the *Titanic* community with his almost photographic-like paintings of the doomed liner and her older sister *Olympic*. But it was Marschall's remarkable attention to detail that shined through in the quality of his paintings that gave the viewer a unique window into a time long gone with his artistic snap-shot of *Titanic*'s legacy either not captured in photographs or etched into the minds of those who survived that terrible night in 1912. Marschall's lifelong interest in *Titanic* and his vast archive of historic material secured him a place on the team to bring *Titanic* to life. This was the perfect opportunity to create the liner in such detail that it surpassed anything previously built. Marschall followed the rule of if it's worth doing, it's worth doing right. His knowledge on the liner, her build, her sinking, and analysis of what the wreck could look like based around survivor accounts were fundamental to the production. With Stanley Kramer as director on the project in 1977, Marschall's valuable input would also play a key role in how Kramer was to visualize other aspects of the story from the intended sinking prologue, *Titanic*'s late arrival in New York to advising on how the wreck could look in modern times.

In 1977 Marschall created a hypothetical version of the raised liner for the production's art department depicting her with a list to starboard; funnel number two intact while the remaining three are missing; her rear mast broken in half and the starboard side of the bridge crushed from the collapse of the forward funnel during her sinking. With Marshall on the project as one of the technical advisors, his work continued in 1977 when art and production designer William "Bill" Creber who was leading the model-building team over in California had Marschall storyboard the earliest version of the intended sinking sequence that would open the film. The scene starts with lookouts Fleet and Lee high up in the ship's crow's nest as *Titanic* steams into the night. Suddenly Fleet spots something emerging from the darkness; an iceberg. As Fleet rings the bell, *Titanic* begins to turn in response. First Officer Murdoch rushes out onto the starboard bridge wing just at the moment the two giants collide. As the liner grinds its way down the mass of ice, a member of the crew bolts across the forecastle as dislodged ice cascades across the deck. Marschall quickly sketched only one storyboard of the sinking *Titanic*, seen from her portside with lifeboats in the water and a distress rocket erupts high above the liner. The depiction of the sinking in the sketch was to uncannily resurface when Marschall created *Her Last Hour* painting in 1998. During the 1912 storyboarding process Marschall also sketched out several scenes of the salvaged *Titanic* as she is towed into New York in an updated and more film-friendly version of the derelict. His depiction of the wreck had her with a noticeable list to starboard, her masts almost intact and only her number one funnel broken away.

John DeCuir took inspiration from Marschall's original renderings, transferring the look into his style and having his *Titanic* intact, minus a funnel, but in a relatively good state of preservation. One concept was to have one side of the *Titanic*'s hull that faced into the ocean currents with a silver sheen to the hull plates as if the hull sides had been polished by marine life passing over the wreck. Thankfully this unusual idea never came to fruition other than on paper. The 1978/79 designs from Bramham and Hurley were a combination of ideas from the book and what was agreed upon to be used in the movie with full masts and funnels. Some artworks were more fanciful than others with views of *Titanic*'s decks littered with debris, fallen rigging cables draped over buckled lifeboat davits and railings. One occurring theme with the concepts is that they all depicted *Titanic* largely intact, stained but still showing much of her White Star Line livery and the hull with a heavy list to starboard as she sits on the ocean floor.

More sci-fi than Reality

DeCuir's vision for *Raise the Titanic* did share a lot of similarities to Cussler's story with some of the submersibles taking their names from those in the novel. The *Sappho* was designed as a cigar-shape craft with a pair of long crab-like claws placed beneath the main body of the vehicle that resembled more of a towable deep-water sonar device. Another design was based on the U.S Navy cable-controlled recovery vehicle *CURV III* with the craft being upscaled in size to allow for crew to sit within and control the vehicle. The 1964 constructed *Aluminaut* also became the inspiration for another of the deep-sea vehicles for the film with the main tubular hull reshaped to look like four spheres with viewports for the crew. Other conceptions were more science fiction with some looking like 1950s stylized U.F.O and one resembling something that would fit within an episode of *Space: 1999*. These early concepts represented a time during the production where no real submersibles had been secured with intended scenes of the craft to be finished with miniatures and interior sound stage sets of interiors. During these early stages of preproduction, the submersibles that were finalized to be crafted for the movie did share some aspects of Cussler's novel; the *Sappho* being one example.

The submersible design was more on the lines of the imagination with elements of previously existing submersible craft brought together into one deep-sea vehicle. As time went on and the models began to take shape the *Sappho* was renamed *Rufus II* and finally replaced with the *Deep Quest*. While the latter was achieved it was the former that went through major changes when the studios were permitted to use the designs of the actual working submersibles D.S.V. *Deep Quest* and the twin sister subs, *Sea Cliff* and *Turtle*. One key design to the *Turtle* was that the sub was to be rigged with a Remote Operated Vehicle (R.O.V.) that was named *Eagle*; later changed to the more comical yet appealing *Snooper*. Although the R.O.V. was down as one of the vehicles to be modelled in miniature it is unclear if it ever came into being, and, if it was created by the model FX unit and filmed with the large *Titanic* miniature.

One last D.S.V. was built based on the *Turtle/Sea Cliff* design that became the ill-fated *Starfish*. The model was just another carbon copy of the *Turtle* with a name change and a different livery placed upon the hull. The early stages of the *Deep Quest* were to include a separate operational vehicle that could be attached to the front of the submersible when required. This smaller vehicle sat connected to a pair of solid tubular arms that slid back and forth into the main body of the *Deep Quest* allowing for the smaller vehicle to be extended out from the main submersible while still being attached. The small craft contained a single operator cockpit where the crew member could control the pair of manipulators, lights, video cameras, and a welding machine used to secure the steel plates over the iceberg damage on the wreck. The vehicle did make it into the final stages of the movie, albeit made smaller, and which was held by the arms of the *Deep Quest* as it worked on the wreck. The excessive editing the film underwent before its general public release resulted in these scenes with the craft ending up on the cutting room floor.

Get it Up!

One of the most interesting aspects of the preproduction stages for *Raise the Titanic* was the varying ideas put forward on how they were going to present on-screen the *Titanic* being salvaged. The movie's important raising sequence is what the audience was paying the price of an admission ticket for. Not only was the scene to be near as perfect to look convincing enough but also one that had to look plausible and within the possibilities of the studios and the studios model effects teams. The concept artworks from DeCuir, Hurley, and Bramham came directly from the pages of the Clive Cussler novel with *Titanic* being raised stern first. The concepts were certainly eye-catching, adventurous, and bold, and though they looked spectacular on art paper it is questionable if the effects unit could pull off such a sequence in having *Titanic* making her grand entrance amidst a fleet of navy vessels with their shell-shocked crew looking on. The early designs had *Titanic* bursting up stern first to claw her way skywards, water erupting from the innards of the vessel as she towers high into a laden sky, her funnels coming lose to sway back and forth like snakes as the huge ship slams down into the hurricane churned waters of the Atlantic. As the navy vessels pitch around in the turmoil the huge tidal surge created by *Titanic* impacting the sea rushes upon the other shipping, sending the crew running for cover in all directions. As the wreck vanishes into the white heavy swells, she reappears rising up on an even keel to reveal her battered and rust-stained hull. If the movie was being made today, I am sure that such a CGI-packed scene would feature all, and much more, in delivering a sequence that would probably be so overcomplicated that the main star would be lost among the confusion of waves and spray.

From the offset, the movie's big money shot was the moment the wreck is raised. Getting the look, the feel, and the combined effects packages in unison were greatly important as the entire production rested upon that sequence. Previous ideas for the on-screen raising of the *Titanic*, in typical Hollywood-style, were, somewhat dare I say — lame. One was to have the wreck fitted with a series of lifting bags that when filled would rise one-hundred-feet over the ship while attached to a series of cables making the hull look as if it were a steel gondola suspended beneath an airship. The wreck would then gradually rise to the surface and once it reaches a depth of 200ft it would be pumped with lifting foam and the lifting bags removed to allow for the *Titanic* to sit, partially waterlogged, allowing for towing on to New York where pumps would, presumably, stabilize the wreck for extracting the vault from within. Whatever the motive was behind ditching this idea was that of a sensible one as it meant the lifting bags were swapped out for a series of salvage tanks. Again, change was incorporated into the design for the wreck as *Titanic* became a ship missing her first funnel, her masts still intact and the hull fitted with six huge Hydrozene tanks that would lift her clear of the sea bed and bring her to the surface and keep her afloat once raised. As the wrecked forward funnel was switched to the second funnel, the salvage tanks were scaled down in size, but increased in numbers from three per side to that of eight, making a total of sixteen Hydrozene gas salvage tanks.

It is sometimes asked if the idea of *Titanic* being raised stern first was ever considered for the movie adaptation. Cussler's dramatic take on the moment the liner makes her appearance makes the inner child in all of us wanting more as Cussler describes the scene as the rusty leviathan erupts from the ocean depths in a reversed sinking; her stern rising and clawing its way higher into the air before gravity takes over and her hull comes slamming down into the ocean sending a tidal surge to swamp the nearby salvage fleet. The raising sequence for the movie was the most challenging part of the entire production and while all these ideas put to paper were adventurous, they were, at the best of times, not very practical. Dozens of ideas on how they were going to depict the raising of the *Titanic* were passed over the table during the months of preproduction. And, yes, even the idea of raising her like the book. Once FX supervisor John Richardson had joined the production to take over the crucial miniature work, it was down to Richardson to come up with the most logical way in lifting such a cumbersome recreation of the *Titanic* up and out of a great volume of water. The production crew did toy with the idea of having the film showing *Titanic* emerging from the Atlantic stern first. The idea was carried over in official promotional advertising used to tease the general public as the studios hinted on something big coming up in theatres soon. And once the model work had been completed and the deep tank finished, tests were carried out with the *Titanic* replica to see if her grand appearance in front of the camera could look as good in person than words from a book.

Two Titles with One Meaning

Raise the Titanic was not the movie's intended original title. Even though the film was based on Clive Cussler's bestselling novel, the early working title was *The Raising of the Titanic*. Stanley Kramer's handwritten shooting notes dated 29 June 1977 uses that very title as the header. Two days later on another hand-written series of notes Kramer again uses *The Raising of the Titanic* as the header for the page confirming that the former was not any sort of typo. The title is not seen again in use until two years later when it appeared in a list of film productions not yet crewed in a February 1979 technical publication. Despite ITC already publicizing the movie as *Raise the Titanic*, *The Raising of the Titanic* was being circulated within the film industry. The latter could be considered as misinformation as included in the list of other films in production was one titled, *The Sinking of the Titanic*, which previously had been named as *Titanic Down,* and eventually renamed *S.O.S. Titanic* for its November 1979 release.

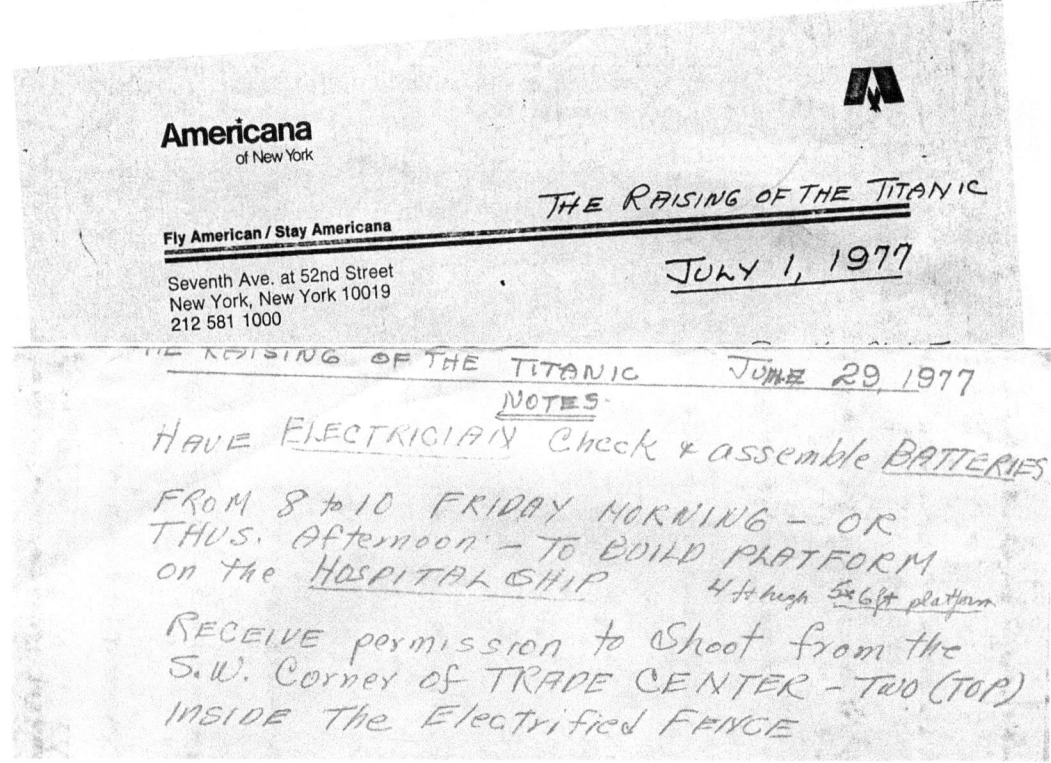

Two examples of documentation from the Stanley Kramer period of *Raise the Titanic* with the working title of *The Raising of the Titanic* being used. *(Author's collection)*

Preproduction Visualisation of *Raise the Titanic*

Having a screenplay is good for building up the characters and subplots of the story for delivery to the screen. But what is just as important, if not more, is how certain scenes had to look from a visual point of view. During the production of *Raise the Titanic* the studio needed to create a believable visual story of bringing the legendary *Titanic* to life in several dramatic sequences. To see what could and couldn't be achieved it took a team of artists to previsualize elements of the story for the studio to determine if the film's budget, producers, director, and host of FX personnel can pull off the challenge. Presented here for the first time is a selection of some of the film's original early concepts from sketches to fully accomplished artworks that give a tantalizing glimpse into the world of science fiction and possible reality.

Concept artwork for *Raise the Titanic* and a scene featuring pilots in a helicopter hovering over the Atlantic Ocean waiting for the wreck to emerge. *(Author's collection)*

Chapter 5: Preproduction Begins • 111

The Oscar award winning production designer John Francis DeCuir fine tunes one of the matte foreground miniatures for *Raise the Titanic*. *(Author's collection)*

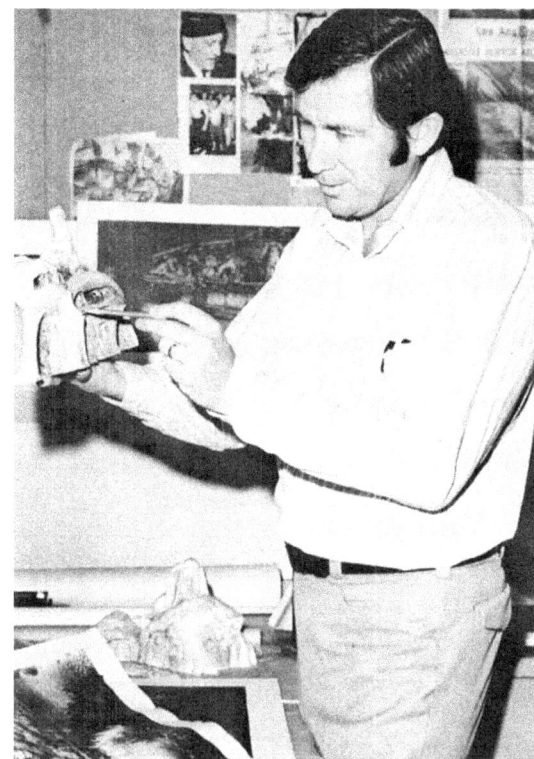
Art director William "Bill" Creber. *(Author's collection)*

This early concept art for the movie production is based around the Clive Cussler novel with the *Titanic* being raised stern first. *(Author's collection)*

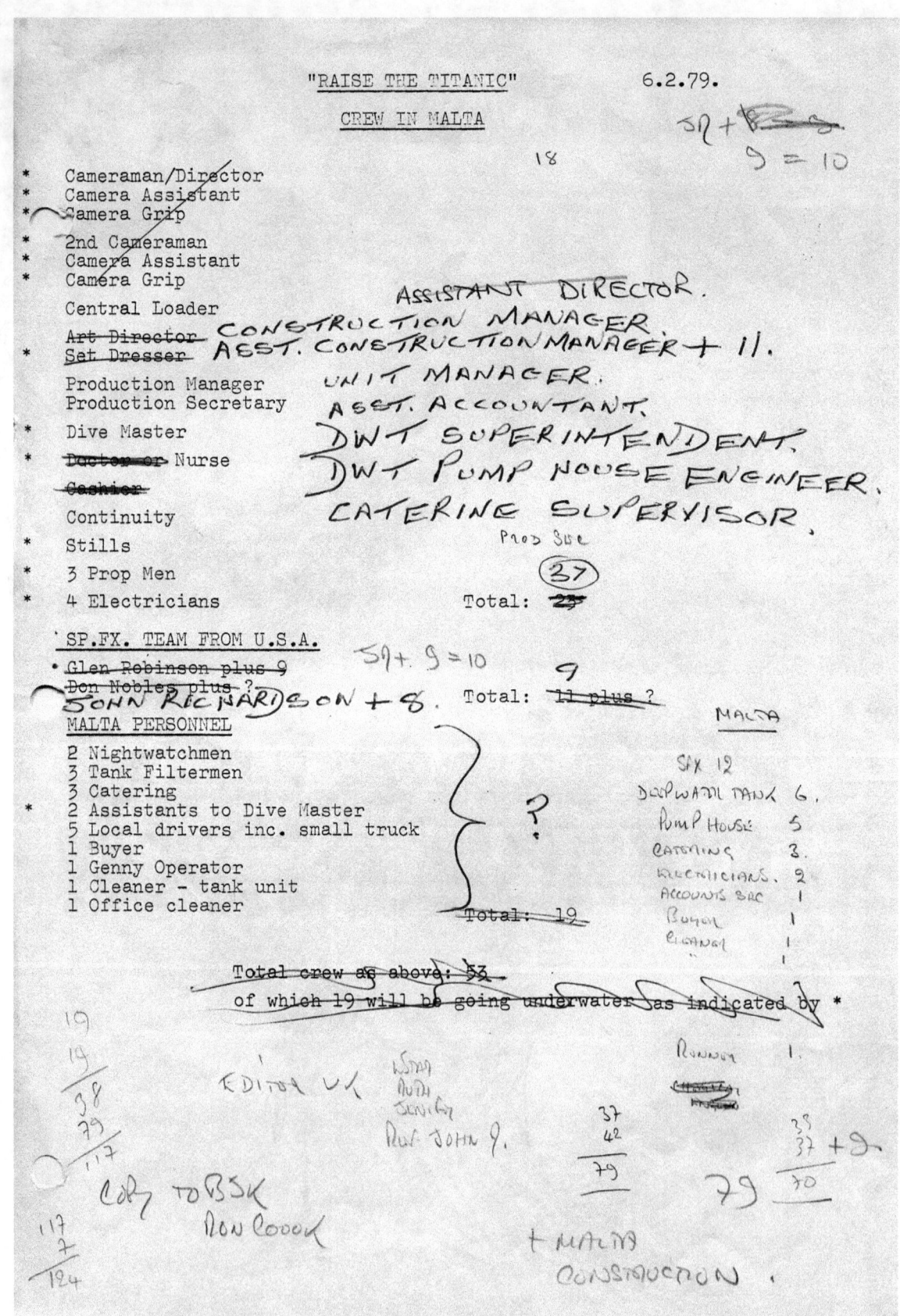

Production crew list for Malta and those to attend work at the Mediterranean Film Facility in February 1979. *(Author's collection)*

Chapter 5: Preproduction Begins • **113**

Series of original preproduction concept sketches for *Raise the Titanic* and the movies intended 1912 sinking prologue. *(Artwork © Ken Marschall - Author's collection)*

Original preproduction concept sketches of the raised *Titanic* as she arrives in New York. *(Artwork © Ken Marschall - Author's collection)*

Chapter 5: Preproduction Begins • 115

This preproduction sketch features an intact version of *Titanic* with the exception of her forward funnel missing. It is interesting to see that the wreck has just six oversized salvage tanks attached to keep her afloat. *(Author's collection)*

Preproduction concept artwork for the *Sappho II* submersible. Fans of the Cussler novel will recognise the name having been lifted from one of the fictional craft that worked on the wreck in his 1976 novel. *(Author's collection)*

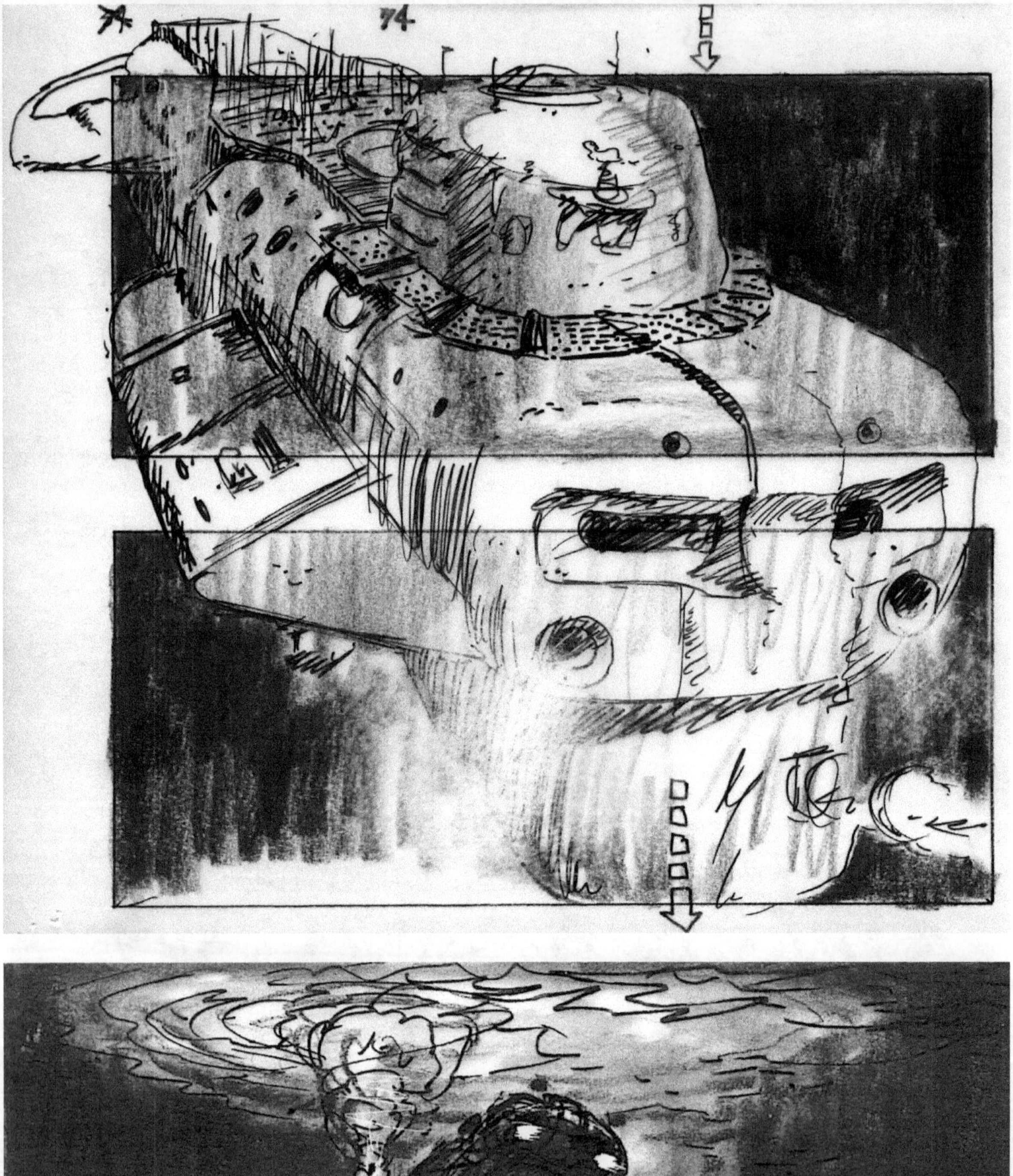

Submersible concept design. Its features were based around deep sea laboratories where the craft could spend days below the surface compared to the much shorter time scale of other submersibles. *(Author's collection)*

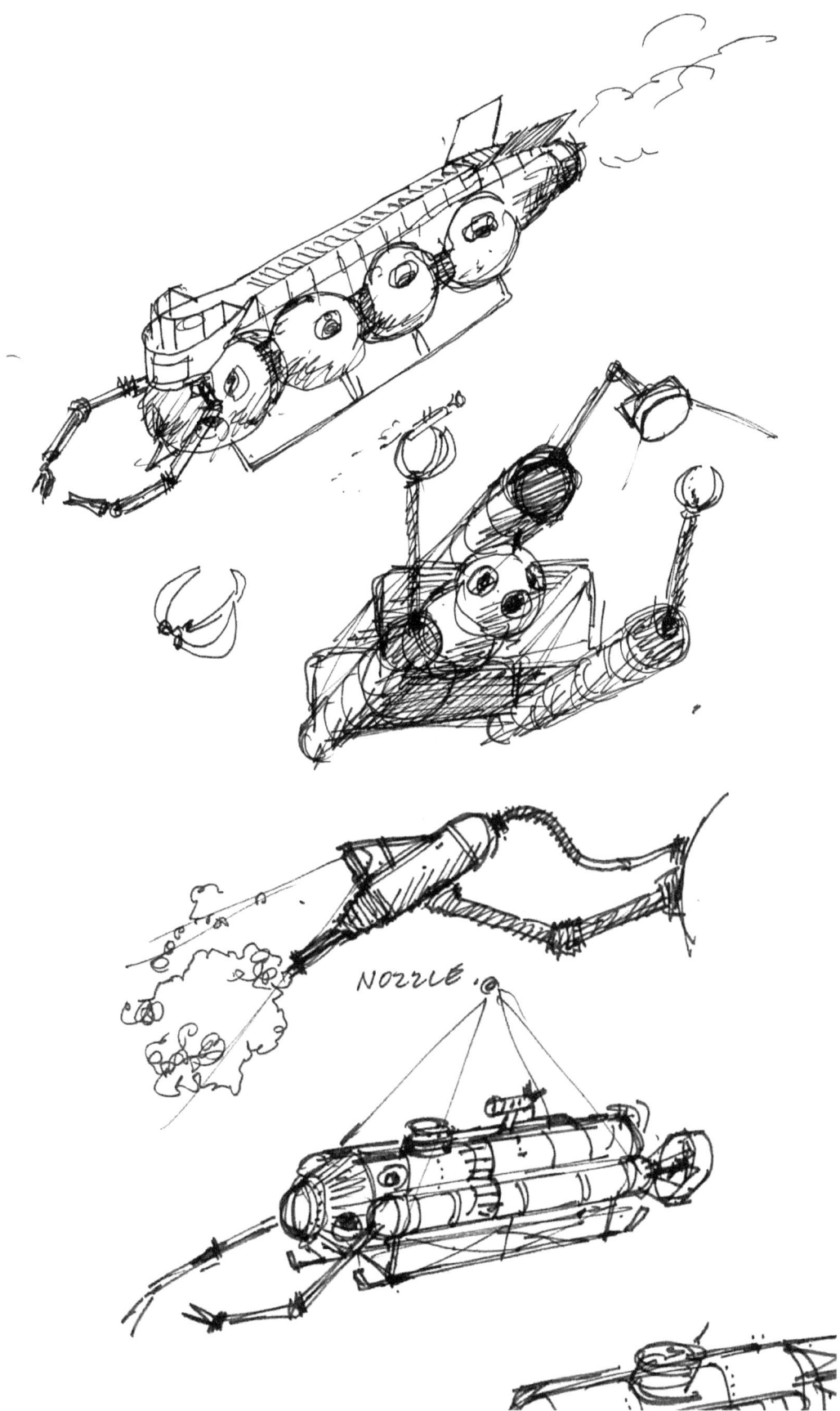

118 • *Raise The Titanic*

This series of concept sketches for *Raise the Titanic* show how the submersible designs not only varied but also tied the books story to the films look during the early stage of development. The submersibles were to be equipped with grappling arms and claws, metal detectors and high-pressure water nozzles to clear sediment away from the wreck. *(Author's collection)*

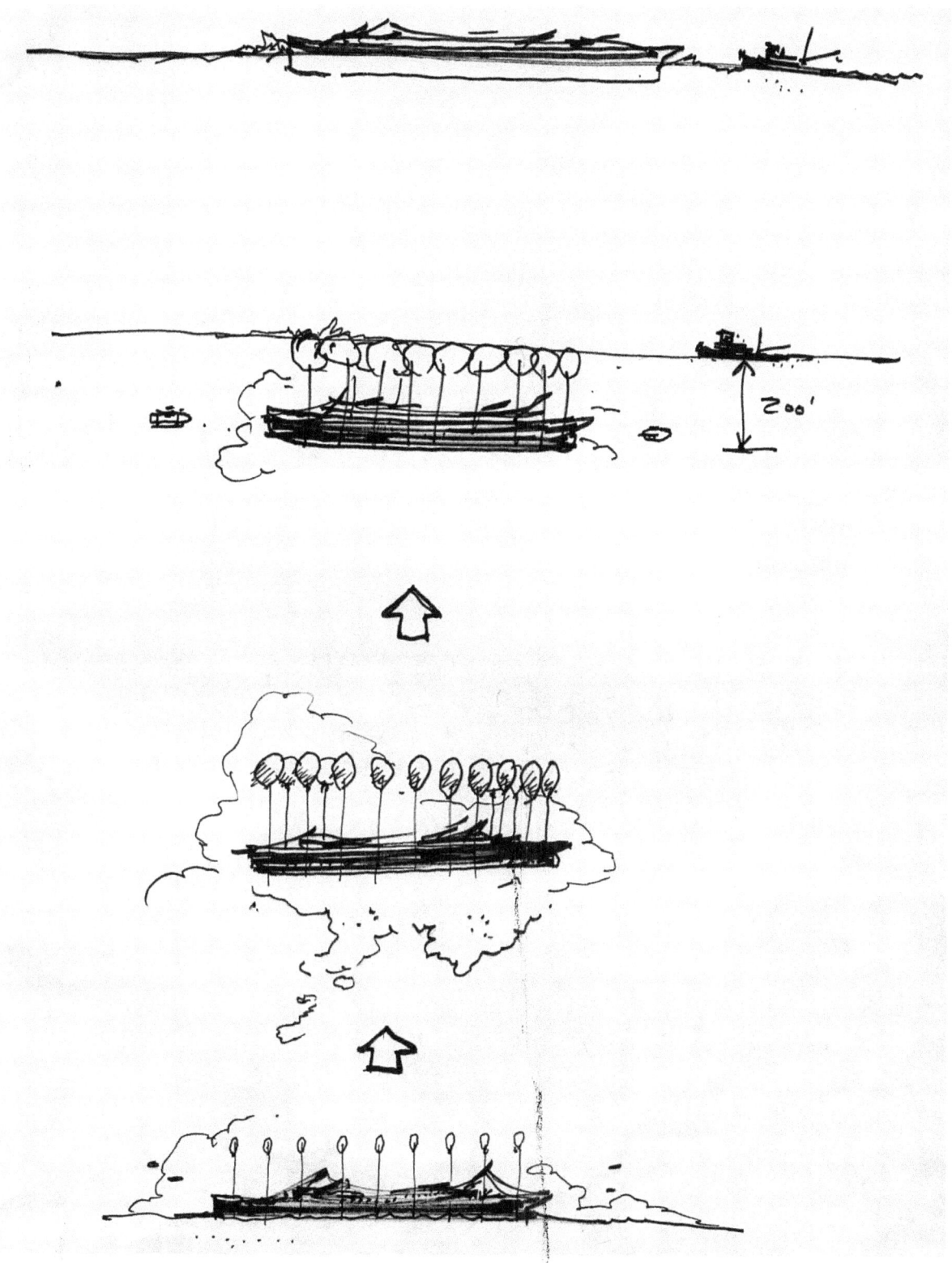

This unique sketch from the early period of *Raise the Titanic* is far removed from what would eventually be put on screen come the summer of 1980. When comparing the arrival at the surface of the wreck in the book; bursting up stern first in an eruption of spray, the idea portrayed here of the wreck coming up on a series of balloons strung up over the hull to a surface depth of 200ft is devoid of impact required for an action movie. In comparison to what would be seen on screen of the salvaging of the passenger airliner in *Airport '77*, interesting as it may have been for a plane, it did not seem that appealing for the most important part of the film for when *Titanic* is raised. *(Author's collection)*

Flight 23 slowly breaks the surface of the waters in a scene from *Airport '77*, the third instalment of the Universal Pictures disaster movie franchise that was directed by Jerry Jameson. *(Universal Pictures © 1977)*

Early publicity teaser for the film that appeared in the October 1976 issue of *Variety*. *(Author's collection)*

INFORMATION RECEIVED

'SCUM'
- Cameraman: Douglas Hill
- Operator: Mike Proudfoot
- Focus: Graham Hazard
- Loader: Paul Jordan
- Grip: Joe Felix

'SUPERMAN II'
- Cameraman: Denys Coop BSC
- Operator: Peter Hammond
- Focus: Not finalised
- Loader: Not finalised
- Grip: Not finalised

'NIJINSKI'
- Cameraman: Dougie Slocombe BSC
- Operator: Chic Waterson
- Focus: Robin Vidgeon
- Loader: Danny Shelmerdine
- Grip: Colin Manning

'SATURN III'
- Cameraman: Billy Williams BSC
- Operators: Dave Harcourt / Mike Roberts
- Focus: Ted Deason
- Loader: Jeremy Jones
- Grip: Dicky Lee

'PORRIDGE'
- Cameraman: Bob Huke BSC
- Operator: Freddie Cooper
- Focus: Peter Biddle
- Loader: John Ignatius
- Grip: Not finalised

'THE BITCH' *
- Cameraman: Denis Lewiston
- Focus: David Wynne Jones
- Focus: Colin Davidson
- Loader: John Bremer
- Grip: Jake Wright

* Operator not finalised at time of going to press.

Productions not yet crewed:
'THE SINKING OF THE TITANIC'
'THE RAISING OF THE TITANIC'
'STAR WARS II' ('THE EMPIRE STRIKES BACK')

Raise the Titanic is still being announced under its old shooting from the 1977 Kramer period in this crew listing from February 1979. The other *Titanic* production was *Titanic Down* that would again undergo a name change to *S.O.S. Titanic*. (Author's collection)

Ken Marschall's 1976 hypothetical rendering of the salvaged *Titanic* that was inspired by Clive Cussler's novel and which served as inspiration for the art department during the early stages of preproduction on *Raise the Titanic*. (Painting © Ken Marschall 1976)

Advanced promotional poster from October 1979. *(Author's collection)*

Lew Grade in his main London office of ATV House in 1978. *(Author's collection)*

CHAPTER 6

The Building of a Legend

"Most of the time I was tolerated by the set designers and construction crew, but of course I didn't always get my way."

Ken Marschall

It would be naive to say that the film industry of today is a CGI laden enterprise where almost everything that appears on screen is the creation of computers and their programmers. Much practical is still used from small budget productions to the multi-million-pound Hollywood blockbusters. While huge sweeping landscapes are born in the safe environment of office spaces as digital artists work on creating biblical devastation as vast cities fall to the power of major earthquakes and volcanoes, such as those created for major summer popcorn blockbusters; Roland Emmerich's disaster epic *2012* for example, or the more recent Bret Ratner movie *San Andreas* from 2015. It should be remembered that despite all what is seen with overblown computer-generated spectaculars, large portions of the scenes will still require the technical challenges of practical effects and props. During the filming of James Cameron's *Titanic*, large amounts of practical were used with tremendous effect; from the large 45-feet hero *Titanic* recreation to the sinking models and the monster 775' exterior tank set of the ship. The application of CGI worked extremely well in bringing what is essentially a static model to a mighty ocean liner charging across the waters of the Atlantic. But there is one major factor that CGI lacks that actual physical models still possess; character.

In 1980, the birth of CGI technology was still five years away. The only way to recreate the ill-fated liner in the film industry was through the use of model work. The building of the *Titanic* for this new post-disaster epic was something that had never been done before in any production. The tremendous scale of the model work required, not just with the *Titanic*, but also with the other vessels and salvage equipment, was monumental, impressive, and extremely challenging.

Titanic in Name & Stature

For *Raise the Titanic* the leading star of the movie was none other than the mighty replica. Before 1977 there were only a couple of large-scale models of *Titanic* available for public viewing. But all were deemed as museum pieces except one, the model built for the 1953 Fox production. The model was currently in storage at this point and despite being a decent 28-feet in length it was not a practical option for this kind of production due to the number of structural errors incorporated into the build from twenty-four years previously. The lavish FX movies to hit theatres during the 1970s are largely attributed to the Master of Disaster; Irwin Allen. His 1972 blockbuster *The Poseidon Adventure* for 20th Century Fox gripped the public's imagination as Gene Hackman and Ernest Borgnine came to blows within the claustrophobic interiors of the capsized hull of the S.S. *Poseidon*. Allen's *Poseidon*, regardless of the impressive special effects, did endure water scale problems that today stand out like a flashing neon sign. The movie was based on the 1969 adventure novel *The Poseidon Adventure* by Paul Gallico and tells the story of the tragic capsizing of the once luxury ocean liner on New Year's Eve after being struck by a giant rogue wave from the results of a sea earthquake. To accomplish the Academy Award-winning special effects a 21ft replica was created by the studios and based on the former Cunard liner R.M.S. *Queen Mary*, crafted under the supervision of the films production designer, William "Bill" Creber.

While audiences were enthralled by the scenes of disaster on-screen, it soon became apparent that, even at 21ft in length and highly detailed, there were shots of the liner as she battles the stormy seas that showed water being over scaled in comparison with that of the model work. This was something that could not be repeated in the production of *Raise the Titanic* given the close proximity that some shots were envisioned by the art department. The film's primary sequence of the rusting hulk as she erupts up from the ocean depths had to look both realistic, to a degree, and at a scale that worked with nature's elements on both big and small screens. Creber decided to have the replica *Titanic* built to a scale of 1:16th making it large enough to work with while also being at the junction of scale and size with water which the camera department could get away with.

The starting point for the model work began in America with film model makers assembled to design, manufacture, and piece together the large replicas. The manufacturing process was on an industrial scale as eight fully hulled ships were commissioned for *Raise the Titanic* that included the 55ft and 9ft *Titanic*'s, three U.S Navy vessels, two tug boats, and a fireboat. As the production required varying camera angles of the miniature work the models could not be built to show just one side of the vessel. Designing, building, and detailing the vessels was time-consuming but essential as each of the miniatures was a carbon copy of actual existing vessels including those secured and contracted out to the film production company. Each of the miniatures was crafted from the keel up using a wealth of archival imagery, plans, and photographs taken during the preproduction stages. A team of FX artists was hired to manufacture and assemble the vessels with those involved in fabricating moulds, welders for steelwork, painters, and an array of those assembling these large-scale kits. But to get the main star of the movie looking accurate, it required *Titanic* experts who had already devoted time in thorough research and recreating the unsinkable legend for their own projects. Of those who came forward to help was 26-year old *Titanic* historian and artist extraordinaire, Ken Marschall. Marschall's attention to detail in taking the subject of *Titanic* and putting her in a series of paintings akin to photo-realism that no photograph of the liner could ever provide, proved that his visionary flare was essential in getting the film model as close to perfection as humanly possible. Marschall's passion for the *Titanic* started at an early age and blossomed over the years that included his assistance in the design stages of the 1:350th scale model kit of the liner released in 1976 by Entex. The model went on to become one of the bestselling and largest model construction kits of the *Titanic* until its scale was surpassed by the 2019 release of the liner in 1:200 scale by Trumpeter Models.

Marschall came to the project early into the film's development stages where he advised and produced pre-production material for use in *Raise the Titanic*. In 1976 he created a painting based on Clive Cussler's novel depicting a hypothetical view of the wreck in one piece, her masts cut short, the bridge crushed from the collapse of the forward funnel while funnel number two is the only one left intact. The painting would serve as inspiration for the art department during these early production stages. Marschall's involvement did not stop there. With the film being directed by Stanley Kramer, Kramer turned to Marschall as the advisor to the model department in recreating the *Titanic* in miniature alongside *The Poseidon Adventure*'s production designer Bill Creber. This was Marschall's first outing in the movie industry. And what a catch for the young ocean liner enthusiast. Reproducing *Titanic* in minute detail was Marschall's natural gift. This could now be achieved with the model work for the movie.

To cut back on water droplet scale issues, the *Titanic* model had to be greater in scale than anything previously built. Before *Raise the Titanic*, previous film studios had constructed and sunk varying scale models from 28-feet to 40-feet. The 40-feet Shawcraft Models replica built for the 1958 Rank Organisation movie *A Night to Remember* was constructed to be split into two sections, bow, and stern, and rigged to sink in the indoor tank at Pinewood Studios. Even the 1979 EMI tv-movie *S.O.S. Titanic* cheated by using hand-tinted unused footage from *A Night to Remember* and a couple of photographs they had obtained of the 20-feet Bassett-Lowke *Titanic* display model which they edited to show the liner in her distressed state on the night of the disaster. Unlike those previous films, the *Raise the Titanic* model had to be something never constructed before and one that had to be put through a huge amount of stress during the raising sequence. The last thing the film studios wanted was to keep throwing cash into the build on every shoot as the model popped a vent or lost a funnel. This *Titanic* was to be constructed on a titanic scale, with a relatively healthy budget, and by the hands of a team of skilled experts.

The size chosen for the model was 1:16th scale which turned the original 882ft.9in *Titanic* into one scaled down to 55ft. 4in for this adaptation, working to ¾ inch to the foot. However, due to miscalculations by the studio resulted from the improper upscaling and printing of plans had the model come out slightly under scaled making the replica 54ft. 6in. Before work could begin on creating the physical model a series of scaled plans had to be made by the model department which covered window sizes and styles, deck fittings, deck structures, lifeboat davits, ventilators; every little detail required to be replicated to make the model as realistic as possible. Thankfully at the time of production, the shipyards of Harland & Wolff Ltd in Belfast who built the original *Titanic* in 1912 still operated and had in their archives many surviving plans used for the liner's construction in which copies could be obtained and studied. The surviving plans were scaled down to 1:16th and printed out and where needed new versions were created for use. One of the Olympic-class side profile plans was adapted to show a fully-hulled ship in 1:16th scale combining two main plans of the *Titanic*; a detailed waterline rigging plan and that of a general arrangement profile of the ship. This mish-mash of two lots of plans provided the model builders a basic understanding of how the liner would have looked externally back in 1912. With the profile printed out it was then pasted up on a huge wooden partitioning wall in the studio tent set up within the grounds of the backlot. While the monster plan was of tremendous use it also inadvertently became a headache as the plan represented the starboard side of *Titanic*, but was printed out flipped, turning the starboard side into an incorrect portside. I should add here that both port and starboard of the ship were not mirror images as window arrangements and deckhouse shapes differed greatly.

The plans offered much detail required for building a faithful replica of the ship's hull shape which included the hull's correct shear, spacing of plates, and porthole locations. Additional plans of the decks were on hand and a wealth of archival photographs of *Titanic* were available for the finer details. And where areas of the *Titanic* were not covered in photographic format, her sisters *Olympic* and *Britannic* could fill in the blanks. This wealth of archival material was taken during construction and captured on plates by Belfast photographic studios such as William Alfred Green and Robert John Welch who became the official photographer for Harland & Wolff. With the original glass plate negatives still in the archives, the company, who were now struggling as shipbuilding decreased at the yards, made available much of their archival material. Already holding a wealth of these prints in his collection, Marschall was hired to assist the model unit on the build and guide them through varying stages of design, construction and assembly. Marschall arrived at the CBS Studio Center facility located at the Studio City district in Los Angeles on the October 3, 1977 to begin work on the models. With a team of special effects personnel needed to build such replicas, the project was carried out on stages 3 and 7, with fabrication done at the special effects mill, the paint shop to hand and the studios art department crafting plans and illustrations. Earning $250 per week while building the world's largest and most accurate replica of the *Titanic*; "I was having a ball" recalls Marschall. Working with Kramer and Creber on the *Titanic* project was a dream job as the attention to detail is what mattered most for Marschall. Creber would jest, "what Ken says goes – within reason". Marschall recalls the working conditions of the studio at the time.

"Most of the time I was tolerated by the set designers and construction crew, but of course I didn't always get my way. And, because there was only one of me and I couldn't be in several places at once, inevitably some minor mistakes were made. But, generally, I was quite proud and excited about the progress."

With the studio set up and manufacturing in full swing, the models soon began to take shape on the concrete floor of the two sound stages. Weekly updates and talks between the model unit and the production team kept things relatively on track. Stanley Kramer did visit the stage to check on the progress of the model builds and inject some enthusiasm and ideas into the sets he had pushed to be crafted. For the many hard at work, this was just another film production even if they cared little for the subject being replicated. The impact of the disaster nearly 66 years previously became more realistic when a special guest arrived at the studio on December 7, 1977. Edwina "Winnie" Mackenzie, born in Bath, England, in 1884, boarded *Titanic* at Southampton docks as a 2nd class passenger for the journey to Auburndale in Florida to be with her sister. Mackenzie was originally booked to take the Atlantic crossing on board the White Star liner *Oceanic*. But from the upheaval from the coal strikes that had ravaged England during the spring of 1912, many vessels operating from Southampton were laid up until fuel stocks were plentiful to return to normal service. Vessels laid up would see their passengers, cargo and some crew bumped over to other ships that were still required to sail. *Titanic's* maiden voyage was deemed far too important to delay.

Winnie was awoken when the liner struck the iceberg. Leaving her cabin, she went to investigate. Once upon the boat deck, the sight of the crew uncovering the lifeboats was enough to convince her that something terrible was unfolding. She quickly made her way back down to her cabin to inform her traveling companions, to put on warmer clothing, and to return to the boat deck where she was guided into lifeboat No. 16 to leave the sinking vessel clutching a prayer book, her toothbrush, and a 5-month old child who she begged the crew to hand over when they refused to let the parent board the boat. Onboard the rescue ship *Carpathia* she slept on a table until the passage to New York turned foul when storms struck. She became hysterical, was given brandy to calm her nerves, and offered comfort in a bed. She remained in America marrying three times during her life and residing in later life at Redondo Beach in California until her passing on the 3 December 1984 at the age of 100. Winnie made the accompanied 45-minute journey from her residence to the CBS Studio Center to see the progress of the model build, to meet and talk with members of the team and answer questions posed to her about the *Titanic* and the night of the disaster. As surreal it must have seemed to the crew at the time, her brief tour cemented the need to honour the ship and her legacy.

Titanic Resurrected

The replica came in two main sections of a hull and superstructure that were designed and built purposely to be separated when required. The reasoning behind this was that the hull had to include a series of floatation tanks that would be fully operational by the model FX unit and if the upper deck sections were fixed in place it would restrict access to the tanks should anything go wrong. Having agreed on the design of the hull, the superstructure was designed to remain entirely intact yet easy enough to be lifted off and away from the main hull and seated down on the ground. For this to fully work both the main hull and the superstructure had to be built to withstand the weight of the accompanying structures, being transported around and the pressures applied to the model when submerged for lengthy periods in the water. So, let me take you on a tour around the studio and the construction of the world's largest *Titanic* model ever committed to screen.

Hull

The hull was designed as a plank-on-frame build of vertical hull frames cut from hardwood and secured to a central wooden keel. Each frame was shaped and cut differently to its neighbour and once laid in place, starting with the first frame being the prow, they came together to form the principal shape of the hull. To add stability to the hull where the stern and bow come together a ½ inch steel plate was cut to shape and bolted into place between the wooden frames. Over the frames were attached the planks that ran horizontally down the entire length of the hull from bow to stern, port and starboard. These frames would be used as anchorage points for the skinning process that was to follow. Using 1/4-inch ply, the boards (skin) were screwed down onto the planks and frames. With the joints sanded down the next level of the build was to apply the layers of glass resin over the entire exterior of the hull. It would have been a long process as each layer was applied, left to dry and the next layer mixed for applying. Once the exterior side of the hull had been resin coated and sanded into shape, the hull, which had been assembled upside down, was then righted to allow access into the interior side. Balsa wood was cut and inserted in between the exposed wooden frames so to fill the recess before the inside of the hull was boarded with timber and resin skinned.

Next was the adding of resin adhesive backed strakes that were rolled out along the hulls contour in marked off locations before the next series of plates were added to mimic the shell plating. For the hull plates that featured exposed domed rivet heads the dome of the rivet was created by tapping out the other side of the resin plate to form a raised head on the exposed face of the plate. This process was repeated along the D-Deck area of the hull where the superstructure would sit along with the forward and aft well deck hull sides. The finish detail of the hull was something to behold with intricately detailed hull plates with their overlapping joints perfectly modelled; portholes with inserts; mooring cleats; coal ports; shell doors; wash ports and hull plates along D-Deck with nearly one-hundred-thousand exposed rivet heads.

On the port and starboard side of the bow, the name **T I T A N I C** had been perfectly laser cut out of brass plate while **TITANIC** and **LIVERPOOL**, her port of registry, were carried over to the stern. At the stern located port and starboard was a set of propeller shaft wings and propellers. The wings of the shafts, known as a wing boss, were made from fiberglass and detailed with plating, and modelled with a hollow section that had a steel shaft passing through it for the attachment of a brass moulded propeller. An identical machined shaft was also created for the four-bladed centre propeller. The rudder was fabricated from steel with a machined steel rudder stock at the top and resin moulded details to simulate the bolt joints between each section of the rudder. Attached to the rear of the rudder was a machined frame with eyelets where the rudder could be mounted upon another stern frame inserted into the hull where gudgeon pins allowed for the rudder to swing to port or starboard while secured at all times to the stern's centreline.

One detail that was made separately for the bow was a cast resin hawser; an opening like an eye which, on the real *Titanic*, allowed for a towing cable to be passed through when the liner was tugged in and out of port. Located just above the hawser was the anchor well where the liner's largest of the three anchors sat. The anchor well was made of steel and within it sat a replica of the large Hall's anchor made from cast resin. Smaller-scale Hall's anchors were copied from moulds, cast in resin and brass, and seated on either side of the bow in their hawsers. To keep the model to scale the panels of the forward and aft well decks had been purposely cut out from the fiberglass hull and replaced with metal counterparts that retained the correct thickness to the hull when filmed up close. Detailing with steel was carried over on the hull when it was used to cover over the existing fiberglass of the raised sides of the forecastle, poop deck, and C-Deck. With the portholes drilled out the steel was screwed in place and finished with overlapping joints cast from resin for the bow and stern and left blank for the area of C-Deck where the superstructure would come down to rest.

Internal Frames, Tanks & Piping

Due to the size of the hull the model makers could not leave the hull without including a steel framework that required to be seated inside the structure. This frame not only added support to the hull overall but allowed for the installation of flotation tanks, their internal pipework and even lighting. The tanks spanned the width of the internal lower space of the hull and were rigged and sealed so air could be pumped in for buoyancy and released for when the completed model was being filmed in a specially built sinking rig in the studio water tank. At this stage of the build the steel frame was fixed to a number of brackets bolted in place inside the hull and positioned so the forecastle, poop deck and well decks could be seated down and secured. More extensive brackets were fixed in place for the frames to support the top of the hull where the heavy superstructure would be sat down. These frames were to stay in place during the filming of the model in Malta for the movies intended 1912 prologue. But as the production progressed and changed, so did the needs of the models which, in the case of the *Titanic* replica, required the innards of the model to be ripped out and completely replaced.

Forecastle, Poop Deck & Well Decks

The forecastle deck on the bow had a one-inch thick hardwood foundation cut to fit inside of the aperture of the hull footprint. Attached to the top of the timber there sat a 3mm thick plate of steel that slightly overlapped the wooden foundation to visually remove any joint between the deck and the hull and hiding all traces of the timber beneath it. At the aft end of the deck beneath the location of the forward mast, the 3rd class entrance was crafted from steel folded into shape, fixed into position, and detailed with resin cast watertight doors. Upon the deck the model unit replicated the many deck fittings using resin moulds of mooring bollards, capstans, windlasses with their runners and anchor chains, the No. 1 cargo hold combing with hatch cover and breakwaters, the sets of steam-powered winches, swan neck, and cowl ventilators, the four sets of control pedestals, cable reel, three different sets of fairleads, a pair of resin and metal deck stairs and an anchor crane machined from solid brass. And standing proud over the deck there rose a rolled metal mast that was completed with the large cargo derrick, crow's nest with supports and, just visible, a machine-tooled replica of the bell which on that cold April night back in 1912 lookout Frederick Fleet struck three times to warn the wheelhouse of the approaching danger ahead.

The poop deck at the stern received the same extraordinary attention to detail as that of the bow with resin cast fittings of bollards, fairlead rollers, capstans, cargo winch, a pair of electric cargo cranes, some eights sets of cowl vents, a machine turned jack staff, a steel-cut docking bridge with cast resin docking equipment, three sets of metal and resin stairs, pair of cable reels and eighteen sets of intricately made brass deck benches; all of which were screwed down to hardwood and steel topped decking. Copying the forecastle construction, the stern deck also had its 3rd class entrance made from shaped steel and finished with cast resin doors. Railings made from 1mm diameter brass were built, shaped, and fitted to the leading edge of the decks. One interesting detail added to the model was a red signage board with white lettering that warned others that the liner was fitted with triple screws.

Positioned fore and aft were the well decks that formed part of the liner's 3rd class open spaces. For the model, these were replicated in great detail that included the cargo holds No. 2 and 3 in the forward well deck, and holds No. 5 and 6 for the aft well deck. The deck itself was cut from one-inch hardwood. But unlike the fore and aft these were covered with steel. From cast resin eight sets of mooring bollards were produced and secured to the deck with a pair of threaded screws from beneath. The distinctive Stothert & Pitt electric cargo cranes were lovingly recreated to such minute detail they included the fuse boxes on the towers, the operating platform, control levers, and cargo lifting cables with tackle. Even the securing cradle that held the crane booms in place was intricately fabricated. An unusual feature that is not instantly recognizable on the model, but was necessary, were a pair of access panels in the well deck which gave entry into the hull at the stern and bow. The panels were cut from the hardwood used for the decking with one located on the starboard side of the forward well deck and another located on the port side of the stern well deck. As these access points were cut into the timber, the removal of the panel meant that it gave quick access into those locations of the hull where the panel could be simply dropped back down in place with little seen of the cut aperture.

Superstructure & Deckhouses

To take the weight of the heavy superstructure the hull had to be fitted with a steel frame that was bolted together in place above the floatation tanks of the hull. The frame allowed much of the weight of the superstructure to sit upon it, distributing it evenly so that the sides of the hull did not move or warp from the weight. The frame spanned the width and the length of the hull from the location of the bridge to the aft end of the superstructure where the boat deck ended. Within this frame were seven thread sleeves to allow a threaded bolt to be passed down from the boat deck, through the superstructure, and into the sleeve where the bolt is tightened up securing the upper structure to the main hull and preventing movement when the model was to be put through its rigorous stages of water submergence. With the main hull now complete the equally enormous superstructure could now be constructed. With the principal idea behind the superstructure and hull being two separate entities it meant that the model offered access into the main hull and for storage if the model could not be stored as a complete structure. The removal of the heavy superstructure also meant that the structure could be lifted free from the hull cutting back on long periods of the upper structure bearing down on the framework of the hull beneath it in which, over time, could cause stress resulting in fractures appearing in the materials, something the film studios would not appreciate this early into the film's production before principal photography on the sinking could begin.

Unlike the hull which had both a bow and stern that was almost streamlined in appearance, the superstructure was a large slab-sided structure that would need to be sturdy enough to take the stress of being flung up and out of the water tank many times. The decision was made to make the entire superstructure out of steel with no main fiberglass structures. The structure contained the boat deck with deckhouses, A-Deck and B-Deck which would sit upon the hull's framework, and already fabricated C-Deck portions that contained the forward and aft deckhouses for 1st and 2nd class passengers. B-Deck came first allowing for the more detailed A-Deck to be welded down on top. Except for the forward and aft ends of B-Deck with the deckhouse walls detailed with cast resin window frames, doors, and handrails from brass, the midships (middle) section contained no internal structures and leaving the space open for the addition later on of pipework that would be used in pumping up water up and out of small outlets built into the decks that can be seen in action during the fly-past sequence after the wreck is raised. On either side of the 2nd class smoking room sat the No. 4 cargo holds which were accessible via two hatches located port and starboard and modelled from resin along with the pair of cowl ventilators that were located forward of the hatch.

Next was A-Deck and its open and partially enclosed promenade deck with the screened-off forward end that differentiates *Titanic* from her older sister *Olympic*. Within the promenade deck were the internal deckhouse walls carefully replicated for the planned close-up views envisioned by the art department that would show this area of the ship's compartments from the forward 1st class cabins, grand staircase, lounge, smoking room, and palm court cafes. While these rooms existed on the real ship, they were not recreated for the model and left to the imagination behind the deckhouse walls and windows. The decking here was steel giving strength to the deckhouse structure that would hold up the boat deck above and the superstructures side walls with the rectangular windows. The open promenade deck areas of A and B decks were finished with c-shaped steel beams in the larger openings that mimicked the vertical supports. The use of steel continued over to the boat deck and the main deckhouses where the funnels would sit. At this stage of the build progress, the production company required that the 55ft model was to be finished off the day she was handed over to her owners the White Star Line. This process meant that the model's upper exposed deck areas needed to be a close as possible to the real ship for when close-up views of the ship were needed to be captured on film. Although the storyboarded scenes of the sinking *Titanic* were to show the ship at a distance, the details of the replica had to be exact for when the model undergoes its transformation to the wreck. If the finer details were already there for the model unit responsible for the transformation then it was to be a much quicker breakdown and aging process without the need to reproduce the larger percentage of the deck details, albeit parts that were earmarked as breakaway parts that would have been prone to easy damaging.

The boat deck was crafted from steel sheets secured down to the inner structures of A-Deck below. Starting from the bridge and working backward, the bridge front was fabricated from 2mm thick steel and rolled out to form the bridge wings that swept back to a pair of bridge cabs on the port and starboard sides of the superstructure. The cabs were fitted out with a set of resin cast navigational lights, red for portside and green for starboard, and complete with bulbs and wiring for illumination at night.

On the roof of the bridge cabs sat the Marconi lamp and like the other navigational equipment they too were produced to emit light. Working back from the bridge was the area of the Officers' Quarters and the 1st class passenger cabins which had been included on *Titanic* at this part of her career, but not a feature of *Olympic* until her 1913 refit. The window frames and doors were produced from resin casts that even included door hinges and handles. If that wasn't detailed enough, they even went as far as to include the sets of locking mechanisms for the windows. The details continued on the deckhouse with deck lamps, handrails, and crew ladders. Upon the deckhouse roof, the many ventilators were a mixed combination of both metal and cast resin. The stokehold vents that sat at the base of the funnels were fabricated from machine-cut metal sheet and fitted with a diamond-shaped fine wire mesh to match the originals. The swan neck ventilators that sat around the footing of funnels one and two were from cast resin that included the electric motors and feet. This method was carried over to the cowl vents with Sirocco motors that sat upon the roof.

Between funnels one and two sat the weather covering over the 1st class Grand Staircase ornate dome, a feature that was replicated for the model but never actually seen. On the model, the covering was formed from metal sheet plate with the window panels cut out and Perspex attached to the underside to act as glass. On the real *Titanic*, this weather covering was made to protect the wrought-iron and glass dome that sat directly above the solid oak staircase that would allow natural light to filter down in daylight but back-illuminated at night. One lot of the features that did not make it onto the model in this location was the skylights for the Marconi room and the Officers' Quarters lavatory. This may have been down to time scale during the model's construction. But as the plans used were taken from those for *Olympic*, pre-*Titanic* disaster, these skylights were not widely known until after the discovery of the real ship in September 1985. But one detail in this spot made it to the film model; the awning bar that was connected from the top of the stokehold vent at the rear of funnel number one and which passed over to a small Gibbs vent that sat directly in front of the weather covering. On *Titanic*, this awning bar could be used to attach a canvas cover for use in protecting items stored upon that area of the deck or to create shade for the crew if they wanted to utilize that area of the deckhouse during a voyage or if the liner was in port or back at the shipbuilders in Belfast.

Moving midships of the model is the raised roof that sat between funnels two and three. The roof here sat directly over the 1st class lounge and the Reading and Writing Room and featured a raised boxed structure that on the real *Titanic* was an interior recess where a 16-light chandelier in the lounge sat. On the model, this area was fabricated from 2mm metal plates, cut, folded into shape, and internally welded down at the seams. Sat atop of the boxed structure was a cast resin Sirocco electric motor with the cowl vent. And rising above the vents was the compass tower. Made from metal it included simulated timbered wooden board joints for the main structure and brass turned leg supports and feet. It was even completed with a notice board aimed towards passengers instructing them not to climb the steps and enter the tower. To finish off the tower's detail was a set of upright supports for attaching a canvas wind deflector and a cast resin compass. Accompanying the compass tower, the raised roof was fitted with a series of resin electric motors with cowl vents, swan neck vents, and Thermotank's.

The deckhouse for the third funnel was a steel fabrication of outer walls and decking with details of windows, doors, and deck lights from cast resin parts. The next section of the deckhouse that sat between the third and fourth funnels was the Tank Room with the Engine Room skylight and the adjacent weather covering over the aft 1st class staircase. Again, steel was used in its construction with resin windows, doors, skylight covers, and ventilators. They were built as two pieces consisting of the main Tank Room with a skylight that, as a unit, could be removed to give access to controls hidden out of sight within the superstructure. The skylight over the aft staircase was a fixed structure with openings cut into the steel to represent the windows of the skylight and Perspex fitted to the underside to appear like glass. At the aft end of the boat deck was the raised roof over the 1st class Smoking Room that contained the deckhouse for the fourth funnel. Both structures were fabricated from steel and dressed with cast resin window frames, doors, air trunking, deck lights, Thermotank's, panelled vent openings, ventilators and their electric Sirocco motors, and tubular piping that replicated the chimney flue that came up from the fireplace of the Smoking Room. The final structure at the very end of the boat deck was the 2nd class entrance. The deckhouse was made from steel with a steel-formed elevator motor housing on top and steel-cut vent tops with a wire mesh grille insert. Window frames, doors, deckhouse lights, and the pair of Gibbs extractor vents were made from cast resin to detail this deckhouse.

The deck benches made for the boat deck and the poop deck at the stern were all made from brass with decorative sides and lattice slats coming together to form a single bench. Resin was to play an integral role in the detailing of the model, and with moulds of the parts made, it afforded the model unit to make multiple spares to which the film production units could revert to if anything got damaged or lost. More commonly known as break-away parts, additional cowl vents, window frames, benches, and lifeboat davits were produced and placed into storage in case of an emergency. These spare parts would accompany the model to where ever it was going to go for filming. One drawback to reproducing many of the deck details from these moulds was that the *Titanic* model was eventually finished with ventilators not fully authentic to the build as many of these units were carbon copies of other vents. The production of vents and their motors resulted in a number of units that did not perfectly match those seen in archival photographs as those on the original *Titanic* differed in appearance with no one unit being the same. But this was the film industry. This was of no importance to the model unit as in the case of many motion pictures, the building of such miniatures had to come within budget while the studio was aware that 98% of the audience would not know the difference if any technical errors were to appear in the build. The carbon-copying of details did not stop with the vents as during the construction of the superstructure the starboard window configuration was carried over to the portside. It was not until Marschall successfully persevered with presenting the case that the mistakes needed to be rectified.

At the Officers' Quarters end of the boat deck was partition railings that split the deck between the officer's area and that of 1st class passengers. On the real ship, these were to prevent passengers from crossing over into areas of the vessel where passengers were not generally permitted. These and the rest of the railings for the model were made from lengths of brass rod and constructed according to which area of the ship they were to be fitted as the *Titanic* had varying railing sets that differed between single hand bar railings to those with three or five horizontal bars and those over in 1st class that was topped off with teak handrails.

At the aft end of A-Deck, port and starboard, were a pair of slightly smaller cargo cranes of the exact type fitted to the stern and the two well decks and made from resin and detailed with fuse boxes and the control levers. One feature that was included in the model was a set of hooded-type weather coverings that sat over the single set of stairs on the port and starboard side of the bridge area that went down to the enclosed forward section of the A-Deck promenade. The coverings, however, were not correct to the *Titanic* as they were modelled from those installed on the *Olympic*. But given the documentation at the time of the model's build and that changes were made to *Titanic*'s design during her final stages of building in 1912, it was easy for such errors to appear. It would not be until the discovery of the *Titanic* in 1985 where the real wreck revealed such a change between the two sister ships.

Lifeboats & Davits

When *Titanic* entered service in April 1912, she was equipped with a total of twenty lifeboats that were approved by the British Board of Trade. The lifeboats had been designed to carry a questionable 1,178 persons to safety from an ocean liner designed to carry a little over 3,000 passengers and crew. For the movie replica three types of lifeboats were needed that were based on the original specifications; four Engelhardt collapsible boats, two emergency cutters, and fourteen main lifeboats. The collapsible boats were designated as boats A, B, C, and D with A and B to sit atop of the Officers' Quarters roofs on either side of the first funnel while C and D sat on the boat deck directly behind the bridge cabs. The 25ft length emergency cutters were numbered 1 and 2 and sat partially swung out over the bulwark behind the bridge cabs. The remaining 30ft main lifeboats were numbered 3 to 16 with a set of four positioned to port and starboard at the aft end of the boat deck and a set of three located port and starboard forwards alongside the Officers' Quarters area of the boat deck. The lifeboats for the model were all made from cast resin as a one-piece unit that was hollowed out inside to include the seating-slats and finished with wood trim to match those supplied to *Titanic*. Each of the miniature lifeboats came supplied with scale rowing oars that would be used with figurines placed into the lifeboats for filming the sinking of the *Titanic*. To complete the lifeboat miniatures the thirty-two Welin davit arms were made from cast resin from moulds and intricate enough when assembled that when attached to their base the fully working worm gear included allowed the davit arm to be cranked out and back in again like the original units.

Before each lifeboat could be seated down on the deck it required thirty-two sets of lifeboat chocks cast in resin and adhered down to the steel boat deck of the model. These chocks acted as a cradle in which the lifeboat would sit upon and be nestled securely preventing it from tipping over onto its keel. Inboard of the lifeboat chocks was the funnel guy wire securing shackles. On *Titanic*, the guy wires acted as additional support for the funnels in which the guy wire was connected to a pad eye beneath the rim of the top of the funnel where the White Star Line "buff" and the black upper section separated the funnel colours. The guy wires were stretched down to the boat deck and secured in place with a hemp cable and shackle and deck-mounted pad eye. For the *Titanic* model, the fifty connectors were replicated with the use of stainless-steel cable hardware pieces with an adjustable thread so the cables could be tightened up.

Funnels

The *Titanic* would not be *Titanic* without those distinctive towering funnels. The construction was a simple one and one used many times in model boat construction. A wooden frame was crafted in which a thin wooden skin could be wrapped around to form the elliptical shape of each funnel. The next step was to add the exterior funnel skin which was rolled sections of 1mm thick metal sheeting that was then secured in place over the wooden skin and frame. The funnel skin rivet pattern was reproduced by laying lengths of thin aluminium strips which had been pressed in from the reverse side to form, on the exterior side, the rivet heads running in lines. The strips then adhered in place directly onto the metal skin of each of the funnel units. To add more realism to the funnel the structure's inner skin was replicated from rolled 1mm metal and formed into a narrower tube structure that followed the internal contour of the outer skin. This inner funnel can be seen in the overhead views of the model in the film's raising sequence. A metal rim was attached to the top leading edge of the funnel with a second rim positioned lower down in the location of where the pad eyes attachments would be for the funnel rigging down to the boat deck. Mounted forward and to the rear of each funnel was the steam exhaust that was modelled from a metal tube and bolted down in place to the funnel skin. The forward steam exhausts were detailed with a set of machined turned brass whistles, a metal platform, and brass fabricated ladders. Where the funnel was to be seated the area of the deck was cut out in the footprint of the funnel that allowed the funnel unit to pass down into the deckhouse structure and be mounted and bolted securely down onto an internal steel frame that stopped the funnel from moving. This procedure followed a similar pattern to the *Titanic*'s real funnels, albeit on a smaller scale, but done so to withstand the funnel's overall height, weight, rake and being thrown off balance when the model is sunk and then later raised.

The tallest of the four funnels for the *Titanic* model stood a few inches short of five feet in height. Impressive in terms of model scale but not as impressive as *Titanic*'s original funnels. Those on *Titanic* varied in height based on the location they were seated and the nature of the liner's hull shear as the bow and stern were higher than the midship section of the liner. Funnels 1, 2, and 3 were connected directly to the boiler casings and inner funnel that passed down to boiler rooms numbered one to six. Boiler room number one was located beneath funnel No.3 with the room numbers going up towards the bow. These boiler rooms were fitted out with 29 Scotch marine boilers, 5 single-ended 50-ton boilers in room one, and the rest as 105-ton double-ended boilers resulting in 159 furnaces that could consume an estimated 650 tons of coal every 24 hours. It would take, on average, a total of 12 hours from the time a boiler is lit to it being ready to be brought online to power the vessel. Funnels No.1 to 3 carried away the waste gasses from the working boilers while the fourth funnel, commonly and very much incorrectly termed the "dummy" funnel, had several uses. The funnel was used to exhaust access gases from the engine room, to expel foul air from the interior of the ship. The funnel also contained the chimney flue from the working coal fire in the 1st class smoking room on A-Deck. From the boat deck level, funnel

No.1 measured 70ft in height making it the shortest of the four. Funnels No.2 and 3 both towered 74ft from the boat deck and funnel No.4 came in at 73ft in height. However, all four funnels measured the same in diameter, that being 24ft, and big enough to pass a locomotive through. As one worker at the Harland & Wolff shipyard that built her proclaimed, "everything about her was on a nightmarish scale."

The Final Touch

The model unit was aware from the start that the model would need to be submerged in water for extended periods so the exterior surfaces of the model had to be treated to slow the rate of deterioration during filming. Painting the replica was carried out in stages. The raw resin of the hull was treated first with a primer filler before the undercoat could be applied. Once cured the model could receive its familiar White Star Line livery that graced *Titanic*'s sleek hull. Given the scale of the model, it was decided that semi-matt paints were used for realism and scale. The lower half of the hull was finished in a colour close to the original ship's anti-foul red. Above the waterline, the hull was treated in black, and the sides of the forecastle, poop deck, and C-Deck were painted in white. A bright yellow shear line was added to divide the black hull to the white superstructure while gold paint was used for the ship's name on the bow and stern; a minor inaccuracy as the real ship's name and port of registry was painted in yellow to match the shear line. The use of semi-matt paints was crucial for keeping the model to scale and not having it appear toy-like; something that using gloss paints would have done if they had been used.

The superstructure was treated with a primer, then a grey undercoat before the topcoats of semi-matt white was applied. With the superstructure and deckhouses all in white the resin window frames were hand-painted in the required brown to simulate a mixture of wooden and coated bronze frames with a similar brown used on the masts and jack staffs. The steel deck for the deckhouses of funnel three and four was finished in grey to match with the *Titanic*'s colour scheme of 1912. All the mooring bollards, fairlead rollers, cargo winches, capstans, and deck gear were finished in matt-black for better scale. And those impressive funnels? Much is debated still over the actual colour that was used on *Titanic*'s funnels. The top was finished in semi-matt black like the hull but the White Star Line "buff" is something that has never been fully established as the mixture for the real ship was constantly changing. The "buff" used on the film model was a mixture based on Ken Marschall's research for the colour tone he used for his artworks during the 1970s. It was, for the time, the best educated guess for the "buff" that the White Star Line used for all their fleet during the period of the 1910s. As a near-completed replica, the *Titanic* model was certainly an eye-catching movie prop and one of the largest and most accurately crafted miniatures of the unsinkable liner.

Choppy Seas Ahead

Down at the CBS Studio Center facility in Los Angeles as the models continued to take shape, cracks were beginning to appear. As time passed, the complications between the movie's original producer/director Stanley Kramer and the productions financier Lew Grade was mounting; mainly due to the ever-increasing costs, resulting in heated arguments between the stalwarts. The model work alone was rapidly eating away at the original $7m budget as Kramer and Creber pushed for historical accuracy with the model work and set pieces. Kramer wanted sets of the Grand Staircase, cargo hold, boiler room, 1st class corridor, and a section of the Smoking Room built for the opening sinking prologue. Grade, on the other hand, felt it was an unnecessary expenditure for something that was going to be on screen for a matter of seconds. But back in London Grade continued to call the shots unaware that some sections of the sets had already been started. But when news reached his offices, he was soon calling for a halt to the construction. The repercussions from all the arguments between Grade and Kramer soon began to affect the production and Kramer began to question his future on the project.

When work began on the large *Titanic* replica, it was thought that the model would only be used for the sinking scenes, then aged and broken down with the use of constructed wreck parts, and filmed in water for the sequences on the discovery and preparations leading up to the raising of the wreck. The 55ft model was never actually going to be raised. This would be achieved with a smaller version of the *Titanic* built to an estimated 25ft in length and equally detailed. The plan was to film the smaller model on its journey to the surface then revert to overhead shots with the same model to capture the movies climatic raising sequence. The big *Titanic* model would then be returned in front of the camera and used as the wreck on the surface following salvage. But circumstances changed as uncertainty arose around the studio when the number of studio personnel decreased and rumours circulated that Kramer was getting ready to walk. Grade, hesitatingly, could only throw more money at the project. While it was a relief to see the production getting an increase in budget, it did not remove the atmosphere around the studio stages that something was wrong. One glaring error was apparent from the offset. There was no tank big enough for the *Titanic* model to be sunk, or even raised. The existing tanks, even those at 20th Century Fox, were nowhere near substantial enough to accomplish such large-scale FX work. And to make matters worse, the huge *Titanic* miniature was nearing completion.

The film project was capturing the media attention as snippets of news began to slowly filter through to newspapers and magazines outlining those approached to work and star in the feature film. Grade, delighted by the attention his movie was receiving, was proud to announce the production was "big business" for the movie industry, especially for Great Britain. But among the positives of the production, there were also the many concerns that grew over the budget restraints the model team in Los Angeles were having to deal with. Slowly the workforce began to decrease to a level of a skeleton crew. Kramer and Creber had envisioned a lavish production for *Raise the Titanic* and they felt that the $7 million Grade had set aside for the project was no longer realistic. Observing from the side-lines was Ken Marschall.

"I remember I went to Beverly Hills with Art Director Bill Sully one day to talk with a car collector/expert about recreating first-class passenger William Carter's new Renault town car in *Titanic*'s hold. I storyboarded a whole prologue sequence at Bill Creber's request involving guys chasing about in the Siberian snow with rifles and such. Creber liked them and said something to the effect 'We'll use these. This is good.' That whole prologue idea in the screenplay was eventually dropped."

By late fall of 1977, it was decided that a water tank could be constructed within the backlot of the CBS Studio Center where the sinking and raising sequences could be filmed. An area of the studio land a stone's throw from stages 18 and 19 had been secured and work began on preparing the groundwork for the tank. But it all came to a close when the ground in that location kept flooding, and eventually collapsing in on itself, rendering the tank build a failure during this time of production. Luckily for Grade, these miscalculations with the geography of the land came early with minimal effect on the already strained budget. The search was back on for land to buy that would be substantial enough to design and construct a water filming tank big enough for the project. Grade sent Bernard Kingham of ITC on the trail to find a place suitable. His search would lead them to the shores of Malta. If Grade had thought that things couldn't possibly get any worse, December was to deliver the first major blow to Lew Grade's *Raise the Titanic*. After several months on the project, Stanley Kramer finally threw in the towel and left the production. He looked upon Grade's budget as too much of a constraint for what he, an Oscar-winning director, could achieve. He could not justify crafting such a lavish visual on a suffocated budget in which those in financial status tried at every turn to cut back. The prospect of losing money to keep the film on track was not an option anymore and Kramer walked taking his film crew with him and pulling the employment plug on those on an advisory payroll.

"My last day in the studio" recalls Marschall "was March 10, 1978, that's when I took my last photos of the almost complete model. On that day I strayed from my usual black and white and used Kodak's new ASA 400 color print film to capture the paint job. My pre-production work helping the set draftsmen and overseeing the model building was certainly the most exciting thing I'd ever done to date. I was allowed an unusual degree of authority and freedom. Creber would say 'If Ken says it's wrong, let's try to fix it. Within reason.' That 'within reason' caveat led to a lot of artistic license, like their deciding early on to break off the second funnel and leave the first one intact when eyewitnesses described the forward funnel collapsing during the sinking. I, of course, protested but was told that audiences needed to see the full extent of the four funnels – the first and last. Losing the correct *first* funnel, it was felt that audiences would think it was a three-funnelled ship and would look odd. Working with Stanley Kramer was of course a thrill, his being such a legendary director. We were all devastated by his unexpected departure. It was awful, a real shame. Under Kramer, the sweeping sets, scenes, and visual effects originally anticipated would have been eye-popping."

The winter of 1977 into 78 was certainly looking cold and bleak for Lew Grade back in London as his *Titanic* film was attracting the wrong kind of attention and looking as if it too was on a disastrous collision course. That January, ITC and Marble Arch Productions had already invested well over $7 million, exhausting the projects original budget. Grade was not one to back down on such an adventure, not with so much expenditure at stake. In traditional showbiz style, he straightened up his tie, fired up a match for his cigar, and stepped forward to announce that he was steaming full speed ahead in looking for a new director for *Raise the Titanic*. Unfortunately, the zeal was dwindling fast over in Los Angeles, when that March, another major change came about as Jerry Jameson took to the director's chair bringing in his own film crew that resulted in those who had been part of Kramer's contingent to be withdrawn from the *Raise the Titanic* movie project.

Unfinished Business

Contrary to belief, the huge *Titanic* replica was never fully finished when it left the CBS studios in Los Angeles for its long journey to Malta. It should have been a forewarning when crews from MGM joined the production and set to work on finishing off the models. With all their good intentions, filmmaking was indeed their forte, *Titanic* modelling was not. Their inexperience on the subject of *Titanic* began to reflect on the model during the latter stages of its construction when previously assembled parts were either wrongly placed on the decks, some details missed, and questionable details that made no sense. One example of this were the raised window frames that were fabricated from resin and fitted to the rectangular window apertures on A, B, and C-Deck of the superstructure. While they stand out distinctively as being window frames on screen, they were in fact incorrectly scaled rivet patterns that followed the shape of the window. The over scaled nature of the resin casts to each window gave the undesired effect that the windows had protruding frames when in reality these would have been a single line of rivets encircling the window to hold the window opening mechanism in place. While these frames were fitted prior to Jameson taking over the project, the crude nature of the parts still spark debates to why they were ever installed in the first place.

Another error incorporated into the film model was the sets of coaling outriggers that were attached to the lower section of the A-Deck superstructure. These triangular structures replicated the outriggers that were used in the dock when the *Titanic* was being fuelled. With the coal barges tied to the side of the ship, the coaling crews could have the bags of coal lifted on a pulley and tackle that was attached to the coaling rigger that had been swung outboard. For the model, sixteen outriggers were made out of brass rods, with eight units placed at intervals on the port and starboard side of the superstructure. Those on the starboard side were correctly placed and pointing towards the stern of the replica. But those that were late in being installed on the port side were now attached to incorrectly face towards the bow. Also missing from the build were the wire mesh inserts to the swan and gooseneck ventilators with motors located on the roof of the Officers' Quarters and the port side of the Tank Room between funnels three and four.

During the model's principal construction, the windows that were glazed on the real ship were to be repeated on the miniature as some windows do have a clear plastic attached to the inner side of the structure. While nearly all of the windows are devoid of window panes in the wreck version, some window frames do still have the plastic "glass" pane inserted. One can be located in the Officers' Quarters covered in sediment on the wreck during the sweep past of the raised ship. But the others are more hidden from the viewer as they appear in the starboard C-Deck windows to the 2nd class enclosed promenade deck. One oddity is the missing yet visible three-bar gratings that were fixed to the tops of the funnels. The grating is completely missing on the remaining standing funnels when the ship is raised, but the broken smokestack that is discovered by the crews of the *Deep Quest* and *Sea Cliff* clearly show that the fallen unit has the grating still intact when Bohannon responds to Pitt's question about the funnel with; "whatever it is, it has ten-layers of sea critters on it." These bars were fitted to the funnels when the model was built over in California. But as the model underwent its transformation to a wreck the bars were removed and never put back.

Other omitted details from the model included the window frames of the open bridge; the port and starboard sets of railings that divided the boat deck areas between the 1st class, aft, Engineers deck, and 2nd class deck, and the handrails to the railings on the aft end of the Boat Deck, A, and B Deck promenades. Of all the items that never made it onto the model was the ships pitch pine decking. A conscious decision was made to not include any timbered exposed decking as the model being submerged for lengthy periods of time in water would result in the timber lifting and warping. With all the fittings secured in place to the bare steel of the decks, including large steel deckhouses welded into place, it was more cost effective to just paint the steel decks. As no scenes were intended to show the model up close and with the scenes being filmed at night, the audience would not be able to tell the difference between a wooden deck to that of a painted one.

Despite the errors that made it into the model at the hands of the seasoned film crews and the often unsympathetic view that it was just a movie prop where the general audience would not care let alone have enough time to scrutinise such mistakes, the final result was still an impressive recreation of the legendary liner that was finely detailed beyond anything previously constructed. She definitely was *Titanic* in name and in scale.

Towards the end of 1978 as the *Titanic* and other miniatures were all ready for crating up for the long journey to Europe, the news came that ITC had finally secured a piece of land over in Malta for the building of a new filming tank within the grounds of the Mediterranean Film Facility. The question now was if ITC were going to go ahead with having the Malta studio construct a smaller version of the *Titanic* purposely for the raising scenes. They had the facilities, the crew and materials available to them to produce such a model. The decision now rested with Lew Grade.

The Mystery of the other *Titanic* Model

One mystery that surrounds the miniatures built for the film is that of the whereabouts of the 1:98th scale 9ft "white" *Titanic* model that was constructed and used in the drop test sequence of the movie and later again for a couple of brief shots of the wreck being raised. In the Clive Cussler novel, the model was described as being a ceramic built scale replica of the *Titanic* with marbles used as boilers that spill out of the iceberg gash in the side of the hull as the model makes its journey to the bottom of the test tank. For the film, the model could almost pass for being constructed from a ceramic mould as it gleamed under the water and in the camera's lights. But it was made from plastic and was light enough for just one of the operating divers to lift it through the water. The sequence was filmed at the marine pool of Rockwell International Corporation in Anaheim, California for part of the movie's core storylines as Gene Seagram and Dr. Silverstein conduct several tests to see where the hull of *Titanic* may have come to rest after its journey from the surface over 12,000ft above. As if to mimic the actual tests in the novel the model was dropped several times until it was felt necessary that enough footage had been captured for the movie. From there the model was then shipped over to Malta where it underwent a change into the battered wreck of the *Titanic*.

The history of this model is somewhat unusual in that after filming the model was put into dry storage and remained there as the storm burst regarding the future of ITC during the post-1981 years. Sometime during 81/82 the model became privately owned by Australian billionaire Robert Holmes à Court who would become associated with Lew Grade's businesses at the time of the movie's release. The model was displayed in a themed restaurant in Perth that was owned by Holmes à Court's and remained there for some time until his untimely death in 1990. The model then vanished from public view until 2004 when it reappeared again at a film auction staged in Sydney with a $5,000 price tag. In more recent times it is rumoured to be once again in storage somewhere in Australia. One story suggests that its current location is that of a government storage facility. A highly unusual resting place for an obscure piece of movie memorabilia with a story that could have easily been lifted from the pages of a Clive Cussler novel.

Titanic Model Dimensions

Have you ever been curious about how big the models were for *Raise the Titanic*? All models were built to $1:16^{th\,(3/4)}$ scale with measurements at 1" = 50' except for the "white ceramic" *Titanic* drop-test model built to a scale of $1:98^{th}$.

R.M.S. *Titanic* (1/16th)

L – 54' 6"
W – 8'
H – 18' 1" (total with masts)
Cost of build $350,000

R.M.S. *Titanic* (1/98th)

L – 9' 1"
W – 11"
H – 54" (total with masts)
Cost of build (unknown)

The 28ft *Titanic* model for the 1953 Fox production under construction at the 20th Century Fox studio. *(Author's collection)*

Behind the scenes image of the partially capsized model of the S.S. *Poseidon* at the foot of the water dump chute. *(Author's collection)*

One of a handful of shots in the films memorable raising sequence that emphasizes the over scaled water with that of the smaller details of the model. *(ITC/ITV Studios)*

Chapter 6: The Building of a Legend • 141

Employees at model makers Shawcraft work on the 40ft scale replica of the *Titanic* for the 1958 Rank Organisation film *A Night to Remember*. *(Author's collection)*

In this 1977 image, one of the FX crew works on a series of sample hull panels at the CBS studio to establish how the wreck of the *Titanic* and 68 years of decay will appear on screen. *(Photograph © Ken Marschall)*

William "Bill" Creber points to an area on a printed-out Harland & Wolff plan to Bill Sully in the fall of 1977. *(Photograph © Ken Marschall)*

Set decorator Daniel Gluck poses alongside the starboard stern of the *Titanic* hull and the impressive propellers at the stern that he crafted. Gluck also fabricated the hull name plates from brass sheet and the array of brass deck benches. *(Photograph © Ken Marschall)*

Titanic artist, historian and the film model's visual consultant Ken Marschall stands proudly alongside the starboard bow of the partially assembled *Titanic* hull. In the background a team of model makers are working on the upturned hull to one of the scale U.S. Navy vessels. *(Photograph © Ken Marschall)*

Publicity postcard from the 1970s that shows a large portion of the CBS Studio Center facilities. *(Author's collection)*

Chapter 6: The Building of a Legend • 145

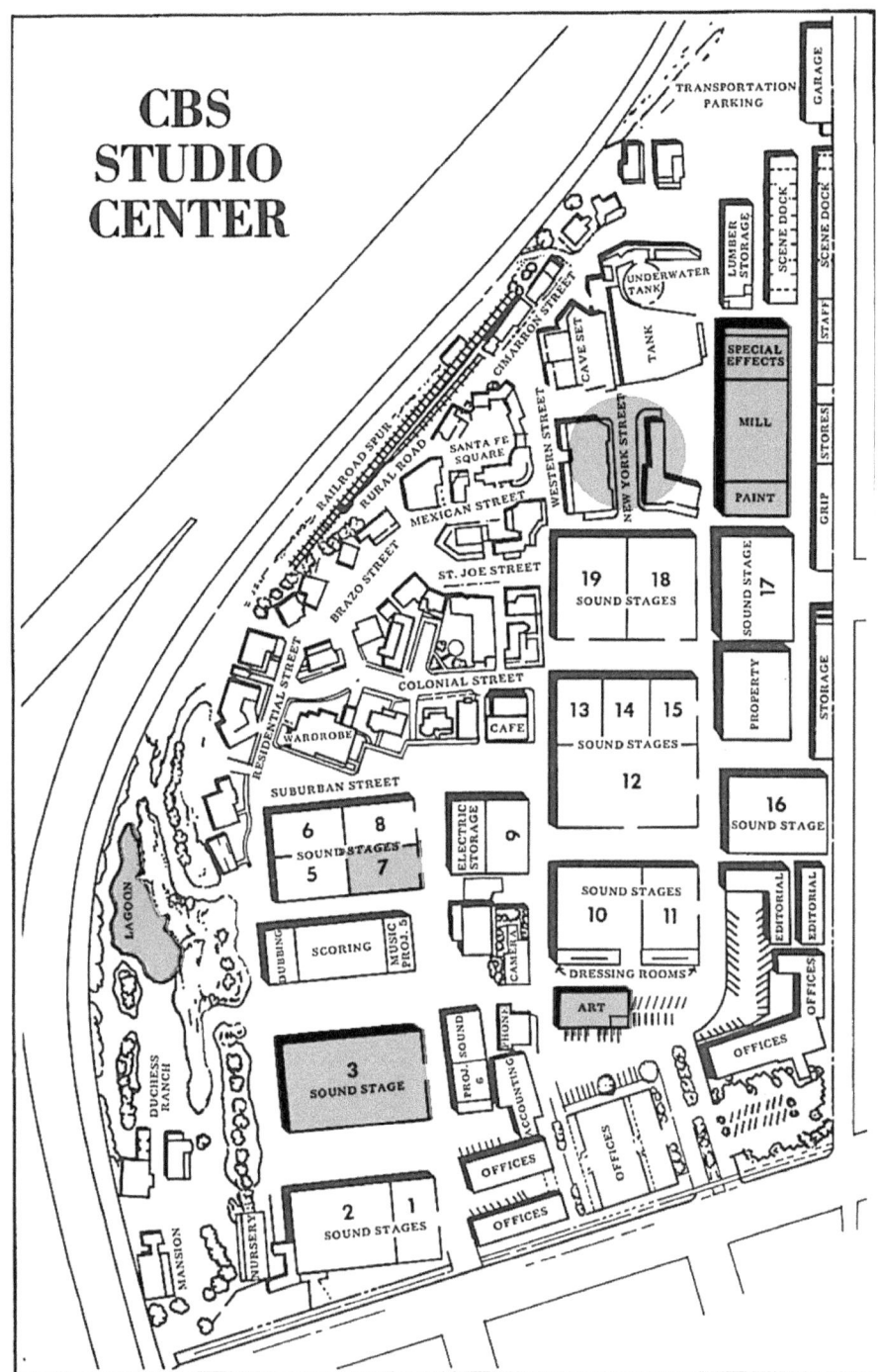

General plan of the layout of the CBS Studio Center created in the late 1960s. Highlighted are the key stages, workshops and other areas that became associated with the *Raise the Titanic* movie model's production. Going clockwise from the top, the circled area had a tent erected for the construction of the huge 55ft hull. Once the hull was completed and moved indoors, the tent was taken down and the ground was prepped for the location of the new water tank where the sinking and raising was to be filmed. A short distance from there is the special effects studio where the superstructure was cut from steel and assembled for painting. The smaller building is the Art department facility where all plans and imagery was created. Next are the sound stages of 3 and 7 where a number of the models came to be assembled and finished off. And lastly the lagoon water set for *Gilligan's Island* that would become the models christening ground for when the miniatures were tested for stability. *(Author's collection)*

October 3, 1977 and a member of the model unit pastes up the 1/16th scale plan of the *Titanic* onto a huge plywood partition wall inside the tent on the backlot of the CBS Studio Center. *(Photograph @ Ken Marschall)*

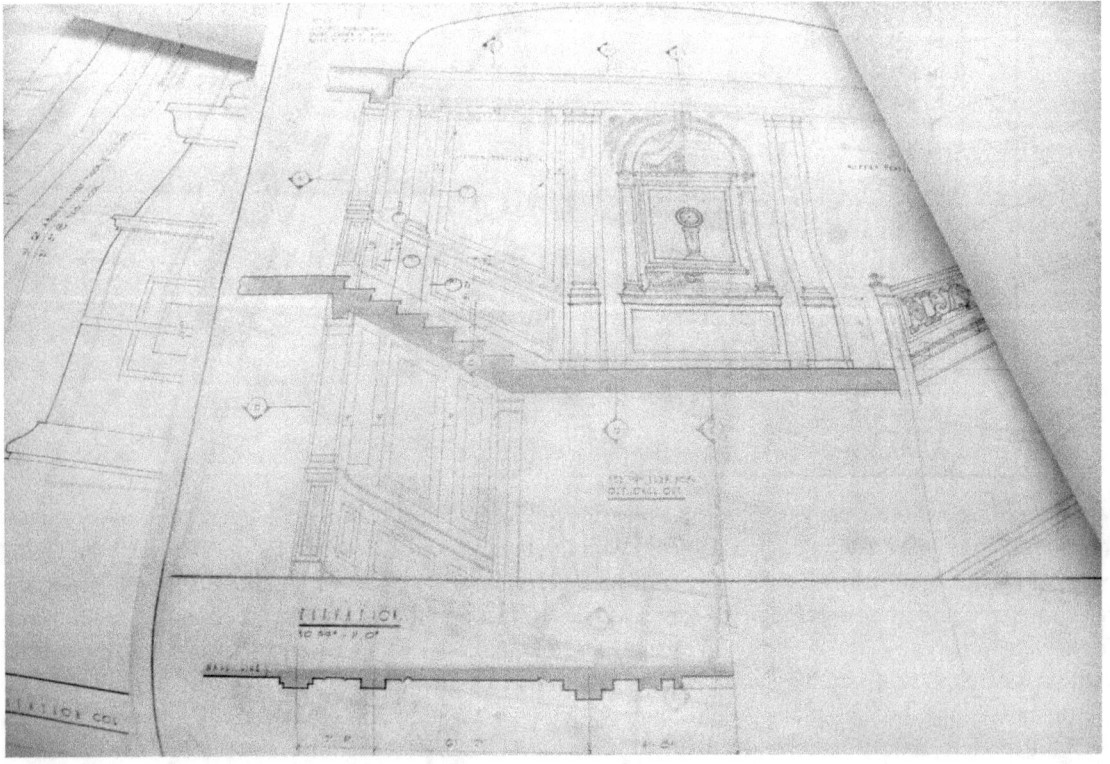

Series of plans take shape in the art department of the CBS studio that was of the proposed 1st Class Grand Staircase set. *(Photograph © Ken Marschall)*

Set decorator Daniel Gluck works on a scale model of the sea bed with an adapted 1/570 scale Revell *Titanic* model kit representing the wreck. *(Photograph © Ken Marschall)*

This interesting image shows a small set section of *Titanic*'s lower starboard hull complete with the jagged iceberg wound for shots that required a close-up view of the damage. *(Photograph © Ken Marschall)*

148 • *Raise The Titanic*

Titanic survivor Edwina Mackenzie photographed during her visit to the studio in December 1977. *(Photograph © Ken Marschall)*

The plank-on-frame hull of the *Titanic* model as it takes shape in the construction tent in the backlot of the CBS studio, October 1977. *(Photograph © Ken Marschall)*

The graceful fantail of the *Titanic* comes together as a member of the model unit skins the hull with timbered boards fixed into position over the frames. *(Photograph © Ken Marschall)*

150 • *Raise The Titanic*

Mid-November of 1977 and the hull undergoes glass resin coating. The crewmember on the left is in the process of scribing the cured resin for the application of the next layer. With the use of a coarse bladed hand planer, any unwanted raised bumps in the resin are sanded down, cleaned off for the next fresh layer of resin to be applied. *(Photograph © Ken Marschall)*

With the hull rendered in resin and sanded down, the first of the hull plates are added. *(Photograph © Ken Marschall)*

Chapter 6: The Building of a Legend • **151**

With the keel and bottom fully plated the hull has now been turned the right way up so crews can fit out the interior with the steel framework. First in place is a heavy steel joist acting as a central keel that will cut down on the hull flexing when the flotation tanks and heavier supports are fixed into place. To the left, close to the plan, two sections of the interior framework awaits installation. *(Photograph © Ken Marschall)*

It is three days before Christmas and crews are still hard at work fitting out the models interior and continuation on plating the hull that has now reached the underside of D-Deck. *(Photograph © Ken Marschall)*

The stern of the *Titanic* model during assembly. The name of the ship and her port of registry is seen here in its original form with each letter cut into the resin plate. Once cleaned each letter was then painted in with gold paint to stand out better. *(Author's collection)*

The port side bow name plate on the model in 2020. This close-up shows how each letter is cut into the plate that would allow for the letter to be filled in with paint. When the model arrived in Malta and was converted to the wreck these plates were covered over with new versions that emphasized the name better for underwater filming. *(Photograph © Jean Pierre Borg)*

The stern name plate with port of registry. Although the original *Titanic* was built in Belfast and sailed from her Southampton, *Titanic's* port of registration was in Liverpool at the main offices of the White Star Line company. *(Author's collection)*

A view inside the hull and the intricate web of tanks, pipes and internal frames. Just visible is the stern poop deck with a member of the model unit working on the piece. *(Photograph © Ken Marschall)*

The stunning level of intricate detail on the hull of the *Titanic* with a comparison image of *Olympic* taken in 1913. *(Photograph © Ken Marschall / Olympic image – Author's collection)*

Chapter 6: The Building of a Legend • 155

At this perspective, the graceful sheer line of the hull is evident with the slightly raised contours of the bow and stern. At this near completed point in the build the hull alone weighed an estimated 4-tons. *(Photograph © Kento Gebo)*

The models stern poop deck in its assembled state waits to be fitted to the main hull. *(Photograph © Kento Gebo)*

This ITC production photograph cataloguing the build of the model shows a rather dusty poop deck awaiting to be fitted to the hull's stern. Also sitting on the table is the deckhouse wall of C-Deck from the stern of the model. To the left is the aft end of the superstructure. *(Author's collection)*

It's a small world. The poop deck docking bridge engine telegraphs were machined from brass and finished with moving command levers and modelled on those manufactured by J.W. Ray of Liverpool and supplied to the *Titanic*. *(Photograph © Ken Marschall / Advertisement – Author's collection)*

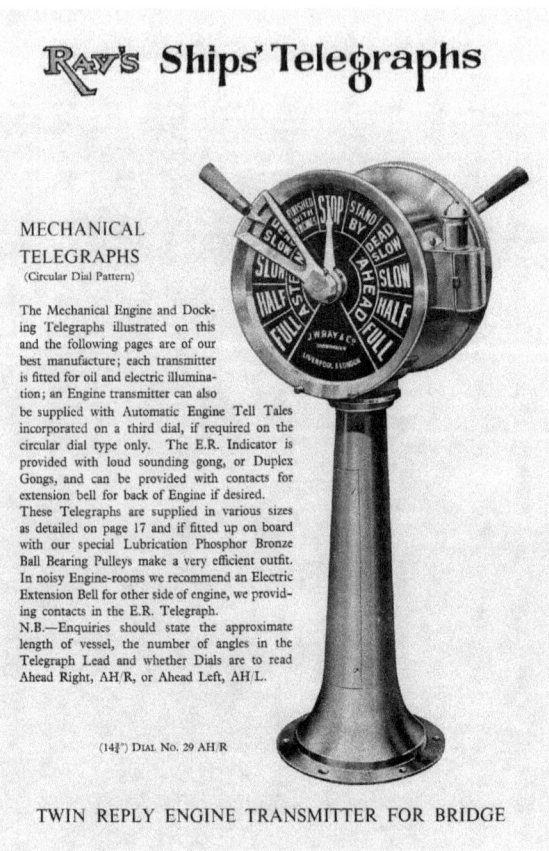

The amazing attention to detail is clear here with this close-up of the equipment on the stern docking bridge showing the port and starboard engine room telegraphs, telephone in its tall box and the steering gear with wheel. After the deck had been assembled it was then dropped in place at the model's elegant stern. *(Author's collection & Photograph © Ken Marschall)*

The forecastle and forward well deck with cargo cranes. Note the access point that has been cut into the well deck; the cut panel now sitting upon the framework to the right. This removable panel would give FX crews access to the operational valves for the tanks when the superstructure was seated upon the hull. An identical panel was cut out in the aft well deck. *(Enlarged from an original photograph © Ken Marschall)*

This view taken inside the special effects machine shop shows the superstructure in the process of being cut from sheet plates for dry assembly before being welded together. At this stage of the build the exposed A-Deck promenade deckhouse wall has been added as a straight unit. Over the coming days the deckhouse wall will be shaped and window apertures cut out of the steel. *(Photograph © Ken Marschall)*

The partially assembled and painted superstructure inside the special effects workshop in February 1978. *(Photograph © Ken Marschall)*

Looking more like a late 1911 Harland & Wolff construction photograph, this view across the portside of the model's boat deck shows the deckhouses taking shape and a number of deck fittings now in place. *(Photograph © Ken Marschall)*

The weather covering that sat between the first and second funnel. Hidden beneath this steel cover there sat, unbelievably, a replica of the dome. The odd-looking wooden board attached to the side of the skylight was copied from archival photographs of *Olympic* and *Titanic*. The board, more correctly boards, were stored port and starboard of the skylight and in reality, would have been most likely used as painter boards for use around the external areas of the liner's deckhouses. More of these boards were located further aft of the superstructure and secured to the engine room skylight between funnels three and four. *(Enlarged from an original photograph © Ken Marschall)*

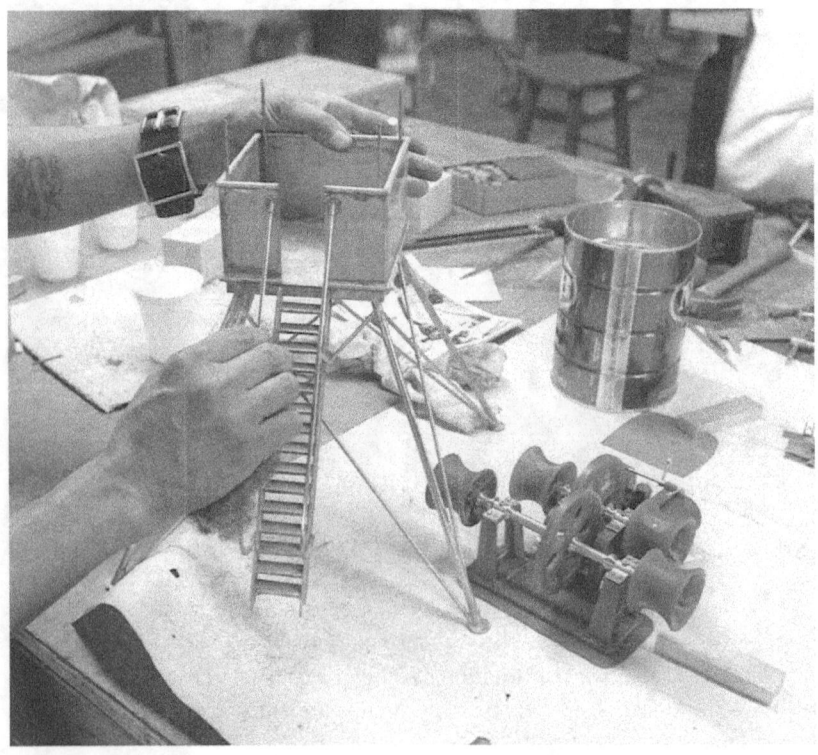

The compass tower that sits upon the raised roof over the 1st class lounge. Sitting alongside on the work bench is a remarkably detailed replica of the steam winch that sat behind the #1 cargo hold on the forecastle deck. *(Photograph © Ken Marschall)*

Chapter 6: The Building of a Legend • 161

Lovingly made from brass by Daniel Gluck, one of the 30+ deck benches fabricated for the model and copied from those supplied to *Olympic* (pictured) and *Titanic*. *(Photograph © Ken Marschall / Olympic image – Brown Brothers – Author's collection)*

Looking across the starboard side of the boat deck as the superstructure, deckhouses and funnels take shape. This photograph shows one oddity that is sometimes questioned; window frames. On the promenade deck the windows have an unusual raised lip like that of a window frame, a feature *Titanic* never had. These were in fact resin cast rivet patterns that had been produced so over scaled that once fixed in place they looked like a raised window frame *(Photograph © Ken Marschall)*

Interesting March 1978 view of the interior of soundstage 7 as some of the *Raise the Titanic* film models come together. From left to right is the *Titanic* superstructure during assembly with the hull just behind and aligned with the roller shutter doors to the studio. Off to the starboard side of the *Titanic* is the scale replica of the U.S. Navy frigate and behind the frigate's stern is the twin-hull of the *U.S.S. Pigeon*; built but never used in the movie. *(Photograph © Ken Marschall)*

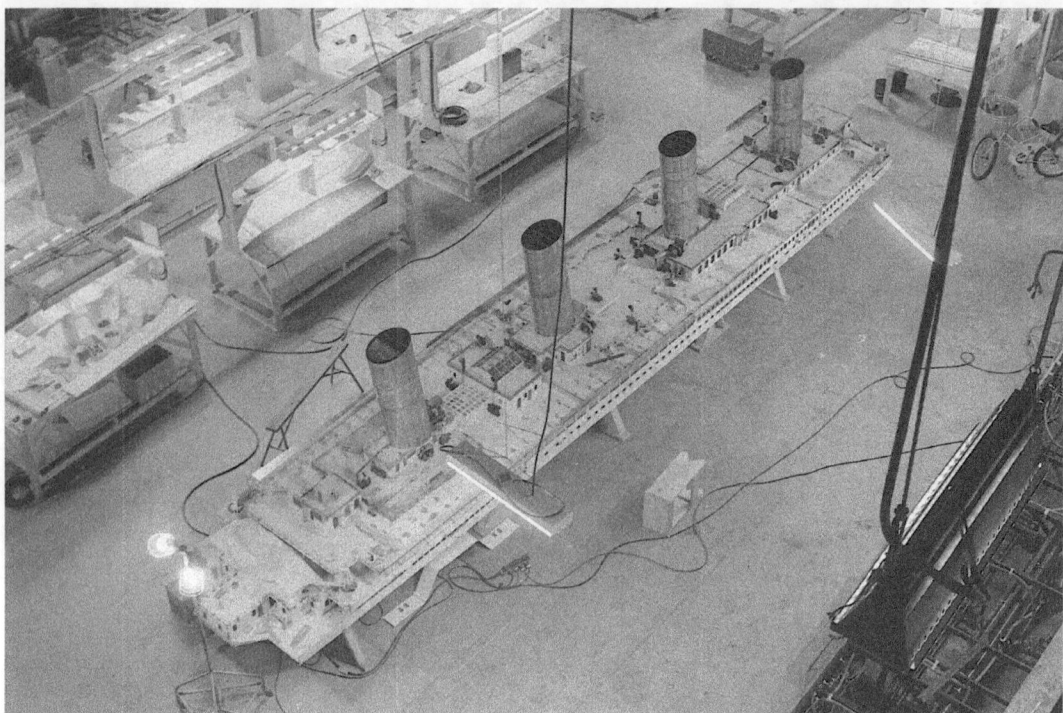

March 1, 1978 and all the funnels are seated and the superstructure is made ready for painting. At the time this photo was taken, Ken Marschall had noted that the inner funnel to the fourth funnel had been fitted the wrong way around. The error was soon rectified by the model unit. *(Photograph © Ken Marschall)*

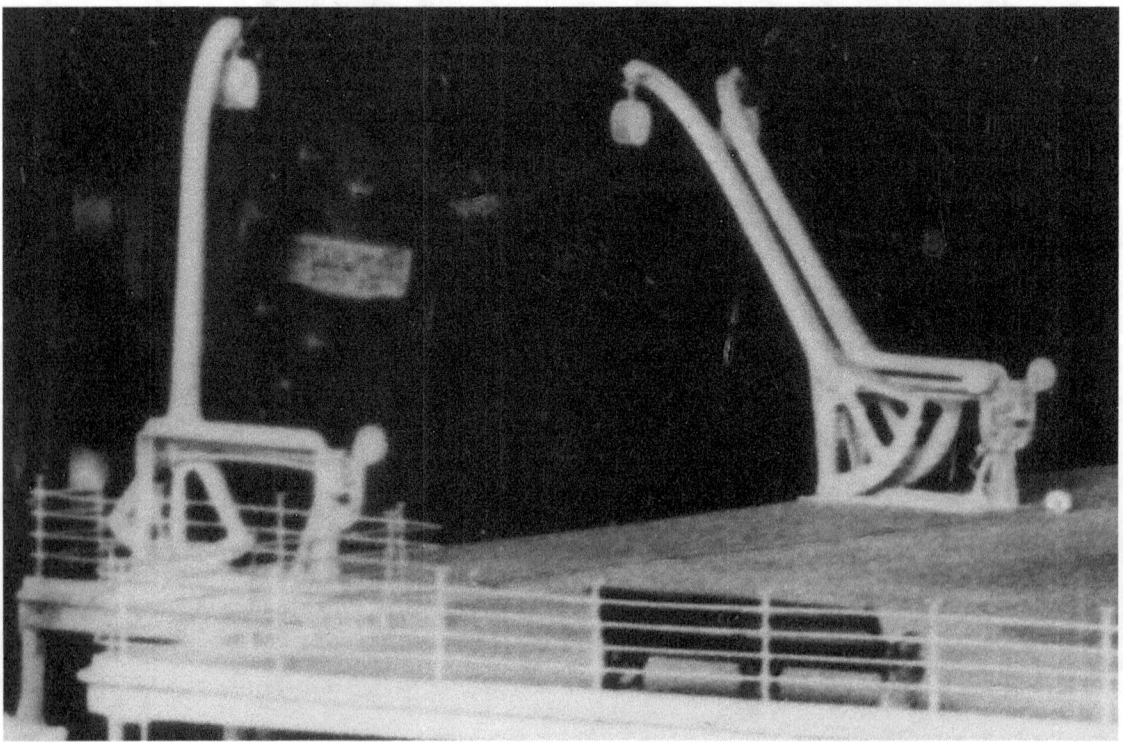

One of the sets of cast resin Welin lifeboat davits on the model. The davits had been designed and produced so when each unit was assembled, the davit arm, on a worm gear, could be cranked out and back in again like the original davits on the *Titanic*. *(Author's collection)*

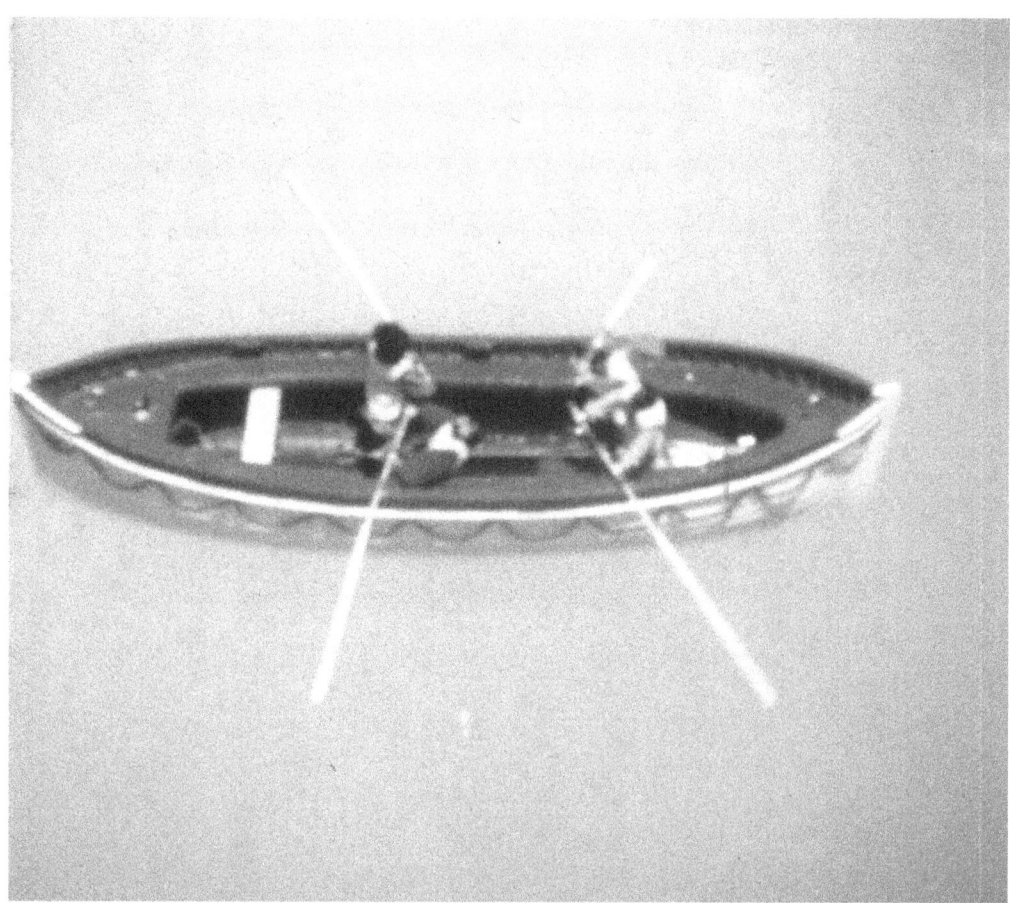

One of the twenty cast resin lifeboats is tested in a fresh water tank with its miniature occupants working the oars. The boats were operated via a battery and a servo connected up to the four working crew/passengers seated in the boat. The mechanism could be turned ON/OFF via a switch (seen to the left) and with extra occupants seated inside the boat, the FX crew members could place the model in the water for the camera unit to film as the little craft rows away from the sinking *Titanic*. *(Mario Cassar collection)*

A sole survivor of the *Titanic* model. One of the 18-inch cast resin lifeboats. *(Joe Sciberras collection)*

The towering first funnel of *Olympic* photographed from the top of the portside ratline of the forward mast following her maiden arrival in June 1911. *(Brown Brothers – Author's collection)*

Chapter 6: The Building of a Legend • 167

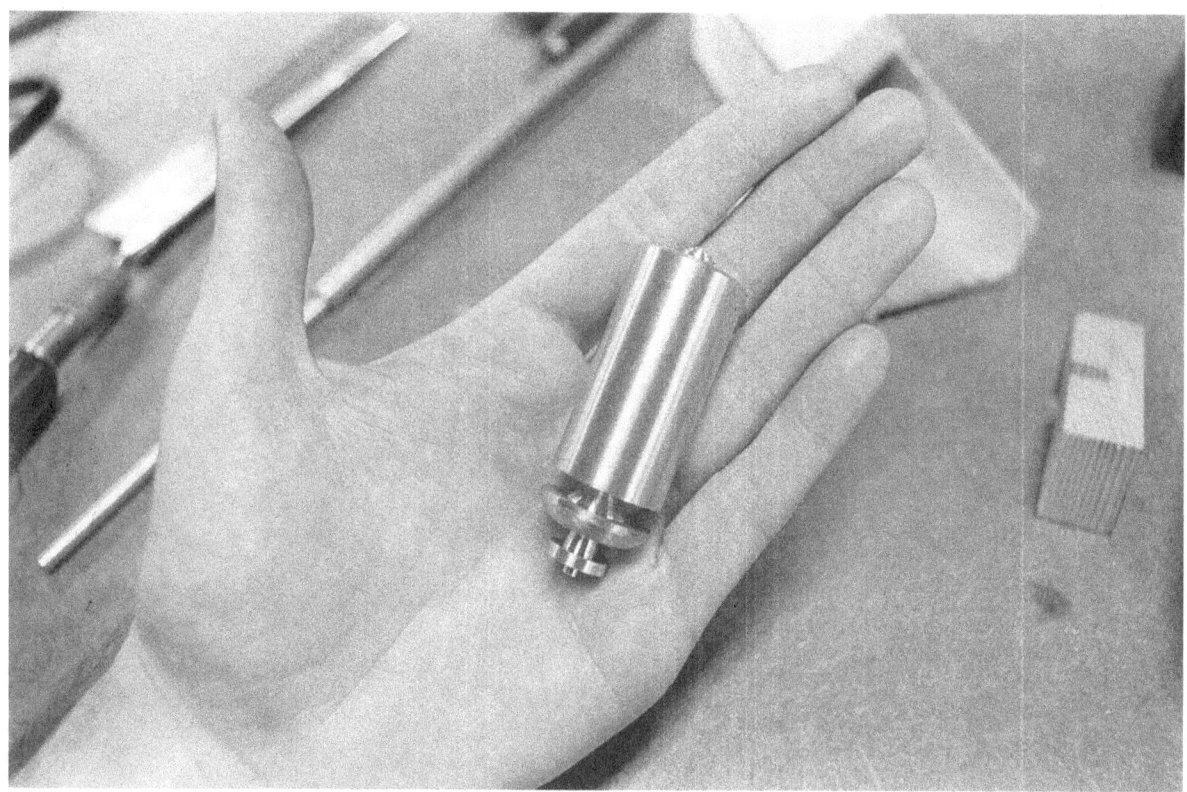

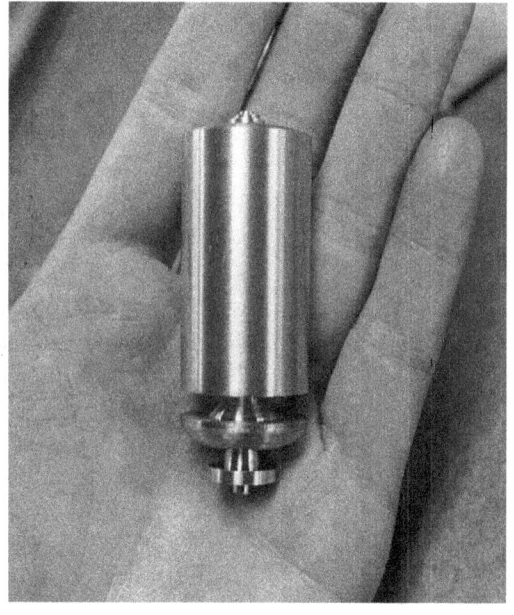

Whistle while you work. The largest whistle chamber from a triple chime set made for the model's mighty funnels and faithfully replicated from the Willett Bruce company versions supplied to the *Titanic*. *(Photograph © Ken Marschall / Illustration from* The Shipbuilder *– Author's collection)*

168 • *Raise The Titanic*

The funnels receive their White Star Line livery. Note the broken resin window frame of the 2nd class entrance. *(Author's collection)*

The first week of March 1978 and the superstructure and funnels are now painted. At this point the funnels were without their guy wires. *(Photograph © Kento Gebo)*

Chapter 6: The Building of a Legend • **169**

March 10, 1978 and Ken Marschall takes the first of several photographs of the model in an almost deserted sound stage on what would become the last day of work at the studio facility following the departure of Stanley Kramer. *(Photograph © Ken Marschall)*

Early concept art for *Raise the Titanic* showing crewmember Bigalow with passenger Arthur Brewster behind him as they make their way down a crew corridor to the flooding cargo hold with the vault, cargo and the automobile. *(Author's collection)*

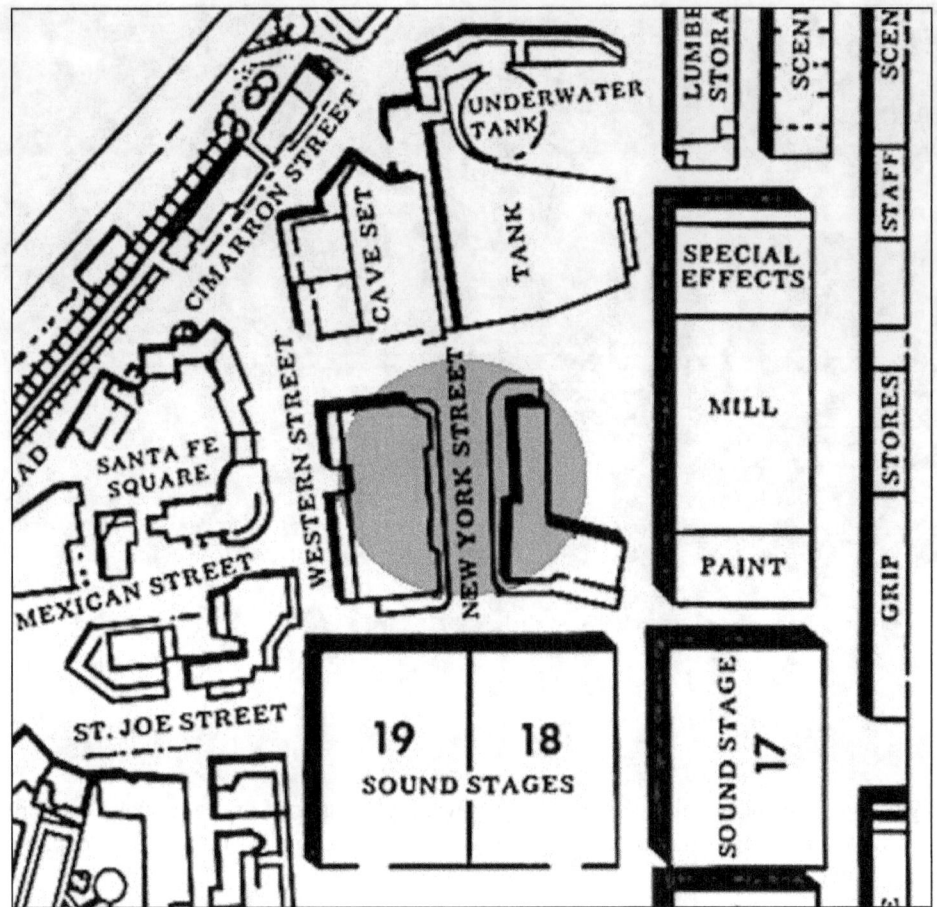

The ground work on the new CBS Studio tank for *Raise the Titanic* began in mid-December 1977. Its construction being closest to the studios existing smaller tanks meant that the new tank would share the water inlet and drainage system of those existing tanks. But as machinery removed the concrete and asphalt, and began to dig down, the problems with the ground reared its ugly head. It soon became apparent that the enormous scale of such a tank was not going to be beneficial for the studio. *(Photograph © Ken Marschall / CBS Studio plan – Author's collection)*

Chapter 6: The Building of a Legend • 171

Another photograph taken by Marschall on March 10 showing the 3-ton superstructure in its latter stages of completion. *(Photograph © Ken Marschall)*

Looking from the bridge over the starboard section of the boat deck, March 1978. One of the lifting hoops can be seen in the foreground. These hoops, a total of seven fitted to the superstructure, were used to lift the heavy structure up and off the hull with the use of straps and a crane. *(Photograph © Ken Marschall)*

Staying on the starboard side, this view is looking from midships and towards the bridge area. One glaring observation is the omission of wooden decking. The decision to not include any was down to the model requiring water submersion. Any wooden decking fitted would succumb to the water resulting in the fine timber warping and lifting and becoming unsightly. Instead the exposed steel decks were painted a light brown. *(Photograph © Ken Marschall)*

The near completed *Titanic* model following its arrival at the Mediterranean Film Facility in Malta in the spring of 1979. *(Mario Cassar collection)*

Chapter 6: The Building of a Legend • 173

The 9-foot "white" *Titanic* model is made ready for its journey to the bottom of the sonar pool during filming at Rockwell International. *(Author's collection)*

CHAPTER 7

Salvage Fleet

"We spent five years on Research & Development. We're a kiss away from the end. We need two hundred ounces of a miserly mineral we can't find. And when we do find it, where is it? It's at the bottom of the Atlantic Ocean!"

Admiral James Sandecker

The main focal point of *Raise the Titanic* was fooling the audience into believing that a successful salvage attempt had been carried out on retrieving the long-lost liner from her watery grave. It was a done deal from the offset that the story required a fleet of salvage vessels that would go out in search for the *Titanic*. This of course had to be on a grand scale given the budget of the production and what ships were needed to look like they could pull off such a marine operation of this size. It is not known in which direction the production was to take when Stanley Kramer was on the project and whether he had plans for using fictional ships in miniature of those built from scratch or abandoned studio back-lot models waiting to be resurrected. It was not until Jerry Jameson was handed the director's chair that the U.S. Navy became involved with the movie. The Navy's role was pivotal to the film, not just in the story, but that of being seen on screen. Marble Arch Productions were very lucky to have been granted the use of three navy vessels and equipment. But while ITC had secured the use of the navy ships there would be scenarios in the movie that could not be fulfilled with the use of the real thing. These would have to be accomplished with the use of miniatures built to match the ¾ scale *Titanic* replica.

It's a Small World

Part One

With the U.S. Navy approving several of their craft to be used on-screen, it was left to William Creber and his model-making team over in Los Angeles to draw up plans and build the 1:16th scale versions of the full-sized counterparts that were docked in San Diego. As the large *Titanic* took shape at the CBS Studio Center, just meters away a fleet of ship miniatures began to rise from the confusion of clanging construction tools. The model work for *Raise the Titanic* was on a tremendous scale that even Stanley Kramer questioned ITC's original budget for the whole shebang. The leading star of the production was the monster *Titanic* replica that was to dominate the screen. The detail on her had to be precise and to the point that she was a near-perfect recreation of the liner. But what became more remarkable was how the model unit carried on over the level of detail to the other ships. Each one was as detailed as the next in that deck structures were a carbon copy of the original. Even the weathering on the models was first-rate. Labelled as the *Titanic Salvage Fleet*, no other term could have been better suited in describing the little ships of *Raise the Titanic*. The model fleet represented in miniature the real vessels that had been built and were currently still in active service and had been perfectly detailed to match the real things. The models were faithful replicas of the U.S.S. *Schenectady*, U.S.S. *Pigeon*, U.S.S. *Denver* and the U.S.S. *Blakely*; a Knox-class escort that was to double as the U.S.S. *Carpenter*; a Gearing-class destroyer. Accompanying these larger ships were a pair of ocean-going navy tugs based on the U.S.S. *Cocopa* that would later undergo several cosmetic changes once they arrived in Malta. The last main vessel built was a New York harbour fireboat that was based on the FDNY *"John D. McKean"* that was to be filmed alongside the *Titanic* and the two tugs for the storyboarded scenes as the raised wreck is pulled past Liberty Island and up to the Brooklyn Naval Base.

The construction of the vessels was not as robust as that of the big *Titanic* build as the navy ships were never going to be submerged. That did not deter from them being incredibly detailed and life-like. The hulls were fabricated from timbered frames and fiberglass so they could be placed within the water of the tanks and controlled via a rig that could pull the vessels by a system of cables hidden beneath the water. Within the hull sat a complex network of pipes that were connected to discharge pumps positioned beneath the waterline at the bow and the stern, and when in use, would kick up water to mimic wash from the bow and water churned up from the stern propellers. The pair of navy tugs were also fitted with a smaller and less complex water pump system for bow and stern wash. The New York fireboat was fitted with a pumping system that would draw up water from the tank, pass it up through the hull, and exit through the several hose and nozzles mounted on the fore, aft, and upper deckhouse of the vessel. The upper structures of the ships were a mixture of wood, moulded fiberglass panels with resin and metal deck and superstructure details. The upper superstructure of the models had been fitted with internal lighting for when they were to be operated in the tank for night sequences at a distance. Unfortunately, these beautifully crafted models were not to be given the screen time they so deserved. For all the work and money invested into the ships, they were only to appear on screen for a matter of seconds with the two lengthiest shots being of the *Schenectady, Denver* and *Blakely/Carpenter* with the just raised *Titanic* followed later with the view of the two tugs pulling at the towing lines as they begin to move *Titanic*. The former sequence of the three navy ships slowly being positioned around the *Titanic* as the Sea King and Super Jolly Green Giant helicopters fly into view did show just how satisfying the use of all these miniatures were when working together; even if the shot was far too short.

The two helicopter miniatures built for *Raise the Titanic* were exact copies of the real machines. The Sea King was constructed to match with the full-size aircraft on loan from the U.S. Navy. The Sea King was modelled on a 1961 Sikorsky SH-3 that was a vital craft for the United States Navy and operated in carrier-based anti-submarine warfare roles and built as the world's first amphibious helicopter. The second and much larger helicopter miniature was the matt green Sikorsky HH-53 Super Jolly Green Giant seen briefly on-screen flying ahead of the Sea King towards the stern of the *Titanic* before the scene cuts to the Sea King dropping down over the poop deck of the waterlogged derelict. That view of the Sea King has fooled many over the years into thinking that what is seen on screen is a real full-size helicopter and filmed using the perspective of the *Titanic* model being in the foreground as the real SH-3 is flown and hovered at a distance from the model. To make others think that it was the real thing is testimony to the model makers' work and the expertise of R/C stunt pilot John A. Simone, Jr who operated the model craft from the side of the water tank. The whereabouts of these helicopter models are unknown. As they were aircraft miniatures, regardless of their working condition after filming, still made them desirable to model aircraft enthusiasts. Since 1980 they may have been sold on to other studios for other productions; stripped for parts or a part of someone's aviation display.

The Ships of the United States Navy

Filming in San Diego took place between 27 November and 10 December 1979 with primary locations onboard the vessels and those on dry land. ITC originally intended to use six ships for the motion picture, all of which were to be hired from the Navy to a set period of days and which coincided with training exercises and manoeuvres staged some 10 nautical miles out in the Pacific Ocean. With rates agreed ITC sweetened the deal by offering to pay the $22,000 fuel cost bill for the running of the vessels over that two-week hire period. Of the vessels on hire one was not part of the Navy agreement having been brought in from the unlikely source of the American Telephone and Telegraph Company (AT&T). Organized by boat master Mannie Louis, a graduate of the U.S. Merchant Marine Academy, the cable-laying vessel C.S. *Long Lines* played the role of the Soviet ship *Mikhail Kurkov*. Built in 1961, the 511ft *Long Lines* was designed to hold 2168 nautical miles of cable and went on to complete 23 cable laying missions before retirement from service and scrapping in 2003. The C.S. *Long Lines* did cause some concerns as she sat at anchor off San Diego as a hammer and sickle prop flag fluttered in the breeze. Speaking on behalf of the U.S. Navy, Wally Schlotter, director of Motion Picture & Television Bureau for San Diego, said "The navy wants the public warned of the harbour cruise so that authorities aren't flooded with calls of alarm." During principal photography, all vessels flew in uniform the same signal flags of a striped red and white flag; the navy code for "Civilian Vessel Nearby". Beneath that was a bright yellow flag with a large black dot indicating "I India" (altering course to port) and a red background flag with a white cross indicating "R-Rodeo" (navigate around). The flags altogether spelled out a code to nearby vessels in those waters that these ships were operating under a special project as civilian vessels and under no circumstances involved in active war duty.

The first full day of filming was scheduled for a 5:30 am start on Tuesday 27 November as some of the fleet sat in dock at the 32nd Street Naval Station. But that soon changed when it became apparent a series of miscommunications resulted in no hotel reservations having been made for the production crew. As the studio rushed around to get accommodation for the crews, all these delays incurred meant that cameras did not roll until 1 pm that afternoon. Actors Robards, Jordan, Selby, Emmet Walsh, and Cannon were in character in the captain's private quarters on board the *Denver* as Jameson lensed the section on the discovery of the spy. Robards got a little too much into the part as during delivering his lines he began to sway slowly back and forth. "Cut!" came the call from Jameson who was not overly impressed with the actor's attempt of creating a rolling motion as if the ship was out at sea. "Why shouldn't I sway back and forth?" asks Robards, who then wised up to redeliver the scene; this time without the need to be more articulate. "Print it" comes the call from Jameson. "Let's break out the peanuts" replies boom operator Glen Lambert. Captain Vincent Edward Cook, master of the *Denver,* was on hand to help out when the utility jacket handed to Robards by the wardrobe department was too small. A quick naval exercise located another better fitting jacket from onboard ship, and, this time, having the correct length sleeves. Speaking on the loan of his private quarters to the actors for the scene, Captain Cook joked "… but you better bet one thing – this cabin's never been this messy even in rough weather."

With the tea growing cold in the silver-plated teapot on the table of the captain's cabin, it marked the end of a day's filming even if some of the actors were unable to properly settle down for the night in the comforts of the local Sheraton Harbor and Sheraton Inn hotels; especially Robards, who discovered his suitcase had gotten lost in transit. Arthur Wilde, the production unit publicist spoke of the issues. "We have a movie crew of 107 people and two-thirds of them are working today aboard ship. We also lost about two-thirds of a day of shooting time and that's, uh, about $40,000 (lost). Sometimes I think that almost everything that could befall a production in one day did." As the fleet lay berthed in San Diego, producer William Frye, lounging in a deck chair on the quay alongside the *Denver*, recalls the relationship between the studio and the navy; "The navy plays an important part in the picture and I feel, generally, we have a good rapport with the navy because they looked good in the 'Airport' movies, helping raise the 747s. So now, they're helping us to raise the *Titanic*."

The time at sea meant that the film production team had the chance to use some of the navy toys available to them. Contrary to belief the floatation tanks and the large three-panel lighting units seen in use in the movie were created for the production and were not equipment in the Navy's salvage arsenal. While the navy was able to assist with whatever equipment they had to hand much of the salvage equipment seen on screen came from the imagination of the writers and prop makers. The lighting rigs are seen in several scenes in the movie, filmed onboard the *Denver* as crews test the system and the lowering of the units into the waters off San Diego before the scene cuts to the miniatures as they gradually drop down to the sea bed. The design of the *Denver* as an amphibious transport ship allowed for the large stern doors to be opened to partially flood the interior to the vessel's utility dock so smaller craft could enter and exit when the vessel was out on manoeuvres without compromising the ship. With the *Denver* partially submerged the lighting rigs were connected up to the overhead monorail and pulled out over the water of the flooded utility dock and lowered down at the stern of the vessel. One other familiar scene from the movie filmed onboard the *Denver* was with Richard Jordan as his character Dirk Pitt boards the vessel from the Zodiac after his return to the surface following witnessing the submersible *Deep Quest* getting stuck in the skylight of the *Titanic*.

Again, the *Denver* and her crew were filmed as they worked on lowering the Navy Salvage Hydrozene tank over the vessel's starboard side and down into the sea to tie in with the movie's story of sixteen buoyancy tanks being fitted, eight per side, to the hull of the *Titanic* in what will give "22,000 tons of lift" as stated by Admiral Sandecker, and lift her to the surface. In reality, no such techniques existed on this kind of scale. The tank used in the film was purposely built for the movie as a workable prop. The realistic-looking device even fooled the navy who thought it was an original piece of salvage equipment on loan to ITC for *Raise the Titanic*. The 40' prop was constructed of steel with eight buoyancy tanks attached to the framework which could keep the unit afloat until the valves were opened to flood the desired tank, to submerge the unit for filming, before being hooked up and lifted out of the sea and back on deck. To keep within a budget only one full-size unit was built with the rest built to match the scale of the 55' and 9' *Titanic* models and switched around depending on the scenes and which model was being filmed. The sequence of the tank being lowered into the sea was split between two locations with the full-size unit with the navy in the waters off San Diego while in Malta the 1:16th scale versions were filmed in the specially constructed water tank as they dip beneath the surface to then switch over to the deep tank for shots of them arriving at the wreck site. To keep with continuity the tanks had lettering that could be peeled off and replaced with a new number so the viewer when watching the tanks being filled with gas would see a variety of numbers from 01 to 16.

We will now take a look at the fleet of ships for *Raise the Titanic*; the real vessels that would take on the fictional role to salvage a lost legend.

U.S.S. *Schenectady*

Exterior & Interior Scenes

On loan from the U.S. Navy was the tank landing ship U.S.S. *Schenectady* (LST-1185). She was 523ft in length, a beam of 70ft, and 8,590 gross registered tonnage. She entered service in June 1970 and remained in active service until December 1993. After being decommissioned she was laid up at the Naval Inactive Ship Maintenance Facility in Bremerton, Washington, until November 2004 where she was used as target practice and sunk. *Raise the Titanic* wasn't the only film she appeared onscreen for as *Schenectady* made a guest appearance in *Airport '77*; another early Jerry Jameson-directed film production.

U.S.S. *Denver*

Exterior & Interior Scenes (at sea)

The amphibious transport dock U.S.S. *Denver* (LPD-9) was commissioned in October 1968 and was 570ft in length, 100ft in beam, and 17,425 gross registered tons. She remained in service until August 2014 where she was decommissioned to the Joint Base Pearl Harbor-Hickam in Hawaii earning her the award for remaining in active service for the U.S. Navy of 46 years.

U.S.S. *Carpenter*
Exterior Scenes (at sea)
The U.S.S. *Carpenter* (DD-825) was a Gearing-class destroyer commissioned in December 1949 with a length of 390ft, a beam of 41ft, and 3,460 gross registered tonnage. She was decommissioned in February 1981 and leased to the Republic of Turkey until November 1997 and later scrapped in 1999.

U.S.S. *Ranger*
Interior Scenes (in dock)
U.S.S. *Ranger* (CV-61) was the seventh vessel for the U.S. Navy to use that name and was the third of four Forrestal-class supercarriers. She was launched in September 1956 and measured 1,046ft in length, a beam of 130ft, with an extreme width of 249ft and a total of 82,402 tons when fully loaded. She remained in active service until her decommissioning in July 1993 where she was laid up at the Naval Inactive Ship Maintenance Facility in Washington until she was towed to the breaker's yard in Brownsville, Texas in November 2017.

U.S.S. *Pigeon*
The U.S.S. *Pigeon* (ASR-21) was launched in August 1969 and operated as a deep submergence rescue vessel for the Navy. She had a displacement of 5,033 tons and measured 251ft in length, 86ft in width, and 26ft in depth. She remained in service until August 1992. Following 20 years of being laid up, she was sold for scrap and towed to the breaker's yard in Brownsville, Texas in January 2012. The *Pigeon* did not make it to screen although it had been originally planned as part of the main vessels in the search and recovery of the *Titanic*. The *Pigeon* was equipped with the latest technology for search and recovery and with the onboard sonar equipment, the production team could have made great use of the hardware available to them. But, alas, even with the money spent in recreating a highly detailed miniature for the movie, the *Pigeon* was not available for the time frame allotted during filming in San Diego. And so, she became the forgotten vessel of the *Titanic* salvage fleet.

... and the surprise package?
One last vessel seen on screen was that of a submarine sent by the U.S Navy to protect the *Titanic* and her salvage crews from the threat of the Soviet torpedo ship. The real submarine was an SSN 594 *Permit*-class nuclear-powered fast attack vessel that was already on a weekly maintenance operation off the coast of San Diego as tests were carried out with the vessel running with removed sail plates and masts and antennas extended during the test cycle. The vessel's master received the call of assistance needed 10 miles off the coast of San Diego. But this was no emergency procedure; just a simple request to help the film industry. Jerry Jameson wanted the appearance of the submarine to be dramatic and so pushed for the sub to be put through an emergency blow; the act of releasing air from the subs Main Ballast Tanks (MBTs) for a sudden ascent. The boat was submerged to 400' and when the crew was told of the cameras running from the deck of the *Denver*, the sub crew released 4500 psi of air from the tanks for 10 seconds that quickly brought the vessel to the surface. With the snorkel mast deployed the submarine replenished the depleted air tanks before being sent back down to 400' for another take. After a couple of attempts caught on film, the operation was brought to a close earlier than expected as the sudden surfacing ended up breaking a set of air compressors that then

took several hours to repair, giving Jameson the chance to film a pair of F-14 Tomcats that had lifted off from the 32nd Street Naval Station.

Submersibles

The search, discovery, and inevitable salvaging of the *Titanic* could not have been completed without the assistance of submersibles. For the movie's screenplay, a total of four submersibles were required to represent the small fleet of vessels under the guise of NUMA (National Underwater & Marine Agency) that would take on the challenges of the deep. In *Raise the Titanic* the four subs were named DSV *Sea Cliff*, DSV *Deep Quest*, DSV *Turtle*, and DSV *Starfish*; the prefix being Deep Sea Vehicle. The models presented in the movie were based on actual submersibles still in operation at the time of the production, even sharing the same name except for the fictional *Starfish*. The real-life *Sea Cliff* and *Turtle* submersibles were part of the *Alvin*-class of fully operational deep-sea vehicles that were owned and operated by institutes associated with the United States Navy who could be relied upon to assist with their equipment at the time of need. Their predecessor, DSV *Alvin*, shares her own real-life *Titanic* adventure story when she was used in July 1986 for the first manned dive to the wreck of the *Titanic* under the expedition's guidance of Dr. Robert Ballard who, with his joint American-French team, discovered the wreck during the early hours of 1 September 1985.

Sea Cliff

The 25-ton DSV-4 *Sea Cliff* was built in 1968 for the United States Navy and at the time it had a maximum dive depth of 6,500ft (2,000m) that remained until her refit in 1984 increasing her limit to an estimated 22,000ft. In 1985 the vessel made history breaking the record for her type of vehicle when she dived to 20,000ft off Guatemala's Pacific Coast. In 1998 the *Sea Cliff* was handed over to its new owners, Woods Hole Oceanographic Institution, where she continued representing the navy until September 2002 when she was removed from active service and dismantled.

Turtle

The 21-ton *Turtle* was the earlier sister to the *Sea Cliff* and was built in 1968 as the DSV-3 for use in the United States Navy. Her name derives from the small Tennessee community of Turtle Town and as a tribute to the former American Revolution submergence craft *Turtle*. The submersible was originally designed to dive at a depth not exceeding that of 6,000ft. But with later modifications to her crew spheres, she was able to reach a respectable 10,000ft limit. *Turtle* operated from the navy's Submarine Development Group (SDG) in San Diego that also housed the DSV *Deep Quest*. In October 1997 the *Turtle* was retired from service and is now on public display at the Mystic Aquarium in Mystic Village, Connecticut.

Deep Quest

The 52-ton *Deep Quest* was designed, built, and operated by the Lockheed Missiles & Space Company in 1967 and operated from their San Diego laboratories as a commercial research vehicle and one accessible to the United States Navy. Before the refit of *Sea Cliff*, the *Deep Quest* held the record for the deepest dive when it planted a U.S. flag 8,310ft down at the bottom of the Pacific Ocean during its historic dive on 28 February 1968. The vehicle's mechanical arms played an important role when the submersible was used to recover the flight recorder boxes from two crashed airliners in the Pacific in 1969. The following year it assisted in the successful raising of a WWII Hellcat fighter plane from 3,180ft of water off

San Diego. The *Deep Quest* underwent her last ever dive in September 1980 where she was removed from service and placed on public display at the United States Naval Undersea Museum at Keyport, Washington, where it remained until 2018 before finally being sold for scrap.

Deep Quest Revealed

Deep Quest and *Turtle* were the only two full-sized working subs that appear on screen in the movie and were used for one sequence only that was filmed at Lockheed's facility in San Diego. Both the subs had been dressed for the movie with a simple set of adhesive transfers added. The *Deep Quest* now sported a large "NUMA" logo to her main hull while *Turtle* had a more excessive make-over with a large number "3" sitting over a double red band that encircled the hull. The studios were granted permission for the use of the subs while they remained in the hanger. But when it came to the subs taking to the water during the filming of *Raise the Titanic* then the studio had to look into other alternatives as the use of the real submersibles was no longer an option as taking the vehicles out to sea would mean the hire of the subs, their operational crews, recovery ships, and their crews and the large fuel bills that would outweigh the budget already set aside for the production which was already being depleted with the costs involved using the navy. The miniatures over in Malta were already to be utilized on-screen for many of the scenes with the scale *Titanic* wreck model in the tanks. What the studio needed were the real vehicles to be seen on screen to fulfil several actions shots that involved humans. In the confines of a studio environment, the interior spaces could be created by the set designers but the exterior views required a little more planning and imagination. Many of the scripted exterior views of the subs on the surface of the ocean had to be drastically reduced as the shots could not be accomplished with the real submersibles. With *Deep Quest* and *Turtle* destined to remain on dry land; with the miniatures filling in for the underwater search and discovery; the production team decided on recreating one of the submersibles as a full-scale prop that could be used in the water in a safe controlled environment.

The scene proceeding the salvaging of *Titanic* is set with a sudden burst of cheering that breaks through the atmosphere as salvage and naval crews crowd the decks of their fleet, dumbfounded by the sight unfolding before them. At the railing of the U.S.S. *Denver* is Sandecker and Pitt. Sandecker is transfixed on the *Titanic* as the wreck stabilizes herself following raising. But Pitt is less impressed. His eyes scanning the ocean for any signs of the *Deep Quest*. Suddenly the submersible pops up from the ocean to a chorus of rapturous applause. Seagram, Munk, Gunther, and Kiel are saved. For the viewer, it would seem that the actors were exiting from a real submarine in the waters of some distant continent. They were partially correct. The shots were filmed in the waters off San Diego between 27 November to 10 December 1979 during the navy exercises co-funded by the film studios. What may come as a surprise revelation is that the *Deep Quest* used in that scene and the previous scene of the sub with the diver were not of the real *Deep Quest*. In fact, it was not a real submersible; it was a convincing mock-up.

The Frankenstein creation was a 1:1 scale replica externally of the *Deep Quest* constructed from the original plans and purposely built for the film production. Weighing a fraction of the original *Deep Quest*'s weight, this craft was essentially built as a watertight floating container in the shape of a submarine that, with the aid of specialist divers, could be floated out, partially submerged to several feet below the surface without any harm happening to its occupants. And, then, allowed to rise to the surface for the camera unit to capture the shots they needed. The interior was basic as the film crews were not meant to film inside the craft. Seating, depth equipment, radio and the controls for flooding and draining the tanks was all that was required and keeping the interior space to a bare minimum. Around the spheres was constructed the outer shell that mimicked the *Deep Quest*, albeit not totally faithful in detail, but enough for the eye to be fooled into thinking it was the real thing. It is not until you take a closer look at the *Deep Quest* inside the Lockheed hanger during the scenes with Jordan, Selby and Cannon, and compare the surfacing *Deep Quest* that the vessel begins to reveal its true identity. One tell-tale sign is that the prop has pronounced raised welded joints on the plates that make up the subs hull. The real *Deep Quest* had no such welded plates as her panels are almost seamlessly bolted together. The film prop --- I will rename it as the *Deep Fake* --- was towed out to sea from the stern of the *Denver* under the assistance of a fleet of navy divers and personnel, followed closely by the actors, stunt unit, and additional divers. Guided from the Zodiacs, the actors and crew entered the *Deep Fake* through the hatch knowing that the craft was safe to be submerged to several feet before being brought back up to the surface again as the cameras rolled. As a safety precaution, the *Deep Fake* was attached to a cable that trailed back to the *Denver* in case anything untoward should occur where the craft would be quickly pulled back to the safety of the mother ship while the occupants were helped by the safety divers and team around them.

Faking It!

The *Deep Quest* prop disappeared shortly after filming and remained hidden under the radar until 2014 when it resurfaced in the press during an unflattering report of fraud following the prosecution of John Re, an art collector from New York's East Hampton, who had made $2.5 million in the sales of fake Jackson Pollock paintings. In 2005 Mr. Re used $70,000 of the proceeds from the sale of the fake paintings to purchase what he told *The New York Times* was the original Lockheed *Deep Quest* submarine. The fraudster had been duped into buying the tarnished remains of the *Raise the Titanic* film prop. Furthermore, Re continued to use the proceeds fraudulently taken from the sale of the fake works of art to convert the *Deep Quest* into a working boat at a cost of $1 million. His lavish deception came to a close when he was arrested by the FBI in December 2014 after flaunting his wealth. The purposely converted *Deep Quest* movie prop was seized by the authorities due to potential worth and put into storage within the grounds of the Greenport Yacht & Shipbuilding Company to await an uncertain future.

So, what became of the real *Deep Quest*? It remained in operational service until September 1980 where it was decommissioned and put on public display alongside the *Trieste II* at the Naval Undersea Museum in Bremerton, Washington. As time passed the museum was unable to keep footing the bill for the maintenance costs of displaying the vehicle and, unable to sell it on, Platypus Marine Inc was awarded the contract to collect it in January 2018 where she was taken to their breakers yard for dismantling and recycling.

It's a Small World

Part Two

To accompany the navy vessels, the *Titanic* miniatures, the models of the salvage equipment, from submersibles to explosive charges, all needed to be designed and fabricated for use in the water tanks. The more obscure models did not have much screen time but still played an important role in the story. The props department built a micro foam tank, a floating device that sat on the surface of the sea, and which was connected via hoses from a navy mother ship that fed the Syntactic foam into the tank. From there, a series of hoses were connected that spanned the distance between the surface and the sea bed. The idea for the micro foam tank was that the foam pumped in from the navy vessel would be sent down at a higher pressure rate from the tank, down through the hoses where, at the *Titanic* wreck, the submersibles would drill holes in the hull of the ship and connect the hoses to pump the foam into her lower interior spaces. Another aspect of the salvage foam story was the patching up of the 300ft iceberg gash in *Titanic*'s lower starboard side. Covering over the gash would form a seal, preventing the foam from escaping from within the hull. As the chemical solution reacted with the water, it would harden into a solid foam. In the story, each plate was welded in place with special equipment attached to the front of the submersibles and controlled from within the sub by a crew member. For the 55ft *Titanic* model several ¾ scale steel plates, 19cm x 11cm, were produced that would be attached to the hull and joined together to form a steel plate blanket that covered the entire iceberg opening. The plates were also modelled in ¼ scale for scenes of them attached to parachutes and heading down to the seafloor where, once they landed in the sediment, the subs would come along and pick each one up and transport it over to the *Titanic*.

The sub crews could not work on the *Titanic* without lighting to aid them. For this two lots of lighting rigs were made in ¾ scale, with one set a miniature carbon copy of the full-sized three-panelled fold-out lighting pods that are seen being tested in the loading bay of the U.S.S. *Denver*. The other lighting rig followed similar lines of the other units with the exception that these had an extending boom which allowed for the base of the rig to sit on the ocean floor while the lighting pods could be cranked up to a higher elevation to light up the superstructure. The 1978 model department plans indicate that 100 lighting rigs were to be made for the production. But on closer inspection of the film that amount had been reduced. It is worth mentioning that the three-panelled lighting pods existed as two variants with some fitted with smaller working bulbs while others, used for close-up views of the lights, had a much larger bulb. The lights were made from a mixture of a cast steel base that acted as an anchor to keep the lighting rig on the bottom of the tank, cast resin upper body, and pods made from sheet brass with a plastic moulded insert where the bulbs would be seated. All the lighting rigs were fully working with each unit connected to a main feed cable that ran around the seabed and up and out of the tank to the surface where regulated voltage was used to light them.

To pry the wreck from her watery grave a number of explosives had to be placed around the hull to blast the sediment away and break the suction caused by seven decades of sitting on the bottom. Each explosive sat within a long tube with a pointed weight at the base and a remote unit at the top that would be primed once the device had been planted. Being a remote device, each unit could be assigned to detonate at set times; remotely triggered from the surface; one explosive, for example, going off on the starboard side of the hull to then be followed moments later by another over on the port side. As the explosives work their way down the mud line the concussion creates a rocking movement to the vessel's hull that will eventually release its grip. Next the salvage tanks and foam will take over and lift the *Titanic* up to the surface. One-hundred miniature explosive models were made for the scenes to be filmed with the *Titanic* wreck while 20 full-size units were built and filmed being removed from their wooden crates and grouped together and dropped into the ocean.

The salvage lifting tank miniatures came in two scales to match the pair of fully hulled *Titanic* replicas. One of the smaller 1:98th scale tanks is used by Jason Robards as his character demonstrates to the reporters how the Hydrozene tanks are "anchored to the *Titanic*'s hull" in the press conference segment. The remainder of the tanks are briefly seen attached to the hull of the 9ft *Titanic* model as she makes her way past the camera to the surface in the film's raising sequence. The larger tank versions were built to match the ¾ scale *Titanic* model and were fully operational with airbags filled with air from cylinders operated by the model FX dive team. However, the story was to include the tanks being operated through several air pressure units placed on the seafloor around the hull of the wreck where air from the surface was fed down, through the units and continuing through more hoses connected to each of the tanks that would be disconnected once the tanks had been filled and reached the required pressure. But as the story changed so did the needs for some of the miniatures. One example of this happening came with the sonar equipment that was planned to be used in the search phrase for the *Titanic*. The sonar device was connected to a tow line and trailed out behind the stern of the U.S.S. *Pigeon* as the vessel zig-zagged across the ocean surface. But as the circumstances changed with the use of the real *Pigeon* it meant that the idea was eventually scuppered.

Salvage Fleet Model Dimensions

Have you ever been curious about how big the models were? Let us take a look into the world of the miniatures behind *Raise the Titanic*. All models were built to 1:16th / ¾ scale with measurements at 1" = 50'.

Ships

U.S.S. *Schenectady*
L - 33' 6"
W - 6' 8"
H - 6' 8"

U.S.S. *Denver*
L – 35' 5"
W – 6' 5"
H – 7' 2"

U.S.S. *Blakely*
L – 28'
W – 5'
H – 6'

U.S.S. *Pigeon*
L – 16' 6"
W – 6' 8"
H – 6' 8"

U.S.S. *Cocopa* (2x tug boats)
L – 13'
W – 3' 9"
H – 5' 6"

New York Fireboat
L – 8' 6"
W – 53cm
H – 2' 8"

Subs
DSV *Deep Quest* (x4)
L – 2' 5"
W – 36cm
H – 20cm

DSV *Turtle* (x2)
L – 49cm
W – 19cm
H – 24cm

DSV *Sea Cliff* (x2)
Same dimensions as Turtle (x2)

DSV *Starfish*
Same dimensions as Turtle (*Turtle* re-decaled as *Starfish*)

Helicopters

Sikorsky SH-3 Sea King (x2)
L – 119cm (overall with blades)
W – 101cm (overall with blades)
H – 30cm (overall with blades)

Sikorsky HH-53 Super Jolly Green Giant (x2)
L – 167cm (overall with blades)
W – 158cm (overall with blades)
H – 32cm (overall with blades)

Cussler's Fictional Fleet

The early days of production on the movie did have several vehicle names carried over from Clive Cussler's novel to the screenplay. But like any film adaptation based around a novel, places, characters, and even mechanical creations can be subject to change. Here are the original names of the surface ships and submersibles as featured in Clive Cussler's 1976 novel *Raise the Titanic*.

Surface Fleet
Monterey Park
Juneau
Modoc
Capricorn
Bomberger
Alhambra

Submersibles
Sappho I
Deep Fathom
Sea Slug
Sappho II

Chapter 7: Salvage Fleet • 185

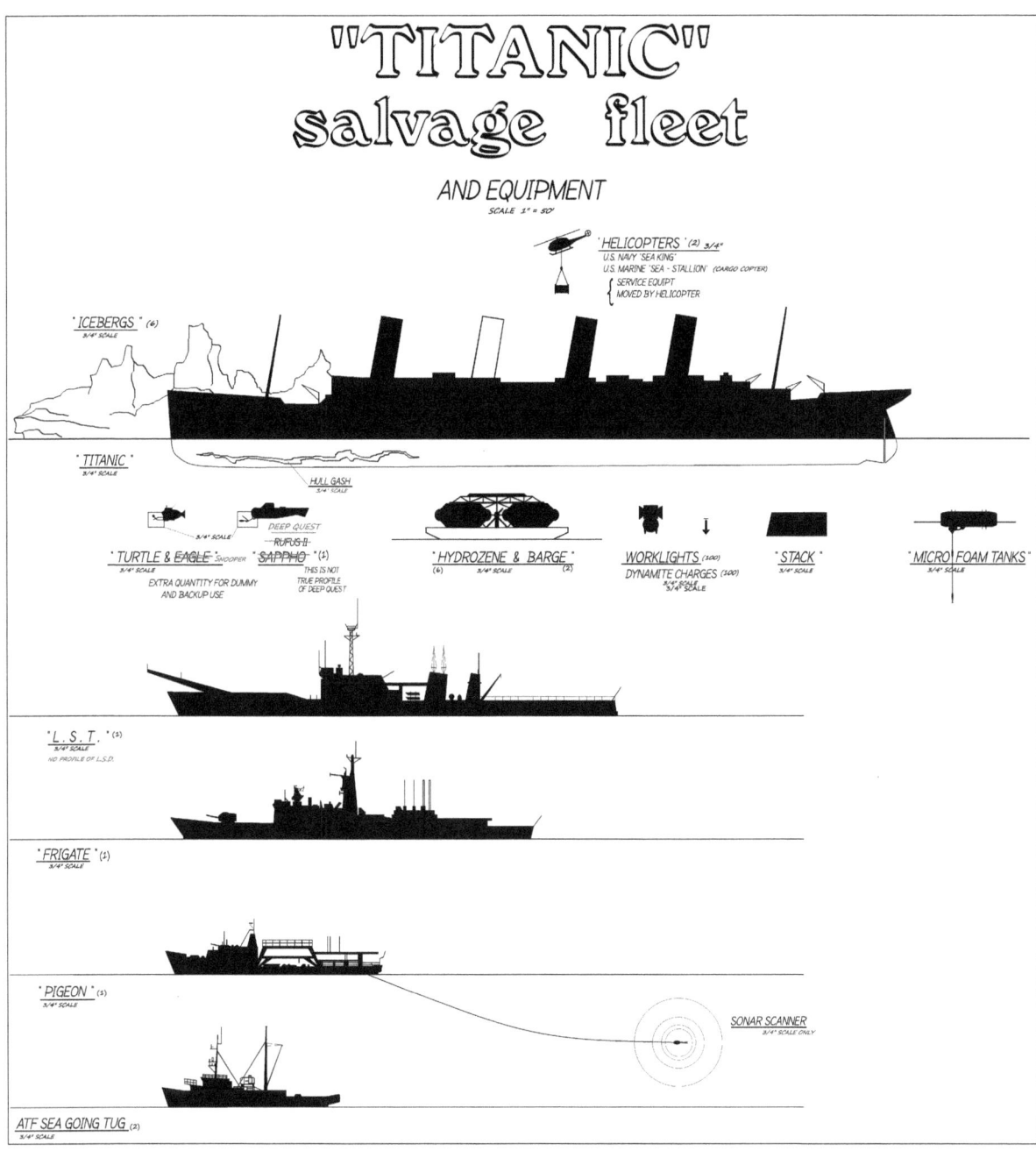

As the original Salvage Fleet plan is badly damaged, this faithful reproduction shows how the vessels all came together. The plan was created during the building of the models over in Los Angeles in stages 3 and 7 of the CBS Studio Center. It was meant to be a basic visual representation of what the facility had to build that included the large *Titanic* model, icebergs to scale and several of the salvage ships. *(Illustration © Jonathan Smith – Based on the original)*

A U.S. Navy frigate takes shape in Stage 3/7. The model is a faithful replica of the Knox-class *U.S.S. Blakely* (1072) and renamed to the role of the *U.S.S. Carpenter*. *(Photograph © Kento Gebo / Postcard by Marine Publishing Co – Author's collection)*

The impressive 1/16th scale replica of the *U.S.S. Schenectady*. *(Photograph © Kento Gebo)*

Built, shipped to Malta but never made it on screen. The model was a replica of the *U.S.S. Pigeon* (ASR-21), a Pigeon-class submarine rescue ship. *(Photograph © Kento Gebo)*

The bridge area of the *U.S.S. Schenectady*. *(Photograph © Kento Gebo)*

Chapter 7: Salvage Fleet • **189**

The pair of ocean-going Navy tugs in their original configuration. The two tugs were based on the *U.S.S. Cocopa*. *(Photograph © Kento Gebo – Author's collection)*

Another of the miniatures built for *Raise the Titanic*. This is a replica of the FDNY *John D. McKean* that was to be used in a scene of when the *Titanic* is pulled into New York with the fireboat ahead of her firing jets of water into the air. The model is pictured with its pump system installed that would draw water up from the tank and fire it through the deck mounted hoses. The model was shipped over to Malta but was never used in any of the scenes. *(Photograph © Kento Gebo)*

Chapter 7: Salvage Fleet • 191

Titanic, tugs, a fireboat and the navy. *(Photograph © Kento Gebo)*

Part of the filming schedule for San Diego dated 26 November 1979. *(Author's collection)*

The 32nd Street Naval Station in San Diego. From here the vessels hired by ITC for the production sailed to the deeper waters some 10-miles out to sea where, during exercises, the fleet was filmed along with personnel on board. *(Postcard by Marine Publishing Co – Author's collection)*

William Frye (right) discusses production details with Jason Robards and set decorator Mickey S. Michaels during preparations at the Naval Station. *(Author's collection)*

The AT&T cable laying ship C.S. *Long Lines* that was hired and used as the Soviet vessel *Mikhail Kurkov*. *(Author's collection)*

Selby, Jordan, Emmet Walsh, Cannon and Robards in character as Jerry Jameson films the scenes when the spy is flushed out. The scene was filmed on board the *U.S.S. Denver* while the ship sat in dock at the Naval Station. The clothing that Robards is wearing was loaned to him by the *Denver*'s captain, Vincent Edward Cook. *(ITC / The Last Great Human Adventure promotional film – Author's collection)*

Chapter 7: Salvage Fleet • 195

The scenes of Pitt explaining that the salvaging of *Titanic* has been brought forward following the entrapment of the *Deep Quest* was filmed in the chart room of the *U.S.S. Denver*. (ITC – Author's collection)

That doesn't look like the North Atlantic does it? This ITC promotional photograph for *Raise the Titanic* was taken in the shallow water of San Diego before the fleet headed out to sea. The shallow waters offered a safer environment for filming with equipment loaned by the Navy. It was also ideal for filming with the *Deep Quest* as the craft breaks the surface and crews prepare to recover it. This photo shows some of the Navy's own salvage tanks being manoeuvred into place for filming. *(ITC/AFD – Author's collection)*

Out at sea and Second Unit Director Michael "Mickey" Moore (left) and Unit Production Manager Robin Clarke get ready to spend a day filming on board the *U.S.S. Denver*. *(Author's collection)*

Chapter 7: Salvage Fleet • 197

Executive Producer Richard O'Connor tries to blend in with the crew on board the *U.S.S. Denver*. *(Author's collection)*

BELOW: "Seagram picked a lousy day to go sightseeing!" Robards, Jordan and Cannon on the hydraulic stern ramp of the *U.S.S. Denver*. *(ITC – Author's collection)*

Filming in the deep waters off San Diego with (clockwise) *U.S.S. Carpenter*, *U.S.S. Denver*, *U.S.S. Schenectady* and the cable ship *Long Lines*. *(ITC/ITV Studios)*

Behind the scenes on the bridge of the *U.S.S. Ranger*. *(Author's collection)*

Actor J.D. Cannon looks on, curiously and suspiciously, at one of the crew members in the comms room on board the *U.S.S. Ranger* in this behind the scenes photograph. *(Author's collection)*

Behind the scenes on the bridge of the *U.S.S. Ranger* as Richard Jordan jokes around on set. *(Author's collection)*

Jerry Jameson (seated with chequered shirt) discusses an exterior deck scene to be filmed before filming the crew of the *U.S.S. Denver* for a scene in the movie when they take up cheering as *Titanic* arrives at the surface. *(Author's collection)*

200 • *Raise The Titanic*

Jameson lensing Jordan, Selby and Robards on board the *U.S.S. Denver* for a sequence where the three men discuss the potential damage created by Merker, the U.S. spy, who, when found out, was arrested, put aboard the *Denver*'s helicopter and flown back to the U.S. *(ITC / The Last Great Human Adventure promotional film – Author's collection)*

"There she is!" Jordan and Robards being lensed on board the *U.S.S. Denver* for their scene of looking out to sea as *Titanic* is raised. *(ITC – Author's collection)*

Chapter 7: Salvage Fleet • 201

One of the Hydrozene tanks begin its journey down to the wreck of the *Titanic*. The tank was actually a one-off, a prop fabricated for use in the film. It is seen here being offloaded from the deck of the *U.S.S. Denver* in the shallow waters of the Pacific Ocean off the coast of San Diego. Once it had settled on the bottom, within diving distance, Navy divers could dive down, attach cables and hoist it back up on board ship. *(ITC/ITV Studios)*

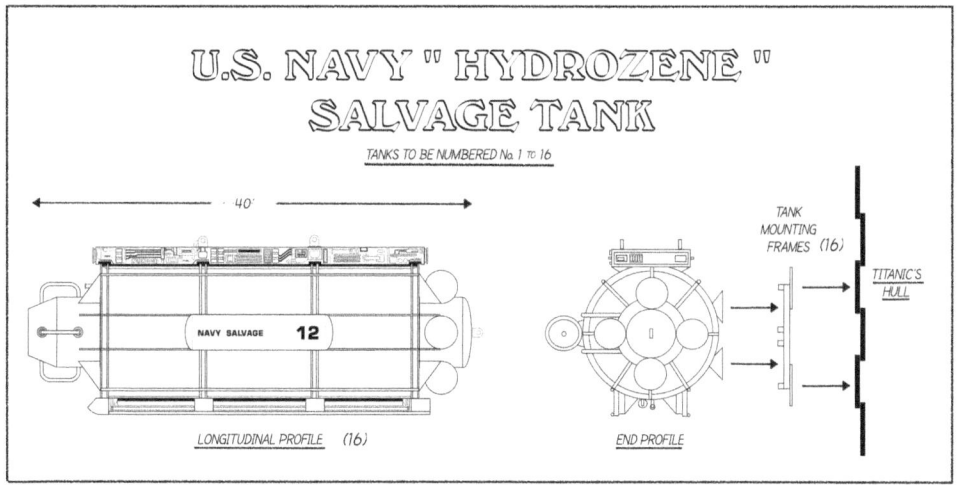

Plan of the movies fictional 40ft U.S. Navy "Hydrozene" salvage tank. *(Illustration © Jonathan Smith)*

U.S.S. Schenectady (Postcard by Marine Publishing Co – Author's collection)

U.S.S. Denver *(Postcard by Marine Publishing Co – Author's collection)*

U.S.S. Carpenter *(Postcard by Marine Publishing Co – Author's collection)*

U.S.S. Ranger *(Author's collection)*

Chapter 7: Salvage Fleet • 203

U.S.S. Pigeon (Author's collection)

SSN 594 *Permit*-class nuclear-powered fast attack submarine. *(Author's collection)*

Sandecker (Robards) and Prevlov (Brundin) watch as a U.S submarine appears between the *Titanic* and the Soviet ship. The effect was simple. A section of railing had been mocked up and aged (visible lower left of frame) and placed on the outer edge of the deck of the *U.S.S. Denver* as the actors were filmed from behind. *(ITC/ITV Studios)*

Behind the scenes photograph of M. Emmet Walsh, Richard Jordan and J.D. Cannon taking a break between filming in the submersible hanger of the San Diego base for Lockheed. Behind them are the real working deep sea vehicles *Deep Quest* and *Sea Cliff* (right) that belong to the Lockheed company. *(Author's collection)*

The real *Deep Quest* inside the San Diego hanger and sporting the *NUMA* logo on the side for its film role in *Raise the Titanic*. During the brief filming schedule in the hanger with the submersibles, not once did any of the subs ever enter the water. The aerial view shows the Lockheed Laboratory on Harbor Island in San Diego where the interior shots were filmed. Just visible is the stern tail of the *Deep Quest*. *(Author's collection & Lockheed publicity brochure – Author's collection)*

Chapter 7: Salvage Fleet • 205

David Selby takes a moment to be photographed in the Lockheed hanger. *(Author's collection)*

D.S.V. *Turtle*; the inspiration for the miniature version that would also become the *Starfish*. *(Author's collection)*

D.S.V. *Sea Cliff* is plucked from the ocean in this publicity photograph from the early 1970s. *(Author's collection)*

Crew jacket patch. *(Author's collection)*

D.S.V. *Turtle* (Author's collection)

D.S.V. *Deep Quest* rests on board the support ship *Transquest* in 1968. *(Author's collection)*

This special First Day cover from February 1970 marks one of the dives accomplished by the *Deep Quest* when she was piloted to a depth of 2,080 feet. *(Author's collection)*

Deep Quest in her retirement days when she spent her last years on public display at the United States Naval Undersea Museum in Washington. In 2018 the submersible was sold for recycling and was sent to a commercial company to be scrapped. *(United States Undersea Museum)*

Chapter 7: Salvage Fleet • 209

Navy divers atop of the *Deep Quest* after the submersible has returned from another dive to the ocean depths. But not everything is as it seems. As detailed as the top of the submersible is, and as accurate to the real *Deep Quest*, this is a full-sized dummy vessel that was built solely for the movie. *(Author's collection)*

Divers in Zodiac's from the *U.S.S. Denver* wait for the *Deep Quest* film prop to submerge and the call of "Action" so they can spring into life and swarm around the vessel to retrieve the half-suffocated *NUMA* crew members after their terrifying ordeal of being trapped on board the *Titanic*. *(Author's collection)*

Behind the scenes during the filming of the emergence of the *Deep Quest* out in the shallows of the Pacific Ocean of San Diego. *(Author's collection)*

Chapter 7: Salvage Fleet • 211

Behind the scenes during the filming of the emergence of the *Deep Quest* out in the shallows of the Pacific Ocean. *(Author's collection)*

In this publicity image of David Selby exiting the *Deep Quest*, the open hatch reveals some of its secrets. A simple twist locking mechanism was used to secure the hatch lid down when the craft was submerged. The hatch lacks any substantial watertight features that would allow the vehicle to dive to a depth of 10,000ft. As the prop was already watertight to allow it to be submerged to a maximum of 10ft below the surface, and with safety crew on board and with divers just metres away, anything untoward should happen, then all on board would be10safe. *(ITC/ITV Studios)*

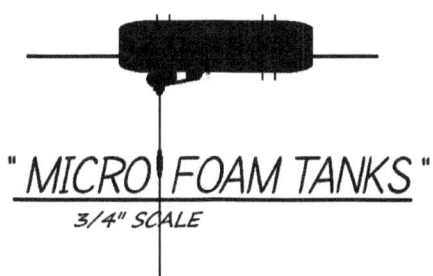

One of the Navy's fictionalised Syntathic Foam Pumping Station's that were built but never made it into any of the edits of the film. *(Illustration © Jonathan Smith – Based on original production material)*

Submarine or a gun ship? A victim of fraud, the former *Deep Quest* film prop for *Raise the Titanic* was purchased and turned into a river boat. Following the arrest of the owner, the vessel was ceased and put into storage in Greenport, near New York. *(All photographs © William Van Dorp)*

This publicity photograph of the large *Titanic* model in the bottom of the Deep Tank in Malta is one of the rare occasions where the salvage plates are in place over the iceberg damage on the hull. *(Author's collection)*

Chapter 7: Salvage Fleet • 213

Some of the original surviving steel salvage plates that were rescued from the model. *(Author's collection)*

LEFT: Electricians at work on testing the full-size lighting pods before being loaded aboard the *U.S.S. Denver*. ABOVE: As believable as these units looked and worked, they were completely fabricated from scratch just for the production. *(Author's collection / ITC)*

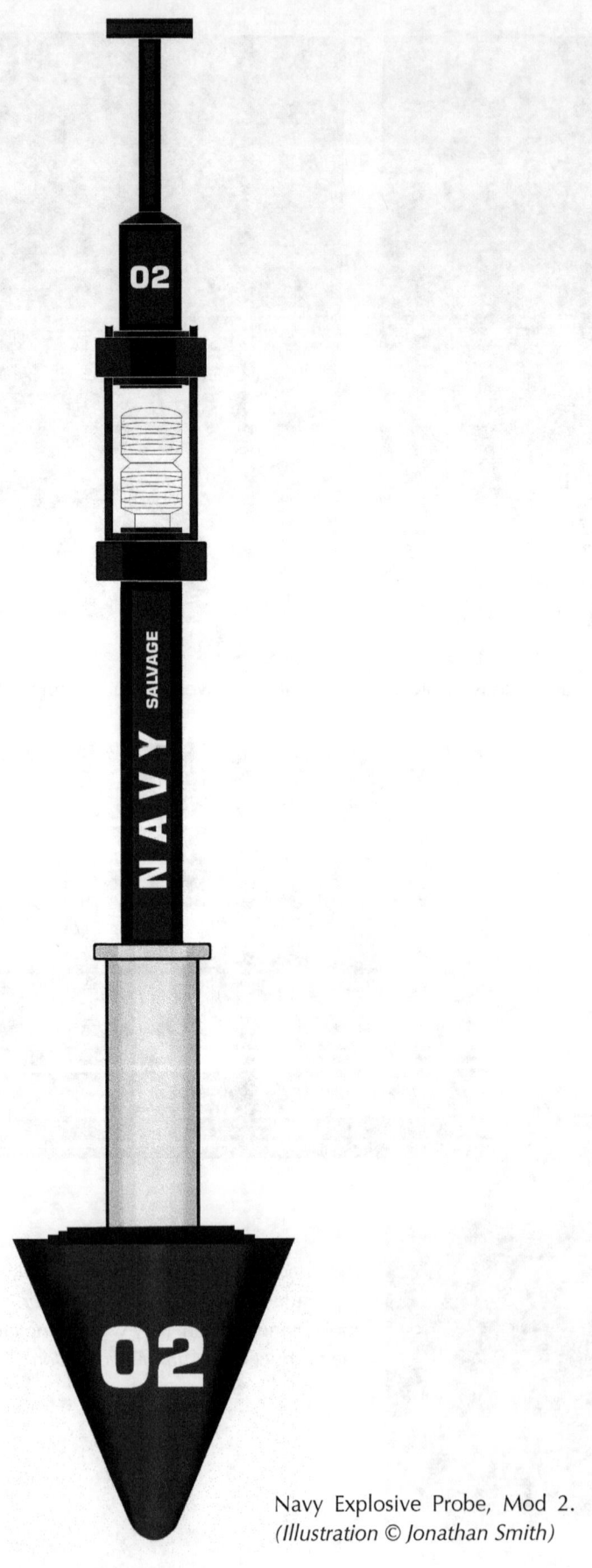

Navy Explosive Probe, Mod 2.
(Illustration © Jonathan Smith)

Chapter 7: Salvage Fleet • 215

Blink and you may miss it. These three frames from the movie reveal one of the hidden pieces of equipment. Sitting side by side behind the crates containing the Explosive Probes are a pair of Sonar devices that would have been attached to a cable and dragged behind one of the Navy ships. *(ITC/ITV Studios)*

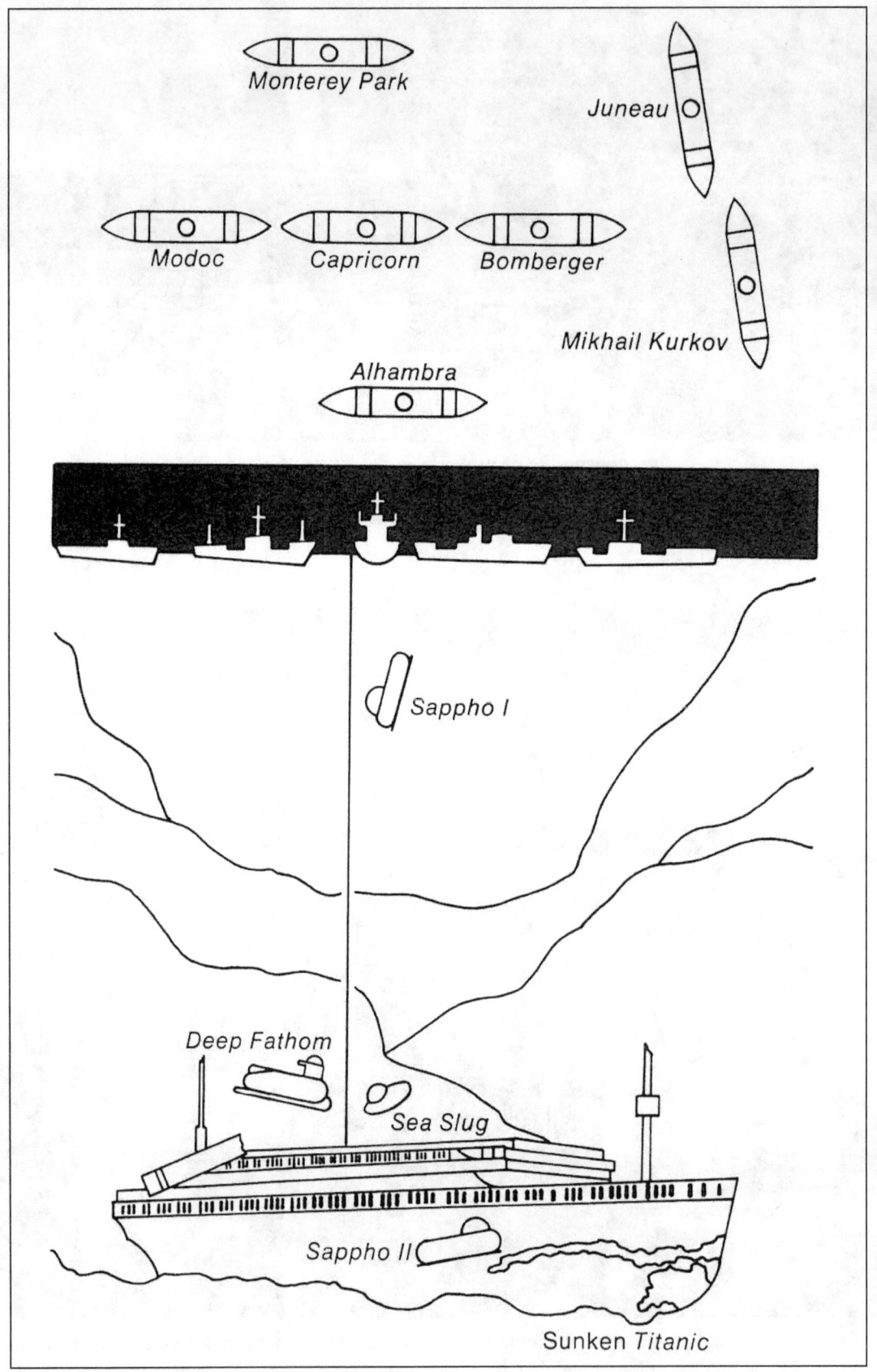

Clive Cussler's salvage fleet. *(Viking Press)*

The Salvage Fleet

The following library of images were taken in early 1979 outside Stage 5 of the CBS Studio Center when the Navy ships and tugs were ready for crating up for the shipment to Malta. The photographs show the Navy tugs, U.S.S. *Pigeon*, U.S.S. *Blakely* and the U.S.S. *Schenectady*. *(All photographs – Author's collection)*

```
MODEL
U.S.N. TUG "AFT *101"
L - 13'
W - 3'9"
H - 5'6"

PLEASE NOTE WE HAVE TWO TUGS
```

Chapter 7: Salvage Fleet • 219

MODEL
U.S.N. TUG "AFT" "101"
L - 13'
W - 3'9"
H - 5'6"
PLEASE NOTE WE HAVE TWO TUGS.

MODEL - U.S.N. PIDGEON
L - 16'6"
W - 6'8"
H - 6'8"

Chapter 7: Salvage Fleet • 221

```
MODEL.
U.S.N. FRIGATE
L - 28'
W - 5'
H - 6'
```

222 • *Raise The Titanic*

Chapter 7: Salvage Fleet • 223

MODEL
U.S.N. FRIGATE
L - 28ft.
W - 5ft.
H - 6ft.

MODEL.
U.S.N. L.S.T.
L - 33'6"
W - 6'8"   H - 6'8"

Chapter 7: Salvage Fleet • **225**

This series of photographs were taken by an official for ITC when the company arrived in San Diego in late 1977 during scouting for vessels for use in the production of *Raise the Titanic*. Of interest to the company was the *U.S.S. Denver* and its accompanying Sikorsky SH-3 Sea King helicopter. *(All photographs – Author's collection)*

Chapter 8

Mediterranean Film Facility

"A very famous noted director who had won numerous Oscars built the Titanic and there wasn't a tank in the world large enough to hold it. So, we had to find a place in Malta next to a smaller tank. And they told me it would be finished in January. The only mistake they made is they didn't tell me which January."

Lew Grade

Reality began to dawn on ITC and Marble Arch Productions that their *Titanic* model was without a tank to raise it in. The model taking shape may have been the largest of its kind in the world but what good is that when the film production it was crafted for was without the fundamental water tank to accomplish the film's title. William Creber's choosing in building the *Titanic* replica at 1:16th scale meant that the model would be at the lowest scale possible when working with actual water and also presenting a large-scale miniature that was big enough to look realistic on camera. From the very start of the production, the studio was in agreement that the model work had to incorporate water, that all sequences where subs were looking for the wreck, where the underwater action and crucial raising had to be completed with the use of a vast water tank. But this was not the only option available as the studio could have gone with a dry for wet, a simple technique of filming in a controlled studio environment using smoke, coloured filters, and lighting effects without the need to submerge in water.

Early examples go back to the 1950s with the release of the original 1954 *Godzilla* movie of scenes with the monster moving underwater. Gerry Anderson used another example of dry for wet during the filming of *Stingray* in 1963 by positioning a clear water tank with fish between the camera and the submarine model with the model passing behind the tank of water while remaining dry. Wet for dry with the use of smoke was particularly effective when it was applied to the filming of the *Titanic* wreck with submersibles for the opening sequence to James Cameron's 1998 blockbuster *Titanic*. Two years later the techniques were used again for the underwater footage of the wreck of the U.S.S. *Arizona* for the Michael Bay war drama *Pearl Harbor*. What the Cameron and Bay movies share is that their main principal stories are focused on events that dominate the screen time on the surface of the ocean unlike *Raise the Titanic* where half of the film is set in the ocean depths. The film's underwater segments, although plentiful, could have been successfully achieved with the use of dry for wet. The building of the tank would be costly, and more so if the tank was built just for a segment that was to last a matter of moments on screen. What eventually swung the decision was that the tank not only would be used for filming the raising segments but also doubled as the environment of the ocean floor. For the studio, the tank offered them the benefits of staying in one location to film both the underwater scenes and those of the raising and post salvage stages of the story. But where were they going to build the tank and how much was it going to cost?

Location, Location, Location

One can only imagine the reaction from Grade when he was informed that the costly fleet of model ships being assembled in California was without a bathtub big enough to put them all in. Grade was already troubled with the spiralling costs of the production as the original budget of £6m was diminishing fast. Grade was left with no choice but to go along with budgeting for a specially built water tank that was large enough to incorporate depth and substantial surface coverage that would work with the *Titanic* model while never revealing to the audience that much of the cinemaphotography was completed in a water tank. What was an issue for the *Raise the Titanic* production was that ITC had to be on-site for a period of months filming. With no studio facilities offering such a large and deep tank, it was left to ITC to come up with an alternative. What would work in favour was if a pre-existing studio allowed an outsider, in this case, another production company, to build an extension to the studio facilities while always having to hand the appropriate backdrop of the sea and an endless supply of water to fill the tank. Thankfully that thinking reduced the list of studios already in operation as ITC required one located on the coastline. The penny dropped in October 1978 when one studio location offered half of what was required to complete *Raise the Titanic*; Mediterranean Film Facility, otherwise known in its abbreviated form as MFF.

The MFF is located on the island of Malta, one of the Southern European groups of islands located in the waters of the Mediterranean Sea. Close to the capital of Valetta, on the east coast of the island is Kalkara, the ancient ruins of Fort Rinella that overlook Malta's Grand Harbour and the studio's grounds of the Mediterranean Film Facilities. The MFF began operation in 1963 when the facilities were devised by the British special effects specialist Jim Hole and built by Maltese construction manager Paul Avellino. Hole wanted to help directors to film safely in the confines of a controlled studio tank that offered a seamless transition between tank and sea horizon while being large enough to allow productions to take place in a water tank with much surface coverage but shallow enough to house sets while allowing personnel to stand in the fully filled tank without the need to get their head wet. The MFF opened in 1964 with the impressive surface tank being used for the first time in the cold war naval drama *The Bedford Incident*. ITC approached MFF in mid-1978 to secure the use of the surface tank during the period of mid to late spring 1979. While the surface tank would be beneficial for scenes post-salvage, the problem lay in that the tank lacked the depth to raise the large *Titanic* model. The surface tank did come with a well, an area in the middle of the tank that was dug out deeper to allow for set pieces to be submerged deeper than the 4ft depth of the main section of the tank. The well did work for the 55ft *Titanic* model during filming the movie's intended 1912 sinking prologue, as the model was controlled to slip beneath the tank's surface depth of 4ft and down into the well, while all the time not being allowed to be fully submerged. The studio could complete the scene with a miniature set of just the stern as it slipped beneath the waves. But the well was not big enough to hold the entire *Titanic* model, the artificial sea bed, lifting gear, and a host of divers who were to work during lengthy periods of time in the tank, and in safety.

It was suggested that the surface tank could be deepened. But as a working studio, it was not practical to put out of action one of the key facilities for the benefits of one motion picture, regardless of its high budget. The MFF concluded that to carry out such a major refurbishment by one film production company meant that half a dozen other productions that required the use of the tank would have to be turned away, resulting in potential financial loss. The only other viable solution was the building of a completely new tank, from the ground up, that offered ITC what they needed for their production while becoming part of the existing Mediterranean Film Facility. And so, with the assistance of the MFF, ITC approached the Maltese government to begin negotiations in buying the land adjacent to the surface tank on the east side of the island where the deep tank, outbuildings, and office building would be constructed.

Guinness World Record Tank

By late summer of 1978, Lew Grade had his lawyers in talks with the MFF and the Maltese government in trying to secure the land. Grade had devised a plan of action to have his company located with the main office in Malta, specifically in the grounds around the deep tank. As the negotiations neared completion, Grade registered his new film business with Companies House in Cardiff; Pimlico Film Ltd, c/o Mediterranean Film Facilities, Fort St. Rocco, Kalkara. The new company now formed part of a franchise of Grade companies for the entertainment industry that included ITC, Marble Arch Productions, and Associated Communications Corporation (aka ACC). The early days of negotiating the land was a headache for all involved. At first, the Maltese government was apprehensive, thinking that the studio in its present state was enough to sustain an income to the island and that any further expansion, such as a new tank, would be viable only for a short term after which the expenses of the new facility and maintenance would outweigh profit margins. Grade's lawyers slowly began to win over the Maltese government when they included in the deal a cash injection of £900,000 for the economy and having the laborious work of building the tank and outbuildings given to local contractors and builders.

Despite some communication breakdowns between the two parties, they did share the same predicament as neither wanted to lose out on a good business deal with the Maltese government and not wanting to drag their heels in case Grade decided to take his business elsewhere. For Grade, it was the need to deliver the film production he was greatly indebted to. The finalized deal between Grade, the MFF, and the Maltese government was that the tanks' design, construction, and workforce would be completed through local companies at the expense of ITC. Upon completion, the tank would be subject to Grade's companies for future productions during a ten-year contract which covered expenses for maintenance and operating. And when the ten-year contract had expired, the tank would become the property of the Maltese government. The submitted and approved plans dated 27 October 1978 presented a water tank in such a grand scale that it dwarfed anything currently in existence and earning the completed tank an entry into the 1981 Guinness Book of Records.

Local Maltese architect and civil engineer, John M. Gambina, was approached to oversee the construction of the deep tank. He drafted up a concave design tank that consisted of three main units of a bottom sump of reinforced concrete with expansion joints, the sloping sides of asphalt and bituminous sealing compound, and a top rim of reinforced concrete making up the weir and horizon wall. The depth of the tank from ground level at the base of the weir wall and down to the sump measured 39ft (11.8m), once filled the depth from the surface down to the tank floor above the sump being 36ft (11m) with the tank floor dimension of 160ft (49m) across and 354ft (108m) at ground level within the rim of the weir and horizon wall. The tank had a filling time of ten hours and thirty minutes with a capacity to hold 9,750,000 imperial gallons of pumped in seawater, the equivalent to 44,324,395 litres of water, which gave the tank facility an estimated 58,400 square feet of surface area. The drainage time for the tank when filled to capacity was four hours and thirty minutes.

The groundwork for the tank began in autumn 1978 as the landscape was cleared off and excavators and dump trucks were brought in to begin the removal of thousands of tons of rock and soil from the natural valley. The tank's location was to be positioned at a higher elevation inland of the island. As the natural layout of the land had a gradual sloping valley from inland down towards the coast, the area of land where the three main sides of the tank were to be constructed now required a new footing, so tons of Maltese globigerina limestone was brought in and offloaded around the foremost outer edge of the tank's footprint, creating a cone-shaped structure. With each new load dumped the earthmovers would push the sides up to create a raised embankment, mixing in rocks and boulders and compacting down the earth with each new layer. The addition of the globigerina limestone at depths between 250mm to 300mm added to the integrity of the structure, as, when water was added to the limestone, it began to solidify, allowing for further compacting down by 35-ton D8 Tractor units. With the artificially-made banks facing out over the Mediterranean Sea, the area inland of these banks would become the internal footing of the tank as all sides, now raised and compacted down, could now be smoothed off with tons of crushed limestone for the next stage of the tank's main body of construction. As Christmas came the heavy plant machinery at the deep tank continued as the laborers worked on the inner side of the tank forcing down the earth and compacting it down to form a solid core footing that would allow for the next materials to be seated upon without the concerns of ground movement.

On the 9 February 1979 the film's executive producer, Martin Starger, revealed the *Raise the Titanic* production budget had increased from the original £7m doubling to £14m with an expected June start for filming with the actors and sets while labelling the film as "the biggest picture we're involved in, both financially and in terms of its potential." That February the tank sides were nearing the point of skinning, the floor of the tank had now been prepared for the installation of the concrete sump with supporting columns, four lots of 2ft diameter drainage pipework with junction box, the dump valve system, and the drain ducting channel. The concrete floor, known as the top slab, was designed to sit over the sump like a lid with an access point covered with a removable grating that gave entry to the sump below. The sump measured 20ft in length, 10ft in width with a 6ft depth. With the top slab in place, the larger area of the main tank floor had an additional height of 5ft where it levelled off parallel with the secondary tank floor. The design of the floor was one built up in eight sections with each piece joined together with a series of 9" thick hollow block connecting walls that acted similar to that of an expansion joint. The tank walls of consolidated filling core were firstly covered with 2" thickness of draining asphalt. Once it was set two layers of hydraulic asphalt were applied at a maximum depth of four inches. And where the sides of the tank fitted flush with the concrete floor the joint was treated with a bitumen sealing compound.

At the top of the tank sat the weir, with a combined drainage sump that also included both the parapet and horizon walls. The weir was designed with three walls consisting of the inner tank wall rising 2ft above the lip of the tank side, the inner horizon wall that measured 4ft in height, and the outer 2ft parapet wall of the drainage sump. The inland section of the weir was completed with a higher outer wall that had the weir sump passing beneath it and a sectional cut out with a foot pool and equipment assembly point and a ramp to allow ease of access from the studio grounds down into the filled water tank. Incorporated into the weir's design were ten dummy contraction joints that reduced any shrinkage points that could appear in the concrete during settling. Located on the tank floor, at the foot of the sloping walls, were twenty forged steel ringlets placed around the inner parameter of the tank that were seated down into the concrete, allowing them to be used as anchor points for submerged sets and the lowering of heavy equipment when the tank was empty. On the studio inland side of the tank wall, adjacent to the studio road, was a galvanized track system that was used to send equipment down with the use of a winch that was bolted onto the floor of the tank. One last feature installed into the tank was that of a galvanized stair which allowed the crew to enter and exit from the tank floor or the main studio ground close to the main deep tank outbuilding and offices.

To accompany the full working arrangement of the deep tank and assist with film productions, outbuildings were required to be constructed that housed the tanks pumping system, water chemical treatment facility, the "*Titanic* Storage & Assembly Shed", paint shop with stores, and model makers workshop. The plans drawn up in April 1978 for the main factory building with offices was that of a two-story building with 25,000 square feet of floor space with 10,000 square feet designated to offices. The main building was to house several facilities to cater for much of the crew and studio personnel while being within a stone's throw of the deep tank. As the construction of the deep tank progressed the main office building changed, being reduced from the original intended two-story construction to a single-story building with the offices and main factory as a single complex. The main building was fitted out with camera storage facilities with a darkroom and film racks, ladies locker room with changing room, showers and toilets, divers air tanks facility, air-conditioned conference room, open-sided rest area, men's changing room with toilets and showers, additional toilet facilities for surface tank workers, open-sided restaurant and camera electrical store with camera unit washdown.

The Workings of the Deep Tank

The following material is taken from the May 1980 ten-page document on the overall workings of the deep tank. It is reproduced here verbatim for the readers with the hope of a better understanding of how the tank was operated and the procedures of how it was filled, its working arrangements, and how the tank was drained.

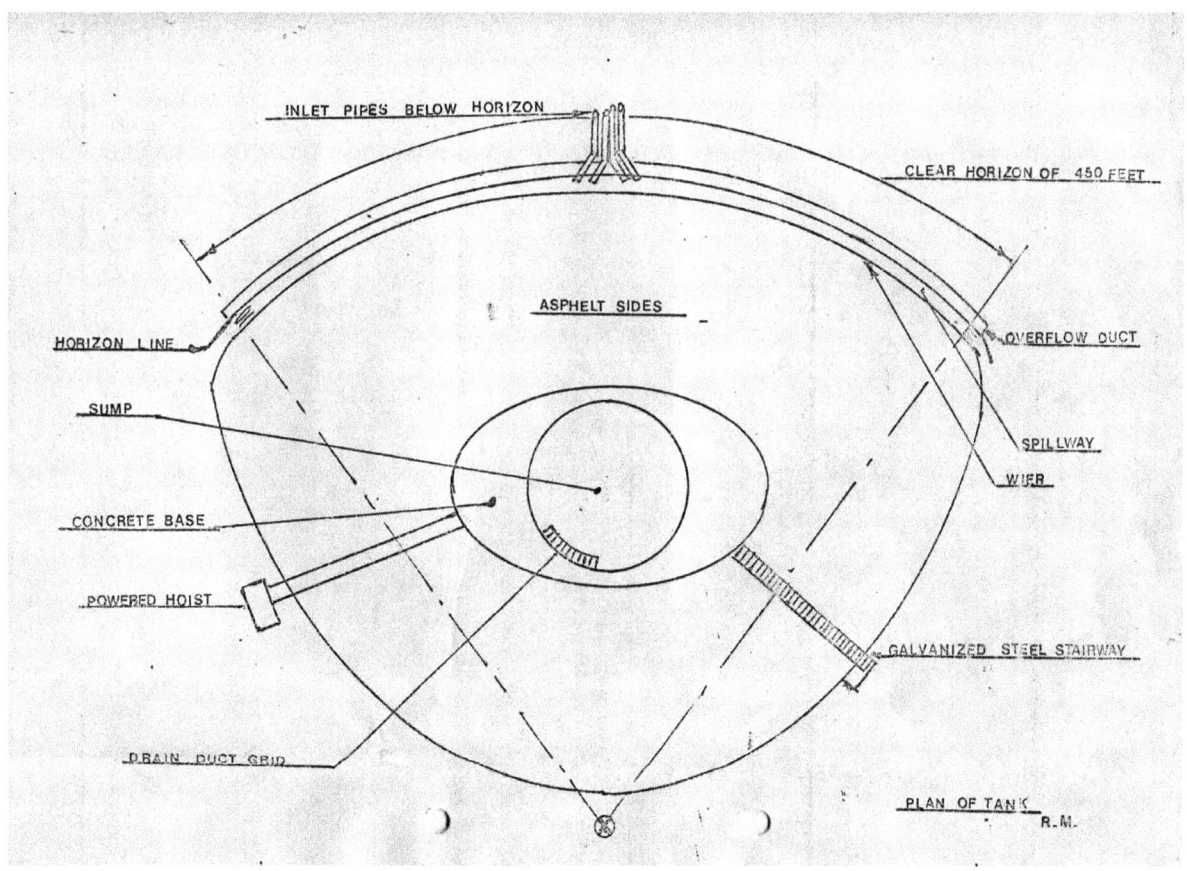

Tank Construction – *(Illustration by Roy Maisey, Deepwater Tank Superintendent, May 1980 – Author's collection)*

232 • *Raise The Titanic*

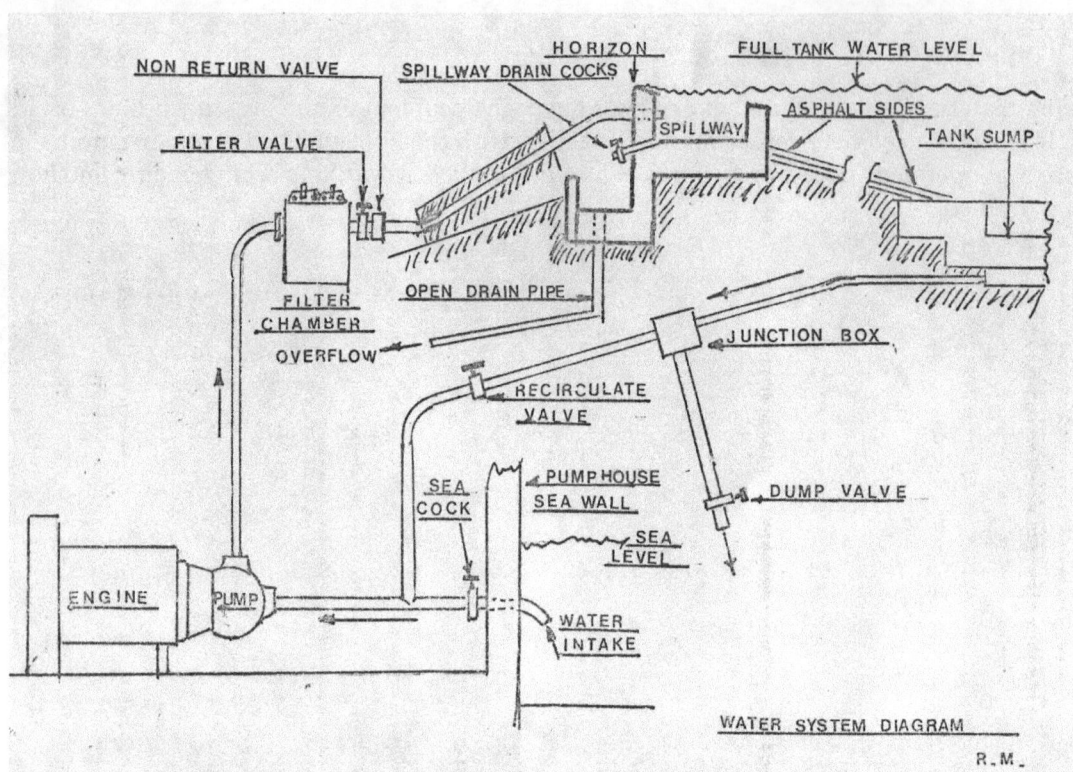

Tank Construction – *(Illustration by Roy Maisey, Deepwater Tank Superintendent, May 1980 – Author's collection)*

Intake pipes, May 1980 *(Author's collection)*

Chapter 8: Mediterranean Film Facility • 233

Filter chambers, May 1980 (Author's collection)

Drainage outlet, May 1980 (Author's collection)

Diesel engines, May 1980 *(Author's collection)*

Disinfection system, May 1980 *(Author's collection)*

Chapter 8: Mediterranean Film Facility

THE DEEPWATER FILMING TANK
FORT ST. ROCCO
RINELLA
MALTA
May 1980
GENERAL DESCRIPTION

CAPACITY
Ninemillion, seven hundred and fifty thousand imperial gallons.

SURFACE AREA:
Fiftyeight thousand, four hundred square feet.

DEPTH
From false seabed, to horizon line – thirty nine feet.

FILLING TIME:
Ten hours, thirty minutes

DRAINING TIME:
Four hours, thirty minutes

PUMPING:
Four – two hundred and fifty H.P. Diesel engines each driving a sixteen inch bore centrifugal pump.

FILTERING:
Each pipeline, from the pump to the tank has a four element filter box installed.

DISINFECTION:
Chlorine gas is used as a disinfectant. This is carefully controlled by the most modern equipment and the content is monitored each day that the tank is in use.

TANK CONSTRUCTION

(a) The tank is made in three main units; The bottom, or sump, which is made of reinforced concrete with expansion joints. The bottom has two levels; the top follows the general configuration of the tank and the lower, or sump, is circular and approximately six feet lower than the top level. This contains the tank drain pipes; four sixteen-inch bore pipes lead to the drain control wheel valves. The outlet from the tank is protected by a heavy steel grid.

(b) The sloping sides consist of two layers of asphalt, the top layer being coated with a bitumous sealing compound.

(c) The top or rim is made of reinforced concrete with expansion joints and consists of a spillway or wier and the horizon wall. All joints between the asphalt and the concrete are made with a thick preformed fibreglass fillet which is heat-sealed with a bitumous compound.

    The space between the spillway and the horizon wall being ten feet wide occupies more than one third of the top rim of the tank. The seawater is pumped into this spillway and then flows over the wier which ensures even distribution of the chlorine solution in the water.

    At the outside of the horizon wall is a concrete through which collects water pumped over the horizon line and it is then piped back into the sea.

(d) The tank has a built-in motorised winch for conveying heavy items to and from the sump area and a galvanised steel stairway with two handrails.

(e) In the tarmacadam surrounding the tank, set about two feet from the outer edge of the wall, are twenty heavy mooring rings and on the inside of the top wall there are fifty six-inch diameter steel rings, set in staples, equally spaced around the complete edge of the tank. These are fitted approximately one foot up the wall from the asphalt joint. A similar number are anchored in the concrete of the bottom of the tank.

THE WATER SYSTEM

Water is taken from the sea, via a man-made channel in which is installed first a course filter frame made up of one-inch diameter steel bars fitted at five-inch centres. This is to retrain large pieces of the usual flotsam that is always present at the edge of the sea.

Secondly, a storm gate or barrier is fitted which completely blocks the channel. This barrier is in steel slides set in the sides of the channel and when pumping is required it is raised five feet. The bottom of the barrier at this height is still below the sea level thus forming a wave damper.

Last in the channel is a relatively fine filter screen. This again is a steel frame with bars positioned with a five-eighth inch gap between them.

The channel is then turned through some forty-five degrees and is widened to correspond with the full width of the pumphouse, thus forming an extensive pool from which the pump intake pipes get their supply. The intake pipes are some six-feet below the water level and angled downwards to prevent a vortex forming. The internal diameter of all the water supply, recirculating and discharge pipes is sixteen inches (40cm.)

The intake pipes pass through the specially reinforced wall of the pumphouse and are coupled directly onto wheelgate valves which form the sea-cocks of the system. From the sea-cocks the pipes are attached to the four Dasnithski centrifugal pumps. Between the sea-cocks and the pumps a "T" piece junction is fitted to carry the water from the tank when recirculation is required; pipes to the "T" piece have wheelgate valve fitted between the junction and the sump of the tank.

From the pumps the water is then passed through the filter chambers. These chambers each contain four filter elements which are easy to remove for cleaning or change of element from course to fine or visa-versa.

Immediately after the filter chambers a wheelgate valve is fitted. This valve closes the pipeline when it is indicated that the filters are becoming clogged and that a change or clean out is required. This indication is shown on a differential pressure gauge which is installed across the inlet and outlet of the filter body.

Coupled directly to the filter gate valve is a non-return valve which has a spring-backed double valves. This Check valve which is entirely automatic, prevents the flowback of water from the tank should an engine failure occur. A flowback would make the pump turn the engine in the opposite direction, causing its destruction.

From the filter chambers the pipelines pass to the tank spillway. This portion of the pipeline in some three hundred feet in length and it rises some forty feet to its discharge point in the spillway.

When the tank is drained water passes from the tank sump to a three-way junction box. One direction leads to the gate valve in the recirculation circuit; the other leads to gate valves at the discharge point.

Driving the pumps, which are rated at four thousand three hundred gallons per minute against a sixty-five feet head, are four of the latest type turbo charged Dorman diesel engines of two hundred and fifty H.P. These engines have fitted a very sensitive governor control unit.

This unit keeps the engine speed constant should load fluctuation occur. Also installed is a thyrestor controlled safety device which will automatically shut down the engine should an oil pressure temperature failure or a coolant pressure temperature failure occur.

Fuel for the engines is stored in a four hundred and fifty gallon tank which can be filled direct from a road tanker or by hand rotary pump from forty five gallon barrels. Each engine uses approximately seven gallons per hour at full power.

THE DISINFECTION SYSTEM

Chlorine gas is used as a media for destroying any bacteria which is present in the sea water and which contaminate the tank water from the atmosphere. The chlorine is obtained in liquid form in steel drums which holds eight hundred and fifteen kilograms of liquid chlorine. The drums are used in batches of four. One drum for each of the four pumps. One batch of four drums will give ten to fourteen complete fillings of the tank and the highest rate of discharge available at a ratio of four and a half parts per million of chlorine to water. The rate of four parts per million was recommended by the British Thames Water Authority, who carried out a survey and analysis of the sea water in the vicinity of the tank intake channel.

The metering system used to control the flow of chlorine into the pumping system is of the latest type and was recommended by I.C.I. the chlorine manufacturers and the Thames Water Authority.

The chlorine is stored in a fireproof and well ventilated building some one hundred and fifty feet from the pumphouse. Accommodation is provided for twelve drums in the gashouse as supply from the UK is ten or twelve weeks delivery (ref: I.C.I. Malta Agents)

The metering system is of a unique design. It displays the amount of chlorine flowing into the system which is controlled by vacuum. Should a break or loss of pressure across the venturi occur, the supply is immediately terminated.

In the gashouse a weighing machine is provided to assess the quantity of chlorine in any drum as when gas is withdrawn the pressure drops, the liquid chlorine boils and re-establishes the pressure.

CHARGES FOR USE OF TANKS 1979 – 1980

Charges for the use of the Surface Tank
Inclusive Monday to Saturday – 6 days   £3,000
Filling of tank   £150
Chemical Treatment   (at cost)
Colouring of water   (at cost)

Charges for the use of the Deep Tank
Inclusive Monday to Saturday – 6 days   £4,000
Filling of tank   £150

* * *

Tires, Fines & Other Problems

The building of the tank wasn't without controversy; from internal struggles and conflicts between the studio and the construction company, to local residents and questionable tank apparatus. On 23 July 1979 ITC received a letter of complaint from the UK crew working on the deep tank after they discovered damage to plant machinery. It was "the latest in a series of deliberate acts of vandalism" to be carried out on-site at the studio with personnel being approached for information and the police to assist with preventing further damage. As the damage caused was carried out during the time the machinery was left unattended it could not be established if these acts were the result of disgruntled Maltese or British construction workers or unruly local residents who had gained access to the studio grounds. Regardless, with a large percentage of Maltese construction workers in attendance on-site, the overall construction of the tank and surrounding buildings were overseen and largely financed by the British side of the tank project. The escalating problems of vandalism may have been an act of retaliation from those loyal to the heritage of the British Empire, when in 1814 Malta was handed over to the British under the Treaty of Paris. It was not until September 1964 that Malta was handed back to the Maltese

Government achieving its independence as the State of Malta after lengthy and intense negotiations with the United Kingdom, leading to adopting a policy of neutrality by 1980.

Some Maltese locals objected to the redevelopment of the studio facility, despite the studio being a major contributor of income to the island. Concerns were raised about a breakwater in development that, once completed, was to be placed in the channel leading into the inlet of the pumping station for the tank. The proposed breakwater was to be constructed from scrap tires secured together of fourteen tires per bundle totalling twenty-one bundles and secured via cables attached to the rocky shoreline and allowed to float at the entrance of the seawater intake. The breakwater was deemed unsightly with local residents objecting to this pontoon of old vehicle tires left to free float and catch any flotsam that should come its way. However, the residents were in luck when the August 1979 submitted proposal fell foul with the Commissioner of Lands. The barrier, although approved, had a completion date of no later than 31 July 1980, set and agreed upon by all parties involved in the deeds. By May the breakwater had not yet been started, forcing the Commissioner of Lands through the courts to slap a £50,000 fine upon ITC to compensate for the expenses that the Maltese Government had incurred during the handling of the barrier agreements. But the Maltese officials were not quite done yet, as someone waited in the wings with a proverbial spanner to be thrown into the works. The purpose of the deep tank, like the older surface tank, was created for the sole purpose of having a perfect unhampered view of the ocean, that when filled to capacity and with the tank's overspill in full working mode, there would be a seamless integration between the tank water and the distant waters of the Mediterranean Sea. But not all could grasp the serious nature of such a multi-million build like the deep tank and the economical benefits to the area. Domenico Mintoff, the Prime Minister of Malta, wanted to incorporate fir trees around the coastal end of the tank adding colour to an otherwise bland concrete structure. While the idea was discussed, thankfully, it was dropped – discreetly. Maybe the Prime Minister came to his senses after realizing that fir trees cannot grow in the middle of an ocean.

Turntable & Bridge

As the deep tank approached the final stages of completion, attention was turned towards the construction of steel framework staging's that would be used in, and above, the tank. The two main pieces were designed to work with the specifications of the tank, with one being a gantry bridge system suspended over the water and which would span the width of the tanks surface area. The more crucial structure was the turntable, that, once assembled, would sit and be operated on the floor of the tank via a pulley system. The turntable was not to be a permanent fixture of the tank, having been designed for use only with the *Raise the Titanic* production, where it would be broken down, removed from the tank and the tank floor prepped for the next studio production. The Californian-based steel manufacturer D.C. Mesner Associates were the designers and suppliers of both the turntable and bridge. The turntable was designed to operate on a rail circle with an additional drive unit. With the tank bottom finished level, a steel rolled angle track would be laid down onto the concrete bed of the tank with the first rail being 20ft from the centreline and the outer track at 70ft from the centreline and encircling the inner circumference of the tank floor while allowing for the turntable to rest and move upon the track.

The main structure of the turntable was designed to represent a decagon; a ten-sided polygon, with each section, ten sections in total, fabricated to bolt together to form the decagon shape that would be attached to a central circular plate. Each segment consisted of two main radial trusses with nine stabilizing struts placed at intervals, two of which were fabricated with staggered lacing for extra stability. With all ten segments bolted together to form the decagon, the framework of the turntable would resemble a steel deck which would allow for the artificial sea bed to be assembled on top. Fixed to the underside of the turntable were a total of twenty upright posts secured at the joints of each segment of the turntable. At the track end of each of the upright supports there was a cast steel wheel that ran upon the rail giving the turntable a clearance of 3'.4" from the floor of the tank. Once the turntable had been assembled and seated upon its lower sprocket drive the wheels that sat upon the track would take the weight of the unit where seven men could turn it around on its axis. To eliminate the use of manpower a hydraulic unit was incorporated into the design that would pull the turntable clockwise or anticlockwise depending on the positioning required for filming. This was achieved by a chain cable that ran around the outer edge of the turntable, over a series of chain engagement sprockets with guards to then pass through the hydraulic power unit as a set of gears cranked the turntable along. With the turntable erected and operating accordingly the final phase was to weld up all the joints so as not to rely solely on the securing bolts holding the unit together.

During the early stages of the construction of the tank, it was thought that a pivoting bridge could be built that extended out over the entire width of the tank surface that would allow for the film crews to walk on the bridge and control models and equipment. The land end of the bridge was to be mounted upon a weighted four-wheel bogie than ran on rails embedded into the groundwork around the edge of the tank and with access onto the bridge via stairs. The 10ft wide platform allowed crews to work in safety while suspended 5ft above the surface of the water. To create a counterbalance that prevented the bridge from tipping down into the tank when in use, the land end of the bridge with stairs was additionally weighted with a steel-framed riser towering 17ft above ground level. At the very end of the platform were to be a set of staging legs that would be swung down to stabilize the unweighted end of the bridge. When the bridge was required for use it would be moved into position, the platform swung out over the water, and when the opposite end of the platform had cleared the inner wall of the tank, the legs would be dropped to sit inside the weir, allowing for crew to walk up from the apron around the tank, onto the platform and carry out their work. When the bridge was not required it would be moved to the side of the tank where it would not interfere with the view out towards sea.

Problems begin to Surface

The building and completion of the tank were without issues when a series of problems became apparent that would have severe side effects for the production of *Raise the Titanic*. The first major setback came with the bridge when it was offloaded at Malta docks and brought into the Mediterranean Film Facility for assembly. With the parts of the bridge laid out on the ground the crews who fingered through the instruction documents realised that something was amiss with its design; the bridge was going to be too short. Following double-checking of the tank and bridge plans with the specification documents sent to the manufacturer, all appeared to be correct. However, the roughly assembled and laid-out bridge sections contradicted the specifications. With the main bridge platform bolted together according to the assembly instructions from the manufacturer, it was all too evident that the dimensions were all out. Then the penny dropped. It appeared that the Californian-based engineering company D.C. Mesner had failed to grasp the British metric system used in the design of the tank that was carried over to the plans, copied, and then sent on to Mesner's when the order for the bridge was placed. But they were not fully responsible for the mix-up as the plans sent over to the company were older versions of the tank before the structure, at ground level, was redesigned. The finished structure that arrived in Malta was of a bridge 20ft too short and unusable at this point. On the telephone to the contractor the studio explained the situation in Malta; "can you send us an extra 20ft please?" The response was not what they wanted to hear as "no" came the reply, "we have to build the whole thing again because it will change the dynamics and won't be strong enough." For the studio, the idea of the entire pivoting bridge having to be built again from scratch was not an option anymore as the production was already running behind schedule. Embarrassed and defeated, ITC had no choice but to dump the bridge on the studio backlot grounds turning the $200,000 structure into a pile of scrap metal that would gather dust and rust over the years to follow.

The troubles with Mesner's did not stop with the bridge. Down in the bottom of the tank, the huge turntable was proving to be difficult as the wheels to the track system were dragging over the inner raised lip of the track causing friction that affected the structure from being turned. The cast steel wheels supplied did not give enough clearance for the side plate inadvertently allowing the exposed head of the axel to grind over the raised lip of the track. With the problem identified, the Maltese engineering company Licari, produced a new set raising the wheel units giving a few millimetres of clearance that was enough for the turntable to be operated without issue. But this was not to be enough as the biggest problem was days away. With the turntable steelwork all assembled and the wheels no longer being a headache, it was time to start the assembly of the fiberglass base that would become the sea bed. The decagon shape of the turntable would be completely covered over once the sea bed was seated down. The fiberglass sea bed came in sections that could be bolted together forming one huge set-piece upon which the *Titanic* model would be rested upon. The sea bed was designed to represent the baron rocky landscape of the North Atlantic with areas of flat lifeless plains broken up with areas of raised outcrops, ledges, and cliff sides like natural steps. The outer edge of the set-piece followed the contour of the concrete floor of the tank with an 8" gap between the edge of the set and the floor of the tank allowing for the turntable to be turned around when needed.

The design of the turntable with its artificial sea bed meant that the inland side of the set, being open, meant that crew could pass between the legs and frames of the turntable, and enter the sea bed, from beneath the set, while a small section of the sea bed large enough for a person to pass through was cut into the fiberglass in the form of a trap door. Before the tank is filled with seawater the huge *Titanic* model would be craned down into the tank and seated upon the sea bed, while a mixture of sand, gravel, and Fuller's Earth was laid around to simulate the natural environment of an ocean floor. But before the tank could be filled, before any diver was allowed into the water, before the *Titanic* replica was submerged, safety tests had to be carried out. The stability of the set, the working conditions the divers and crews would be subjected to, all required testing. With lessons learned from the miscalculations of the pivoting bridge, the plans for the turntable and sea bed came under scrutiny; and not a moment too soon.

When Alex Weldon and John Richardson's model unit arrived in Malta in the autumn of 1979 to begin work on *Raise the Titanic*, it was following the departure of the American unit, who had completed filming the model in the surface tank for the opening 1912 sinking sequence. With the groundwork in progress as outbuildings and landscaping took shape the deep tank was now in the latter stages of completion for first series of filling and draining trials. It was important that the turntable was designed and assembled to withstand the huge amounts of pressure that the filled tank would create. Before the American unit departed Malta for home, they had worked out the look of the sea bed, putting the design to paper and sending the plans with dimensions off to California for the model makers at the CBS Studio Center to fabricate the huge set in sections that would be shipped out to Malta for final assembly inside the tank. The U.S units' idea for the turntable was to place cameras at certain locations where they could film the underwater sequences without having to spend more time hauling the cameras around. Angles can be achieved by rotating the sea bed while the *Titanic* model sat on the set. The film's art director, John DeCuir, had proposed the building of a filming tower with windows acting as viewports that could be submerged into the tank. A staircase within the tower would allow for camera crews to ascend at various levels and film out into the tank. The jury is still out on whether it was a good idea or not, as they could not have predicted at such an early stage of the production the lighting conditions in a tank filled with over 9 million gallons of water and being blacked out if they wanted to mimic the ocean floor at 12,500ft down. As they worked out the logistics of such a structure, they decided it was not feasible, and the tower idea was dropped.

It was during the assembly of the sea bed that, yet again, the miscalculations reared their ugly head once more. When Richardson's model unit started assembling the turntable at the bottom of the tank it became clear the earlier film crews were off with their calculations. The crew had designed the turntable, track, and sea bed to act as a single structure when bolted together. As fundamental as it was, they had not taken into account the stresses asserted onto the set when the tank was filled with water. Although the set was sitting 36ft down, the design of the tank with its sloping walls and colossal water storage capacity produced a great amount of pressure that pushed down onto the turntable rendering the structure immobile. To further add to the growing list of problems the original sea bed was found not to be substantial enough to cope with the weight of the *Titanic* model when the tank was drained of water. New calculations revealed that when the model sat upon the sea bed during the period the tank was filled a small amount of buoyancy kept the set from failing until the point the tank was drained. With the water pumped out and the ten-ton *Titanic* was left to sit on the structure, the combined weight of the model and the turntable could result in structural failure. Unable to move the turntable, even with the hydraulic machinery installed to operate it, the only way forwards was to make the most of what they had, keep the turntable as static, and add extra steel shoring to the existing design locking the turntable in one position and giving additional strength to the structure while a new fiberglass sea bed was constructed and seated over the top of the existing one. The addition of more supports under the turntable may have fixed one issue but as the tank was filled and the dive team entered the water all these new supports would become a problem when access was needed to the underside of the tank; as John Richardson would later find out during one particular scary dive into the abyss.

These monumental headaches were not looked upon favourably over in London as Lew Grade signed off cheque after cheque, courtesy of ITC and Marble Arch Productions. The press who had picked up the stories of the escalating problems over in Malta delighted in publishing the details of Grade's troublesome sea saga that had now pushed the budget up even more. By the middle of October 1979, Lew Grade had announced that *Raise the Titanic* was "my biggest production to date" as the costs spiralled to a staggering £20m and confessing the problems faced with such a mammoth movie of this scale had pushed the production way behind schedule, blaming the issues with the screenplay and ongoing hold-ups with the tank build. Bernard J. Kingham, production manager for ITC, was concerned over the alarming rise in the film's expenditure. Kingham perceived that Grade was slowly losing control of the company finances and oblivious to the outgoings which were being flagged up by executives and questioned by shareholders. Kingham's concerns were enough to warrant advising Grade to cut his losses once and for all and to stop throwing good money after bad. Whatever Grade's response was to Kingham's financial objections towards *Raise the Titanic*, it was far too late for the film company to shelve the production.

They Wanted a Tank, Not a Colander

These problems were nothing compared to the biggest glitch; leakage. The rather unique conical design of the deep tank with a concrete bottom, concrete ring at the top, and the concave skin in between made from tarmac, a bitumen viscous material that acted as the tank's internal water-retaining skin, gave way to construction workers struggling to maintain a seal between the top and the bottom of the tank. Wimpey Laboratories had already calculated the evaporation process when the tank was filled and left to stand during the ever-changing weather and seasons of Malta. They had taken into account the volume of loss through the summer months and the addition of rainwater into the tank during times of bad weather. But what they had no control over was the loss of water through structural imperfections brought about by the construction and settling of the tank. The issue was so severe that when the tank was filled and monitored a loss of 135,000 gallons of water over a 24-hour period was recorded to have exited through a combination of joints, seals, and building materials used. On 11 October 1979, now frustrated with what was happening in Malta with the tank, Production Supervisor Malcolm Christopher wrote to Bernard Kingham at the London offices of ITC strongly suggesting that Kingham engages in appointing a company of auditors to get to the bottom of the issues citing that "the time has now come to employ a company of competent engineers to take over. I feel that Gambina is guilty of professional incompetence and has to be stopped immediately." After weeks of debate, the situation was finally resolved when a team of engineers was sent to Malta from the UK to fix the problems by laying down a high-graded sealant coating that was used in the construction of airport runways.

These mounting complications with the build hampered the process of securing insurance for the facility if the quality of the construction and materials used did not meet the criteria of the appointed insurance company. Another factor of ITC appointing surveyors was that a claim had been put in for the loss of expenses as the delays with the tank were eating into the productions budget as Grade demanded an explanation as to why his *Titanic* project was experiencing unnecessary starts and stops at the expense of others. "And they told me it would be finished in January" quipped Grade. "The only mistake they made is they didn't tell me *which* January." At the end of November, ITC had sent surveyors from Bayly, Martin & Fay of London over to Malta to carry out their assessments of the deep tank. The compiled report handed to ITC on 7 December had uncovered dozens of problems with the build with seven major issues flagged up for immediate attention by the inspector. Large rocks that were exposed on the downstream face of the embankment gave them doubts over the compact nature of the earthworks as materials laid around them would have proved difficult to compress down, leading to voids appearing and compromising the stability of the embankment when the tank was filled and settled under the pressure of the water. It was of the inspectors' opinion that the vital seals between the sides of the tank to the concrete floor had been laid down by unskilled laborers and, to him, was "somewhat haphazard", bringing to question how the seals could work when the tank, once filled, had an estimated 1.2 tons per square feet of pressure applied to them. The seal between the weir and the sides of the tank indicated locations where water was seeping down into the foundation below. The pipeline to the pumphouse roused suspicion when it came to light the pipes had not been tested before being entombed in concrete.

During the inspection, it was discovered that the pipeline was leaking. More importantly, the outlet drainage pipes had also not undergone any testing before being landscaped over. The inspector concluded that if the drainage pipes had suffered any identical leakage it would lead to the embankment becoming unstable and "dangerous". The biggest problems were those that could not be seen. The tank floor and sump foundations on the provided documentation of the build were not clear to the inspector if sufficient drainage had been incorporated into the ground that would prevent the concrete base from moving during filling and draining as the pressure changed in the tank. It was hoped that the fissured rock was enough to dissipate these pressures and prevent any movement that would lead to cracks appearing in the concrete. The surveyors' report acknowledged that the issues raised were not substantial enough to cause instant catastrophic structural failure. But the issues were enough to warrant immediate action in rectifying the problems addressed which, if left, would lead to progressive failure to the overall structure as finer materials became washed away from the embankments.

On receipt of the letter from Bayly, Martin & Fay, ITC sent instructions to Malta for the immediate start on the repairs. John Gambina and his crew had very little time to complete them as the tank was to undergo its first main operational tests between the dates of 10 – 14 December. A troublesome incident occurred during the 12 December trial run when the Teddington mechanical equipment that was installed to carry out an emergency shutdown encountered difficulties when it automatically went into reverse, running at 2,000 r.p.m and overheating the unit. The solution was to install a heavy-duty clutch between the engine and the pump and being robust enough to withstand the shock load. Then to add to the growing list of problems, members of the film production unit discovered, at their displeasure, that the electrical shocks they kept experiencing were due to the steelwork in the tank not being properly earthed. As the electricians handed over a bill of £800 for their troubles, the surveyors on site continued to make notes as the tank was put through a series of tests that would form part of responding to the claims triggered by the complaints from ITC. In the meantime, Gambina was left to put right the issues during the festive season for the finalized tank trials that were to commence the second week of January 1980 which would determine if the facility was ready to be approved and handed over to the studio for filming.

Tank Trials

On 9 January the deep tank and facility underwent its official testing trials under the watchful eye of the engineering surveyor D. R. Harwood from the London-based Sun Alliance Insurance Group, tank architect John Gambina, the film production supervisor Malcolm Christopher and the managerial team of Pimlico Films Limited. The trials had been delayed for 24 hours when on the previous day testing one of the recirculation pipes had suffered cracking attributed to a bulldozer used for replacing fill material during the repairs. For the first time, the tank was to be filled in one sitting and not in stages carried out during earlier tests. At 0800 on the 9th of January the trials began. Although some teething problems were encountered, the test filling was successful from the engineering viewpoint with the four pumps running consistently for 9 hours at the manufacturer's recommended speed of 1500 r.p.m. with each pump delivering 4300 gallons per minute. The installed seepage filter was monitored to be collecting water at 1 gallon per minute when the tank was being filled to 30 gallons per minute when full. Harwood concluded that this amount of seepage was reasonable for a structure of this magnitude with the leakage points slowly becoming sealed over time as fine materials carried in the water passed through. A dye test uncovered leakage along the top embankment of the concrete weir with an estimated 6 to 10 gallons of water exiting over an hour from a faulty seal in the chamber. As the chamber filled with water it rose through the shaft to exit at the top of the weir floor to run down the embankment facing out towards the sea.

With the tank full the important water clarity tests could begin. During filling with the use of course filters the water clarity was found to be greater than expected despite previous trials where a fine filter used was severally clogged leading to the filter blowing out under the pressure; an issue easily rectifiable if pressure gauges were fitted into the system. Overall the water clarity did prove sufficient enough for divers and equipment to be used in the filled tank. It would be the addition and balancing of chlorination into the water that would determine a workable environment. Chlorination chemicals were imperative for the working conditions of the tank to eliminate bacteria and viruses within the seawater. In September 1979 the Directorate of Scientific Services of Thames Water authorities in London were flown to Malta to carry out a series of tests with collected samples of seawater retrieved over 1000 meters out at sea, in line with the currents to the entrance to the inlet pipes for the tank. The area was chosen because the sewage outlet that dumped sewage effluent of 75% of Malta's population out into the Mediterranean Sea was located 700 meters in direct line of the shoreline at the foot of the tank inlet. Six locations were picked where samples were taken, including the entrance of the Grand Harbour, where the bacteriological analysis could cover contamination ranging between that released from the sewage systems to surface run-off and trade discharge such as that from the harbour waters.

The test results submitted to ITC were positive with no traces of E.coli being detected given the areas where samples were obtained from. That was not to say traces may occur from time to time depending on how strong currents were in taking sewage out to sea. Thames Water included in their findings their proposed methods of including the correct levels of disinfectant into the tank either directly through a side pump supply or passed from a trough installed in the wier. Chlorine gas was also recommended for use in the tank, during filling, and during circulation, with its use as part of the disinfectant stages rendering the water germ-free. While the added chlorine to seawater had its advantages in germ reduction it also had the potential to cause harm due to its extremely volatile nature when being shipped, stored, and used. Adding the chlorine through a direct pump circulation into the intake system to the tank was Thames Water's suggestion for maintaining a carefully managed routine while access remaining chlorine would be quickly removed due to the action of direct sunlight allowing fish to be used in the tank water during periods of filming.

The January 1980 tank trials were deemed satisfactory, albeit not complete, as the inlet pipeline pumping system was still yet to be fitted out with the requested automatic non-return valves. But it was enough for the surveyors to sign off the tank for the production crews to begin the preparations to spend the next 12 weeks on-site filming in the tank for *Raise the Titanic*. On 15 January, D. R. Harwood filed off a 4-page report into the tank trials with a copy sent to ITC for their records. The report outlined the tests carried out during the 8 and 9 January to include a breakdown of positives and negatives, highlighting potential problems while rectifying others and giving ITC a simplified view of the workings of the facility. Harwood closed his report in addressing the claims made by ITC for the losses incurred by the problems over in Malta. Harwood concluded "As a result of the testing, I now consider that the likelihood of a claim arising from consequential losses incurred by the production company due to the lack of tank availability for this particular film is now no greater than the claims potential from other influences outside the scope of this report. The long-term effectiveness of the tank remains dependent upon the factors noted in the initial report."

Playing the Blame Game

With filming now underway the crew still experienced several teething problems with the tank and surrounding facilities. The night filming in the tank was tiresome as crews struggled with the lighting, or the lack of, as floodlights had not been installed around the grounds of the tank. If the film crews felt that they had been purposely left in the dark, the tank operators must have been extremely frustrated, as the pumphouse was still without any lights as of the end of January. The lack of lights in the pumphouse was unacceptable given that come dusk the gauges and machinery were submerged in darkness. The film's Production Manager, Ray Frift, wrote to the studio about the lighting issues at the tank and outbuildings. A meeting was set up between personnel of the Mediterranean Film Facility, the tanks architect, and Pimlico Films as an agreement was met for the MFF to cover the £3,621 costs for permanent lighting while ITC paid £2,000 for the loan of temporary floodlighting and a further £35 per week for the hire of a generator. The twelve-week filming schedule at the tank was planned to come to a close by mid-April in time for the production to go through its editing stages for early screenings before being approved for its world premiere date pencilled in for the last week of July followed by the 1st August general release. However, this could only be achieved successfully with the full cooperation and workings of the tank, facility, and production unit.

As the weeks passed the tank still proved to be as unforgiving as once again came the stories that the tank was still leaking and, now, showing new signs of problems with fresh fault points appearing in the structure that hampered filming to becoming an inconvenience when repairs and maintenance were required to be carried out. Correspondence between studio crews painted a picture of around-the-clock maintenance needed for the tank with little in the way of spare hands to work on other issues elsewhere in the facility. On 22 February John Gambina wrote to Malcolm Christopher to inform him that the contractor responsible for laying the concrete floor in the pumphouse had not finished the job. The contractor was penalized for not completing the screeding to the floor with Gambina stepping in offering to complete the job when his team had time to do so. As *Raise the Titanic* neared the last crucial stages of filming many must have been eagerly waiting for that final day to come when "that's a wrap" marked the end of production and crews packed up their belongings to head off to the next big film project. For some that coming April was to turn events around on a much more personal level.

As part of the construction agreement between the Mediterranean Film Facility and ITC, once production on *Raise the Titanic* had come to an end, the tank with adjacent buildings would be handed over to the MFF for continuation into the future. But not before maintenance work to the tank post-filming had been completed by ITC. In a letter to Ray Frift dated 23 April, John Gambina addressed some of the key points of repairs needed to be done in the tank before the handover from ITC. One concern raised was damage that had occurred to the membrane over the concrete joints at the turntable level with Gambina blaming the damage on the "explosives that were carried out in the bottom of the tank to break up the ocean bottom." The proceeding letter on the 26th from Gambina now included that the tank had been test-filled to the horizon line and during monitoring over 48 hours the wier had gone from losing 3 gallons per minute to 45 gallons per minute as a result of excessive seepage from the damaged floor membrane, allowing water to pass into the structure and through one of the internal chambers in the embankment, creating a discrepancy of 20 gallons per minute in which the materials of the embankment were soaking it up. The combination of the damage to the tank floor membrane and the high rate of water being passed into the embankment was enough to cause much concern as the tank's stability was now brought into question, along with a costly bill to rectify the problem. Gambina concluded that "the tank is not behaving satisfactorily and unless the damage is found and repaired, I cannot assume responsibility for the safety of the tank. In view of the above I am deeply concerned and would solicit you to give this very serious consideration." And to make matters worse, the *Raise the Titanic* unit was still on-site filming in the tank as delays pushed the production yet again past its scheduled completion date of mid-April.

The production office received another letter of complaint from Gambina on 30 April when he aired his grievance's over the way he is treated during repairs to the tank. These filming timeslots were not to his liking when on one occasion as he worked on sealing an area of the tank and was given one hour to complete it as the tank was required to be filled for the *Titanic* model to be dropped back no later than 3 pm. The model, he writes, was not put back in the tank until 5 pm. A 3" hole was then discovered in the weir which Gambina attributed to the careless handling of a wave machine. But with holes and cracks sealed up, Gambina turned once again to question the damage to the membrane from the use of explosives. Gambina wrote "I understand you have a film to finish. I cannot agree with the stand taken, every time I try to discuss the matter to arrive at some working arrangement. I am totally fed up with the situation, and I hope that this will make you act sensibly both in my regard and in regard to the tank." He continued, "Real explosives were never part of my brief in designing and constructing the tank. I am not an explosives expert." Gambina signed off that the issue should be passed over to a qualified expert for their conclusion. The letter was soon to catch the attention of Bernard Kingham at the main ITC offices in London. Whether Kingham decided to bring the problems to the attention of Lew Grade is unclear. But Kingham now had been handed more proof to show the board of executives that Grade was losing control of the company.

So, what were these explosives that Gambina spoke of? If his observations were to be believed then the fiberglass sea bed attached to the top of the turntable was forcibly broken down into easy-to-remove sections with the use of explosives. A somewhat excessive way to do things when cutting equipment would have been used for a controlled and safer environment for crews working in the tank. Was Gambina mistaken? After all, he does not acknowledge being present during the dismantling of the sea bed and only spoke up about the damage after the tank had been drained for him to walk upon the membrane while inspecting the tank floor. Gambina addressed his concerns over the damage to the membrane on 23 April citing that the cracks were done after the use of explosives in the tank while breaking up the sea bed set. Then three days later he brought up the subject again that prompted his 30 April rebuttal. But it would appear that his letter was in response to a request from the studio when Malcolm Christopher inquired about the use of explosives for a sequence in the film. Christopher's letter dated 29 April was asking to the maximum amount of explosives the FX unit could use during the filming of the scenes when the *Titanic*, during salvaging, has the sediment blown away from around her hull to free her from the bottom suction that will eventually lead to the wreck starting her journey to the surface. Christopher went on to say "Incidentally this is one of the sequences for which the tank was designed and built." It was evident that Gambina had got the wrong impression of the type of explosives to be used confusing that to the more commonly known destructive explosive devices to that of a film unit FX department replicating explosions with the use of none explosive materials. Gambina's suggestion that the studios turn to an explosive expert was enough to warrant a closer look at the architect's abilities considering previous and ongoing problems with the build and Christopher's October 1979 letter to Kingham questioning Gambina's competence.

With Gambina shifting the blame towards the FX unit for their filming techniques, the accusations of the unit causing damage to the tank did not sit well with FX supervisor John Richardson. On receipt of receiving copies of the letters, Richardson wrote to Christopher, copying Kingham into the response, to defend the unit and explain exactly what these explosives were and making it clear that he had twenty years of experience handling and using explosives in the film industry. These qualifications outweighed those of the tanks architect who had not even been present on-site when the FX materials were used. Richardson outlined the procedure of what was used and how it was installed and controlled in the tank.

"The charges were, in fact, very small amounts of Aquaflex, a type of Cardtex which is, in fact, detonating fuse. This was spread out in thin lines across the ocean floor and was fired in four separate lots. There was 6 to 10ft. air space between the charge and the floor of the tank and in no place was it in contact with the tank. The structure supporting the sea bed to the tank floor was not rigid enough in any place to transmit any great shock to the tank and the only place the sea bed was damaged or cut was within 1 to 2 inches either side of the charge. It was, therefore, a very local effect which was its sole intention and I can quite categorically state that in no way could it have damaged the structure. It would not even have been strong enough to increase any structural faults which may already exist in the tank."

Clearing the FX unit of any wrongdoing, Richardson had not finished with pointing out potential causes to the damage sustained to the tank's important membrane.

"The pressure from the water on the base of the tank when filled to the top must be a thousand or more times greater than any charge we have used. In fact, as we have already discussed, the dynamiting of the rock in the Pump House area carried out by Mr. Gambina AFTER the main structure was completed would potentially have a far, far greater effect on the tank than our small charges could ever have. This is obvious from the newly freshly fissured rock around the Pump House area. I would also point out to Mr. Gambina that the tank was built for the purpose of making films and not for use as a decorative fishpond. It should, therefore, have been built to withstand the use for which it was originally intended."

It was becoming clear that Gambina was looking for excuses to cover up possibly bad or incorrect civil engineering design and workmanship which could in the course of time become evident in the tank and Pump House installation.

On the 7 May Gambina apologized for his previous letters citing that the content was only "intended to give a down-to-earth representation of facts. I sincerely hope that this will in no way jeopardize our relationship." If he had felt that the letter would mend wounds between himself, his company, and that of ITC, then it was to be short-lived. On 21 May he wrote to Bernard Kingham and the film's Executive in Charge of Production; Richard O'Connor, listing the damages and works required in the tank. Again, Gambina brought up the issues of the cracks in the tank floor expressing they were not the result of the tank's normal loading stresses "for which the tank was designed and built." This time he avoided pointing the finger of blame, removing his company from the spotlight, but emphasizing that the damages could not be repaired under normal maintenance. What complicated matters were restrictions being enforced by ITC as the company tightened the hold on the productions budget. ITC wanted the workforce at the tank reduced leaving Gambina to scale his crew down to just four personnel. The ongoing works in maintaining the tank during its first year operational were something that could not be achieved with just four workers given the scope of the structure. All involved with the production were fully aware that time was of the essence and any studio committing to such a huge project, and a costly one at that, could not afford to push the production beyond schedule as the accumulating fees would eat into returns from the films initial release. Another issue that went against the repairs was the times being allotted to carry them out while all the time working around the production unit who had to stick to their own time schedules for filming in the tank. And there lay the dilemma. Each time that a repair needed to be carried out to the membrane or surrounding floor or tank sides the tank had to be completely drained of water and then left to dry. This was workable on dry sunny days but completely useless on days of rain. Then the areas under repair that had been exposed were again left to dry before repair materials could be used and left to set properly before the tank was filled once again.

It was understandable as to why Gambina had got to the point of being fed up with the project; wanting to be paid for the work he carried out and move on to new build projects elsewhere. But as the architect and engineer of the tank and ancillary facilities, he was obligated to see it through to the very end regardless of the number of obstacles he had to hurdle in the process. The design stages, building, and workings of the deep tank were a monumental feat of engineering. The time frame and mounting pressures to get it completed for filming were always going to be against all involved. The Mediterranean Film Facility had to continue to work as a fully functional film studio so had to make allowances that there would be occasions that the building of the new tank would have some effect on the established facility. Lew Grade wanted his tank finished and put in use; the film units wanted the tank to produce a multi-million-pound sea adventure, and Gambina and his company wanted to complete and be paid for the work carried out. There were always going to be clashes and plenty of disagreements between all involved, and the building of the tank and facilities proved that, despite all the odds, something amazing can come of it; even if it went on to cost Lew Grade a whopping £3.5 million, three times its original estimate, to complete.

Beyond *Raise the Titanic*

When production on *Raise the Titanic* finished on the 19 May 1980 it also marked the moment when ITC could fulfil their obligations under the terms of the contract signed in September 1978 and hand the deep tank over to the Mediterranean Film Facility for them to continue, contractually, with providing the many studios around the world the opportunity to film in the world's largest water facility. Over the years, the deep tank has undergone many facelifts to keep the huge structure up to date, fully operational, and available to meet the demands of modern studios and their equipment. Since 1980 the MFF has been used for many classic films from the mythological beasts in *Clash of the Titans* through to music videos, commercials, and television game shows. But it has not all been smooth sailing for the studio over the decades, with some periods of financial gloom as the company overheads increased becoming almost unsustainable during the 1990s.

The opening of a theme park adjacent to the studio grounds in 1998 became a weight around the studio's neck that almost bankrupted the facility. The theme park was to be a combination of amusements for all the family woven around several film productions realized in Malta. Of those films *Raise the Titanic* was to have its place with plans earmarked to preserve the model to some degree for displaying. As the park haemorrhaged money, the investors backed out and the park closed its doors for the final time in 2000. The escalating financial problems at the studio through the 90s cast doubts over the continuing support of the facility through privatization and bringing to light the controversial news that the studio's owner, the German entrepreneur Jost Merten, had not paid any of the ground rent for some years under his ownership leading to disputes between him, the studio, and the Maltese government. As profits dwindled, Merten even resorted to proposing a plan of action of turning the two tanks into a fish farm to recuperate some of the losses.

Merten remained in position until 2014, when, through the courts, he was ordered to vacate the land. Since then the studio has been owned by the Maltese government and continues to run under the government until a more permanent investment plan falls into place. Today the facility thrives under the name of the Malta Film Studios with both the surface and deep tanks offering uninterrupted filming experience courtesy of these unique horizon tanks. And with the government continuing to lead the studio into a new decade the facility is going from strength to strength with the studio and grounds undergoing much-needed renovation and construction works making the facility more accessible to meet today's demands in film production. The forty years that have passed since the tank was first used have proven that the Malta Film Studio has become the go-to studio for all major aquatic filming amenities; regardless of scale and production.

* * *

Filmed in Malta

The following list consists of selected productions completed at the Mediterranean Film Facility/Malta Film Studio from the first film in 1964 right up to the current times and the release of the survival thriller *Jetski*.

The Bedford Incident (1965)
The Trouble Shooters (1965)
Casino Royale (1967)
A Twist of Sand (1968)
Vendetta for a Saint (1969)
Mosquito Squadron (1969)
Battle of Britain (1969)
David Copperfield (1969)
Hell Boats (1970)
Adventures of Gerrard (1970)
Mister Jerico (1970)
Eyewitness (1970)
When Eight Bells Toll (1971)
Murphy's War (1971)
Zeppelin (1971)
The Protectors (1972)
Pulp (1972)
Young Winston (1972)
The Golden Voyage of Sinbad (1973)
The Mackintosh Man (1973)
The Investigator (1973)
L'invenzione di Morel (1974)
Shout at the Devil (1976)
Sinbad and the Eye of the Tiger (1977)
The Black Pearl (1977)
Orca: The Killer Whale (1977)
Midnight Express (1978)
Warlords of Atlantis (1978)
Force Ten from Navarone (1978)
North Sea Hijack (1979)
The Martian Chronicles (1980)

Raise the Titanic (1980)
Popeye (1980)
Clash of the Titans (1981)
The Last Shark (1981)
Samraat (1982)
Erik the Viking (1989)
Leviathan (1989)
Der Skipper (1990)
Les 1001Nuits (1991)
Burning Shore (1991)
Christopher Columbus: The Discovery (1992)
Cutthroat Island (1995)
White Squall (1996)
U-571 (2000)
The Emperor's New Clothes (2001)
Asterix & Obelix: Mission Cleopatra (2002)
Pinocchio (2002)
Troy (2004)
Open Water 2: Adrift (2006)
Ein Fliehendes Pferd (2007)
Sommer (2008)
Largo Winch (2008)
U-900 (2008)
Vicky the Viking (2009)
Vicky and the Treasure of the Gods (2011)
Kon-Tiki (2012)
Captain Phillips (2013)
Fort Ross (2014)
Thugs of Hindostan (2018)
Das Boot: TV series (2018–)
Jetski (2020)

The Malta Film Studios in 2017 with the facilities world-famous water tanks. *(Author's collection)*

The studio under its earlier name of the Mediterranean Film Facility. This image shows the surface tank during filming of the 1976 Roger Moore WWI film *Shout at the Devil*. What is of importance with this picture is that the studio is shown with the surrounding landscaping intact in the period before ITC came forward and secured the land adjacent to the surface tank for ground work to begin on the deep tank facility. *(Malta Today, October 1979 – Author's collection)*

The Bedford Incident from 1965. *(IMDb)*

Inside the surface tank during the set construction for the 1980 Paramount Pictures version of *Popeye* starring Robin Williams and Shelley Duvall. *(Author's collection)*

Pimlico Films Limited company letter header from 1979. *(Author's collection)*

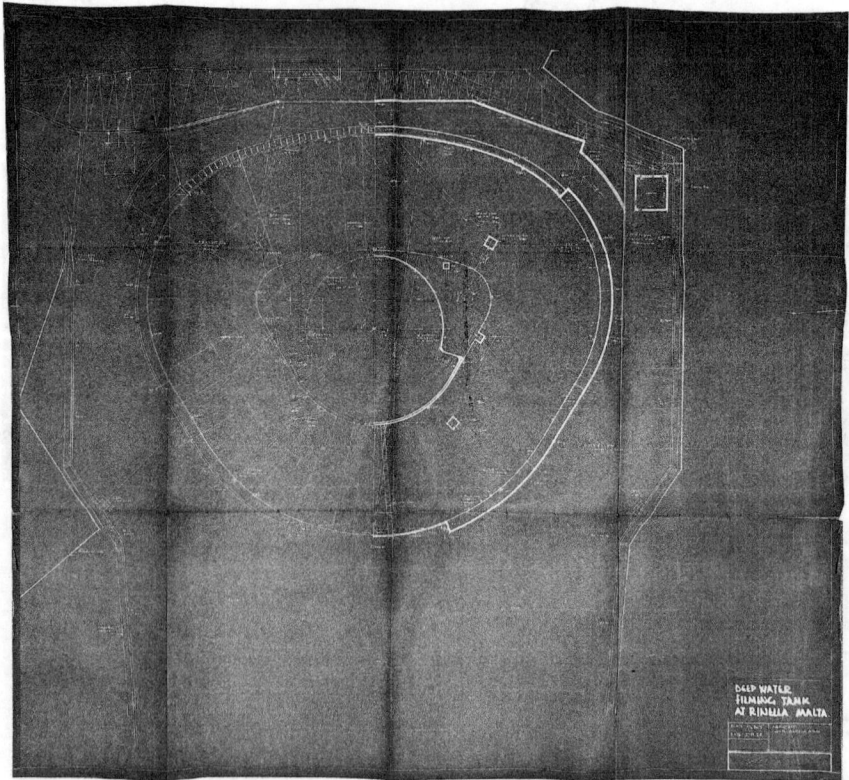
The original blueprint of the deep tank drafted by architect John M. Gambina. *(Author's collection)*

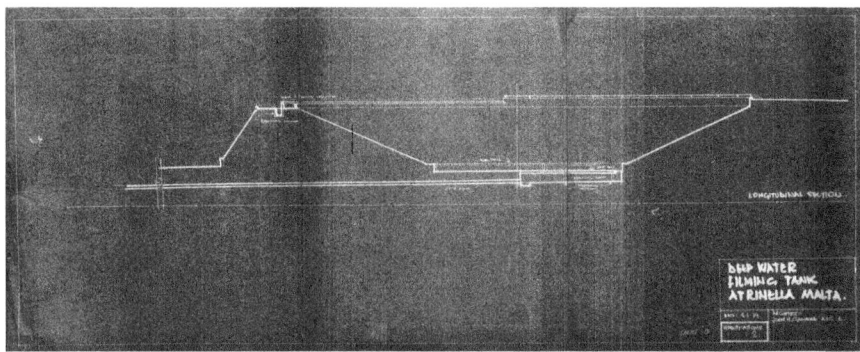

Early draft of a longitudinal cutaway of the deep tank from January 1979. The raised wall to the right at ground level forms part of the retaining wall at the inland end of the tank where crews would operate from, such as entering the tank, the camera equipment pool and the grounds around that area of the tank where workshops and offices would be built. *(Author's collection)*

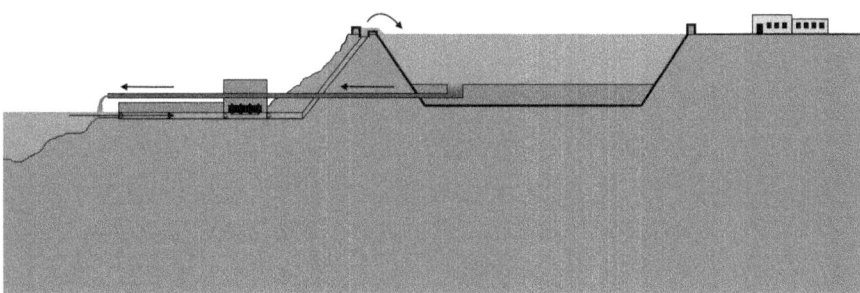

This illustration demonstrates the basic principle of how the tank would operate. Sea water would enter into the pumping station where it would be filtered and treated before being pumped up to the surface of the tanks spillway where it would flow over the top of the inner spillway wall and down into the tank. When it came to emptying the tank, the release valves were opened up for the water in the tank to pass down through a sump and out through a series of pipes to be discharged back out to sea. *(Illustration © Jonathan Smith)*

Panoramic #1: In the first of a series of images created using a number of photographs taken on site and stitched together. It is the autumn of 1978 and the groundwork is underway as heavy plant machinery begin the long and laborious job of moving tons of earth, rocks and sand into place on the levelled area of the former fields to create a series of raised embankments which would form the foundation for the world's largest water tank. *(Author's collection)*

Panoramic #2: The footings for the tank sides begin to take shape. *(Author's collection)*

Globigerina limestone being added to the coarse foundations of the side walls to the tank sometime in December 1978. *(Joe Sciberras collection)*

Chapter 8: Mediterranean Film Facility • 253

Panoramic #3: It is the new year of 1979 and the D8 heavy plant tractor units are at work compacting down the limestone over the coarse foundations to the tank's inner walls. This view would be looking towards the south west of the island with the waters of the Mediterranean Sea to the right. *(Author's collections)*

Panoramic #4: With the tank taking shape, other areas of the new facility are now in progress. To the right of the photograph can be seen the pump house in early stages of construction. *(Author's collection)*

The main inlet channel to the pump house is pictured here in January 1979 after crews have blasted out sections of the rock. As the build of the pump house progresses, the channel will be lined and coarse filters fitted at intervals. *(ITC/Author's collection)*

Panoramic #5: This photo was taken from the direction of Triq Santu Rokku (St Rocco Street) and looking west across Fort St Rocco with its surface tank and Marine studio, over towards Fort Rikazoli with Valleta, Malta docks and the St. Elmo West Breakwater. *(Author's collection)*

This photograph shows the partially removed section of the north wall of the tank as the four main 2ft diameter outlet pipes for draining the tank are being assembled ahead of the installation of the concrete sump. *(Author's collection)*

Looking down into the pump room of the pump house. At this stage of the build the upper section of the walls that will hold the roof have not yet been completed making the assembly of the pumping units much easier for the engineering crews. *(Joe Sciberras collection)*

Chapter 8: Mediterranean Film Facility • 255

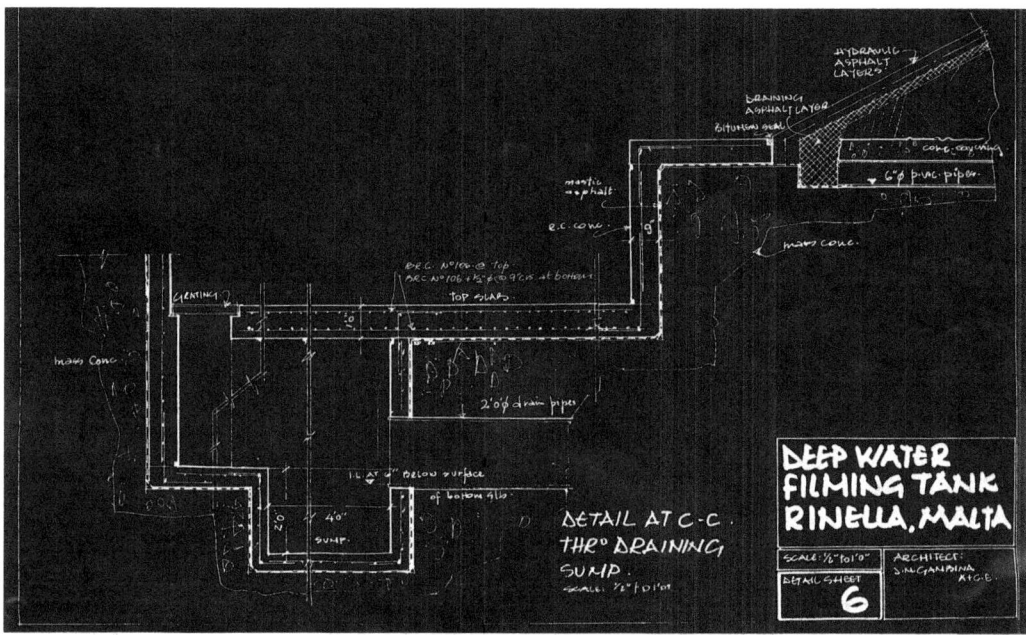

Gambina's blueprint of the concrete drainage sump with one of four of the 2ft diameter outlet pipes. *(Author's collection)*

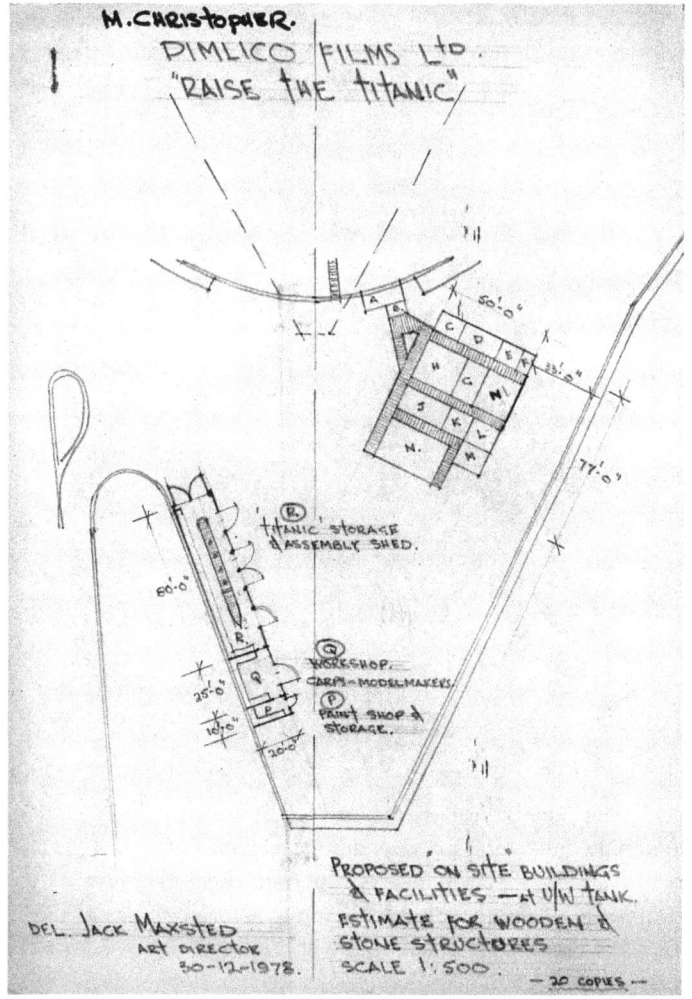

This plan from December 1978 shows the general layout of the original proposed deep tank facility. The deep tank is positioned top centre with the main office building alongside it. What is interesting with this plan is that it also shows additional buildings for model makers, paint shop and, more importantly, a designated storage building for the 55ft *Titanic*. *(Author's collection)*

The final layers of the limestone are compacted down to make way for the heavy coarse layer of draining asphalt. *(Author's collection)*

With the finer crushed limestone now added, crews with portable rollers can be seen at work smoothing out the walls of the tank while (foreground) the first of the layers of drainage asphalt is being laid down. Around the inland parameter of the tank, the groundwork is underway in levelling out the landscape for the building of the concrete retaining wall that will encircle half of the tanks top. Behind can be seen the new office building taking shape that will house offices, toilets, restroom, conference room and storage areas. *(Author's collection)*

Chapter 8: Mediterranean Film Facility • 257

This June 1979 view is looking north over the tank towards the Mediterranean Sea. To the left is one of the large asphalt machines at work while behind it a cement mixer truck is pumping concrete down through pipes to construction crews working on the floor of the tank. The photograph also shows the spillway being built. There is one revealing little detail in this image that the reader may overlook if not prompted. In the distance, just left of the propane gas tank is the corner edge of the surface tank with two large icebergs just visible. With work progressing on the deep tank during daylight hours, come the night, over in the surface tank, the U.S. film crews were hard at work with the *Titanic* model filming scenes of the ships tragic demise during the night of April 15, 1912. *(Author's collection)*

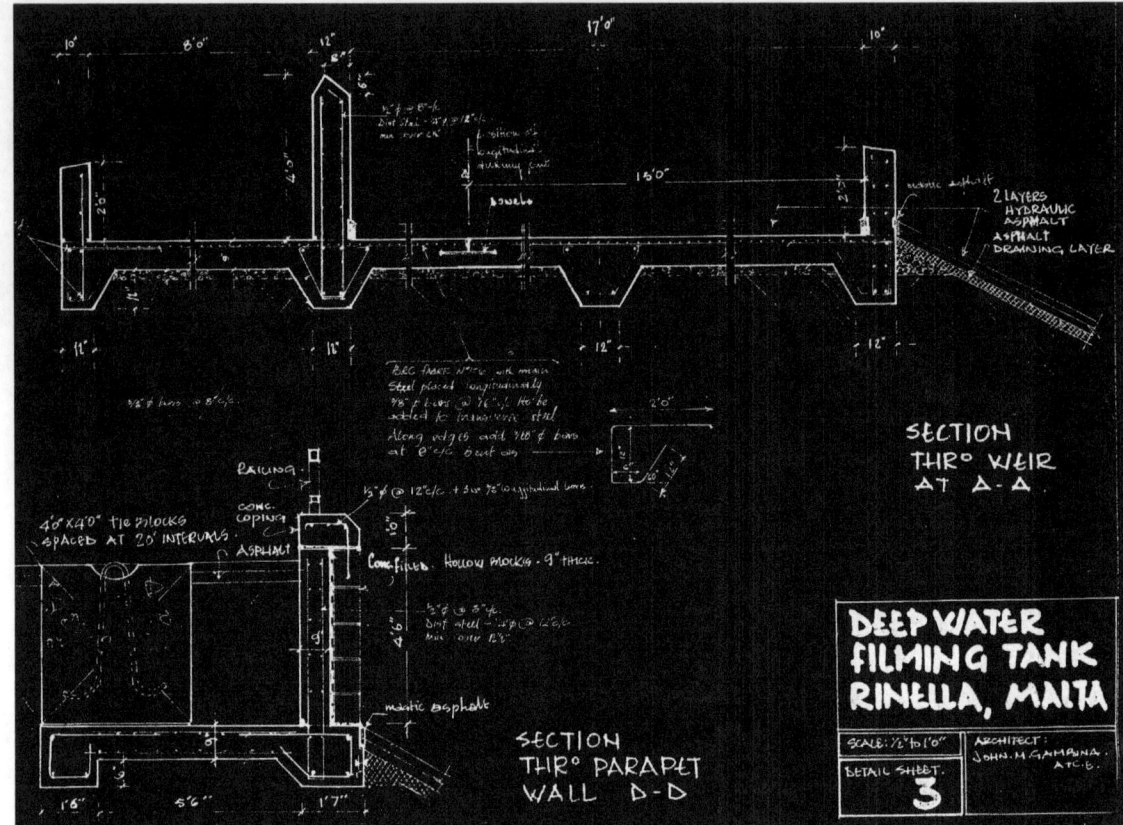

Cross-sectional blueprint of the spillway that was built on the north facing side of the tank. The parapet wall was designed with three purposes in mind; the inner tank wall to retain the water when the tank was full and to allow pumped up water to spill over the top, the middle wall to act as the main retaining wall and stop water from the spillway channel from flowing backwards towards the sea. The outer wall formed part of the top of the embankment that also acted in a channel for access water to be passed through should the main retaining wall develop a leak. *(Author's collection)*

The entrance to the chamber and sump with the grates waiting to be put in place. *(Author's collection)*

Chapter 8: Mediterranean Film Facility • 259

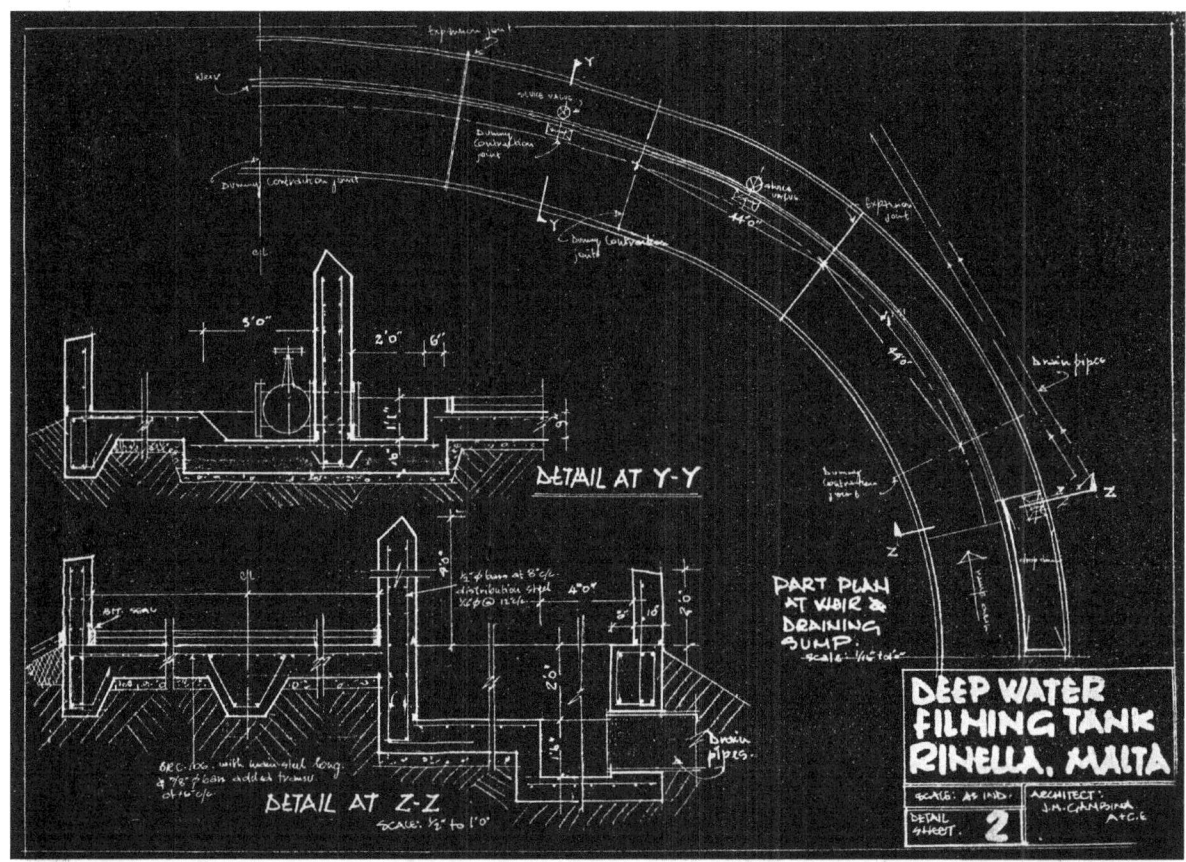

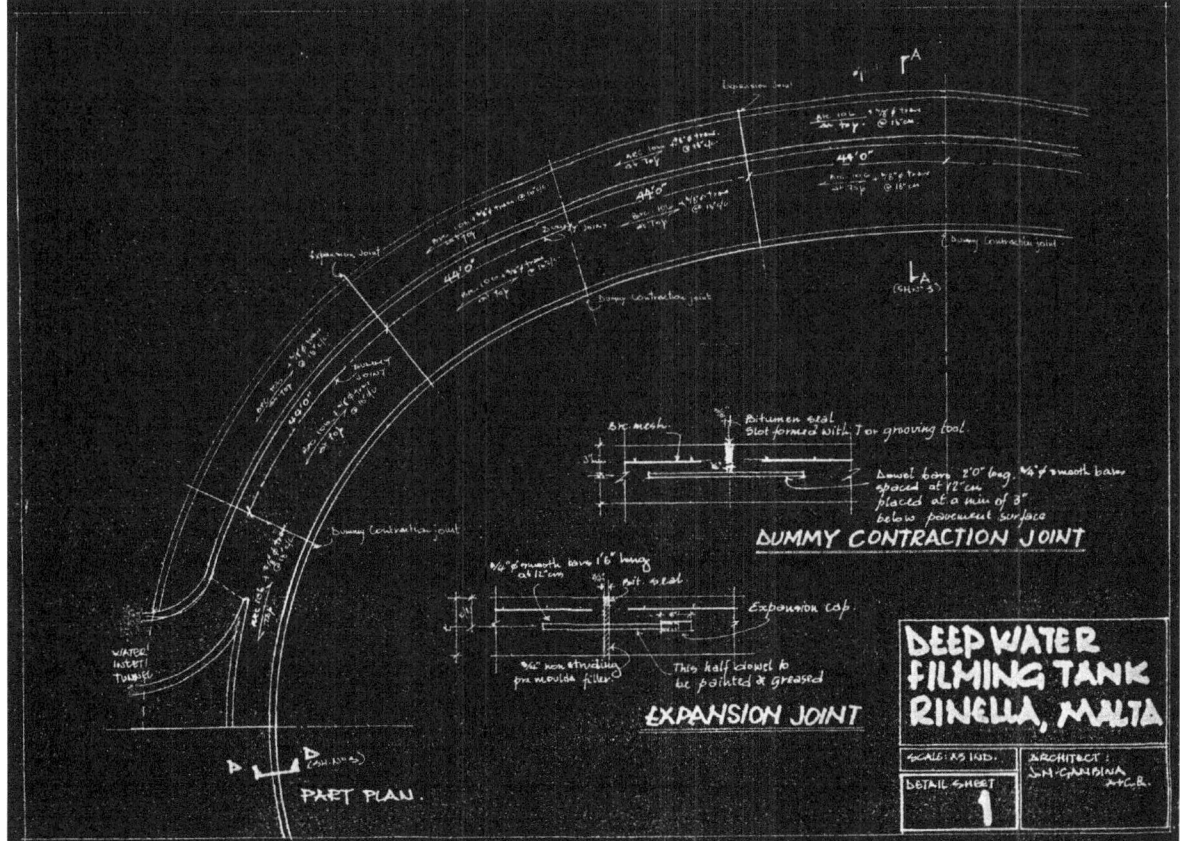

Blueprints of the spillway and locations of the expansion joints in the concrete structure. *(Author's collection)*

Another June 1979 photograph showing the progress of the office building and the skinning of the deep tank. *(Author's collection)*

This segment is taken from a series of photographs glued together to form a panoramic view across the tank. It shows a rare glimpse into the construction of the concrete base of the tank prior to the final skin being applied to the walls. The lowest section of the floor is the water chamber that is connected to the sump with drainage pipes (just visible, centre). To the left, construction workers are laying down the reinforced flooring to the tank. Once this is done a number of vertical support columns will be put in place in the chamber where a large slab-like lid will be lowered down over the open chamber to form a ceiling to the chamber but also a floor to the tank base. Located to the right of the chamber, running alongside the curvature of the floor where the worker is seen with the roller, will be an entrance/exit point to the chamber that when complete will be finished off with a set of galvanized grates. *(Author's collection)*

Close-up of the sump and the four lots of 2ft diameter drainage pipes. *(Author's collection)*

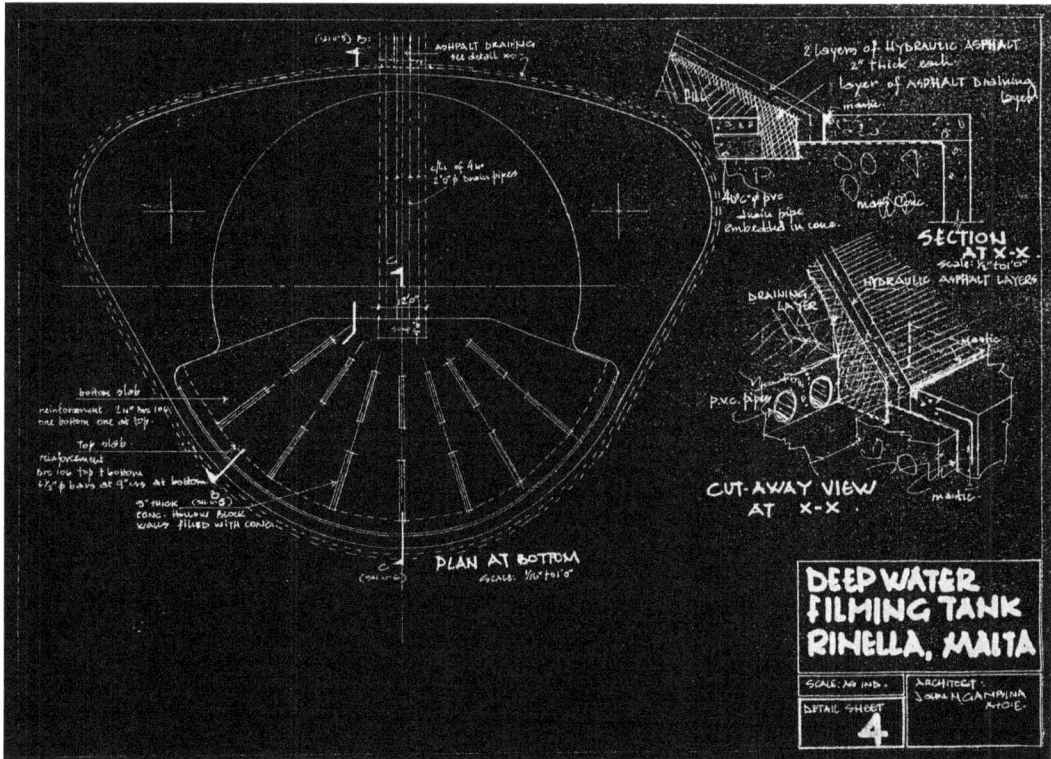
Architect John Gambina's plan of the layout of the tank and floor that demonstrates the materials used for the walls and the location of the drainage pipes for the sump. *(Author's collection)*

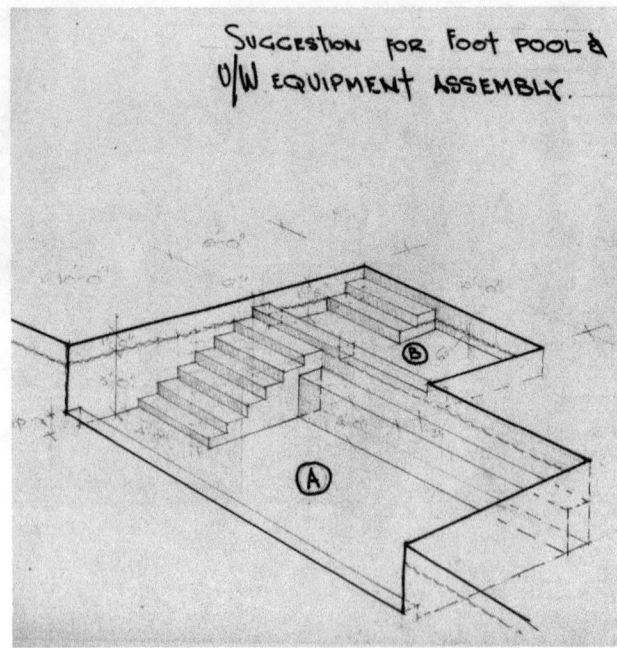

Original plan for the equipment assembly pool that was put into the tank at ground level and just metres away from the main office building. The pool would serve as one of the entrances into the deep tank for filming crews as well as an area where equipment to be used in the tank would be checked and assembled. *(Author's collection)*

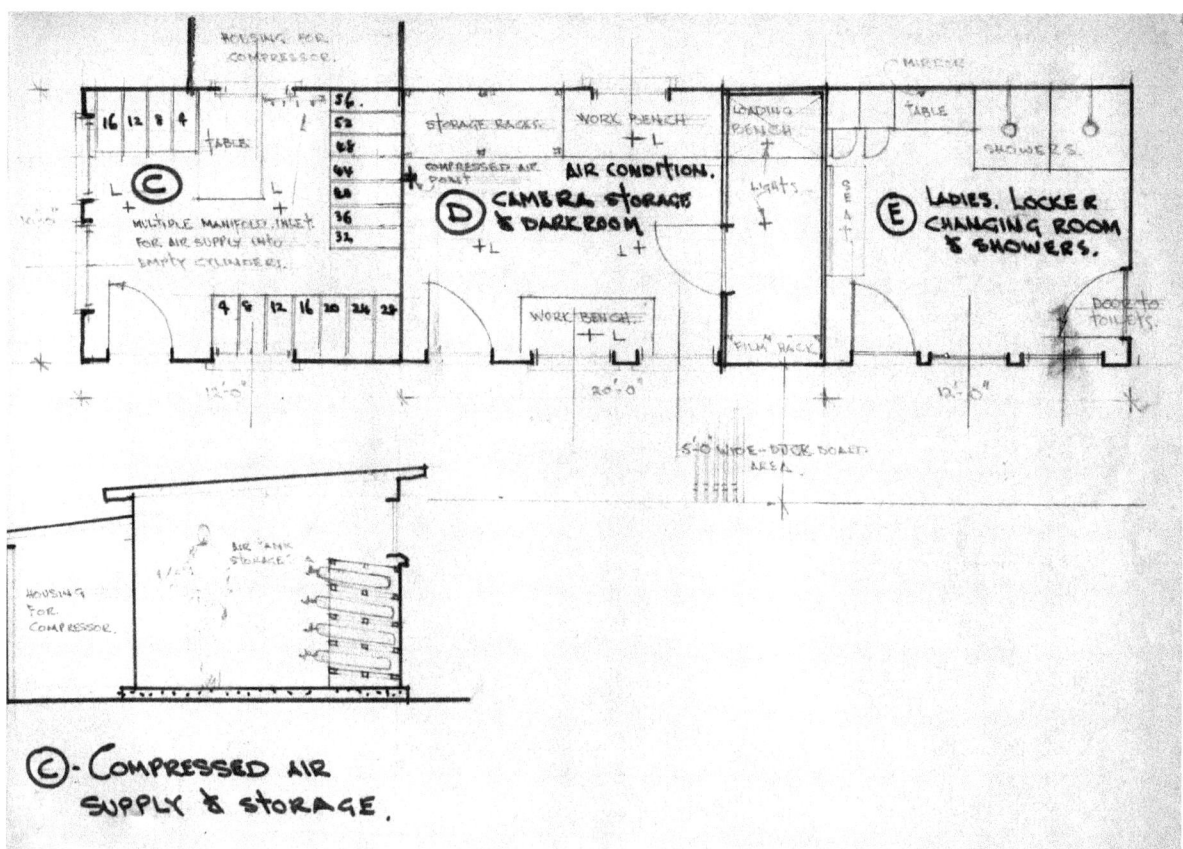

Early floor plan of a section to the main office building. *(Author's collection)*

Panoramic #6: It is August 1979 and the tank has received its two layers of hydraulic asphalt. With the composite in place it acted as a skin in the same way hydraulic asphalt is used on the core embankments of dams. The proof of its success now lay with the first filling of the tank which was still several weeks away as the pump house was not yet up and running. Around the concourse to the tank work is still largely underway in levelling off the grounds. Over in the surface tank the set for the feature film *Clash of the Titans* is being used for filming the sequence on the arrival of the mighty Kraken. *(Author's collection)*

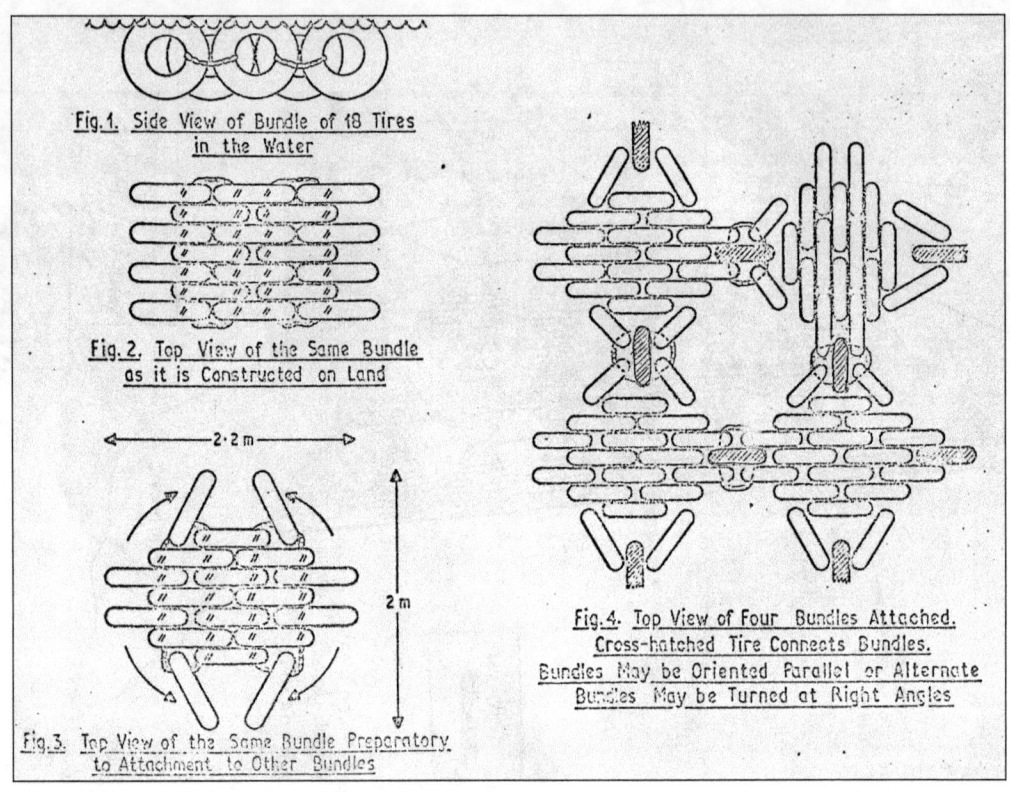
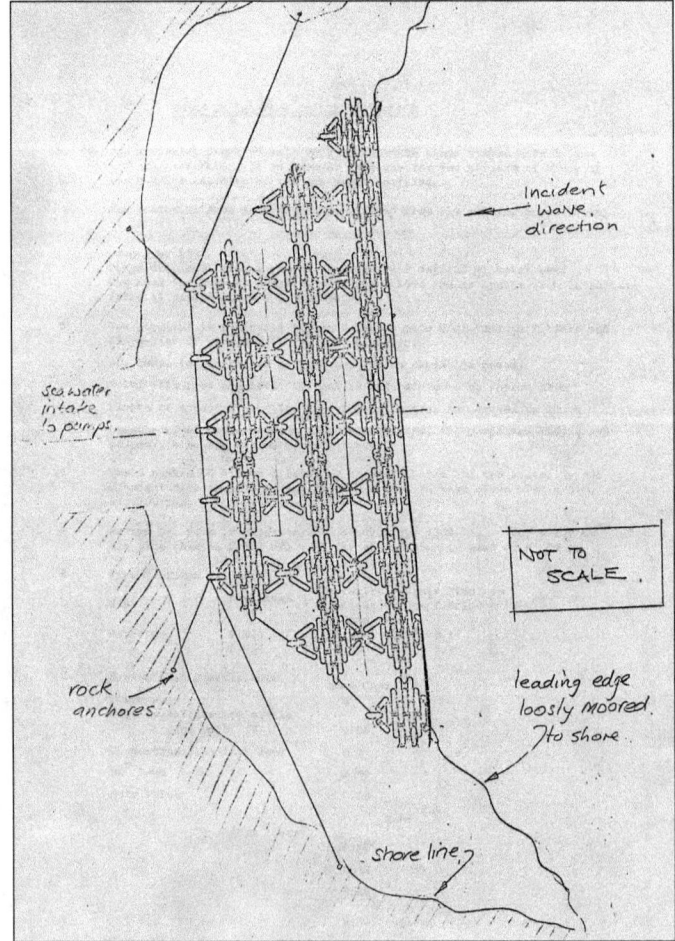

The proposal for the tyre breakwater. *(Author's collection)*

Chapter 8: Mediterranean Film Facility • 265

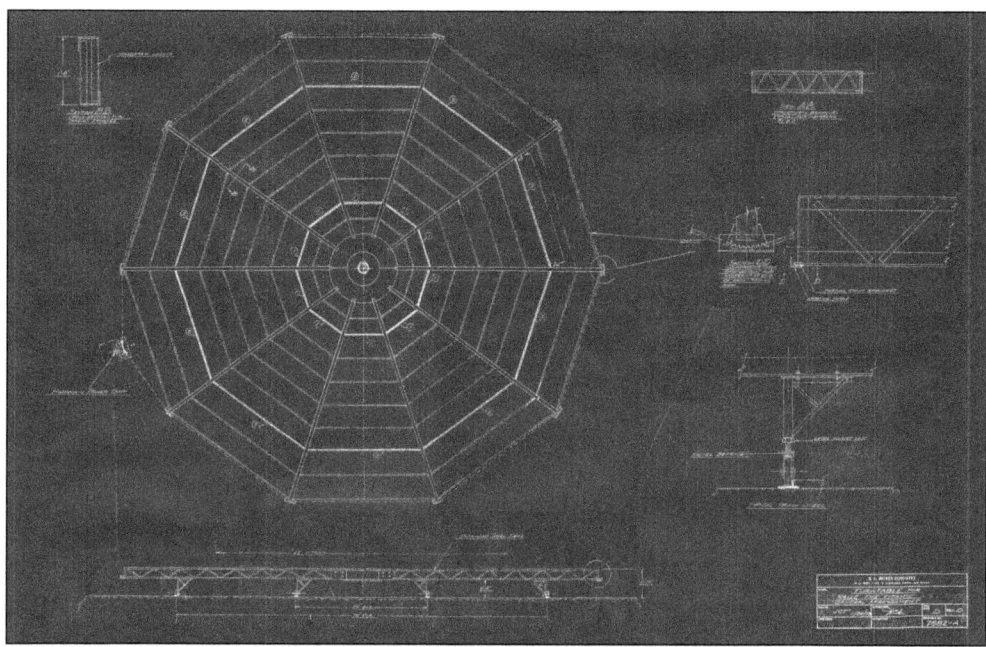

Original general arrangement blueprint of the enormous turntable designed and built by D.C. Mesner Associates of California, approved on the 20 November, 1978. *(Author's collection)*

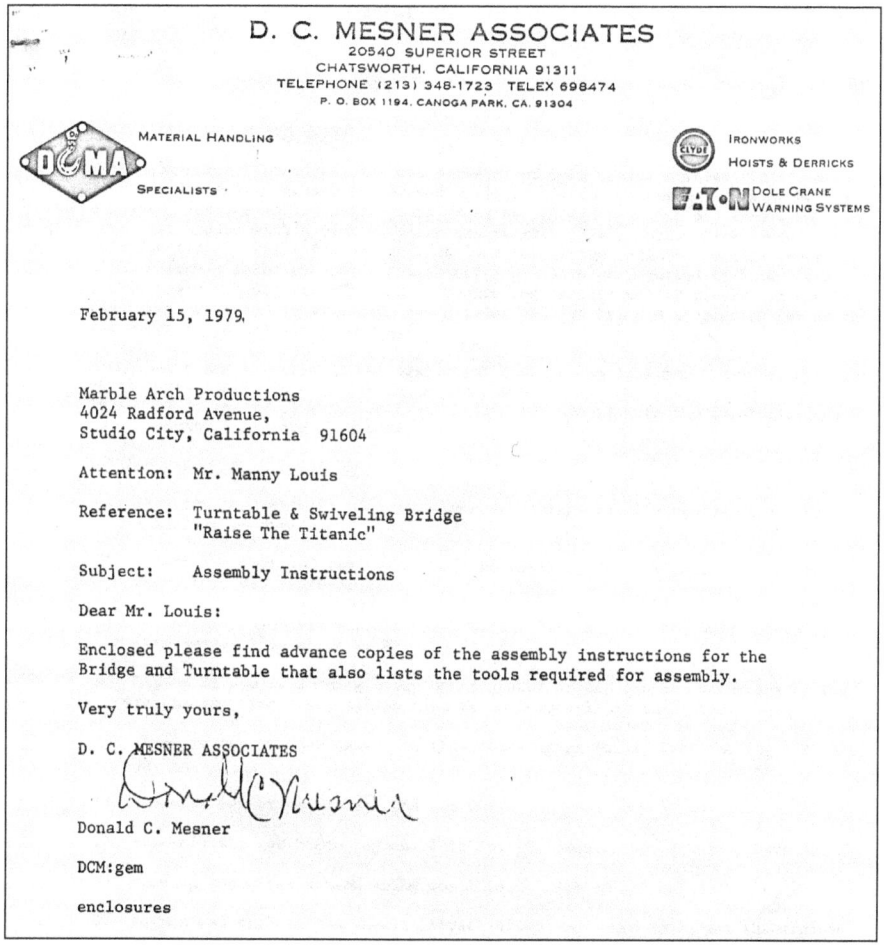

Correspondence sent to Marble Arch Productions for the assembly guide to the turntable and tank bridge, February 1979. *(Author's collection)*

A single section of the turntable sitting on the ground next to the deep tank. *(Author's collection)*

One of the turntable sections awaits to be lifted down into the tank. *(Author's collection)*

This photograph shows the complexity of the turntable during assembly at the bottom of the deep tank. Just visible on the concrete floor of the tank is the single track that the turntable on its wheels would follow allowing the steel structure to be cranked clockwise and anti-clockwise. *(Author's collection)*

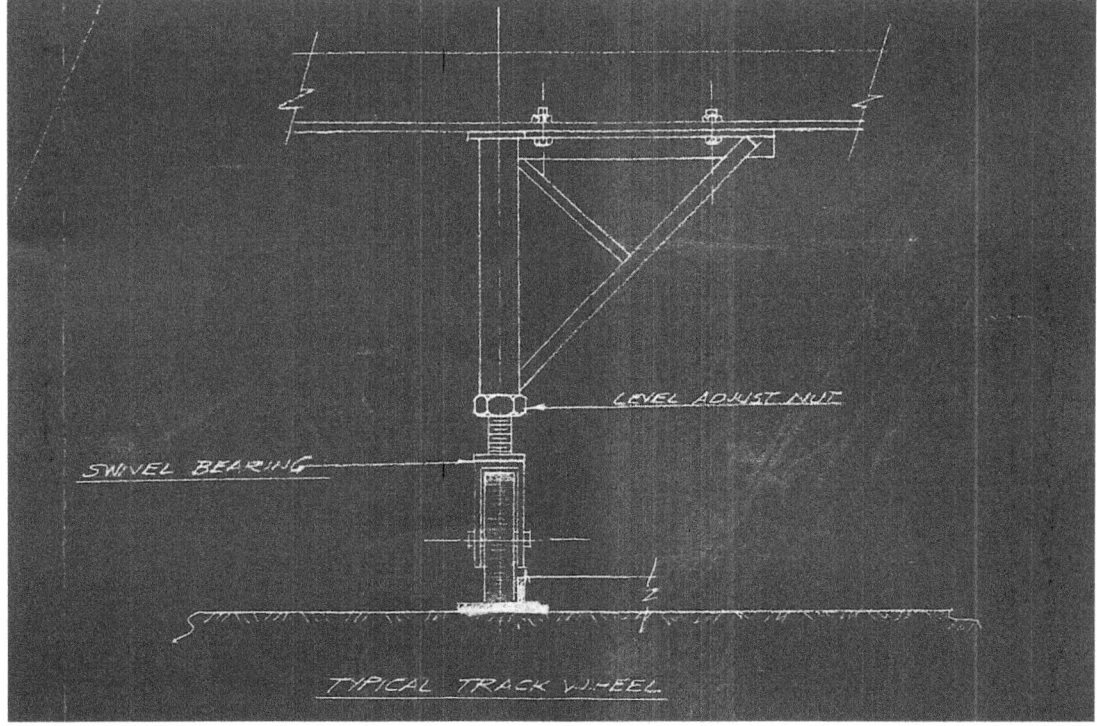
One of the track wheels on the turntable. *(Author's collection)*

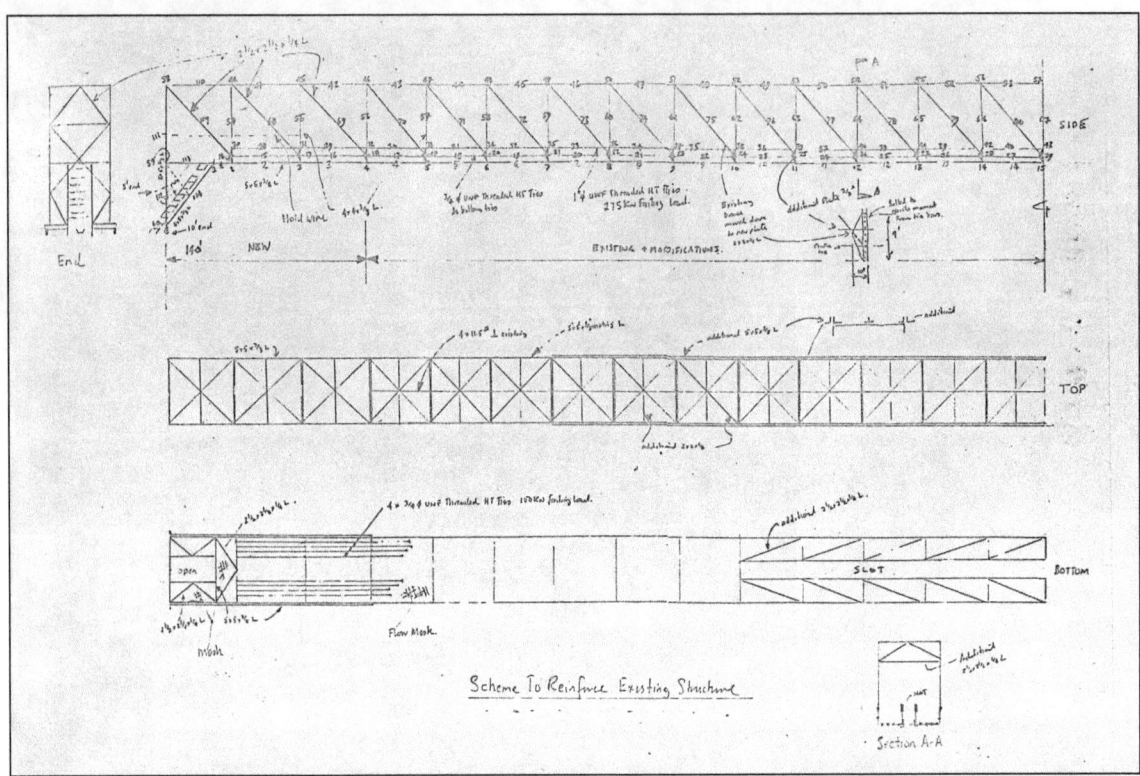

The D.C. Mesner schematic of the tank bridge that was constructed over in California. *(Author's collection)*

Surveyors photographs of the problematic turntable wheels with the securing pin that dragged on the rim of the track. *(Author's collection)*

Chapter 8: Mediterranean Film Facility • 269

The replacement turntable wheels under assembly and pressure testing at Licari Engineering in Malta. *(Author's collection)*

The fibreglass sea bed is assembled and secured down to the steel turntable. At this point of the construction the crews putting the sea bed together had no idea of the problem that lay ahead due to the miscalculations on the weight of the assembled structure, the *Titanic* model once sat upon it and the pressures at that depth once the tank was filled to capacity. *(Author's collection)*

This photograph taken while repairs to the tank were under way shows the turntable being rebuilt as a solid structure to the tank floor. The track for the wheels has been removed along with the mounting point for the turntable. From the chamber beneath the tank floor, a number of threaded bolts have been inserted that will be used to hold the vertical supports to the fixed turntable. As the turntable is assembled and strengthened, a second steel tier is being added giving additional height to the structure and a new foundation for the sea bed that is being fixed down into place. While the new structure was to prove successful in maintaining the tremendous pressure applied to it during filming, it would also prove to be a nightmare for one of the special effects crew during filming. *(Author's collection)*

Despite the increasing costs on *Raise the Titanic,* Lew Grade was still confident in his product as the very subject of *Titanic* sells. *(Author's collection)*

Bernard J. Kingham, production manager for ITC, was not so positive about the production. The alarming rise in costs was enough for him to start questioning Grade's position in the company. *(ITC – Author's collection)*

```
WIMPEY LABORATORIES LIMITED                    BEACONSFIELD ROAD,
                                               HAYES, MIDDLESEX


              REPORT  OF  TESTS


Description: Hydraulic asphalt design for      File Ref.: GRL/JMH/394
             the underwater filming tank
             project at Rinella, Malta.

Tested for:  Wimpey Asphalt Limited


Lab. Ref. No.: ASP/12/79

Date Received: 16.3.79            Date Reported:   25.5.79


1.   INTRODUCTION

     Testing of asphaltic materials has been carried out jointly with Wimpey
     Asphalt Limited, in connection with the design of hydraulic asphalt for
     lining an underwater filming tank at Rinella, Malta. The object was to
     design a mix that would perform satisfactorily in laboratory tests that
     have become accepted as being reliable indicators of the performance
     under site conditions of asphaltic materials used in revetments in
     hydraulic engineering.

     The tests that have been carried out are listed in Table 1.

2.   BITUMEN

     The bitumen used in the mixtures was 70 pen straight run supplied by
     Shell UK Oil and obtained from Wimpey Laboratories stock. The properties
     of the bitumen are given in Table 2.

3.   AGGREGATE MATERIALS

     The properties of the aggregate materials are given in Table 3. Tests
     were made in accordance with British Standard 812, where applicable.
     Details of the coating with bitumen and resistance to stripping test
     are given in Appendix A.

4.   AGGREGATE GRADING USED IN MIXTURE

     The aggregate grading and proportions of constituents used in the
     mixture are given in Table 4.

5.   MARSHALL TESTS

     The Marshall test specimens were compacted with 10 blows of the
     standard hammer to each face.

     The test results are given in Tables 5 and 6, and Figure 1. At the mean
     binder content of 8.5 percent for peak density and peak stability, the
     voids in total mix are 1.5 percent. It is normally accepted that between
     2 and 3 percent voids in total mix are desirable, depending on the mix.
     The corresponding binder content for 2 percent voids in total mix with
     the aggregate grading chosen is 8.2 percent.
```

Before the materials to line and seal the tank could be approved for shipping to Malta, the mixtures had to be thoroughly tested and passed. In the 17-page report by Wimpey Laboratories of Middlesex, England, dated 25 May 1979, the tests carried out had been determined "satisfactorily" leading to approval for the materials to be dispatched. *(Author's collection)*

This rare photograph was taken during the early testing of the deep tank before the tank was made ready to be inspected and signed off for handing over to ITC. What is not so apparent is that the photograph shows how much the water in the tank has dropped over a certain set time due to the issues with leaks. *(Author's collection)*

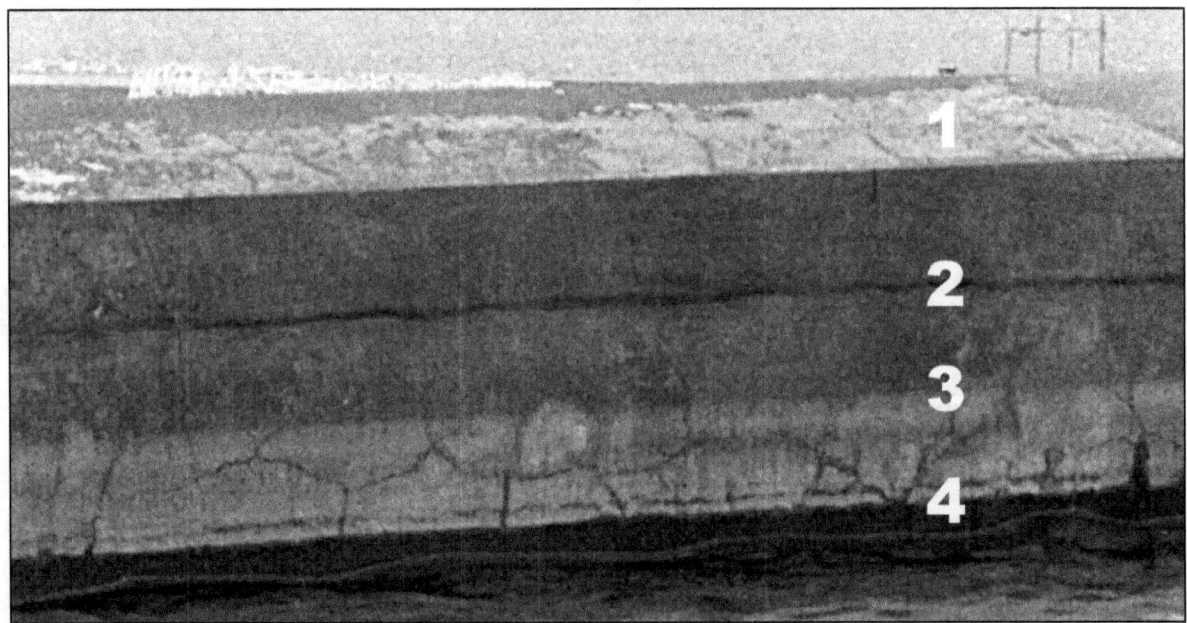

Close up of the inner wall of the tank at the spillway end showing the defined lines left in the concrete from the water levels during the early tests. (1) The top of the concrete centre retaining wall with the inner tank wall just below in a darker shade. When the tank was being filled, the pumped in water would spill over the lip of the inner tank wall and not flow backwards to flow over the taller centre retaining wall. (2) Water deposit line that has left a stain in the concreate of the inner wall when the tank had been filled to near capacity. (3) As water seeps from the tank due to leaks in the spillway it has left another deposit line in the concrete. (4) The water level has slowed down after reaching the top of the tank wall that has been sealed between the asphalt skin and the concrete of the spillway. *(Author's collection)*

Chapter 8: Mediterranean Film Facility • 273

This photograph taken in 1988 during the filming of the sci-fi horror movie *Leviathan* shows the layout of the weir and spillway. *(Photograph © Mike Seares)*

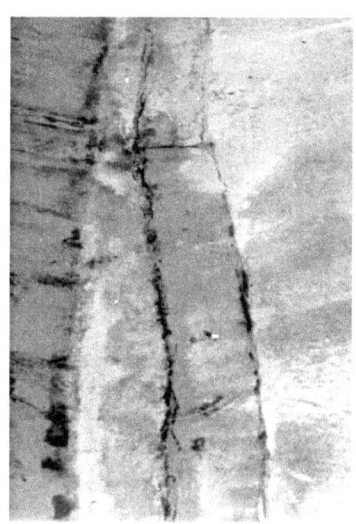

Report on the problems occurring in the tank materials and design sent to Lew Grade's company on the 7 December 1979. Stress cracks at the junction of the concrete tank floor (right) and the footings of the asphalt sides going up the tank initially caused some concerns. *(Author's collection)*

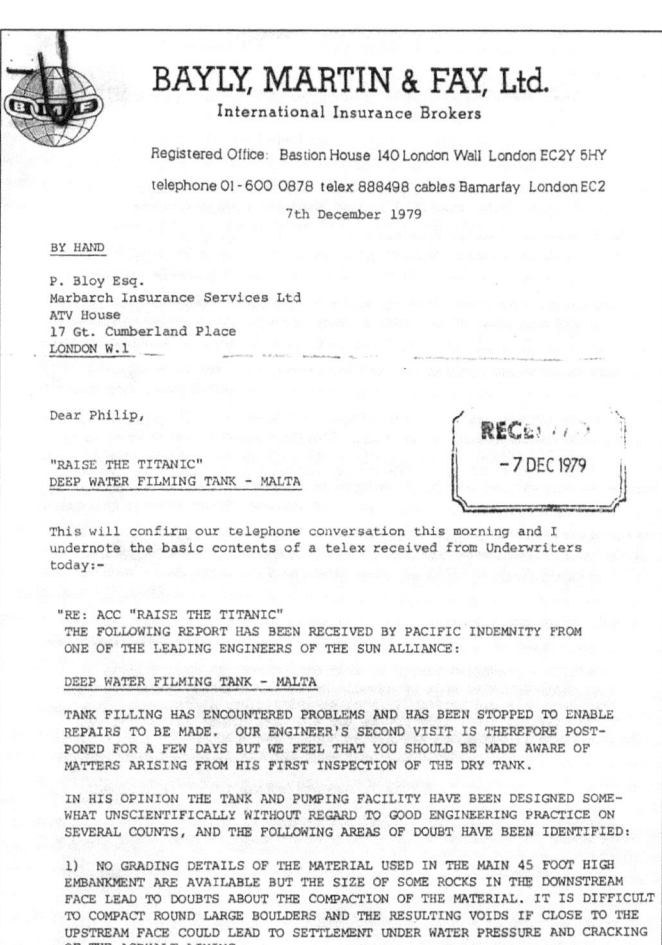

Panoramic #7: It is December 1979 and the tank is now ready for the first series of test trials that will be carried out in front of inspectors. *(Author's collection)*

The official 11 page report carried out by Thames Water in September 1979 on the findings of scientific surveys and tests carried out with samples from key points of the Mediterranean Sea off the coast of Valetta, and to determine the necessary requirements to treat the pumped in sea water as it is passed through the pump house facility and into the tank. *(Author's collection)*

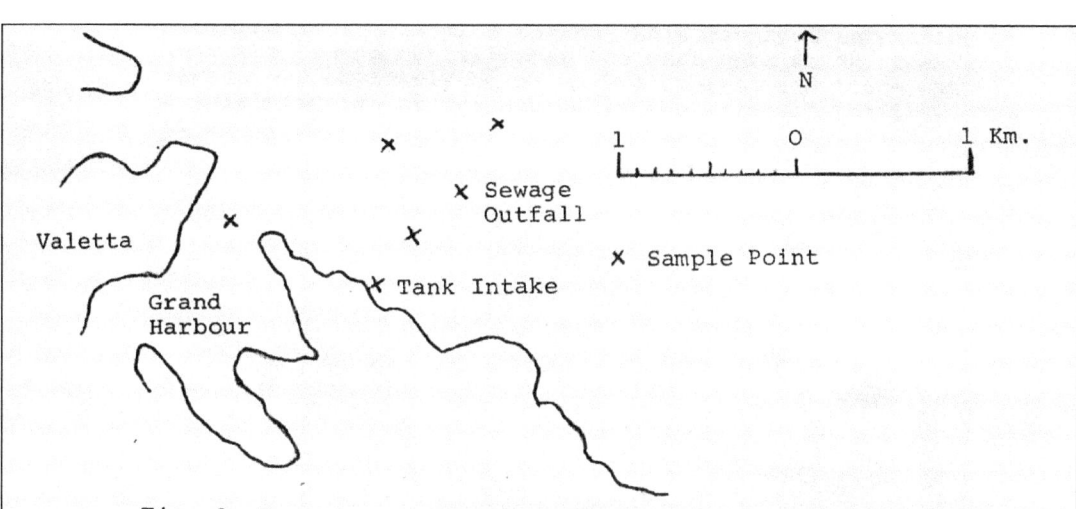

Diagram from the Thames Water report indicating locations of water samples collected. *(Author's collection)*

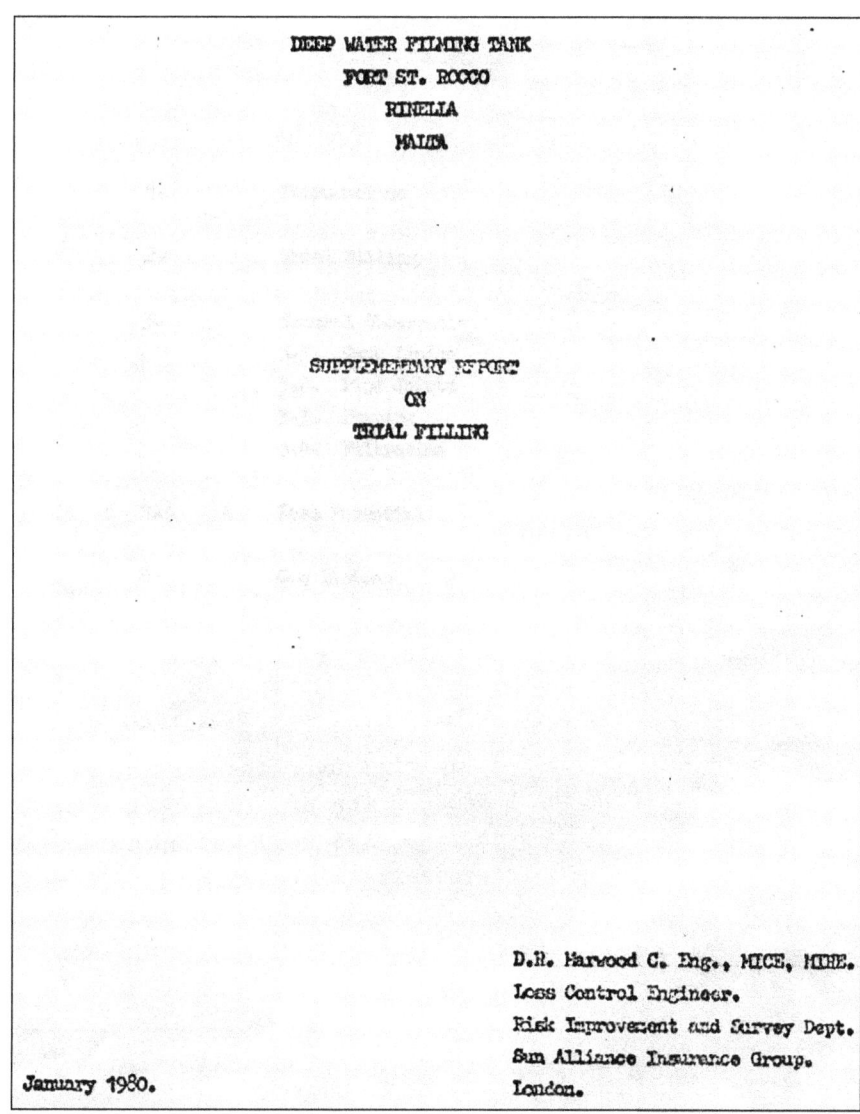

The report by D.R. Harwood that was delivered to ITC and dated January 1980. The tank has passed and filming can now proceed. *(Author's collection)*

```
TO      RAY FRIFT,    c.c. MALCOLM CHRISTOPHER

FROM    JOHN GAMBINA

DATE    23th APRIL 1980.

RE: TANK MAINTENANCE.
```

Just a short note to reconfirm the points discussed during our visits to the tank to-day.

A The laying of the seal coat in the wier is about 75% complete. This work could not be finished as water was let into the wier yesterday afternoon while the maintancance gang was trying to finish the job.

B A certain amount of damage has been done to the membrane cover over the concrete joints at the turn-table level, while set construction works were going on in this area over the past few days. Damaged areas which were in the dry have been resealed. The other damaged areas are very wet and a proper resealing job would necessitate cleaning off all the water in these areas.

cont/2

Letter sent to production manager Ray Frift from Gambina on the 23 April 1980, reporting on the damages within the tank. *(Author's collection)*

PAGE 2.

RE: TANK MAINTENANCE.

This job would require at least one day's solid work. Since this time could not be granted we can only wait and see what effect these damaged areas will have on the tank once it is refilled.

C   The same applies in relation to the explosions that were carried out in the bottom of the tank in order to break up the ocean bottom, viz. a close inspection of the concrete for any haircracks arising from these explosions would necessitate proper cleaning of the bottom from all water and sand. This again is a lengthy job for which time could not be granted and one will therefore have to see if there are any changes in the behaviour of the tank once it is refilled.

signature

JOHN M. GAMBINA A & C.E.

TO   MALCOLM CHRISTOPHER   c.c. RAY FRIFT.
FROM   JOHN GAMBINA.
DATE   30th APRIL 1980.

RE: TANK PERFORMANCE.

Please refer to my memos of the 23rd. April and the 26th April 1980.

Subsequent to my memo of the 26th April the water in the tank was lowered to the top asphalt/concrete joint on two occasions, viz Saturday 26th. at 1600 hrs. to Monday 28th. at 0700 (this gave us one day to work in) and Tuesday 29th. at 1100 to Tuesday 29th. at 1200 hrs. (this gave us one hour to work in). It is worth nothing that in the latter occasion the reason given for wanting the water back in the tank at 1200, on the dot, was that the Titanic had to be lowered back in the water not later than 1500 hrs. This was in fact lowered into the water at 1700 hrs.

From the first occasion the following results were acheived.

Cont/2.

John Gambina's letter to the films production manager bringing into dispute the continuing issues he and his workers were facing in trying to resolve the repairs to the tank. (*Author's collection*)

Page 3.

RE: TANK PERFORMANCE.

Whilst I understand that you have a film to finish I cannot agree with the stand taken, every time I try to discuss the matter in order to arrive at some working arrangement, that you are completely disinterested in the fate of the tank. Please note that you are doing me no favours by allowing me to safeguard your interests. I am only doing this as a duty to a client, for whom I have great respect. Otherwise I am totally fed up with the situation, and I hope that this memo will make you act sensibly both in my regard and in regard to the tank, which you have built at substantial cost.

Finally a short note with regard to your memo of the 29th. April (which was only handed to me this morning). In the light of what has been said above in respect of my memo of the 26th. April, it is obvious that I cannot even entreat the contents of your memo at this stage. However I beg to comment as follows:-

a. Real explosions inside the tank were never part of my brief in designing and constructing the tank.

b. I am not an explosives expert and this memo should therefore be proposed to a <u>qualified</u> expert in this field. If you require any names, I would be more than glad, to forward them to you.

Yours faithfully,

[signature]
JOHN M. GAMBINA A. & C.E.

c.c. Mr. Bernie Kingham.
encl. memos dated 23rd April, 26th April, 29th April 1980.

TO   MALCOLM CHRISTOPHER c.c. RAY FRIFT.

FROM   JOHN GAMBINA.

DATE   26th APRIL 1980.

RE: TANK PERFORMANCE.

Please refer to my memo of the 23rd. instant.
After monitoring the tank for over 48 hours, subsequent
to refilling to the horizon line, the following things
have been noticed.

1 The amount of water coming out from the drainage
culvert, at the toe of the asphalt, has increased from
3 g.pm. to 45 g.pm. This is the result of (a) flow
coming from the top asphalt/concrete joint and (b) added
flow coming from the damaged seals at the bottom of the
tank.

2 Seepage has been discovered in three areas along the
foot of the earth embankment on the air compressor side
of the tank. Since these seepages appeared for the first
time immediately upon refilling the tank to the horizon
line and since the tank had been filled to this level on
other occasions for longer periods and no such seepages
had been experienced, it is safe to assume that damage
has been caused to the tank by the explosions mentioned
in my previous memo.

STUDIO CENTER • 4024 RADFORD • STUDIO CITY, CALIFORNIA 91604 • (213) 763-8411

Gambina's letter from the 26 April 1980 to the production manager expressing his concerns over the amount of water loss being generated by leaks within the tank. *(Author's collection)*

Page 2

RE: TANK PERFORMANCE.

3 There is a discrepancy of about 20 g.pm. between the loss from the tank and the addition of the various drainage flows including the loss from the junction manhole and other quantifiable flows. Since all leakages from the A/C pipes had been successfully repaired, it is quite propable that this discrepancy is being soaked up in the embankment material, with only part of it appearing in the new seepage areas.

After considering these points my suggestions are as follows.

(a) The tank is not behaving satisfactorily and unless the damage is found and repaired I cannot assume responsability for the safety of the tank.

(b) In order not to upset the filming works, at the moment, the water should be drained to the top asphalt /concrete joint and the wier drained as well immediately, in a first attempt at discovering and repairing the damaged areas. If this is not successful, one would then have to consider draining completely and looking for the damage elsewhere.

In view of the above I am deeply concerned and would solicit you to give this memo very serious consideration

JOHN M. GAMBINA A. & C.E.

EUROPEAN AGENTS FOR:-
MARBLE ARCH PRODUC[...]

Please reply to:-
PIMLICO FILMS LTD.
c/o M.F.F., Fort St. Rocco, Kalkara, Malta.
Tel: Malta 622289 & 622880
Telex: MW 212 FFACIL

TO: JOHN GAMBINA

FROM: MALCOLM CHRISTOPHER

DATE: 29th April 1980

We are planning to shoot an underwater explosion in the deep water tank. Would you please let us know the maximum amount of explosions we can use. Incidentally this is one of the sequences for which the tank was designed and built. Your very urgent reply is required in this matter.

MALCOLM CHRISTOPHER
Production Supervisor.

Malcolm Christopher's letter to Gambina from the 29 April 1980 inquiring about the use of explosive devices in the tank for one of the films important underwater scenes. With the problems mounting up over leaks and stress fractures in the material of the tank, the bigger question was if Gambina was incompetent to the point it had put the design of the tank in jeopardy. *(Author's collection)*

Chapter 8: Mediterranean Film Facility • 283

The partially filled deep tank in 1988. *(Photograph © Mike Seares)*

The impressive deep water tank and its adjacent film facilities during filming in March 1980. It is not until you see aerial photographs such as this where all is revealed to how much land there is between the tank and the rocky coastline of the sea. But through the simple techniques with low angle cameras facing out over the water of the tank, towards the weir and its spillway, the backdrop of the Mediterranean Sea would become perfectly blended together. Note the empty surface tank at the top right of the photograph. *(Author's collection)*

Chapter 8: Mediterranean Film Facility • **285**

June 1979 aerial view looking over at the water tanks of the Mediterranean Film Facility. facility. When this photo was taken the deep tank was still undergoing skinning of the walls with the coarse concrete and the first of the layers of asphalt. Here are some key areas of the studio and surrounding land. (1) The great 100-ton Armstrong gun of Fort Rinella that was added by the British artillery in the 19th century. (2) The surface tank that was built in 1964. (3) This area is part of the coast line to the sea that includes the outlet discharge pipes for the deep tank. (4) The deep tank and its main building which are still under construction. The building, once complete, would contain offices, toilets, showers, camera rooms, divers' facilities such as changing rooms and equipment storage, film screening room and eating area. The tanks weir is still largely under construction. From here the pumped in sea water from the pump house would exit up through pipes and into the weir to then spill over the top and down into the tank. The weir also acted as the focal point for camera shots taken from low angles from the point of the main building and out across the water and the horizon point of the Mediterranean Sea. (5) The historic ruins of Fort St. Rocco which, today, also contains the remains of the now decaying movie park. (6) The entrance/exit for the construction crews working on the deep tank that prevented any heavy pant machinery from having to pass through the studios main entrance. *(Original photograph taken from Malta Today, October 1979 – Author's collection)*

CHAPTER 9

Casting the Characters

"What a lovely thing she was. Standing as high in the water as one of your skyscrapers. Longer than two rugby fields. And furnishings to match the finest mansions in England. She was one of a kind. No question about it. And God himself they said couldn't sink her. Then in two hours, she was gone… and fifteen-hundred souls with her."

John Bigalow

While fans had a good idea of how *Titanic* would appear on screen, there were those eager to see which of Hollywood's big stars would portray the book's heroes and villains. In the early days of pre-production, many actors were approached for varying roles in the film and this not only included those who did go on to get the starring roles but also those considered for them and whatever reason during the time of production had to turn the roles down. Some may find it hard to comprehend that any other actor of the time could have played Dirk Pitt other than Richard Jordan. But Jordan was never the first choice to play the leading role. Scouting for actors for the film first started in October 1976. In those early days, Lew Grade reached out to those he had previous or current business relations with. Of those, he first contacted *Death Wish* actor Charles Bronson. It was during a dinner venue at Bronson's home in October that Grade talked *Raise the Titanic*. Grade's idea was to expand on their current movie deal from two pictures to that of four. His commitment to the MGM movie *Telefon* in January 1977 and another film project with Italian producer Dino De Laurentiis for *The White Buffalo* prevented any chance of Bronson committing to the *Titanic* project. But Grade was never the one to give up. In February 1977 he approached Bronson again with not just a copy of the film's screenplay for his perusal but the additional offer for his wife Jill Ireland. But again, Bronson's work commitments elsewhere put an end to appearing in the film in any role, let alone that of Dirk Pitt. Grade was on the hunt again.

During that same January of 1977, Grade had high hopes of grabbing *Patton* (1970) and *The Hindenburg* (1975) star George C. Scott to play the part of the President of the United States in *Raise the Titanic*. Part of the deal would also include Grade financing Scott's then-current Broadway comedy *Sly Fox* written by M*A*S*H creator Larry Gelbart. While Scott was not able to appear in Grade's production, he did finally walk the decks of the fabled liner when he played the role of Captain E.J. Smith for the Konigsberg/Sanitsky Company TV Mini-Series *Titanic* in 1996. In March 1977 the *Hollywood Reporter* magazine published a snippet on Lew Grade sizing up Rocky actor Sylvester Stallone for a leading role in *Raise the Titanic*. While Stallone fits perfectly in the part of a heavyweight boxer, he doesn't quite fit the bill of a trouble-shooting Dirk Pitt. But what Stallone did offer was the characteristics of Pitt's friend and sidekick, Al Giordino, with the Italian-American ancestry like that of the fictional Cussler's novel wise-cracking Giordino. In the end, he decided to raise the Championship belt a few more times to that of a long lost shipwreck with the role of Giordino being swapped out from the early drafts of the screenplay and replaced with Master Chief Walker played by the older M. Emmet Walsh. Then Grade turned to James Brolin in June that same year. Brolin had previously worked on another of Grade's films, the science fiction thriller *Capricorn One* for ITC. Brolin ticked many of the boxes for the leading role of Pitt and was highly recommended by director Stanley Kramer. Yet again fate was on Grade's side as Brolin had to turn down the role on what would have been his second film for Grade due to working on *Steel Cowboy* (1978) and *The Amityville Horror* (1979).

From 1976 to 1979 several more A-listed actors had been scouted to star as the film's leading role of Pitt. Both Paul Newman and Steve McQueen who were no strangers to disaster movies following their blazing on-screen performance in the master-of-disaster Irwin Allen's 1974 blockbuster *The Towering Inferno*. Then in the summer of 76 Lew Grade hosted a rooftop all-star diner party in New York with one prominent figure attending, Robert Redford, who too was offered the same role. But like both Newman and McQueen, Redford was unable to commit to the project due to other filming commitments. Another two actors were considered for starring roles in the film; *Logan's Run* (1976) Michael York and even Blair Brown, the partner of Richard Jordan. It is not known where they would have been placed in the film but Brown may have been the original Dana Archibald, the role that went to Anne Archer in the end. But what about those who were successful? Despite the growing difficulties with the ever-changing script, the film's leading stars had an equally challenging performance to deliver quality from such a lackluster screenplay.

Publicity photograph of Richard Jordan from 1978 during the release of Woody Allen's motion picture *Interiors*. *(Author's collection)*

Death Wish star Charles Bronson and wife Jill Ireland. *(Publicity card - Author's collection)*

Chapter 9: Casting the Characters • 289

George C. Scott in 1977. *(Author's collection)*

"Yo, how you doin?" Sylvester Stallone was being sized up for a leading role in *Raise the Titanic*. Dirk Pitt? Perhaps Al Giordino even? *(Publicity card – Author's collection)*

James Brolin, star of Grade's *Capricorn One*, was a likely contender for the role of Dirk Pitt. *(IMDb)*

Malta Times, 11 February 1979. *(Author's collection)*

Steve McQueen, Faye Dunaway and Paul Newman on the set of Irwin Allen's 1975 disaster epic *The Towering Inferno*. *(Films in Review, February 1975 – Author's collection)*

Robert Redford in *All the President's Men* from 1976. *(IMDb)*

Michael York (right) with Richard Jordan and Jenny Agutter in *Logan's Run*. (IMDb)

Blair Brown in the 1980 movie *Altered States*. (Publicity card – Author's collection)

The Main Cast

Richard Jordan

Dirk Pitt

Richard Jordan was born Robert Anson Jordan Jr on July 19, 1937, in New York City. Jordan attended the Hotchkiss School in Lakeville, Connecticut to then enroll at Harvard University where he graduated in 1958 to then turn his attention to acting in 1961. His early years of acting saw him appear in several television series before taking to the stage on Broadway and start his life-long passion of performing Shakespeare, which led to him appearing in many productions including *The Tempest* and *The Merchant of Venice*. In 1970, Jordan turned to film with his first movie role in the 1971 Michael Winner production *Lawman*. Jordan went through a stage of playing villains and good-guy villains in *Rooster Cogburn* (1975), and his most-recognized bad-guy role in *Logan's Run* (1976). It was during 1976 that Jordan appeared in the leading role for the miniseries *Captains and the Kings* in which he earned a Golden Globe Award for his performance. The 1980s saw Jordan appearing in several films including *Raise the Titanic* (1980), *Flash of Green* and *Dune* (1984), *The Mean Season* (1985), *The Secret of My Success* (1987), and a successful run in the television series *The Equalizer* between 1987 to 1988 as a stand-in for actor Edward Woodward who was recovering from a heart attack.

Richard Jordan *(ITC)*

In 1990 Jordan went on to produce and direct a stage production in New York of *Macbeth* to appear once again on the big screen in *The Hunt for Red October* that same year. Jordan's last on-screen appearance was to be the 1993 epic war movie *Gettysburg* in which he played the doomed Brig. Gen. Lewis Armstead. It was during filming in 1992 that Jordan began to show signs of deterioration in his health. It was during the early stages of filming in April 1993 for the film *The Fugitive* in the role of Dr. Nichols that Jordan's health quickly deteriorated forcing him to abandon the part. On discovery, it was found that Jordan had a brain tumor, which would claim his life on the 30th August 1993 at the age of 56. *Gettysburg* producer and director Ronald F. Maxwell went on to dedicate the film to Richard Jordan.

Jordan joined the cast of *Raise the Titanic* during the late summer of 1979 as the hero of the story. The role, depending on the success of the film, could have lead Jordan down the path as the new James Bond action figure with Lew Grade's intention of turning Clive Cussler's novels into an adventure series. Alas, it was never to be, but while Jordan possessed a vigorous handsome six-foot build, he appears on screen in his character role as Pitt, a man who did not take fools lightly, but still being separate in appearance to that of Cussler's adventurous rogue.

Jason Robards
Admiral James Sandecker

Jason Robards was born Jason Nelson Robards Jr on July 26, 1922, in Illinois, Chicago. While attending the Hollywood High School, Robards was active in sports covering baseball, basketball, and football, and caught the acting bug from drama classes. Following his graduation in 1939, he joined the U.S. Navy to serve World War II as a radio operator and was present when the Japanese attacked Pearl Harbor. During the war, he was assigned to the cruiser *U.S.S. Northampton*. On November 30, 1942, the vessel was attacked and sunk in the waters north of Guadalcanal by Japanese torpedoes. Robards survived the sinking by treading water until daylight when he was rescued. His time during the war earned him a respectable 13 battle stars and the Navy Cross for valor. Robards got into acting after the war with a slow-moving career consisting of small parts from radio programs to stage. The 1950s saw Robards career flourish with successful outings in Broadway productions leading to major starring roles in films throughout the 1960s including *Big Deal at Dodge City* (1966) and *Once Upon a Time in the West* (1968). In 1970 he was given the part of General Walter C. Short in *Tora! Tora! Tora!* had Robards returning to the attack on Pearl Harbor for the cinema screens. Robards went on to appear in *All the Presidents Men* in 1976 and played the part of a fictional President in *Washington: Behind Closed Doors* (1977).

Jason Robards *(ITC)*

By the 1980s *Raise the Titanic* was not the only film that Robards was a part of for Lew Grade, when he appeared in the 1981 ITC production of *The Legend of the Lone Ranger*. With a healthy spate of films under his belt in the 1980s which also included the disaster TV movie *The Day After* (1983) he was to close the decade with one of his most popular deadbeat appearances in the 1989 Steve Martin comedy film *Parenthood*. During the 1990s Robards went through a succession of narrating many television documentaries and one memorable if somewhat all too brief, appearance in the action movie *Crimson Tide* (1995). His final feature film role was in *Magnolia* (1999) where he played a dying man wanting to reconnect with his estranged son. During his career, he went on to receive many awards for his time on the screen including 8 nominations for the Tony Awards, the most for any male actor, the Academy Award for best supporting actor, Kennedy Center Honors for performing arts, and the George Foster Peabody award for broadcasting. In life, Robards had six children over four marriages with his third wife being Lauren Bacall, although the marriage ended due to his alcoholism. In 1972 Robards was seriously injured during an automobile accident due to intoxication leaving him with facial injuries that resulted in reconstruction. The accident ended his years of abuse with drink leading to him going public and campaigning for alcoholism. Jason Robards died on December 26, 2000 from complications with lung cancer at the age of 78.

In *Raise the Titanic* Robards plays the part of retired U.S. Navy Admiral James Sandecker, who is the head of an underwater research agency who, instructed by the President of the United States, has to lead his team of experts to locate and salvage the long lost remains of the *Titanic*. Robards joined the cast in October 1979.

David Selby

Dr. Gene Seagram

Born David Lynn Selby on 5 February 1941 in Morgantown, West Virginia. David attended West Virginia University where his education earned him a Bachelor of Science and a Masters degree in theatre followed by a Ph.D. from Southern Illinois University. He headed for New York and the lights of Broadway as he struck out for stage work. His first major acting portrayal came in the role of werewolf Quentin Collins in the successful *Dark Shadows* television series that ran from 1968 to 1971. His film debut came in 1971 with the film *Night of Dark Shadows* reprising his role of Quentin Collins. His next film came in 1972 starring alongside Barbara Streisand in *Up the Sandbox* followed by *The Super Cops* released in 1974. It was during the 1970s where David appeared in guest-starring roles in the much-loved television series *The Waltons* and *Kojak*. David's versatile character range led to appearing in all six episodes of *Washington: Behind Closed Doors* in 1977, a lavish fictionalized retelling of the Watergate scandal that starred Jason Robards and Robert Vaughn. In 1979, David and Robards would be reunited once again with leading roles in *Raise the Titanic*. The film kicked off the 80s in style for David with the leading role in the 1981 television series *Flamingo Road* followed in 1982 with his most recognizable role to date as Richard Channing in *Falcons Crest* (1982 - 1990). David is still very active on stage and screen appearing as Abraham Lincoln in *Touched by an Angel* (1998), *Ally McBeal* (2001), *Tell Me You Love Me* (2007), *Cold Case* (2007), *Mad Men* (2009), *Legion* (2017) and a guest appearance in the 2012 Tim Burton film adaptation of *Dark Shadows* starring Johnny Depp. Along with acting David is also a successful author with works covering poetry, the return to the *Dark Shadows* series that includes audio dramatizations for Big Finish Productions, and his long time passion for Abraham Lincoln that has seen him play the role on numerous occasions from celebrating the 200th birthday of President Lincoln to appearing on stage with the former President of the United States, Barack Obama.

David Selby *(ITC)*

David joined the cast of *Raise the Titanic* in early October 1979 in the role of Dr. Gene Seagram, the leading scientist behind the development of the futuristic laser defense system nicknamed the Sicilian Project that would create an impregnable screen around the parameter of the United States. But the system can only be fully activated with a vital mineral of which the last known traces thought to be locked within the cargo hold of the unsinkable *Titanic* now resting over two miles down on the bottom of the North Atlantic.

Anne Archer

Dana Archibald

Anne Archer was born on August 24, 1947, in Los Angeles, the daughter of actors John Archer and Marjorie Lord. The Golden Globe, BAFTA, and Academy Award-winning actress began her acting career following studying theatre arts at Claremont College. In 1970 she secured an acting role in an episode of *Men at Law* followed by *Hawaii Five-O* (1970), *Ironside* and *Alias Smith and Jones* (1971), and a couple of reappearing roles in *Love, American Style* (1971). In 1973 she was given the leading part of Carol Sanders in the 12-part comedy series *Bob & Carol & Ted & Alice* staring alongside a very young Jodie Foster. Her first TV movie role was in *The Blue Night* (1973) with Lee Remick and William Holden. For the remainder of the 1970s, Archer appeared in several other TV movies and television series with her first proper big screen movie outing being *Raise the Titanic* in 1980. At this time Archer was running the production company Aster Corporation that she

Anne Archer *(ITC)*

formed with her husband Terry Jastrow. Her second feature film came in 1981 with *Green Ice*, which also was the second movie production she did with Lew Grade and ITC.

In 1982 she and her husband wrote *Waltz Across Texas* in which both would star as the leading actors. In 1985 she was to team up again with *Raise the Titanic* star David Selby to play the part of Cassandra Wilder in all 22 episodes of *Falcons Crest*. The first of her memorable movie roles came in 1987 as Beth Gallagher, the wife of Dan Gallagher played by Michael Douglas in the Paramount Pictures stylish thriller *Fatal Attraction*. In 1990 she was to appear with another *Raise the Titanic* actor M. Emmet Walsh in *Narrow Margin* starring in the leading role alongside Gene Hackman. The 1992 Paramount Pictures action thriller *Patriot Games* gave Archer another memorable moment along with *Clear and Present Danger* (1994) with Harrison Ford. Today Anne Archer is still very active in movies, TV movies, television series, and stage productions. A collector of fine arts and sculptures, she also has a passion for skiing and tennis. In 2006 she founded Artists for Human Rights to raise awareness of the rights as laid out in the Universal Declaration of Human Rights. For her devotion to the cause, she was honored with the Women's Image Network Humanitarian Award of 2017.

Anne Archer joined the cast of *Raise the Titanic* in November 1979 in the role of Dana Archibald; the only actress in a leading role in the entire movie. She is cast as a vivacious reporter and journalist for the Washington Star and who is also the girlfriend of scientist Gene Seagram and the former love interest of Dirk Pitt.

Alec Guinness

John Bigalow

Alec Guinness was born Alec Guinness de Cuffe on April 2, 1914, in Maida Vale, London. While still a drama student Guinness got his first job in a theatre on his 20th birthday. By the age of 22, he was given a starring role in Sir John Gielgud's stage production of *Hamlet*, a position that would lead to a successful run playing various Shakespearean characters. It was during his adaptation to the stage of Charles Dickens *Great Expectations* that one audience member was British film editor, David Lean, who would later give Guinness a role in his film adaptation of the novel in 1946. During World War II he served as a Royal Navy Volunteer Reserve, which saw him become a Temporary Submarine Lieutenant until he was given the command of landing craft during the Allied invasion of Sicily. Following the war, Guinness was

Alec Guinness *(ITC)*

to return to his roots of acting by rejoining the Old Vic in 1946 performing as the Fool in *King Lear* with Laurence Olivier. Having starred in Lean's *Great Expectations* he went on to appear in another of Lean's productions as the scoundrel thief Fagin in *Oliver Twist* (1948). One early performance from Guinness would be in the 1949 Ealing Studios comedy *Kind Hearts and Coronets* where he was given the remarkable role of portraying eight of the film's characters. This would cement his position with Ealing to appear in more of their classic comedy films including *The Lavender Hill Mob* and *The Man in the White Suit* (1951) and *The Lady Killers* (1955). In 1957 Guinness would win both an Academy Award and BAFTA for his performance of Colonel Nicholson in *The Bridge Over the River Kwai*.

Guinness was extremely talented in taking the character given to him and starting from the outside to work inwards to build up the overall appearance of the person he was to play. This can be seen in such films as *Lawrence of Arabia* (1962), *The Fall of the Roman Empire* (1964), *Doctor Zhivago* (1965), *Hitler: The Last Ten Days* (1973), *Tinker Tailor Soldier Spy* (1979), *Smiley's People* (1982) and *A Passage to India* (1984). For fans of science fiction, Alec Guinness would be best remembered in the role of Ben Obi-Wan Kenobi in the original trilogy of *Star Wars* films starting with *Star Wars* (1977), *The Empire Strikes Back* (1980), and *Return of the Jedi* (1983). The remainder of the 1980s into the 1990s saw Guinness appearing in smaller roles in film and television with a part in *Eskimo Day* (1996), which would become his last appearance on screen before retirement. Guinness went on to author three autobiographies on his life and times in acting, *Blessings in*

Disguise (1985), *My Name Escapes Me* (1996), and *A Positively Final Appearance* in 1999. On August 5, 2000, Alec Guinness died from liver cancer while living in Midhurst, Sussex, England, at the age of 86.

Alec Guinness joined the cast of *Raise the Titanic* in November 1979 to play the role of survivor John Bigalow who was in charge of cargo on board *Titanic*. Now retired in a seaside retreat at St Ives, Cornwall, England, Bigalow now lives a simple life in a public house he owns on the seafront.

The Supporting Cast

J.D. Cannon

Capt. Joe Burke

John Donovan Cannon (April 24, 1922 - May 20, 2005) was born in Salmon, Idaho. He was a student of the American Academy of Dramatic Arts in New York City and is best remembered for his portrayal of Chief of Detectives Peter B. Clifford in the long-running television series *McCloud* that aired between 1970 to 1977. His earliest acting appearance was in *The Phil Silvers Show* in 1958. Through the 1960s he was a regular on many television shows including *The Defenders* (1961-1965), *The Invaders* (1967-1968), and *The F.B.I.* (1966-1970). He is best remembered in films such as *Cool Hand Luke* (1967), *Scorpio* (1973), and *Death Wish II* (1982).

J.D. Cannon *(ITC)*

Bo Brundin

Capt. Andre Prevlov

Bo Brundin was born on April 25, 1937, in Uppsala, Sweden. His earliest acting role was in the 1970 war drama *The Baltic Tragedy* that tells the true story of the extradition of Baltic soldiers during World War II. In 1976 he was to have a guest-starring role in the science fiction action series *The Bionic Woman* with Lindsay Wagner along with guest roles in *Hawaii Five-O* (1977) and *Wonder Woman* (1976-1979). Mainly working in television he has also appeared in films including the disaster movie *Meteor* (1979). His most recent acting appearance was in 2012 short *The Light That Dances Across the Sky*.

Bo Brundin *(ITC)*

M. Emmet Walsh

MCPO Vinnie Walker

Michael Emmet Walsh was born in Ogdensburg, New York, on March 22, 1935. In 1958 he graduated from Clarkson University with a Business Administration degree. Walsh has had a varied acting career starring in many well-established series and prominent films including *Starsky and Hutch* (1976-1978), narrating *The American Civil War* documentary series in 1990. The *Home Improvement* comedy series (1994), all 24 episodes voicing Mack in *Big Guy and Rusty the Robot* (1999-2001), *Damages* (2012), and all 46 episodes voicing Olaf in *Pound Puppies* (2010-2013). It is the large array of films that Walsh is most recognized by, *The Jerk* (1979) with Steve Martin, *Blade Runner* (1982), *Fletch* (1985), *Bigfoot and the Hendersons* (1987), *Narrow Margin* (1990), and *Wild Wild West* (1999). At the age of 87 Walsh has no plans of retiring just yet.

M. Emmet Walsh *(ITC)*

Norman Bartold

Admiral Kemper

Norman Hillman Bartold (August 6, 1928 - May 28, 1994) was born in Alameda County, California. He made his acting career appearing in many television series from his first role in *She's Working Her Way Through College* (1952), *Dragnet* (1956-1957), *The Rockford Files* (1974-1977), *Charlies Angels* (1977-1981), and *Falcons Crest* (1985). His film credits include an appearance in Cecil B. de Mille's epic *The Ten Commandments* (1956), *West World* (1973) and *Close Encounters of the Third Kind* (1977).

Norman Bartold *(ITC)*

Elya Baskin

Marganin

Elya Baskin was born Ilya Zaimanovich Baskin on August 11, 1950, in Riga, Latvian Soviet Socialist Republic. He immigrated to the United States in 1976 following attending the Theatre and Variety Arts College in Moscow. His earliest acting part was in 1972 in the Russian comedy film *The Long Recess*. The move to the U.S secured a part in the Gene Wilder comedy *The World's Greatest Lover* (1977) and the Peter Sellers drama *Being There* (1979). Since the mid-1970s Elya has built up an impressive acting career having starred in many films, TV shows, and TV movies including *MacGyver* (1986-1987), *Quantum Leap* (1992), *Walker, Texas Ranger* (1993-1996), *Spy Hard* (1996), *Spider-Man 2* (2004), *Spider-Man 3* (2007) and *Transformers: Dark of the Moon* (2011).

Elya Baskin *(ITC)*

Dirk Blocker

Merker

Dennis Dirk Blocker was born in Hollywood, California on July 31, 1957. He began his acting career in 1974 in the drama series *Marcus Welby, M.D*. By 1976 he was appearing in all 36 episodes of *Flying Misfits*. His film credits also include *Poltergeist* (1982), *Starman* (1984), and *Prince of Darkness* (1987). Today Blocker is well known for his role as bumbling Hitchcock in the long-running comedy series *Brooklyn Nine-Nine*.

Dirk Blocker *(ITC)*

Robert Broyles

Willis

Robert Houston Boyles (January 20, 1933 - February 12, 2011) was born in Sparta, Tennessee. After serving in the U.S. Navy between 1952 to 1956, he went on to Ohio State University where he earned a Bachelor of Arts degree. His early acting career began with the hit TV series *Bonanza* in 1964 followed by appearances in *Mod Squad* (1969), *The Streets of San Francisco* (1972), *The Rockford Files* (1975), and *Police Story* (1977). His film credits include *Close Encounters of the Third Kind* (1977) and *Poltergeist* (1982).

Robert Broyles *(ITC)*

Paul Carr

CIA Director Nicholson

Paul Carr (January 31, 1934 - February 17, 2006) was born Paul Wallace Carr in Marrero, Louisiana. After a period of doing live television work, Carr made his film debut in 1955 with a small part in the Alfred Hitchcock thriller *The Wrong Man*. He worked steadily through the 1960s, 1970s, and 1980s with guest spots on *Rawhide* (1961-1964), *Days of Our Lives* (1965-1966), *Star Trek* (1966), *The Time Tunnel* (1966), *Voyage to the Bottom of the Sea* (1964-1967), *Land of the Giants* (1968), *Mission: Impossible* (1969), *Mod Squad* (1969-1972), *Ironside* (1968-1972). *Mannix* (1969-1974), *Police Story* (1973-1976), *The Six Million Dollar Man* (1974-1978), *Buck Rogers in the 25th Century* (1981), *Quincy M.E* (1978-1982), and *Dallas* (1982).

Paul Carr *(ITC)*

Michael C. Gwynne

Bohannon

Michael C. Gwynne was born in Detroit, Michigan, on October 1, 1942. After moving to Hollywood in 1969 he was offered acting parts in *The Bold Ones* series in both 1970 and 1971. His movie acting break began in 1973 with *Payday* followed by the comedy crime movie *Harry in Your Pocket*. During the 1970s Gwynne appeared in numerous TV-movie roles and TV series including *Kojak* (1975), *Harry O* (1975), and *Rafferty* (1977). For the big screen, he is remembered for his roles in *Private Parts* (1997) and the disaster movie *Knowing* (2009). In 1965 Gwynne was to enter the Guinness Book of Records for his 92 hours of non-stop drumming for "Drum-A-Thon".

Michael C. Gwynne *(ITC)*

Harvey Lewis

Kiel

Harvey Lewis is an American actor and producer. He made his acting debut in the 1977 comedy series *CPO Sharkey*. He went on to star in *Almost Summer* (1978), *Tilt* (1978), *Honky Tonk Freeway* (1981), and *Alamo Bay* (1985). In 2011 Lewis was the producer for the TV movie documentary *Sully Erna Presents: The Journey to Avalon*.

Harvey Lewis *(ITC)*

Charles Macauley

General Dale Busby

Charles Macauley (September 27, 1927 - August 13, 1999) was born in Louisville, Kentucky. Macauley had a long and varied career on the screen starring in the 1961 series *The Rifleman*, his first screen appearance, followed by roles in *Dr. Kildare* (1962), *Days of Our Lives* (1965), *I Spy* (1967), *Mission: Impossible* (1970), *The F.B.I.* (1972), *Columbo* (1971-1974), *Starsky and Hutch* (1975) and several *Perry Mason* TV-movies between 1990 to 1993; and with his friendship with the *Perry Mason* star Raymond Burr they became business partners at Burr's vineyard. During his time on television is most memorable moment was playing Jaris and Landru in the two 1967 episodes

Charles Macauley *(ITC)*

of *Star Trek*. His most popular feature film credits include *The Hindenburg* (1975), *Airport '77* (1977), *The Big Red One* (1980), and *Splash* (1984).

Stewart Moss

Koplin

Stewart Moss (November 27, 1937 - September 13, 2017) was born in Chicago, Illinois. He began his career in acting with his first screen appearance in the television series *The Fugitive* (1964). He went on to appear in several well-known series during the 1960s, 1970s, and into the 1980s including *Rawhide* (1964), *Bonanza* (1966), *Perry Mason* (1966), *Star Trek* (1966-1968), *The Invaders* (1968), *Hogan's Heroes* (1965-1971), *Cannon* (1971-1973), *The Rockford Files* (1975), *The Six Million Dollar Man* (1974-1975), *Quincy M.E* (1977-1981) and *Hart to Hart* (1981-1983). His film acting credits included *Pendulum* (1969), *Fuzz* (1972), and *The Bat People* (1974).

Stewart Moss *(ITC)*

Michael Pataki

Munk

Michael Pataki (January 16, 1938 – April 15, 2010) was born in Youngstown, Ohio. He studied at the University of Southern California where he passed with a double major in both political science and drama. Pataki appeared as a guest star in numerous television productions including *The Twilight Zone* (1961), *Rawhide* (1964), *My Favorite Martian* (1965), *Voyage to the Bottom of the Sea* (1965), *Batman* (1966), *Columbo* (1972), *McCloud* (1974-1976), *The Fall Guy* (1982-1984) and voicing credits to *The Ren & Stimpy Show* (1992-1994). Along with *Raise the Titanic,* his other film credits include *Airport '77* (1977), *Halloween 4* (1988), and *Rocky IV* (1985). Pataki went on to direct the 1977 film adaptation of *Cinderella*.

Michael Pataki *(ITC)*

Marvin Silbersher

Soviet Ambassador Antonov

Marvin Silbersher (June 28, 1924 – December 7, 2015) was born in Millburn, New Jersey, U.S.A, and worked as both an actor and director. His earliest acting credits go to *Lamp Unto My Feet* which he appeared in between 1961 to 1964 and an episode of *I Dream of Jeannie* (1969). His first film role was in the 1973 drama *Life Study* which starred Tommy Lee Jones along with other film credits including *The Taking of Pelham One Two Three* (1974).

Marvin Silbersher *(ITC)*

Mark L. Taylor

Spence

Mark Lawrence Taylor was born in Houston, Texas, on October 25, 1950. He has had starring roles in *M*A*S*H* (1979), voicing a role in *Mork & Mindy* (1982), *Superman* series (1988), *Melrose Place* (1997-1999), *Boston Legal* (2006-2008), *Saving Grace* (2007-2010) and more recently *How to Get Away With Murder* (2016). His notable films roles include *Any Which Way You Can* (1980), *Innerspace* (1987), *Honey, I Shrunk the Kids* (1989), *Arachnophobia* (1990), and *Homeward Bound* (1993).

Mark L. Taylor *(ITC)*

Maurice Kowalewski

Dr. Silverstein

Maurice Kowalewski started his acting career with his first screen appearance in *My Name is Nobody* (1973). He went on to appear in several television series that included *Cannon* (1975), *The Blue Knight* (1976), *Police Woman* (1976-1977), and *Little House on the Prairie* (1982). His first movie appearance was in the 1975 crime drama *The Streetfighter* which was followed by *Raise the Titanic* and *Death Hunt* (1981).

Maurice Kowalewski *(ITC)*

Nancy Nevinson

Sarah Martindale

Nancy Nevinson (July 26, 1918 – January 25, 2012) was an English actress born in Chittagong, East Bengal, British India. She had a long career on both stage and screen with her acting appearances credited to *Dr. Jekyll and Mr. Hyde* (1956), the *BBC Sunday-Night Play* 1962), *The Spy Who Came in from the Cold* (1965) which starred Richard Burton. *The Saint* (1965), *UFO* (1971) television series. *Jesus of Nazareth* (1977), *Tales of the Unexpected* (1980), the BBC adaptation of *Martin Chuzzlewit* (1994), and the BBC long-running soap *Eastenders* in 1996. Her *Titanic* film credits not only include *Raise the Titanic* but also the 1979 TV movie *S.O.S. Titanic* where she played Ida Strauss.

Nancy Nevinson *(ITC)*

Trent Dolan

Isbell

Trent Dolan was born on May 5, 1938, in the United States and has appeared in episodes of *The Six Million Dollar Man* (1974-1977), *Starsky and Hutch* (1978), *CHiPS* (1981), *Dallas* (1981-1985) *Murder, She Wrote* (1989-1993) and *NYPD Blue* (2001). He has had roles in films that include *Capricorn One* (1977) for ITC and *The Swarm* (1978).

Trent Dolan *(ITC)*

Paul Tuerpe

Klink

Paul Tuerpe was born in the United States in 1949. In his long varied career on screen, he has appeared in many well-known films including four separate roles in all four of the *Lethal Weapon* movies (1987-1998). He has also appeared in the disaster movie *Airport 1975* (1974), *Airport '77* (1977), *Superman* (1978), *The Goonies* (1985), *Scrooged* (1988), *Three Fugitives* (1989), *Maverick* (1994), *Free Willy 2* (1995) and *Conspiracy Theory* (1997).

Paul Tuerpe *(ITC)*

Ken Place

Drummer

Ken Place was born in Tulsa, Oklahoma. His acting credits include *More American Graffiti* (1979) and *The Big Chill* (1983).

Ken Place *(ITC)*

Michael Ensign
Lieutenant Northacker

Michael Ensign was born on February 13, 1944, in Salford, Arizona, United States, and is of British/American descent. He trained at the London Academy of Music and Dramatic Art to spend the first decade of his acting career working on the stage in theatres around Britain. His earliest on-screen performance was in *Of Heaven and Home*, a U.S short drama from 1963. His first feature film appearance was in *Assassin* (1973) followed by *Midnight Express* (1978) and *Superman* (1978). His long career in television includes roles in *The Dukes of Hazzard* (1984), *Falcon's Crest* (1986-1987), *Dynasty* (1988), *MacGyver* (1987-1989), *Matlock* (1989-1991), *Friends* (1998-1999), *3rd Rock From the Sun* (1999), *The X-Files* (1999), *Boston Legal* (2004-2008) and more recently with *CSI: Crime Scene Investigation* (2002-2008). Of the films Ensign will be most recognized for are *War Games* (1983), *Ghostbusters* (1984), and the role of millionaire playboy Benjamin Guggenheim in James Cameron's blockbuster *Titanic*.

Michael Ensign *(ITC)*

Craig Shreeve
Gunther

Born on May 30, 1933, in the United States, Craig Shreeve started his acting career in 1958 starring in *J.P. Patches*. His other credits include *The Man from U.N.C.L.E.* (1966), *I Spy* (1966), *The Wild Wild West* television series (1967), *Starsky and Hutch* (1975), and *Falcon's Crest* (1983). He has also appeared in the adventure thriller movie *Ice Station Zebra* (1968) and *Close Encounters of the Third Kind* (1977).

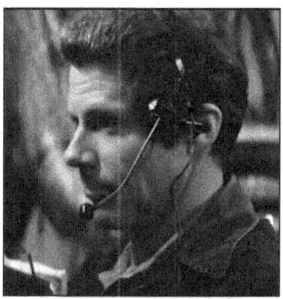
Craig Shreeve *(ITC)*

Brendan Burns
Carter

Brendan Burns is an American actor, producer, and screenwriter. His acting career began in 1971 and has had starring roles in *Kojak* (1974), *The Waltons* (1974), *Cannon* (1973-1975), *The Streets of San Francisco* (1973-1977), *Hawaii Five-O* (1975-1979), *The Judge* (1989) and *The Young and the Restless* (1991-2006).

Brendan Burns *(ITC)*

Jonathan Moore
Capt. Parotkin

John Miller Moore Jr (March 24, 1923 – September 17, 2008) was born in New Orleans, Louisiana. A classically trained actor who worked on the Broadway stage, his onscreen debut was in *Love of Life* in 1951. His film credits also include *Amadeus* in 1984.

Jonathan Moore *(ITC)*

George Whiteman

Beck

George Whiteman began his career on the screen in 1957 appearing in *Highway Patrol* and later in *Shirley Temple's Storybook* (1961), *Kraft Mystery Theatre* (1963), *The Bionic Woman* (1977), and *CHiPS* (1980). His film roles include *King Kong* (1976) and *Airport '77* (1977).

George Whiteman

Hilly Hicks

Woodson

Hilly Gene Hicks Sr was born on May 4, 1950, in Los Angeles, California. His acting career began with the comedy-drama series *Room 222* in 1969. He would later have appearances in *The Bill Cosby Show* (1969-1971), *Ironside* (1969-1972), *Roots* (1977), *M*A*S*H* (1975-1977), the animated TV series of *Godzilla* 1978-1979) and *Hill Street Blues* (1985). His first film role was in *Halls of Anger* (1970) followed by *The New Centurions* (1972), *Gray Lady Down* (1978), and *Go Tell the Spartans* (1978). Hicks is both an actor and a clergyman of the United Methodist Church in Nashville.

Hilly Hicks *(ITC)*

Mike Kulcsar

Russian Sentry

Michael Kulcsar was born on September 11, 1937, in the United States and is known for his appearances in *Herbie Goes to Monte Carlo* (1977), *Megaforce* (1982), and *The Twilight Zone* television series from 1986.

Mike Kulcsar *(ITC)*

Alexander Firsow

Sloyuk

Alexander Firsow is known for his brief role as the Soviet Ambassador at the Soviet Embassy in Washington in *Raise the Titanic*, his only known screen appearance.

Alexander Firsow

Mark Hammer

Polevoi

Mark Hammer (April 28, 1937 – February 15, 2007) was born in San Jose, California. He began his acting career in 1966 starring in *The Journey of the Fifth Horse* and appearing in episodes of *Law & Order* (1991-2003). His first movie role was in Peter Seller's film *Being There* (1979) followed by *Raise the Titanic*.

Mark Hammer *(ITC)*

Sander Vanocur

Sander Vanocur (news commentator)

Born Alexander Vinocur on January 8, 1928, in Cleveland, Ohio, he is well known for his broadcasting and journalism. He did have a brief acting part in the 1952 series *Orient Express* but he is also known for his cameo appearances playing himself, as a reporter, and has appeared in *The Gang That Couldn't Shoot Straight* (1971), *The Last of the Cowboys* (1977), *Dave* (1993), *Without Warning* (1994), *Street Fighter* (1994) and *Weapons of Mass Distraction* (1997).

Sander Vanocur *(ITC)*

Nicos Savalas

Welch

Nicos Savalas is an American actor known for his brief part of Welch in *Raise the Titanic*. He is the nephew of *Kojak* actor Telly Savalas.

Nicos Savalas *(ITC)*

James W. Gavin

Helicopter Pilot

James W. Gavin (March 13, 1935 – August 13, 2005) was born in Denver, Colorado. He was known as a miscellaneous actor due to his profession as a pilot which earned him roles as a pilot for many productions. His film credits include *Dirty Harry* (1971), *Airport 1975* (1974), *Earthquake* (1974), *Lethal Weapon* (1987), *The Dead Pool* (1988), *Lethal Weapon 4* (1998), and *Pearl Harbor* (2001).

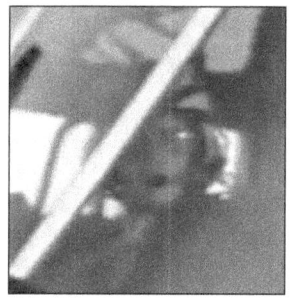

James W. Gavin *(ITC)*

Bert Drake

Helicopter Passenger

Bert Drake is an American actor known for his brief part in *Raise the Titanic*.

Bert Drake *(ITC)*

Roy Evans

Gravedigger #1 (talking part)

Roy Evans was born in 1930 and is a British actor who has appeared in many well known British series including *Doctor Who* (1965-1975), *Poldark* (1975), *Blakes 7* (1979), *The Onedin Line* (1976-1979), the Rowan Atkinson comedy series *The Black Adder* (1983) and *Only Fools and Horses* (1989), His movie credits include *Jabberwocky* (1977) and *The Elephant Man* (1980).

Roy Evans *(ITC)*

Tom Curnow

Gravedigger #2

Tom Curnow was a resident of St Ives in Cornwall who was offered his first and only film appearance as the non-speaking part of the second gravedigger who appears with Roy Evans.

Tom Curnow *(ITC)*

Milton Seizer

Dr. Vogel

Milton Seizer (October 25, 1918 - October 21, 2006) was born in Lowell, Massachusetts, U.S.A. He rose to fame during the 1960s after appearing in such classic television series as *Peter Gunn* (1961), *The Untouchables* (1961-1962), *The Twilight Zone* (1962-1964), *Perry Mason* (1963-1964), *Voyage to the Bottom of the Sea* (1964), *The Fugitive* (1965), *Get Smart* (1965-1966), *The Invaders* (1967), *Mission: Impossible* (1967-1972), *Kojak* (1974), *The Streets of San Francisco* (1973-1976), *Hawaii Five-O* (1968-1978), *Hill Street Blues* (1983) and *L.A. Law* (1987). He appeared in several movie roles including ITC's *Capricorn One* (1977).

Milton Seizer *(ITC)*

Nik Mescherski

Soviet Embassy Official

Nik Mescherski was a Mercedes-Benz car dealer in Washington DC. He was given the unique chance to play a brief part in *Raise the Titanic* as one of the Washington Russian Embassy officials.

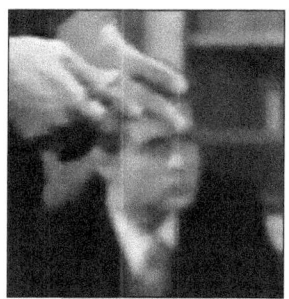

Nik Mescherski *(ITC)*

Garth Inns

Vault/safe cutter

Garth Inns was born on April 12, 1943, in Brentford, Middlesex, England and is known in the film industry as a special effects supervisor and special effects technician. His established career with films include such classics as *The Guns of Navarone* (1961), *From Russia with Love* (1963), *Dr. Strangelove* (1964), *Goldfinger* (1964), *Thunderball* (1965), *You Only Live Twice* (191967), *2001: A Space Odyssey* (1968), *Chitty Chitty Bang Bang* (1968), *Flash Gordon* (1980), *Superman II* (1980), *Highlander* (1986), *The Living Daylights* (1987), *GoldenEye* (1995), *Tomorrow Never Dies* (1997), *Planet of the Apes* (2001) and *Van Helsing* (2004).

Garth Inns *(ITC)*

Press Conference Reporters

Ron David

Mayfair Hotel press reporter - *Raise the Titanic* (1980)

Ron David *(ITC)*

Franchelle Stewart Dorn

Mayfair Hotel press reporter - Born November 6, 1949, in Houston, Texas. Films include *The Pelican Brief* (1993) and *Die Hard: With a Vengeance* (1995).

Franchelle Stewart Dorn *(ITC)*

Claire Lee

Mayfair Hotel press reporter - Jon-Clare Lee is an American actor who has appeared in *Muriel's Wedding* (1994) and *Nim's Island* (2008).

Jon-Claire Lee *(ITC)*

Norvell McDonald

Mayfair Hotel press reporter - Norvell McDonald's film credits include *Raise the Titanic* and *Kennedy* (1983).

Norvell McDonald *(ITC)*

James Scopeletis

Mayfair Hotel press reporter – James "Jim" Scopeletis film credits include *Best Friends* (1982), *Head of State* (2003), and *Voiceless* (2015).

James Scopeletis *(ITC)*

Gabrielle DeCuir

Mayfair Hotel press reporter - Gabrielle DeCuir was born on May 12, 1954, in Los Angeles. She is an actress, producer, and director. Her film credits include *Raise the Titanic* and *Legal Eagles* (1986).

Gabrielle DeCuir *(ITC)*

Clive Cussler

Mayfair Hotel press reporter - Clive Cussler was born on July 15, 1931, and is the original author of the 1976 best-selling novel *Raise the Titanic!* His cameo role was his first and last appearance on screen.

Clive Cussler *(ITC)*

CHAPTER 10

Rewriting History

"You don't make good friends in Hollywood in my opinion. Everybody is too busy looking behind them."

Adam Kennedy

When Clive Cussler signed the agreement in November 1976 with Lew Grade's company Associated General Films/ITC, Cussler relinquished his rights to *Raise the Titanic*. While it appears that the screen rights at the time were not made that clear, Cussler waving his rights to penning the film and the escalating issues with the screenplay, one would think that Cussler's original deal could have been reviewed and renewed to include him. But it was never to happen; he was never approached or asked. Cussler had sold the rights for $450,000 with the understanding that he was to have a cameo appearance and that all-important line of dialogue. The signing of the contract resulted in Cussler dismissing any creative control with the film's production along with a percentage of the film's takings, although the former would have been unlikely as a bargaining chip. His gut instinct was to take the money and run regardless if the film became a flop or a success. When Cussler found out that the screenplay was undergoing yet another rewrite, he took it upon himself to fly out to London to confront Lew Grade and angle for a fresh option in putting himself forward to pen the script. It would seem from the offset that this would be the best possible option all-around but those at the top thought otherwise. What did go against Cussler in terms of writing the screenplay was that he never had any expertise in that field, and during preproduction stages with the studio when searching for someone to pen the screenplay, if Cussler's name had not been found previously associated with any other released productions, then it may account as to why he was not considered.

Dusting off the Typewriter

Adam Kennedy was never the first choice to adapt the novel for the screen. When Grade purchased the rights his first order of business was to produce a workable print. He turned towards director Stanley Kramer who, in July 1977, contacted Arnold Schulman, author, and screenwriter to the 1975 Barbara Streisand comedy-musical *Funny Lady*, the follow-up to Streisand's 1968 classic *Funny Girl*. Schulman was not able to work on the project and so Kramer turned to Kennedy to co-write the screenplay. Kramer wanted the story to be more East-West Cold War thriller which delivered a message on the uncertainty of humanity under the shadow of nuclear war. Lew Grade was more focused on it being a straightforward adventure yarn. Following Kramer walking off the project and Jerry Jameson taking control, Jameson approached Kennedy to offer him the opportunity to continue with the project. Adam Kennedy was born in Otterbein, Indiana in March 1922. He graduated from DePauw University with an Alma mater to then study acting at the Neighbourhood Playhouse in Manhattan. His first screen role was an uncredited part in the 1955 movie *The Court-Martial of Billy Mitchell* with Gary Cooper. During the 1960s and 1970s, Kennedy had several major starring roles on screen from features films to smaller productions for television including programs for the CBS network. He retired from acting during the mid-1970s to concentrate on adapting novels for the big screen, his first being the 1977 released Stanley Kramer motion picture *The Domino Principle*, one of Lew Grades early financed projects. His first draft for *Raise the Titanic* with Kramer in 1977 underwent several rewrites when five other writers were brought in to expand on Kennedy's original draft. When the film project stalled and Kramer walked, the project collapsed. As Jameson picked up the production, he turned to Kennedy asking for his old screenplay to be worked on again. "It's a group activity," says Kennedy. "Everybody thinks they can write dialogue. The reason screenwriting is very pleasant for me is that I understand it. It's a marvellous way to make money. It's not a primary means of expression. Only one script in 30 ever gets filmed. You don't make good friends in Hollywood in my opinion. Everybody is too busy looking behind them."

If Kennedy had faith in his screenplay the proof would become apparent when Eric Hughes transferred it to the screen. *Raise the Titanic* was Hughes's first major project and his inexperience of adapting for movies is all too evident in the final release of the film. In all fairness the adaptation was not all that bad, it just didn't live up to the expectations that readers of Cussler's novel had hoped for. Hughes only had two more film credits to his name after the release of *Raise the Titanic* with the release of the 1984 movie *Against All Odds* and *White Nights* the following year. What went against Kennedy's and Hughes's work was the almost haphazard nature of the editing the production went on to receive. But a dialogue scene is only as good as the performance of the actors. If the actor could not relate to the character then the performance is weakened and the human side of the story then begins to crumble. As a movie *Raise the Titanic* was crafted in a way that the audience was being forced to focus more on the subject of the ships recovery than on the characters in the story who had to pull off that feat of engineering. Grade could not have made it any clearer when he exclaimed that the main character in the film was *Titanic*. And as the film progressed the *Titanic* side of the story overshadowed the human side, resulting in the audience caring less about the human characters and drawing out the weaker elements of the screenplay which had already been exaggerated by the editing.

Raise the Titanic became Kennedy's third and final film, retiring from productions to concentrate more on authoring novels. The numerous rewrites for *Raise the Titanic* probably did more harm than good as the exhausting process far removed the suspense that Cussler's *Titanic* adventure already oozed. And yet despite his previous writing skills and with all good intentions for the project, Kennedy was not successful in adapting this particular story for the big screen in quite the same dramatic flair that the title had promised to deliver on.

Counting the Cost

The earliest draft of the film's screenplay came in while Stanley Kramer was still on board as director. Written by Adam Kennedy the draft consisted of 91 pages with the date of the draft being January 27, 1977. At the request of the Pentagon's principal liaison officer Donald E. Baruch, the script underwent the first of the big changes. A revised edition from Kennedy followed with it now being extended to that of 108 pages with a total of 299 scenes. Again, it was subjected to the scrutiny of the Pentagon who requested more changes resulting in the First revised draft from Kennedy consisting of 131 pages now totaling 473 scenes. This, like the previous, was not dated. And yet again it was not to the Pentagon's liking. The second revised draft dated December 15, 1977, now had a new writer with Eric Hughes joining the production team. This draft had a total of 141 pages and 333 scenes. Off it went to Baruch who outlined more changes required. It is not officially clear exactly how many drafts were created in 1978 as filming was now in its pre-production stages and actors were being screen-tested. But the next screenplay came on July 27, 1979, with Adam Kennedy back at the helm. This time the script was revised to 126 pages with 411 scenes. It was returned for revision and became the first of the Revised Final Drafts on August 27, over 142 pages with a total of 411 scenes. On October 19 new added material was included in the draft which included a Cast of Characters and 20 pages of Revised Shooting Schedules for the San Diego locations slated for November 26, 1979. The final draft from Kennedy was emitted on October 17, 1979, and titled the Revised Final Draft consisting of 143 pages and a total of 411 scenes. For *Raise the Titanic*, from Adam Kennedy's first-completed draft of January 1977 to his Revised Final Draft in October 1979, an incredible and lengthy two-half-years had passed. Nine writers were used, including those brought in by Adam Kennedy to fulfil the story for the big screen.

The following are of the known released editions and revisions of the screenplay from the earliest printing to the Revised Final Draft.

RAISE THE TITANIC
By Adam Kennedy
Stanley Kramer Prod, Ltd
First Draft
January 27, 1977
91 pages
Size: 11.0 x 8.5 inches
(3-hole binding of brass fittings)

RAISE THE TITANIC
Screenplay by Adam Kennedy
Based on the novel by Clive Cussler
First Revised Draft
(no date)
131 pages
473 scenes
Size: 11.0 x 8.5 inches
(3-hole binding with brass fittings)

RAISE THE TITANIC
By Adam Kennedy
A Martin Starger Production of a Stanley Kramer film
108 pages
299 scenes
Size: 11.0 x 8.5 inches
(3-hole binding with brass fittings)

RAISE THE TITANIC
Screenplay by Eric Hughes
Second Revised Draft
December 15, 1977
141 pages
333 scenes
Size: 11.0 x 8.5 inches
(3-hole binding with brass fittings)

RAISE THE TITANIC
By Adam Kennedy
July 27, 1979
126 pages
411 scenes
Size: 11.0 x 8.5 inches
(3-hole binding with brass fittings)

RAISE THE TITANIC
Screenplay by Adam Kennedy
Revised Final Draft
August 27, 1979
142 pages
411 scenes
Size: 11.0 x 8.5 inches
(3-hole binding with brass fittings)

RAISE THE TITANIC
Screenplay by Adam Kennedy
Revised Final Draft
October 17, 1979
411 scenes
Size: 11.0 x 8.5 inches
(3-hole binding with brass fittings)

RAISE THE TITANIC
Post Production Release Script
General Distribution Version
October 1980
80 pages
13.0 x 8.0 inches
(2-hole binding)

Arnold Schulman in 1993. *(Photograph © William B. Winburn)*

Stanley Kramer. *(Author's collection)*

A young Adam Kennedy during his acting days. *(Author's collection)*

Chief of the Visual Production Branch of the Washington Department of Defence; Donald E. Baruch. His crucial involvement in the production on *Raise the Titanic* would see a vast number of changes to the screenplay that would end up having dire consequences on the look of the film once released. *(National Archives - Record Group 330: Records of the Office of the Secretary of Defense, 1921-2008)*

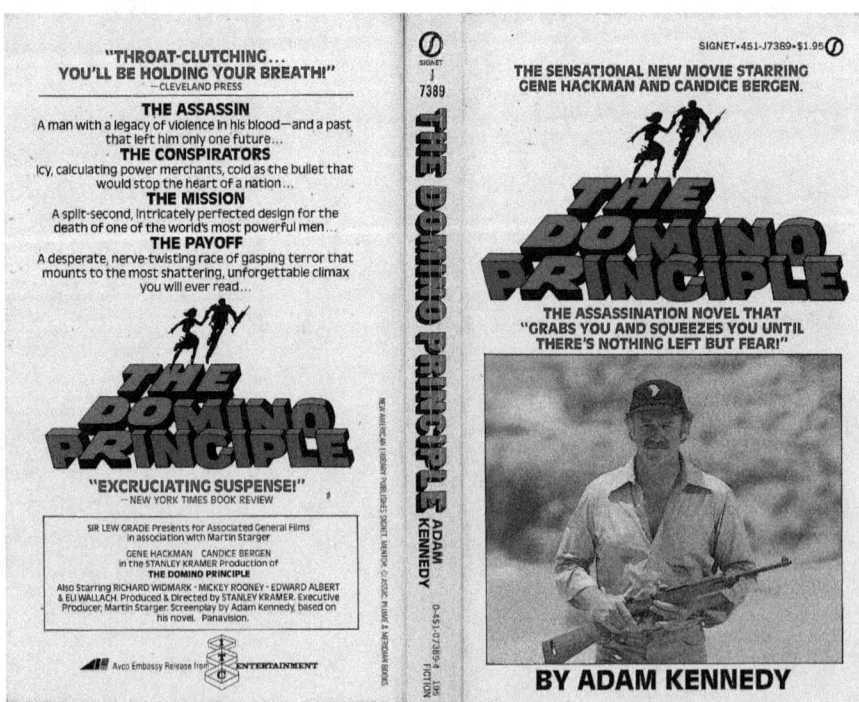

The novelisation of Adam Kennedy's *The Domino Principle* released through Lew Grade's ITC. *(Author's collection)*

Adam Kennedy in 1979. (Author's collection)

Eric Hughes (MUBI.com)

Revised Final Draft issued August 27, 1979. (Author's collection)

Adam Kennedy and his wife, Susan, attending the star-studded special advance screening of Raise the Titanic in Beverley Hills in July 1980. (The Hollywood Reporter, July 1980 - Author's collection)

Eric Hughes (left), Pavla Ustinov (daughter of actor Peter Ustinov) and Ron Parker from Marble Arch Productions attending the advance screening. (The Hollywood Reporter, July 1980 - Author's collection)

Post Production Release Script, October 1980. *(Walter Winterburn collection)*

Chapter 11

Doomed from the Start

"It seems to me that the disaster about to occur was the event that not only made the world rub its eyes and awake but woke it with a start, keeping it moving at a rapidly accelerating pace ever since with less and less peace, satisfaction, and happiness. To my mind, the world of today awoke April 15, 1912"

Jack Thayer, Titanic survivor

Tension mounts as the world's largest ship, the vessel they claimed was unsinkable, begins to dip by the head. Her funnels discharge smoke and steam. Lights flicker, go dim, and then flicker again. Tiny figures litter her boat deck as lifeboats, packed with their human cargo, begin the fear-induced journey down to the water. Across the water sits the cold monster that claimed the life of the stricken vessel. As lifeboats slowly row away from the sinking ship there comes the sound of turmoil followed on the heels by a sudden explosion as one of the towering funnels lifts from the deck and comes crashing down into the sea amidst a tremendous roar and cloud of sparks and smoke. The scene abruptly changes with a loud call from a loudhailer. "Cut!" booms the voice from the side of the water tank. "Can someone *please* swim out and move that iceberg?" comes the disembodied voice once again. From the darkness, a slight splash is audible as a black wet-suited team member slips into the water and makes their way towards the offending iceberg. It is June 1979, still relatively warm at this time of year, and an American film crew from MGM are at the surface tank at the Mediterranean Film Facility located alongside Fort Rinella on the island of Malta lensing the sinking of the R.M.S. *Titanic* for the motion picture *Raise the Titanic*. With the studio's tank facilities facing northeast over the beautiful blue waters of the Mediterranean, it couldn't be any further away from the frigid waters of the North Atlantic. In fact, the tank is not even part of the Mediterranean, not even at sea level, but built on an elevated position some thirty-five-metres from the sea.

The period in Los Angeles with the building of the *Titanic* model had already sparked many concerns that there was no tank big enough to hold such a large-scale creation. Even the tank at the back lot of the 20th Century Fox studio was out of the question because it lacked vista and came with the added complication with the facility having been taken over by the state. The production team was forced to look further afield to then be knocked back every step of the way. It is hard to comprehend that during these stages of the production the studios had no facilities agreed upon to film the movie's most crucial scenes. And yet by mid-1978 that was the case. One saving grace came when the surface tank over in Malta was offered to the production teams. Originally constructed in 1964 when the film facility came into action the surface tank had the bonus of a broad sea view that would serve both feature films and smaller productions very well. The tank measures 301ft breadth; 400ft at its widest point, and built was a depth of 3ft at the retaining wall with the floor of the tank dipping to a depth of 6ft at the center of the tank. Furthermore, a 7ft depth center pit with an overall length of 100ft and 50ft in width gave the tank a total depth of 13ft. The filling time of the tank is an estimated 9 hours where the facility could hold 23 million litres of water that would take an additional 4 hours to drain. Once filled and the overspill was in full operational use, the tank offered a seamless horizon point out over the Mediterranean Sea.

Ship Shipping

By early 1979 as the deep tank construction began to become a reality, ITC was in talks in booking the surface tank for the filming with the huge *Titanic* model for what was initially to be the movie's 1912 prologue of *Titanic* striking the iceberg to begin her sorrowful destiny to the ocean floor. But they were missing their main star – *Titanic*. Stanley Kramer's departure from the production resulted in delays in getting the miniatures in Los Angeles finished to an acceptable time. With Jerry Jameson now in charge, with ITC pushing for production to get back on track, the next problem began to rear its ugly head; transporting hundreds of film equipment, models, and sets from America over to the island of Malta some 6738 miles away. The smaller and more portable items could be crated up and sent via plane. But the problems lay with the huge models and sets that could not fit within the cargo bays of commercial aircraft. Once again, the scale of the *Titanic* model was to prove a headache. Its sheer size and weight contributed to the problems in getting it ready for any long-distance transportation. Even a heavy haulage company was needed to transport the model starting with collecting it from Stage 3 of the CBS Studio Center and hauling it, safely and securely, to the pickup point where it would begin the 6738-mile voyage to Europe. But first, they had one last thing to do before the *Titanic* model was prepared for its long journey; she required christening. Like some bizarre ceremonial ritual, the model was pulled out of Stage 3 and moved over to another part of the CBS Studios backlot where it was then lowered into the waters of the exterior lake set used for the television series *Gilligan's Island*. Satisfied that it floated, to a certain degree, the model was removed, hauled back over to Stage 3, and prepared for transportation.

Now crated up, the studios faced the challenges of getting the large ship models over to Malta. ITC looked towards commercial flight but was hampered by the fact that no commercial aircraft in operation had a cargo bay large enough for an extremely expensive 10-ton film production model in a specially constructed wooden shipping crate measuring 60ft x 20ft x 10ft. There was one aircraft in service that would have been able to take such a cumbersome cargo load; the Lockheed C5 Galaxy. But as the C5 was a military aircraft is was not an option available to the studio. The inability of flying the model out of Los Angeles meant only one other option; transport the *Titanic* model by sea. No one would have given a second glance in seeing a long wheelbase low loader making its way along road and freeway to the Port of Long Beach, thinking it was just another heavy-haulage consignment underway to the port and destined for some faraway shore. Little did they realize that hidden within the crate was the world's largest replica of the *Titanic* that was bound for the docks on board a cargo ship to the port of Valetta in Malta.

Even if the production crew didn't believe in any superstitions, they must have felt that *Titanic*'s legacy was jinxed when it became apparent that the model was too big to be passed down through the vessel's cargo hold. In an undignified manner, the model had to be secured down to the deck of the vessel for its long sea journey. They could only hope that the vessel would not encounter any form of tempest during the voyage. Thankfully they had nothing to worry about when a few weeks later the cargo ship arrived safely in port where the *Titanic* and the other ship miniatures were carefully offloaded at the quayside to await road transportation to the film studios. From this time on Malta would become the permanent home to this particular *Titanic*.

Thank God for Southby

With work now underway on the deep tank and outbuildings, the film production team focused on getting the *Titanic* miniature ready for filming the prologue sequence. Although the model was in a nearly completed stage, the U.S. model unit could not just put it in the waters of the surface tank and sink it while filming. A lot of work was required in getting the model ready so it could be filmed in varying angles of her demise. A steel rig was built that sat at the bottom of the surface tank pit where the *Titanic* model could be seated into it and cranked into a position to simulate the sinking. As the model was 55ft in length and the pit of the surface tank was only 13ft in total depth it meant that the whole model could not be fully submerged. ITC did enquire about the possibilities of reworking the surface tank by adding additional depth. But as time wore on it soon became apparent that carrying out such construction work was not feasible for both the film studios or the Mediterranean Film Facility who hired the use of the surface tank out to other productions. ITC was forced to make the best of what they had, partially sink the *Titanic* model and then use a newly crafted model of the stern as it disappears beneath the waves.

The early day of preproduction for the opening sequence was to incorporate parts from the Clive Cussler novel of the running gun battle between the American mining team and the Russians content in claiming back their property. During the talks between Ken Marschall, Bill Creber and Stanley Kramer, Marschall had sketched out rough storyboards to show Kramer that a stylized version of the novel's prologue could be achieved. The sequence was to tell the tale of the ore arriving in England, the chase across the country to Southampton and Brewster having the crates of ore loaded aboard *Titanic* at Southampton docks. The scene would jump to the night of the disaster as Brewster forces crew member Bigalow down to the flooding cargo hold, and to the waiting vault. Creber was fully on board with Marschall's idea and it would seem that it was taken seriously. But the sudden change of directors soon quashed that planned prelude. And with Jerry Jameson now on the project, and Adam Kennedy penning the new screenplay, the prologue would undergo a new direction.

The new prologue began with a jubilant musical score played out with a series of black and white period photographs of the construction and maiden voyage of the *Titanic*. As the celebrations of her conception build, it is abruptly ended with the sudden appearance of a huge iceberg followed by the sharp clangs of the crow's nest bell and the shout of "Iceberg right ahead!" As the screen goes black a cacophony of screams and hissing steam reveals the stricken *Titanic* listing heavily to starboard as distress rockets erupt in the starlit sky. A dishevelled figure of a man rushes out from the crowd massing on the boat deck and pushes his way forwards to the 1st class entrance of the Grand Staircase. It is Arthur Brewster. He hurries down the staircase and exits onto the A-Deck promenade, past crew desperately trying to assist passengers into lifeboats being lowered past the windows. The bearded man runs aft, enters the interior of the ship, and forces his way through 2nd class to finally come upon an open access door that leads down to the crew areas of the vessel. Unconcerned of what may await, he ventures forwards through the crew areas and enters into the open spaces of the cargo hold. In the dim light of the gradually flooding hold stands a man with his back to Brewster. The passenger pulls a revolver from his jacket and presses it into the crew member's side. At gunpoint, the crew member is threatened with death if he refuses to take the armed passenger to a certain location of the cargo hold. With the deck tilting, the hold flooding, Officer Bigalow guides Brewster to a large steel vault. Producing a key from his pocket, Brewster unlocks the vault, steps in, and tells Bigalow to save himself. As Brewster pulls at the heavy door, he mutters the words "Thank God for Southby". Bigalow makes it to the open deck just as the unsinkable *Titanic* slides beneath the waves. As the stern vanishes out of sight the angle changes to an underwater view of the fully submerged *Titanic* as she free falls through the black waters of the Atlantic. As the ocean depths swallow her up, she emerges once more from the shadows to slam down into the ocean floor. As she settles back, the title RAISE THE TITANIC appears on the screen before the scene fades back to black for the final time.

With the *Titanic* model changing so it could be filmed in the surface tank and ITC laboriously searching for a full-scale vintage ship they could secure for the filming with actors and extras for the 1912 prologue live plates, these short sequences would tell the all too familiar tale of the loss of the liner with the use of live-action sets and footage filmed with the miniatures in the surface tank. April 1979 was earmarked to begin the filming of the miniatures in the surface tank with principal photography with the actors and extras commencing at a much later date once the studio had finalized the human stars of the movie. Until then the focus was on getting the *Titanic* miniature ready for filming in the surface tank. The now completed sinking rig was soon to bring up problems for the U.S team as the extra weight added to the *Titanic* miniature meant that the floatation tanks were not substantial enough to keep the model on an even keel. The tanks that had been built and fitted within the hull over in L.A were ripped out and replaced with newer constructed tanks. If the crew was relying on trial and error, errors were outnumbering the filming process almost every step of the way. As April came closer the realization set in that the model was not ready to be filmed. With the surface tank being leased out to other productions, the sinking of the *Titanic* was pushed back to June.

Sinking Ships & Little Chicks

That summer in Malta the crew from MGM set about re-enacting the night the *Titanic* went down. Each day the model was prepped for an evening shoot. Upon the floating pontoons stretched out across the water of the surface tanks knelt a handful of model unit crew members at work cranking out the lifeboats on their davits and moving about the scores of figurines on the boat deck. As night fell, as the film units waited patiently, as the model unit braced themselves, "Action!" came the call as FX smoke bombs added by fans began belching out plumes of smoke from the ship's funnels. The model certainly looked the part as she sat with a defined list to starboard, ice on her foredeck from the encounter with the monstrous berg, lifeboats hanging from her side as figures silhouetted by the lights from within the liner made the scene look like some macabre nightmare that would be best forgotten. But despite all their best efforts the crews struggled to get the sequences looking right. And what they did capture on film looked outlandish, over the top, and in some circumstances, too comical. For nearly two weeks in the tank, they filmed and prepped and filmed, day after day and night after night. During the day the model was rigged to sit on the water surface at an even keel or if they were working on scenes with the model sinking, the hull could be sat bow-down; as long as the decks of the forecastle and forward well deck were not left submerged in water for extended periods of time.

To add to the human side of the story the production required a large number of figures that would adorn the decks of the liner. The doll-like figurines were without any facial features as they were to be filmed at a distance. They just needed to look – human. Male, female, even children, were made and dressed with little lifejackets and placed around the Boat Deck and inside the lifeboats hanging from the davits. To overcome the prospect of eagled eyed viewers picking out that the figures were too static, a number of them were attached to a simple wire system that ran flush across the Boat Deck and promenade deck. When slowly cranked by a model unit member out of sight behind the model, the figures would appear to be moving back and forth. And any scenes that were to show a lifeboat making its way down the side of the sinking liner would have posable figures with some facial features that would be used again for foreground shots of the lifeboats in the water as they row away from the *Titanic*. These articulated figures did have some screen time when a storyboarded sequence of panic breaking out on the Boat Deck when the second funnel comes crashing down to strike a lifeboat, snapping the rope falls and tipping the lifeboat on its side sending all the occupants crashing down into the sea below. The scenes were to be brief so as not to allow the viewer to spend time scrutinizing if the scene was model work or live-action. Of course, the whole sequence was pure fiction, added for the sake of entertainment value. But at least it was better executed than what was originally planned.

One bizarre incident occurred around the time that the preparation work was underway before filming the sinking scenes. Art Director John DeCuir Jr received a batch of invoices with a post-it note attached that simply read, "what the fuck is this all about?" The first invoice was for 500 baby chickens that would come in from an Italian farm. The second was for a case of Vecchia Romagna Italian Brandy. The third was for six dozen boxes of eye droppers while the last invoice was for a toy manufacturer over in China who would produce 500 Sou'wester rain hats with elastic straps and matching coats with a zipper. Someone in the production office had devised a scenario where the use of the chicks would answer their query on how to mimic passengers and crew on the sloping decks of the doomed *Titanic*. It was thought that dressing the chicks up, administering a drop or two of the brandy via the eye droppers into their beaks, would affect the bird's ability to walk creating the impression of people struggling with the incline of the ship's deck. Surely this was not even taken seriously enough to follow it through? Let's just say that a few fell off the deck, into the tank, got rescued, and spent the rest of their lives distributed to various farms around Malta living a survivor's life with their dignity still intact when the footage was later scrapped. I don't think the "No animals were harmed in the making of this motion picture" rolling credits certification from the American Humane Association would have been void for this production?

A Disaster Waiting to Happen

The director of the model unit in Malta during the production of *Raise the Titanic* was none other than Ricou Browning, the man in the monster suit from Universal studios 1954 monster movie, *The Creature from the Black Lagoon*. His model unit had one advantage with filming the model at night; the darkness could hide any sins that would otherwise be evident. If only the brilliantly lit cruise ships and other vessels out in the waters of the Mediterranean would have been more understanding to the cause. But that was all part and parcel of the location and the vista it gave while the world continued to operate outside of Hollywood moving pictures.

To sink the *Titanic* a special gimbal was built in the surface tank that went from the shallow portion of the tank and down into the deeper section of the tank called the well. The rig was designed like a rollercoaster track that was seated just a few feet off the bottom of the tank floor, over the well and to then suddenly angle downwards. A wheeled dolly was then attached to the track where the *Titanic* model could be seated down and secured in place. A simple cable and pulley system ran from the dolly, through the track, down to the bottom of the tank well and back up to the shallow tank floor where FX crew could crank the model forwards along the track. When the dolly with the model came to the area of the track that bends down towards the well floor, the dolly with the *Titanic* attached to it then follows the downward curve of the track sending the bow of the model downwards and the stern upwards giving the illusion that the model is sinking.

However, limitations to the model unit due to the shallow nature of the surface tank meant that the *Titanic* model could not be fully submerged. This posed a problem. If they were to film the *Titanic* sinking then the sequence would have to abruptly end with no climax to the waters closing over the ship if they could not fulfil such shots with the 55ft replica. The model unit opted to build a small-scale section of the stern where they could set the miniature up on a rig and film the stern as the liner up-ends and dives down beneath the waves. Not much is known about this particular set piece other than it was built and possibly used. But interestingly the stern prop would make a brief appearance on screen when it was later reused for the triumphant reveal of *Titanic*'s name during her discovery.

Filming the *Titanic* miniature in the tank would prove that not everything planned would be accepted. The key to filming the model was not to push the model past its capabilities. The main bulk of the sinking footage was to be filmed showing the starboard side of the model as the broad expanse of the Mediterranean Sea behind acted as an uninterrupted backdrop. With the portside of the model hidden it was an excuse for a large array of special effects equipment and personnel to work their magic out of sight of the cameras and from a control panel attached to the side of the hull. All four funnels had been rigged up at the Malta studio with pipework where a smoke machine attached to the side of the portside hull could feed smoke into the model, up the pipe and out of the funnel. A generator with a blower fed steam up through a hose that snaked up through the deck, up the face of the funnel and exited in the location close to the models static funnel whistles.

The model unit had worked out a slight list to starboard which would link the iceberg damage to the amount of flooding within the vessel. The model was given a 5° list on the dolly that would be identifiable on screen but enough to secure the safety of the model and reduce the stress on the newly constructed funnels. Only one of the funnel units would be required to collapse under controlled conditions. The early artworks promoting the film had the artist envision the wreck on the ocean floor with her number one funnel ripped away and resting a short distance away from the hull. The art department felt it was better schooling to keep the model looking more *Titanic*. Eliminating the second funnel would still give the impression to the viewer that a funnel was missing yet still presenting the ship as a four-funnel ocean liner.

The model unit had rigged the funnel in a way that when the pyrotechnics were set off the unbolted funnel would fall to starboard amidst a cloud of sparks and smoke. It did not matter if the falling funnel would be damaged during the collapse as long as the scene had been set up as a one-take shot. "Action" calls out Browning. Moments later the explosion goes off and the funnel is pulled with the use of a fine wire. With the funnel knocked from its center of gravity, it is left to free-fall down and over the side of the partially submerged hull. "Cut!" booms Browning. During filming one small mishap occurred when the suspended wire that led from the detonator and across the tank to the *Titanic* model shorted out a second after the explosion. The short in the cable was to send a shower of sparks cascading all over the model and water tank. If anything, the model unit could have passed it off as one of the distress rockets being launched as the ship goes down. But the scale of the detonation and the huge shower of sparks revealed that it was less of a special effect and more human error.

Ricou Browning's unit had captured some impressive broad sweeps of the *Titanic* in distress. Certain angles show off the lines of the vessel while others complimented the details of the miniatures, if somewhat fogged out by the darkness of the night shoots. But despite all that hard work and effort, it lacked impact as a whole. The lighting systems put into the model failed to capture the essence of the grandeur of the ship as model crews had rigged up lengths of lighting cable with bulbs attached at intervals that were not correct to the design of the ship. Areas of decking were left in darkness whereas on the real *Titanic* lights would have been present. While the general public would care less about how accurate the replica was, the placement of the lights did nothing to improve the overall look of the ship. It was as if the film crew had just draped a string of garden lights over the model and left it that way. The shallow nature of the surface tank did create restrictions in the way the sinking sequences were to be filmed. But the production crew used the facility to the best of their abilities and did put to film some imaginative and profound moments of a tragic event that had occurred 68 years previously. With the footage in the can and on its way over to Elstree Studios in England, all that could be done now was to wait for the next film unit to pick up the live-action sequences with actors for all the elements to be brought together as a single entity. Speaking in 2019, FX supervisor John Richardson looked back on viewing the footage himself of the sinking sequence in 1979. "It just didn't look right. The icebergs all looked brown instead of white. It generally was a pretty crummy shoot. So they decided not to use it in the film."

In the meantime, a rough cut of footage had been edited together for a preview screening in front of officials from ITC and scheduled for 25 June 1979. Sitting among the officials seated in Stage 5 of Elstree Studios was Lew Grade. One can imagine the build-up to the screening. Grade sitting there, cigar to hand, congratulating those either side of him for a job well done. Now and then, in his polite yet forceful way, pushing for the print to be run so he can evaluate the spectacular that was to unfold on the screen before him. There she is; *Titanic,* that iceberg. They meet. Steam and smoke issuing from all four funnels. Lights flickering. Figures going back and forth across the boat deck. Lifeboats are being lowered down the hull side. Suddenly some break free under the weight and fall to the sea below. An explosion fills the screen as the second funnel breaks free to collapse with a torrent of spray, sparks, and smoke as the doomed liner upends and slips beneath the water.

A murmur began to develop among the crowd who had assembled to watch the test sequence. It was a mixture of bewilderment and muffled conversations. Then the lights come back on as Lew Grade rises from his seat. The businessman in him had not seen the entertainment value of the sequence. The outlandish explosion moments before the funnel collapses mingled with the sight of a faulty fuse wire that sent sparks showering down over the stern of the model was enough to tip the balance. The expression on his face said it all as he and ITC board members exchanged comments on what they had just watched. Disgruntled by what he had seen; a still glowing cigar resting between his fingers; Grade turned to face his colleagues while motioning towards the now blank screen.

"This is a movie about the RAISING of the *Titanic*, NOT the sinking of it. Get rid of it!"

Chapter 11: Doomed from the Start • 317

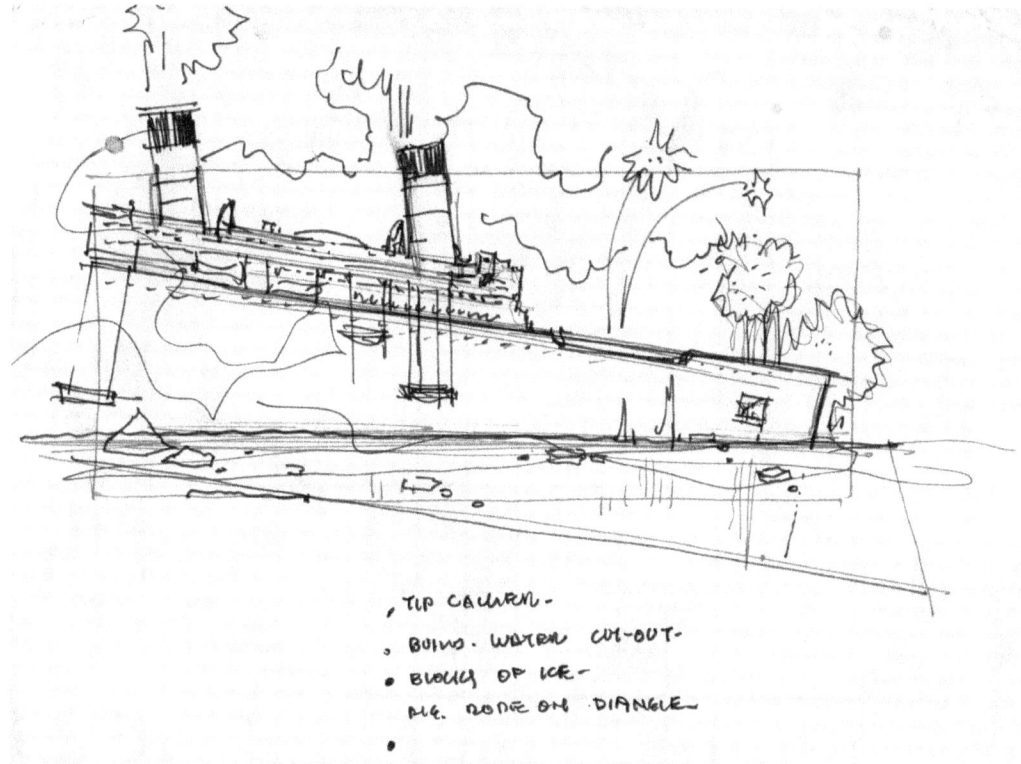

Original production artwork from the prologue. *(Author's collection)*

Lifeboat #15 begins its descent down the side of the doomed *Titanic* in this deleted scene from the prologue for *Raise the Titanic*. *(Author's collection)*

The surface tank at the Mediterranean Film Facility in early June, 1979. *(Malta Today, October 1979 – Author's collection)*

Filming the 28ft *Titanic* miniature for the motion Picture *TITANIC* in the water tank facility at 20th Century Fox studios in 1952. *(Author's collection)*

Directors:
Lord Delfont, Chairman
Andrew Mitchell, Managing Director
E.A. Maxwell
R.A. Webster

EMI ELSTREE STUDIOS LIMITED

EMI STUDIOS
BOREHAMWOOD
WD6 1JG HERTS
Telephone: 01-953 1600
Telegrams: EMIFILMS BOREHAMWOOD
Telex: 922436 EFILMS G

Malcolm Christopher, Esq.,
Pimlico Films Limited.
c/o Pinewood Studios,
Iver Heath,
Bucks.

21st March 1979

Dear Malcolm,

"RAISE THE TITANIC"

With reference to your letter dated 16th March, I confirm that we have booked for your production Stage 5 from 25th June 1979 until the beginning of September.
Should this stage become free earlier than 25th June, I will of course keep this for you.

I note that on your return from Athens you will be contacting me regarding additional stage space, also some office accommodation.

Looking forward to having you back here.

Kindest regards,

Yours sincerely,

ANDREW MITCHELL

c.c. Mr. D. J. Skinner
     Mr. J. R. Shepherd

A Member of the EMI Group of Companies
Registered in England No. 232530

International leaders in Music, Electronics and Leisure
Registered Office: 30/31 Golden Square, London W1R 4AA

This letter from Pinewood Studios dated 21 March 1979 confirms the hire of Stage 5 at the film facility. At this early stage of production, it was thought that *Titanic* interior sets could be built at Pinewood for use in the sinking sequence with actors playing out their roles. *(Author's collection)*

MARBLE ARCH PRODUCTIONS
"RAISE THE TITANIC"
WEEKLY SET COST REPORT

PROPERTY & SET DRESSING

WEEK ENDING APRIL 14, 1979

SET #	DESCRIPTION	BUDGET	COST THIS WEEK	COST TO DATE
N7				
N8				
N9				

* Page 25 of 25 *

One of the Weekly Set Cost reports dated 14 April 1979. The document is blank as filming with the model over in the surface tank was pushed back to June. *(Author's collection)*

Raise the TITANIC!

EUROPEAN AGENTS FOR:-
MARBLE ARCH PRODUCTIONS

Please reply to:-
PIMLICO FILMS LTD.
c/o M.F.F., Fort St. Rocco, Kalkara, Malta.
Tel: Malta 622289 & 622880
Telex: MW 212 FFACIL

8th May, 1979

MEDITERRANEAN FILM FACILITIES
FORT ST. ROCCO
KALKARA   Att. TONY MANICARO

Dear Tony:

This is to confirm with you that we would want to fill the surface tank on or about 1st June.

Would you also please arrange for telephones to be installed in the new offices adjacent to our Art Department.

Many thanks,

FREDERICK MULLER
Production Manager.

STUDIO CENTER • 4024 RADFORD • STUDIO CITY, CALIFORNIA 91604 • (213) 763-8411

Confirmation letter from ITC to the Malta studio on the hiring of the surface tank starting the 1 June. *(Author's collection)*

PIMLICO FILMS LTD.
EUROPEAN AGENTS FOR:-
MARBLE ARCH PRODUCTIONS INC.

Please reply to:-
PIMLICO FILMS LTD.
c/o M.F.F., Fort St.Rocco, Kalkara, Malta.
Tel: Malta 622289 & 622880
Telex: MW 212 FFACIL

22nd May, 1979

M E M O

TO: NARCY CALAMATTA
      TONY MANICARO

FROM: FREDERICK MULLER

Dear Narcy and Tony:

I would appreciate very much if you would as of tonight double the security down at the SFX workshops - in other words two men per night.

Would you further instruct these security men that once members of our Unit have left the premises at the end of the day (6 - 6.30 p.m.) no one, I mean no one is allowed inside our workshops without written permission from myself.

I thank you very much for your co-operation.

FREDERICK MULLER
Production Manager

cc. J. Maxsted
    R. Robinson
    D. Frift
    S. Priori
    M. Higgins

STUDIO CENTER • 4024 RADFORD • STUDIO CITY, CALIFORNIA 91604 • (213) 763-8411

As the model nears readying for filming, ITC ask that extra security is put in place at the Mediterranean Film Facility to prevent none staff members from entering the studio grounds and photographing the ongoing production. *(Author's collection)*

PIMLICO FILMS LTD.
EUROPEAN AGENTS FOR:-
MARBLE ARCH PRODUCTIONS INC

Please reply to:-
PIMLICO FILMS LTD.
c/o M.F.F., Fort St.Rocco, Kalkara, Malta.
Tel: Malta 622289 & 622880
Telex: MW 212 FFACIL

1st June, 1979

M E M O

TO: NARCY CALAMATTA

FROM: PRODUCTION OFFICE - RAISE THE TITANIC

Due to the fact that the Titanic Model will be removed from the Special Effects Stage, where it is under lock and key, to be placed in the Surface Tank, would you please provide us with an extra security guard starting Saturday 2nd June until further notice.

This specifically to ensure the safety of the Model.

Thank you for your co-operation.

PRODUCTION OFFICE

STUDIO CENTER • 4024 RADFORD • STUDIO CITY, CALIFORNIA 91604 • (213) 763-8411

Letter from ITC requesting that more security is hired to be at the tank and workshops starting the 2 June when the *Titanic* model is removed out into the open from the facilities Marine Studio. *(Author's collection)*

The *Titanic* model following its arrival at the Mediterranean Film Facility in the spring of 1979. *(Mario Cassar collection)*

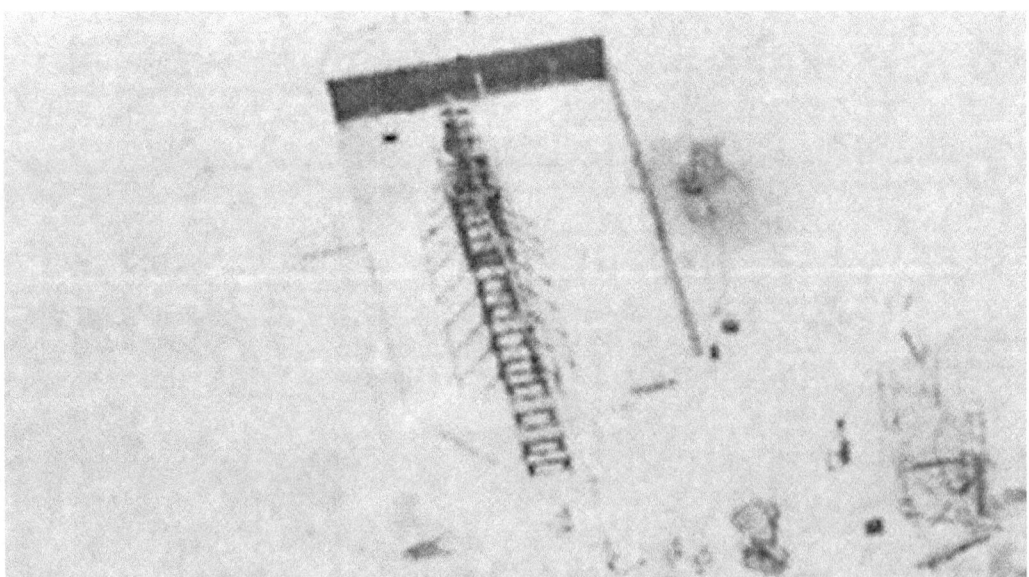

The aerial view of the surface tank floor shows the well that allowed for some set pieces to be lowered deeper than the tanks original 4 feet depth limit. Taken during the first week of June 1979 the image reveals the gimbal during the latter stages of construction. The strange looking objects seen to the right of the cradle and the well are some of the icebergs being assembled on frames. *(Malta Today, October 1979 – Author's collection)*

The *Titanic* model is lowered into place on the dolly, June 1979. *(Mario Cassar collection)*

The model FX unit testing the *Titanic* miniature on the sinking dolly and gimbal. *(Mario Cassar collection)*

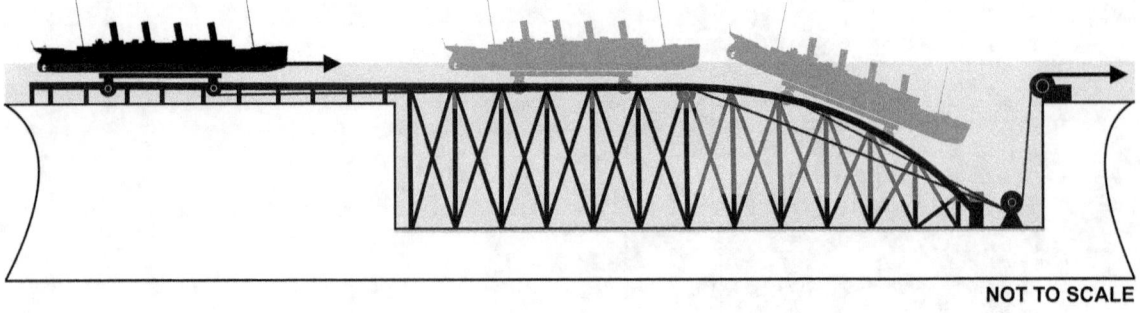

This illustration demonstrates how the model on the dolly and gimbal worked. A simple cable and pulley system rigged up to the dolly allowed the FX unit to crank the model along the track and partially down into the well of the tank. While the tank was not deep enough to completely submerge the *Titanic* miniature, it was basic and worked. *(Illustration © Jonathan Smith)*

The surface tank all set up with the *Titanic* model and a number of icebergs. The second funnel has been completely removed for the model unit to replicate and prepare the model for the filming of the funnel collapse. *(Mario Cassar collection)*

Rare view of the *Titanic* model sitting level on the surface tank gimbal. *(Joe Sciberras collection)*

Even with the water damage to the photograph it does little to take away the impressiveness of the model. *(Mario Cassar collection)*

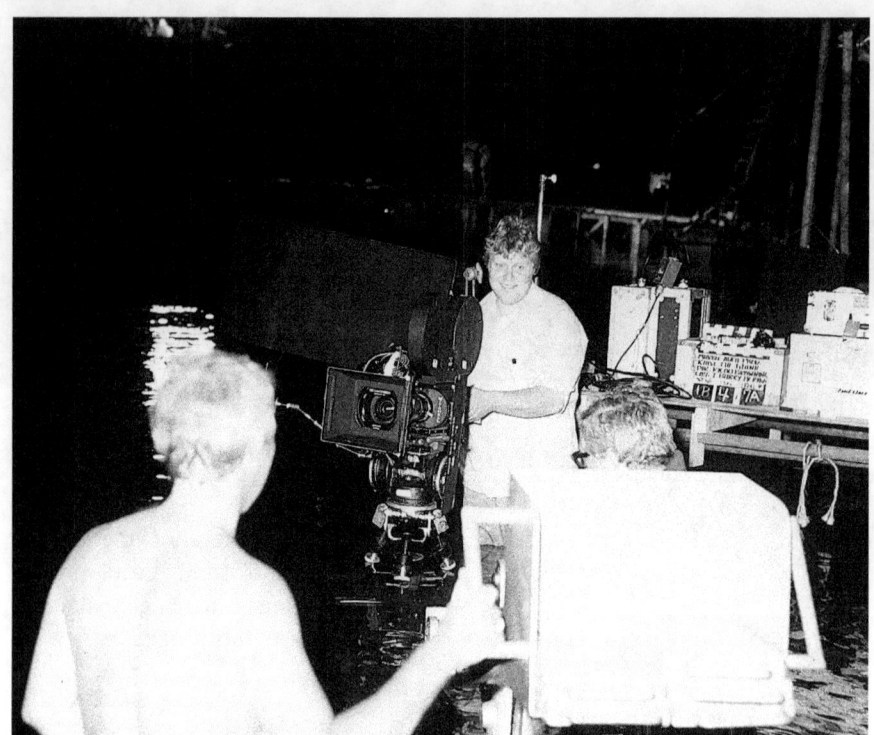

Camera runner Clive Prior and other members of Rico Browning's production crew prepare for a night shoot. *(ITC – Author's collection)*

Last minutes checks before filming resumes. One of the divers can be seen (lower left) returning to the side of the tank after positioning some of the lifeboats floating in the water. *(ITC – Author's collection)*

The wind machines are switched on but the smoke has become too unruly. *(ITC – Author's collection)*

With each night shoot there proceeded a day's work of prepping the model. *(Author's collection)*

Resembling equipment from the laboratory of Dr. Frankenstein, these views of the portside of the *Titanic* model show the complexity of the panel that controls the smoke machines, artificial steam machines and hull lighting switchboard. *(Mario Cassar collection)*

"What a lovely thing she was." The world's largest model of the *Titanic* sits in the surface tank waiting for the sun to set for a night shoot. This photograph shows the incredible length they went in getting the replica as close to the real thing. *(Capt. Lawrence Dali collection)*

Chapter 11: Doomed from the Start • 333

This close up of the model reveals a number of figurines on deck replicating both passengers and crew. Those positioned in lifeboats were completely static with a number also stationary out on the deck. But for some of the closer views of the sinking liner, it required a more practical plan to make them move. After a number of unsuccessful attempts, including the idea of using live-stock, Browning's unit opted for cut out silhouettes connected to wire that ran across the deck of the model and to which members of the crew, out of sight behind the model, would pull the wires to make the figures glide along; unconvincingly of course. *(Capt. Lawrence Dali collection)*

With smoke equipment rigged up to the funnels and ice on her foredeck, *Titanic* is made ready to sink... yet again. *(ITC – Author's collection)*

The model unit carry out last minute preparations before the cameras begin to roll. *(Mario Cassar collection)*

This image of the sinking *Titanic* was captured by one of the officials from ITC for the company archives and shows what was achieved during the June 1979 filming in the surface tank. *(ITC – Author's collection)*

Despite all the best efforts of the production unit, the footage failed to impress Lew Grade. *(Author's collection)*

The over the top explosive end to *Titanic*'s second funnel not only added to Grade's dislike to the model work for the prologue, but also the fact that FX errors got in the way of scenes filmed such as the fuse wire suspended over the model emitting a unwelcomed shower of sparks due to a poor connection between the wire from the model to the wire suspended over the tank. *(ITC – Author's collection)*

PIMLICO FILMS LTD.
EUROPEAN AGENTS FOR:-
MARBLE ARCH PRODUCTIONS INC.

Please reply to:-
PIMLICO FILMS LTD.
c/o M.F.F., Fort St. Rocco, Kalkara, Malta.
Tel: Malta 622289 & 622880
Telex: MW 212 FFACIL

23rd July, 1979

M E M O

TO: TONY MANICARO

FROM: MIKE HIGGINS

RE: DAMAGE TO EQUIPMENT AT DEEP TANK

John Gambina has today received an official complaint from one of the contractors regarding willful damage to plant machinery on the Deep Water Tank site. This was apparently the latest of a series of deliberate acts of vandalism.

I would be grateful if you could check if anyone of MFF personnel has any knowledge of these incidents.

In the meantime we are contacting the Police to see if they can provide a guard for our plant machinery at any times when it is left unattended.

Thank you for your attention.

MIKE HIGGINS
Unit Location Manager

cc. Malcolm Christopher
     Fred Muller
     John Gambina
     David Moore
     Stefano Priori
     Narcy Calamatta

STUDIO CENTER • 4024 RADFORD • STUDIO CITY, CALIFORNIA 91604 • (213) 763-8411

As filming on the sinking came to a close in the surface tank, metres away the troubles with the construction of the deep tank continued. This letter from July 1979 points out that building equipment had been purposely damaged. While no one person or individuals were being blamed, it raised suspicions enough to report the matter to the Maltese police. *(Author's collection)*

The 1912 Prologue

Presented here for the very first time is the series of original production storyboards depicting the intended 15 April 1912 sinking prologue. The sequence was to start an hour after the liner had collided with the iceberg as distress rockets burst above the doomed *Titanic*. The scenes were to be a mixture of both miniature work and live action shots with extras and actors playing the role of passenger Arthur Brewster and *Titanic's* junior officer in charge of cargo, John Bigalow. The storyboards show Brewster as he makes his way through areas of the ship on his route to the cargo holds. When he stumbles into Bigalow, the passenger forces the officer to take him into the hold and to the vault containing the mysterious crates and their deadly cargo. *(All storyboards are from the author's collection)*

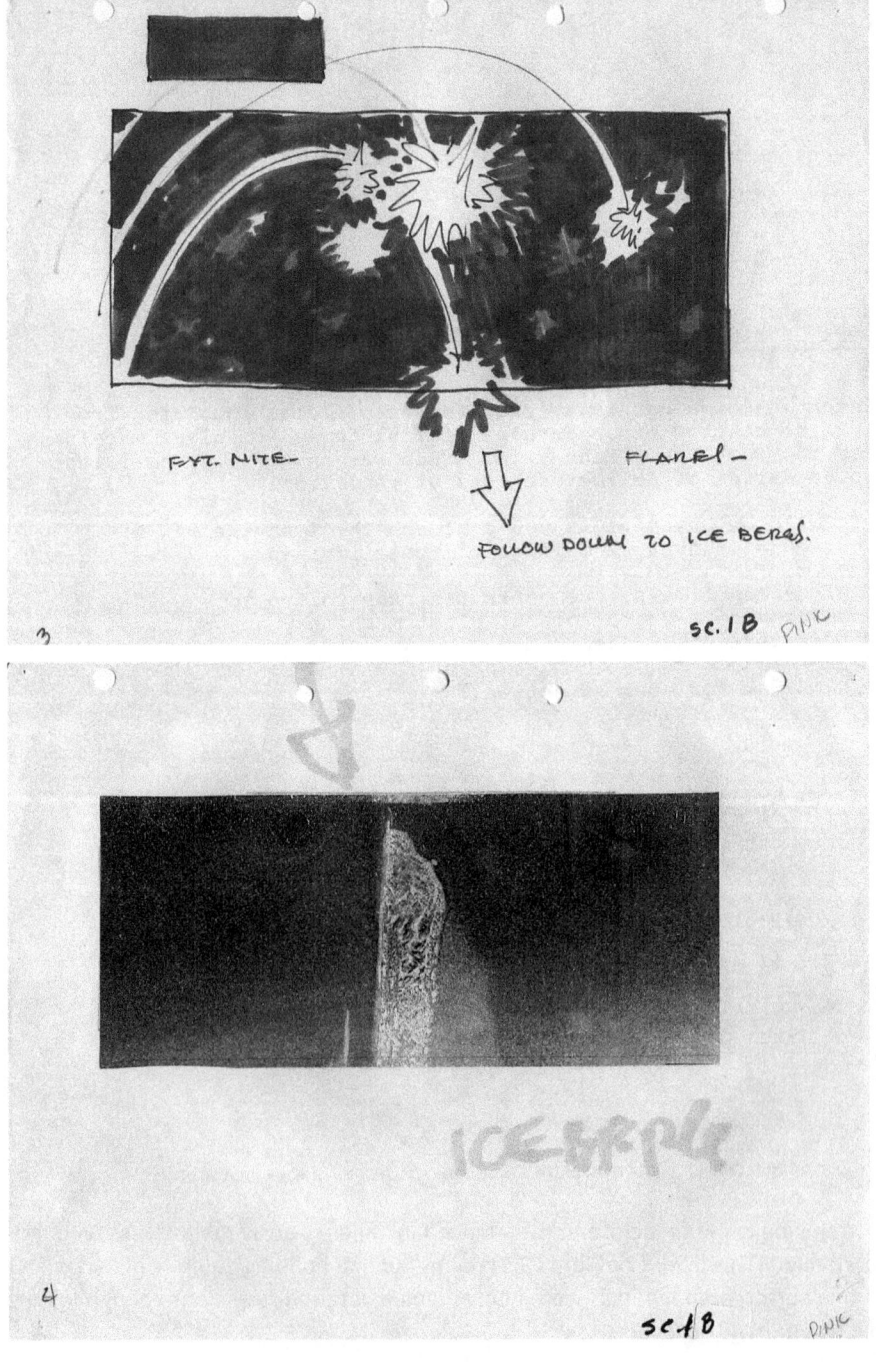

Chapter 11: Doomed from the Start • 339

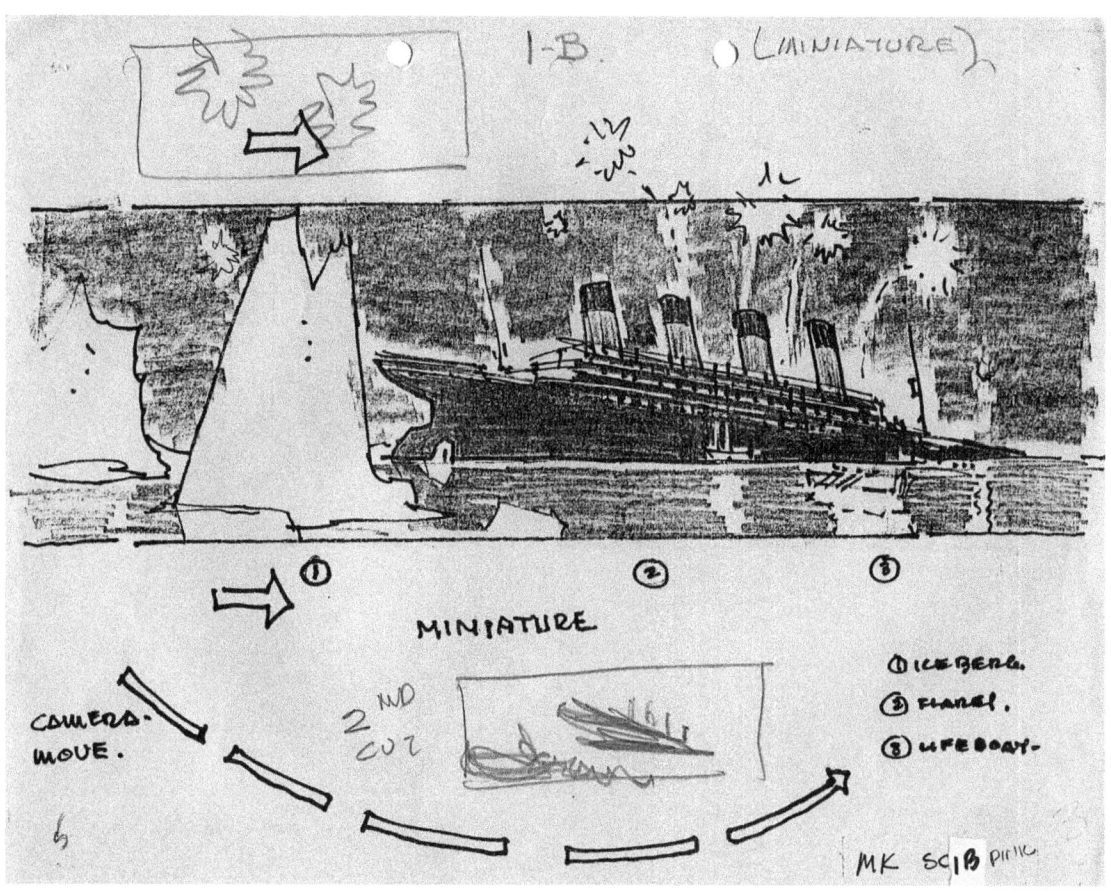

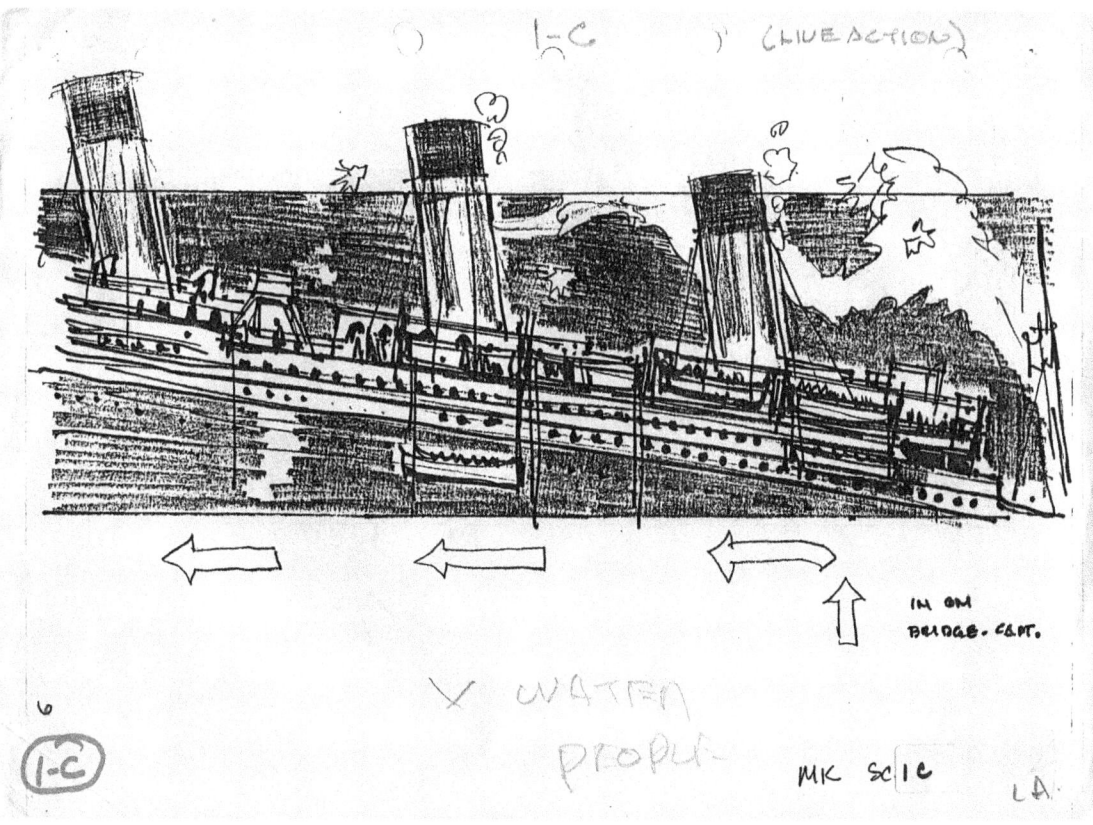

340 • *Raise The Titanic*

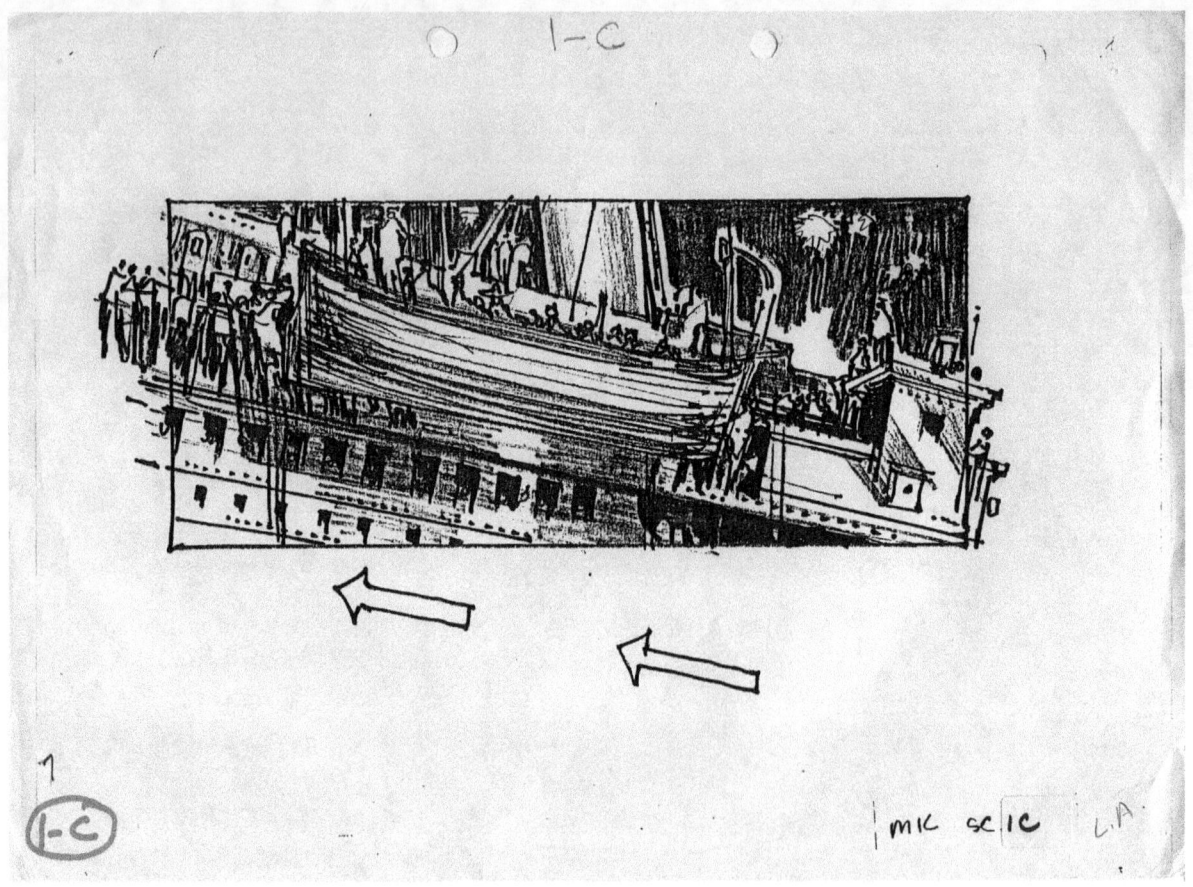

Chapter 11: Doomed from the Start • 341

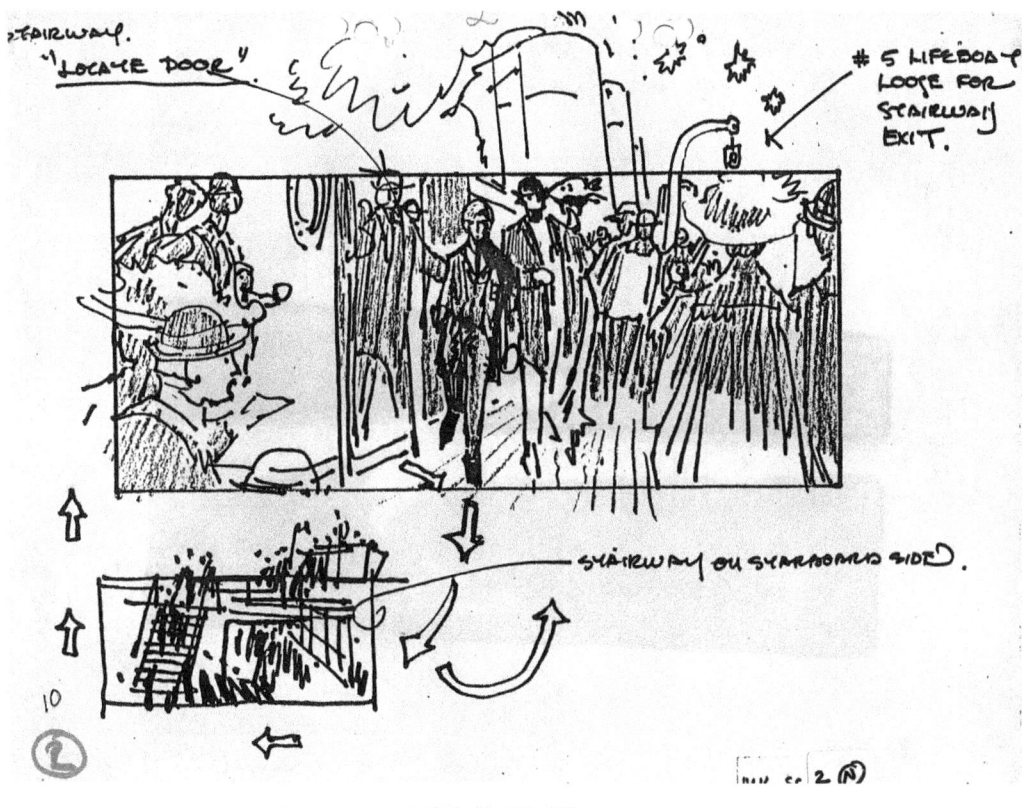

OPEN CAUSEWAY. FOR RUSHING PEOPLE -
SHOT FROM. FLYING BRIDGE SHOOTING DOWN -
* PEOPLE

TO STERN - STOP - LOOK
BACK.

BREWSTER SHOULD
BE FORWARD + DOWN

FRONT OF DECK - TO BOW.
STERN.

ROCKETS. —HORNS—

SC. 3

Chapter 11: Doomed from the Start • 343

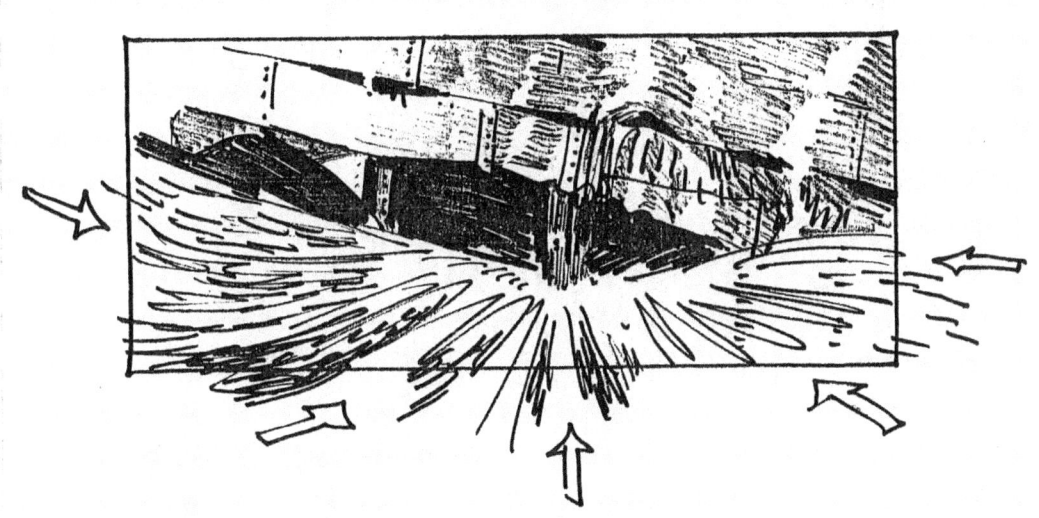

MK SC. 17A

EXPLOSION OF BOILER.

344 • Raise The Titanic

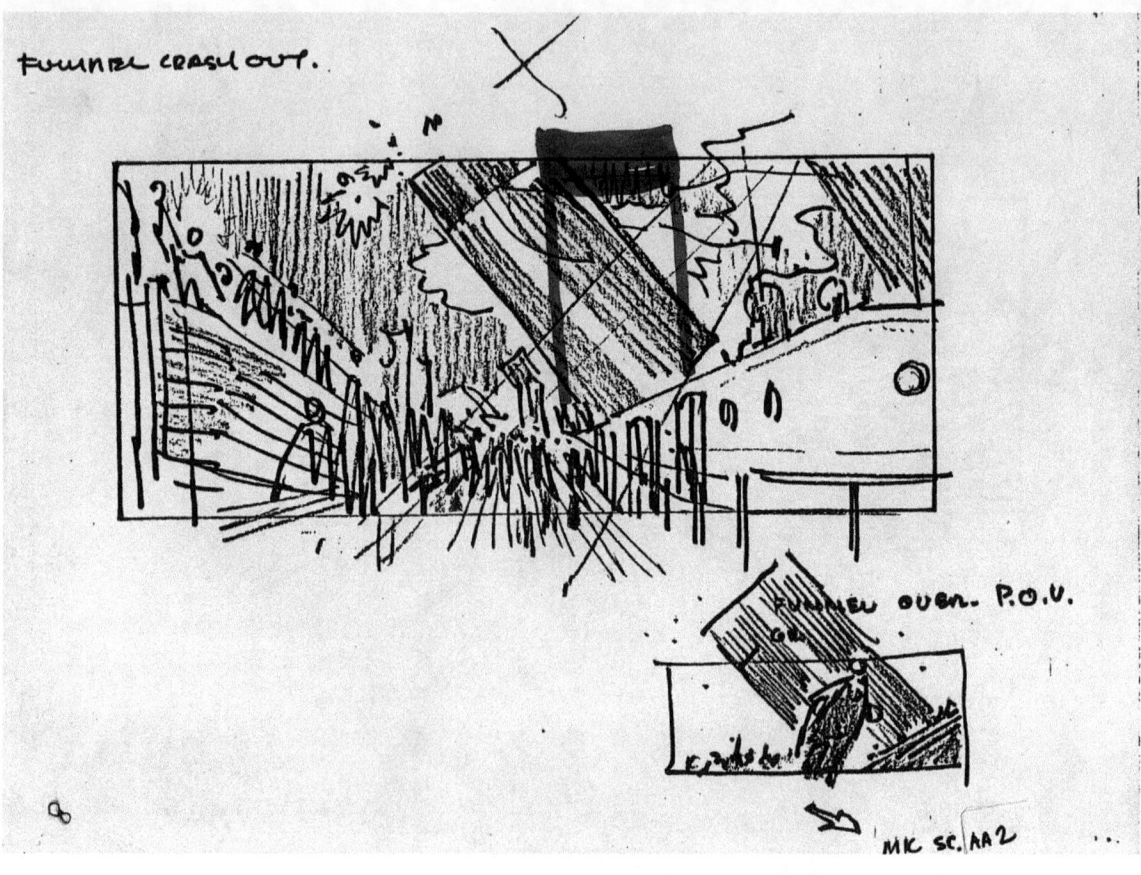

Chapter 11: Doomed from the Start • 345

EFFECT SHOT — BROKEN LINE & TACKLE.
WITH BOW PARTLY IN THE WATER....

STARBOARD SIDE —
PAINT JOB —
ALSO SLOPE ON SHIP —

14

MK SC. 4A

NEW GLAZING IN BALLROOM —
ALSO GLAZING ON WINDOWS —

LIGHTS OFF —

LIGHTS ON —

BOX OFF.

15

MK SC. 4B

346 • *Raise The Titanic*

16   MIC SC. 5

Chapter 11: Doomed from the Start • 347

348 • Raise The Titanic

sc. 6

Sections of glazing on promenade deck —

MK sc. 6B

Chapter 11: Doomed from the Start • 349

SC. 2A –

1)

CLOSE-UP INSIDE STAIRWAY.

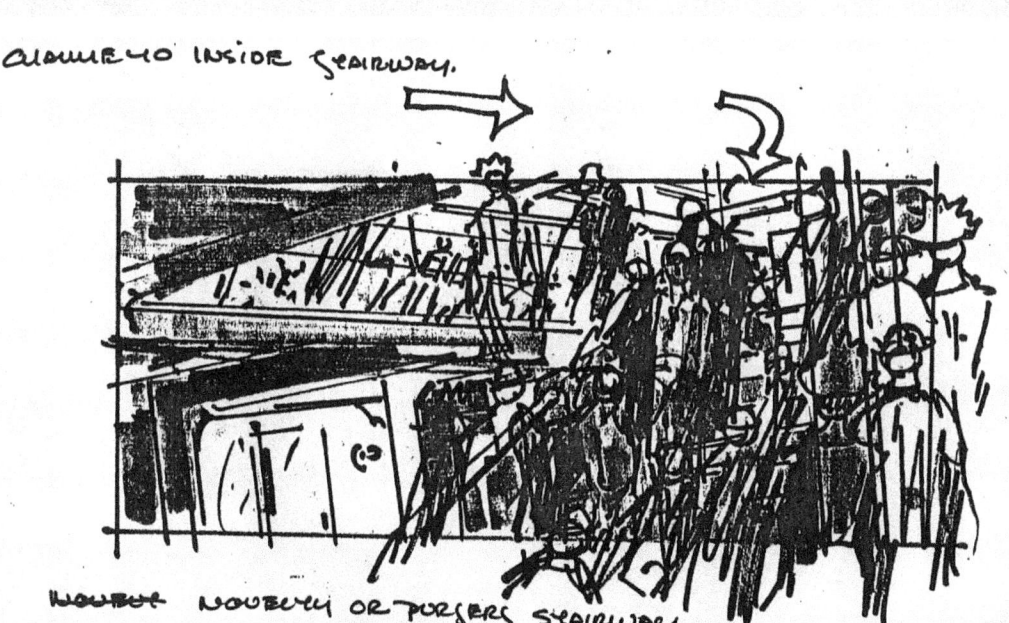

NOVEL NOVELLY OR PURSERS STAIRWAY –

MAY. SC 6-13

350 • Raise The Titanic

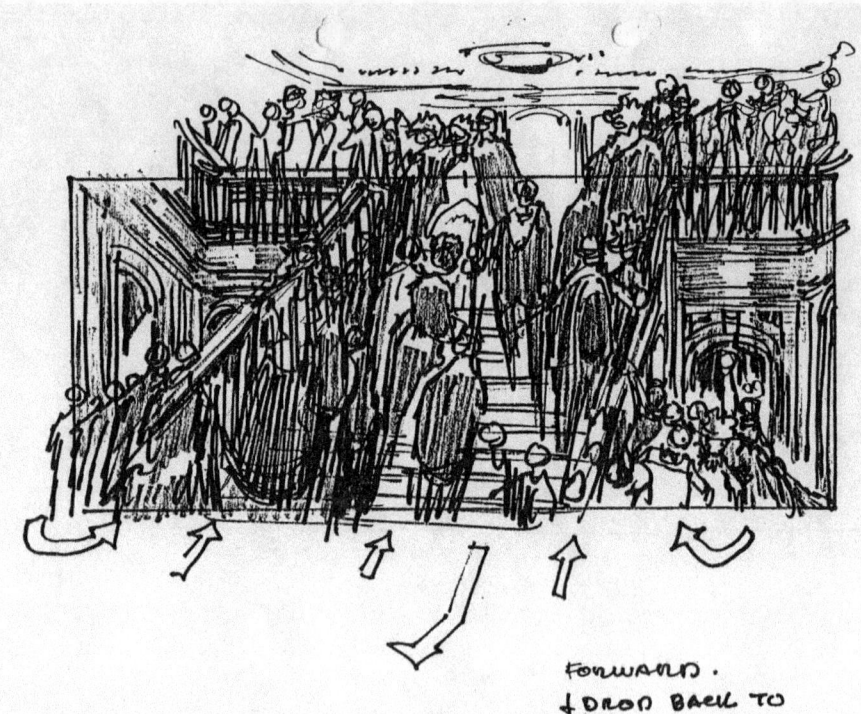

FORWARD.
↓ DROP BACK TO

MK SC. 6-13A

PURSER'S ALCOVE –

SC. 7

Chapter 11: Doomed from the Start • 351

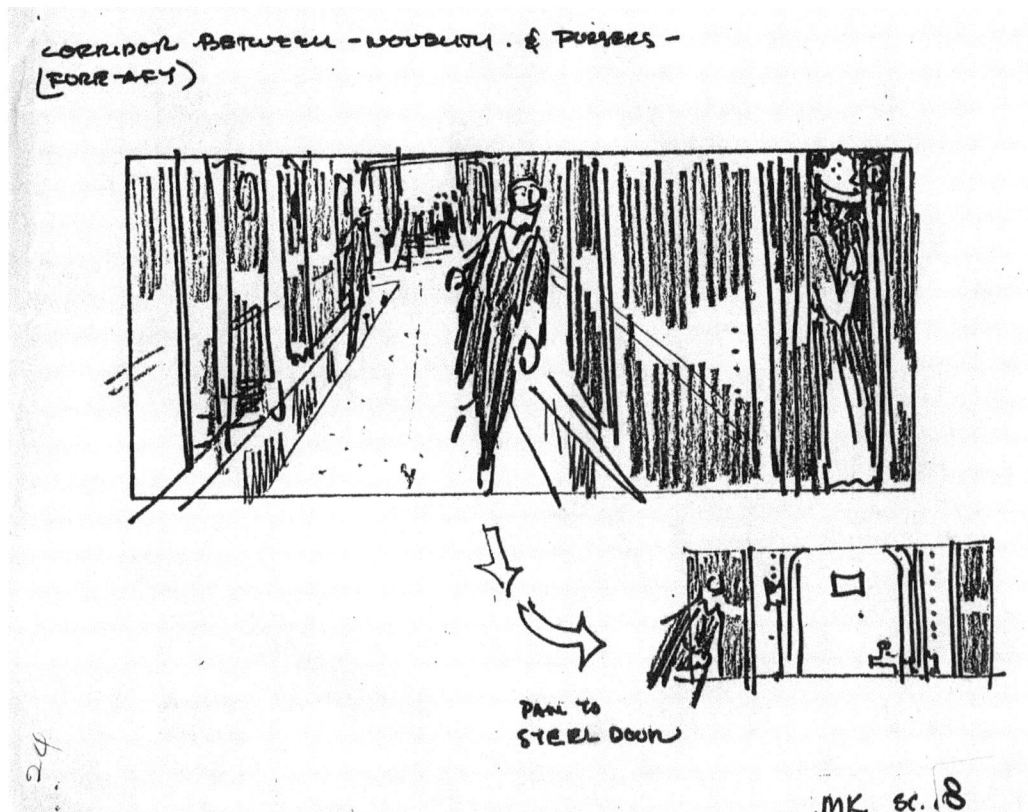

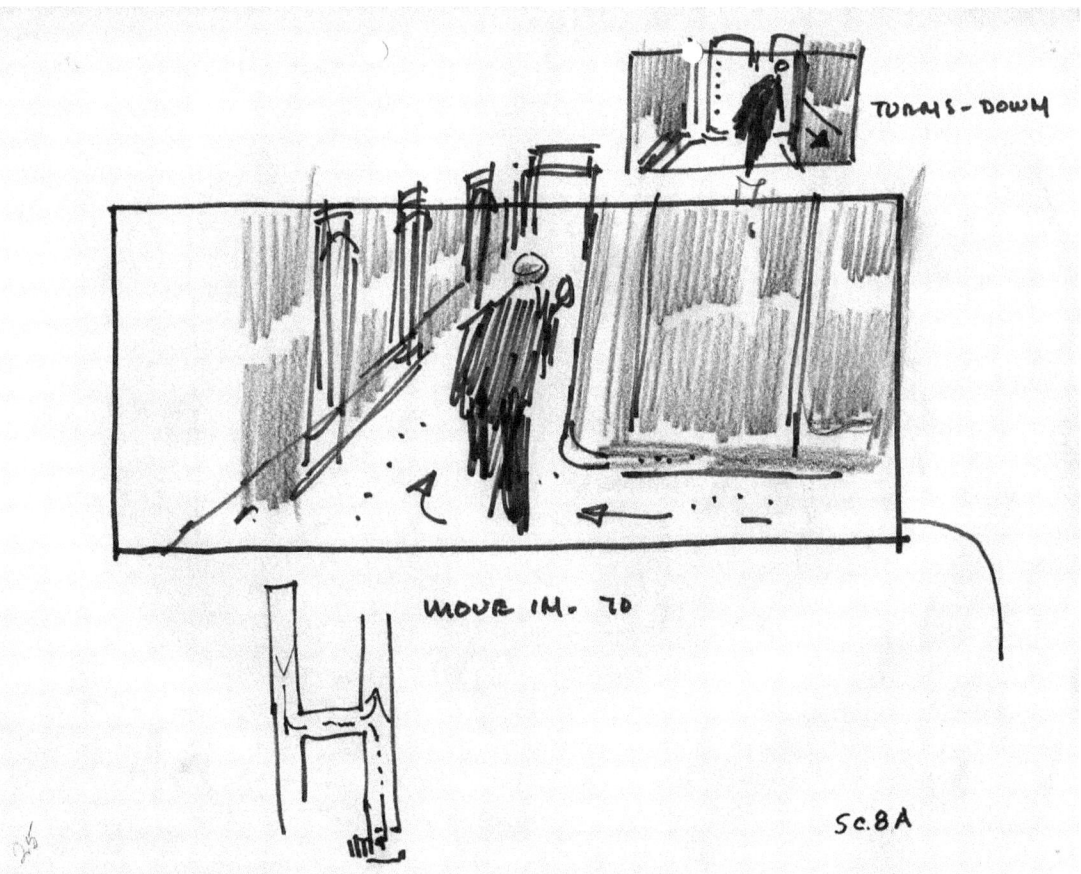

352 • *Raise The Titanic*

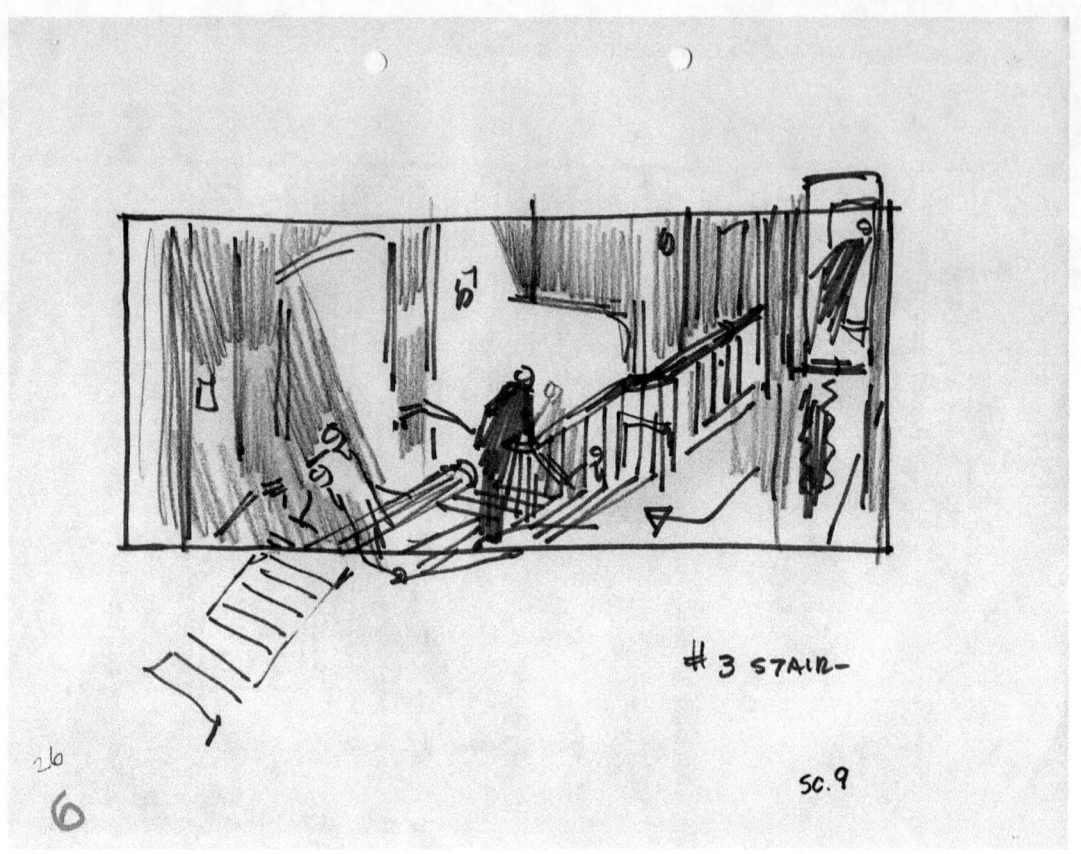

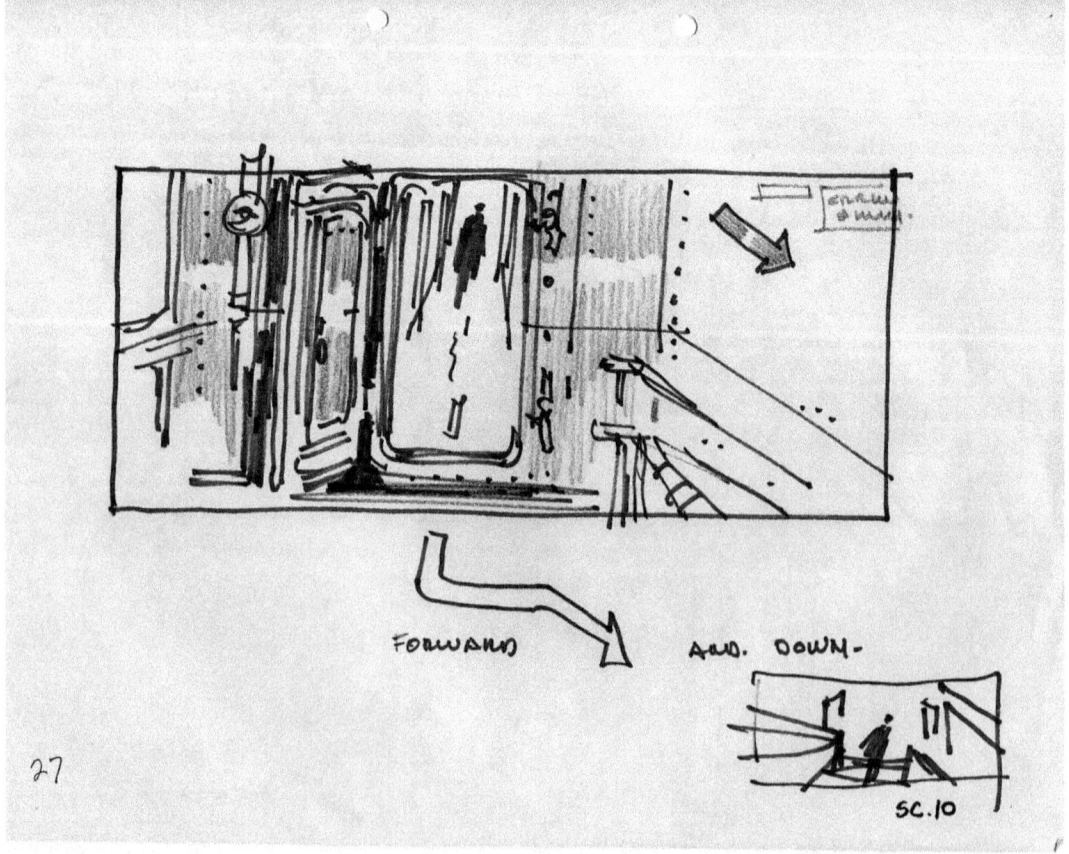

Chapter 11: Doomed from the Start • 353

sc. 11

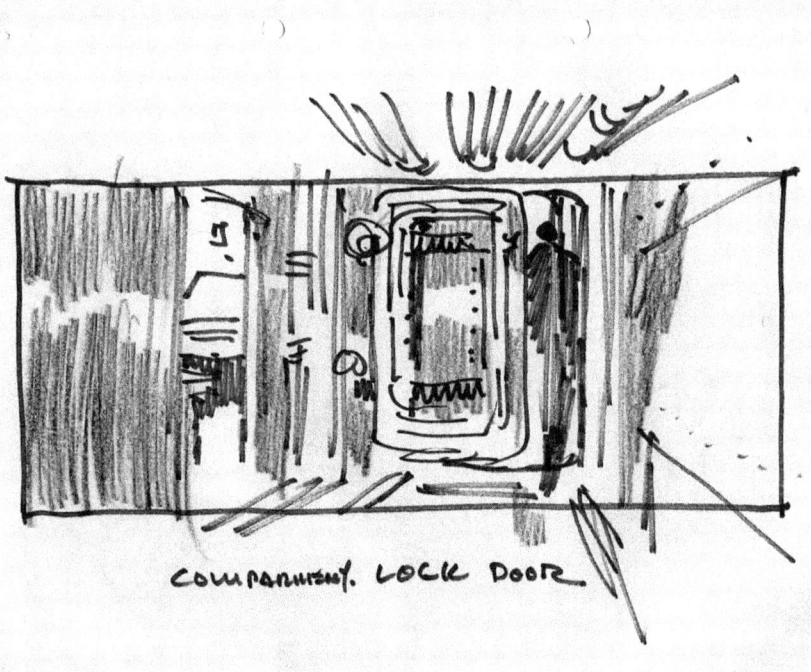

COMPARTMENT. LOCK DOOR

sc. 12

354 • Raise The Titanic

GAWEY

CUT & MOVE F.G. HOT TABLE —
SC.13

30

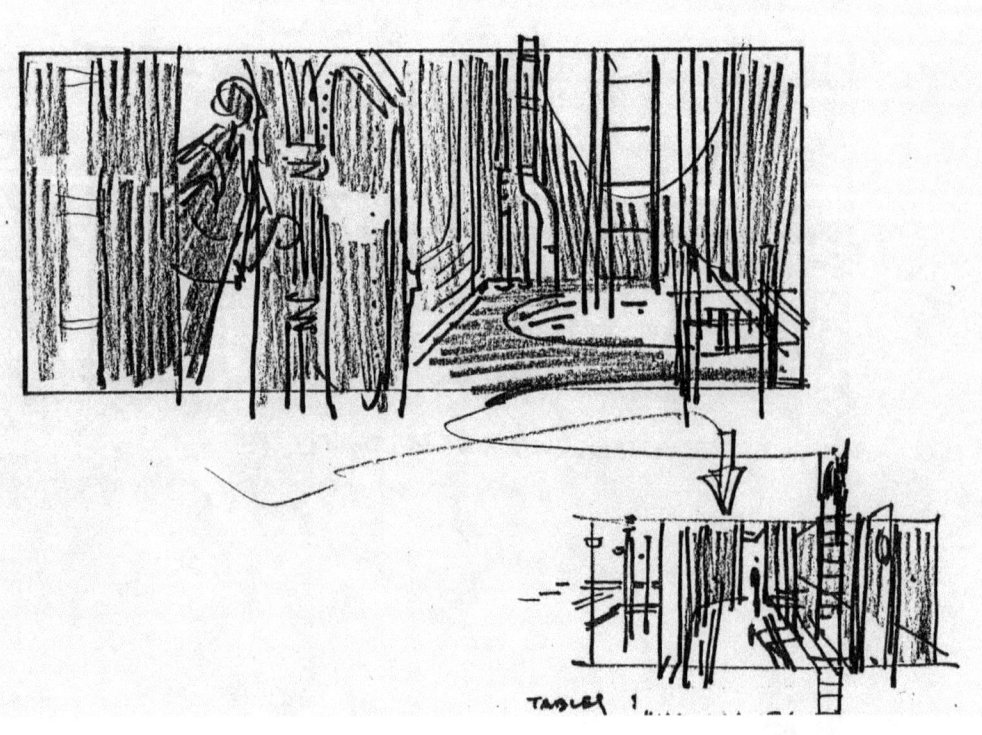

TABLE 1

Chapter 11: Doomed from the Start • 355

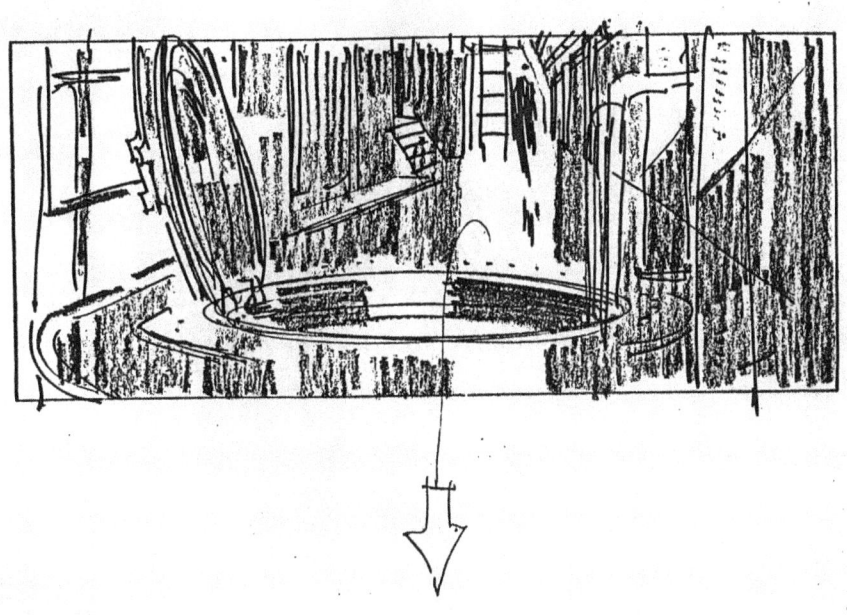

13-D.

MV sc.6-13D

DOOR CUT INTO
SECOND LEVEL CATWALK

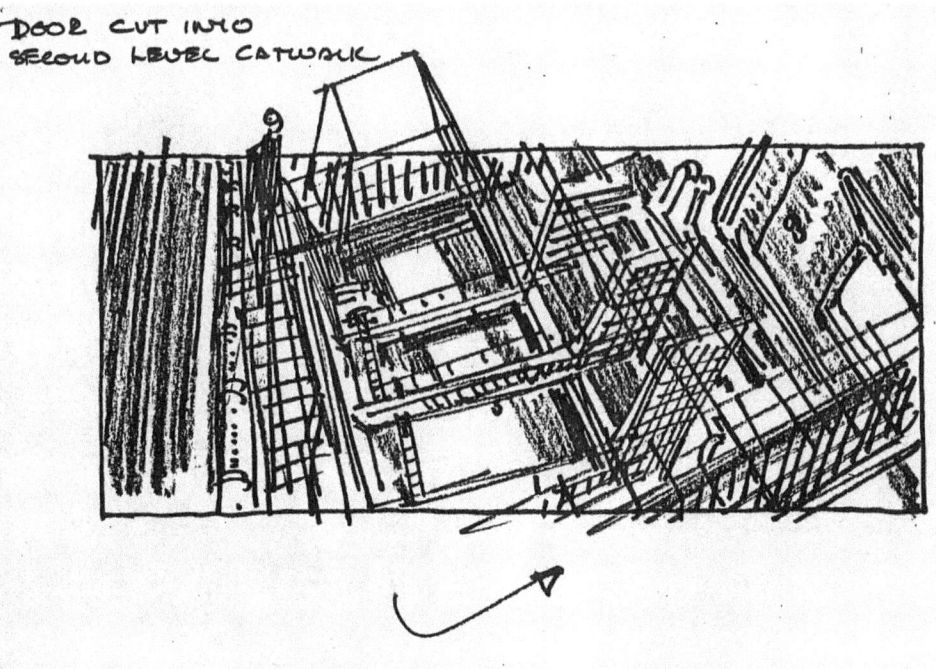

(14)

MK sc. 14

356 • Raise The Titanic

WATER LINE TO A FOOT ABOVE GRATING - ENGIN-

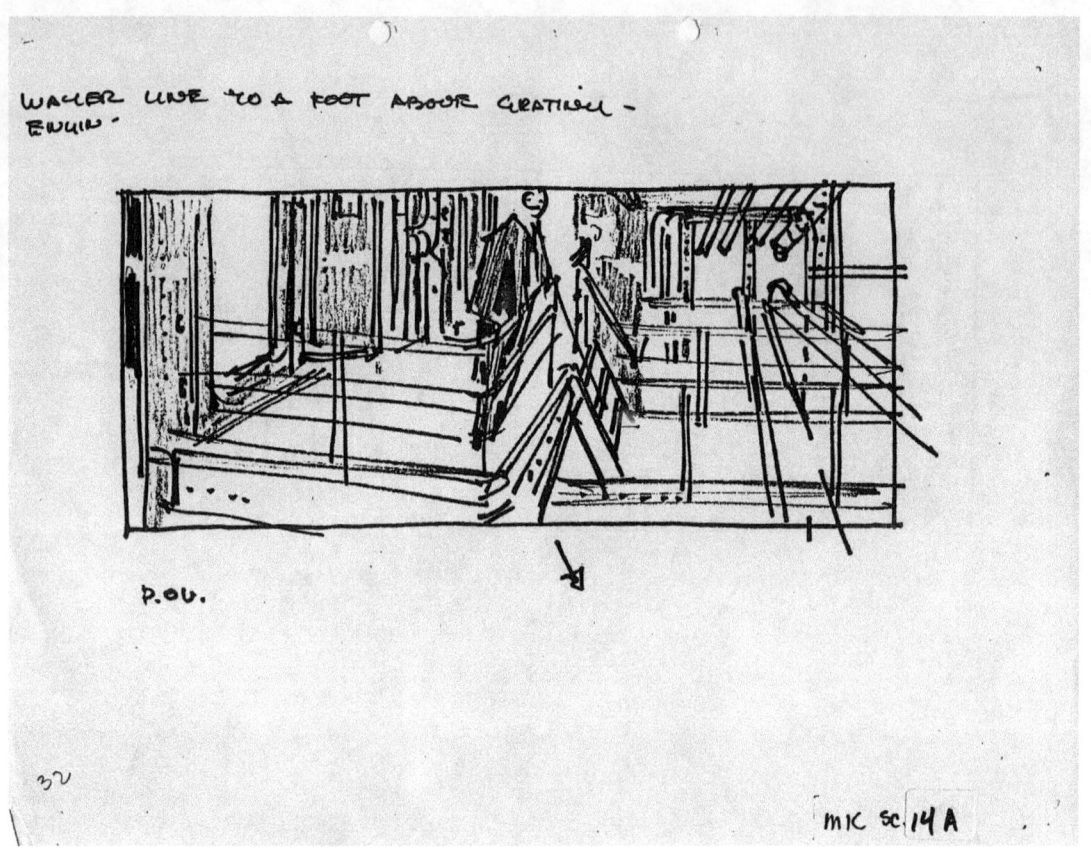

P.O.V.

MK SC.14 A

ELECTRICAL CONTROL PANEL.

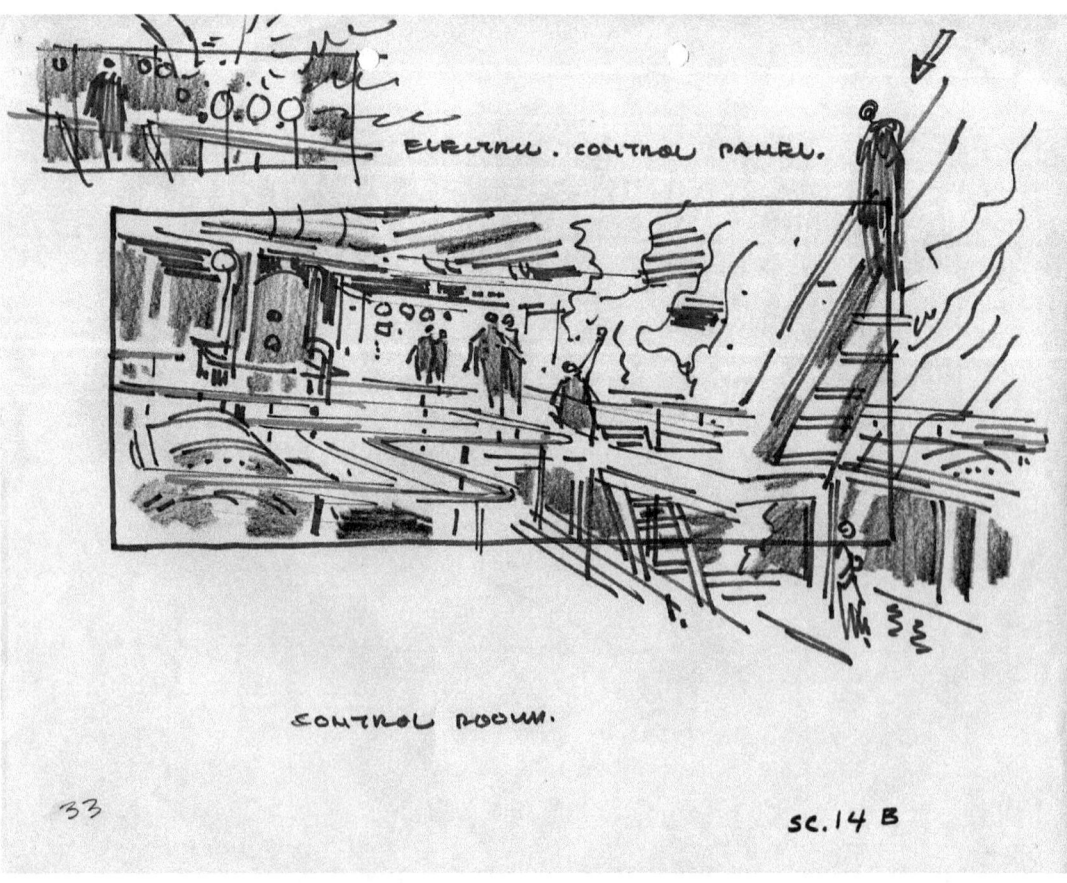

CONTROL ROOM.

SC.14 B

Chapter 11: Doomed from the Start • 357

34   MK sc 15

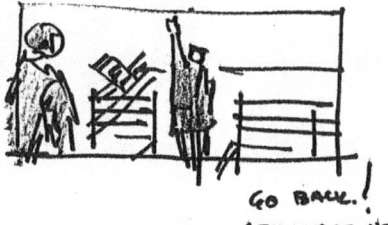

GO BACK!
GET OUT OF HERE!

HOLD AREA — DOORWAY —
POSSIBLY HOLD AREA FW #3
FW #0.

35   MK SC.15A

36   MK SC.16

2

SC. 318 H.S

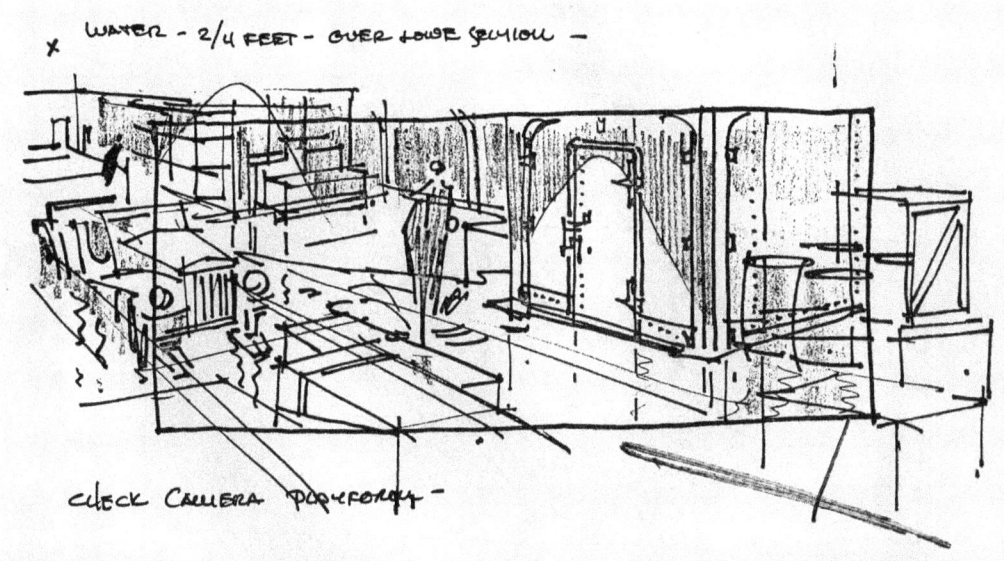

x WATER - 2/4 FEET - OVER LOWER SECTION -

CHECK CAMERA PLAYFORD -

. COAT OF QUICK - SPRAY PAINT -
. WATER EFX -

360 • *Raise The Titanic*

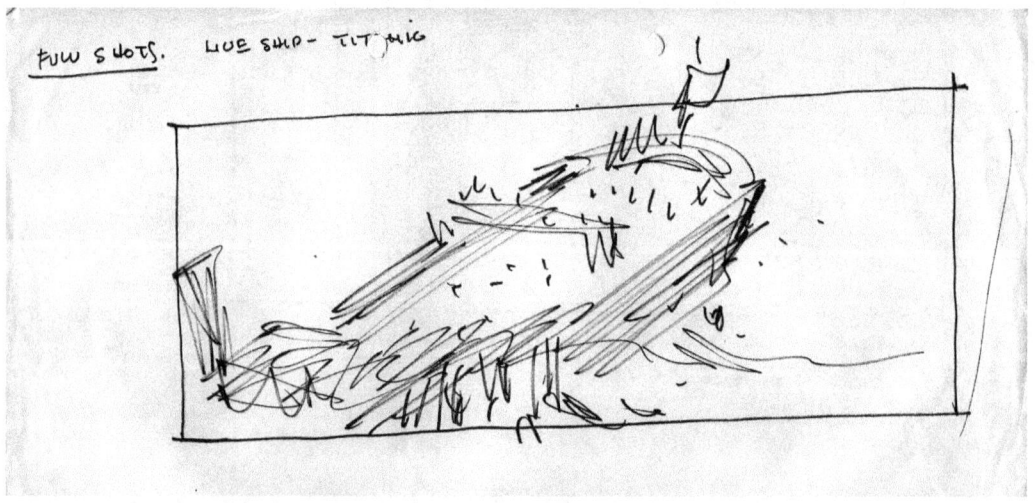

Chapter 11: Doomed from the Start • **361**

362 • *Raise The Titanic*

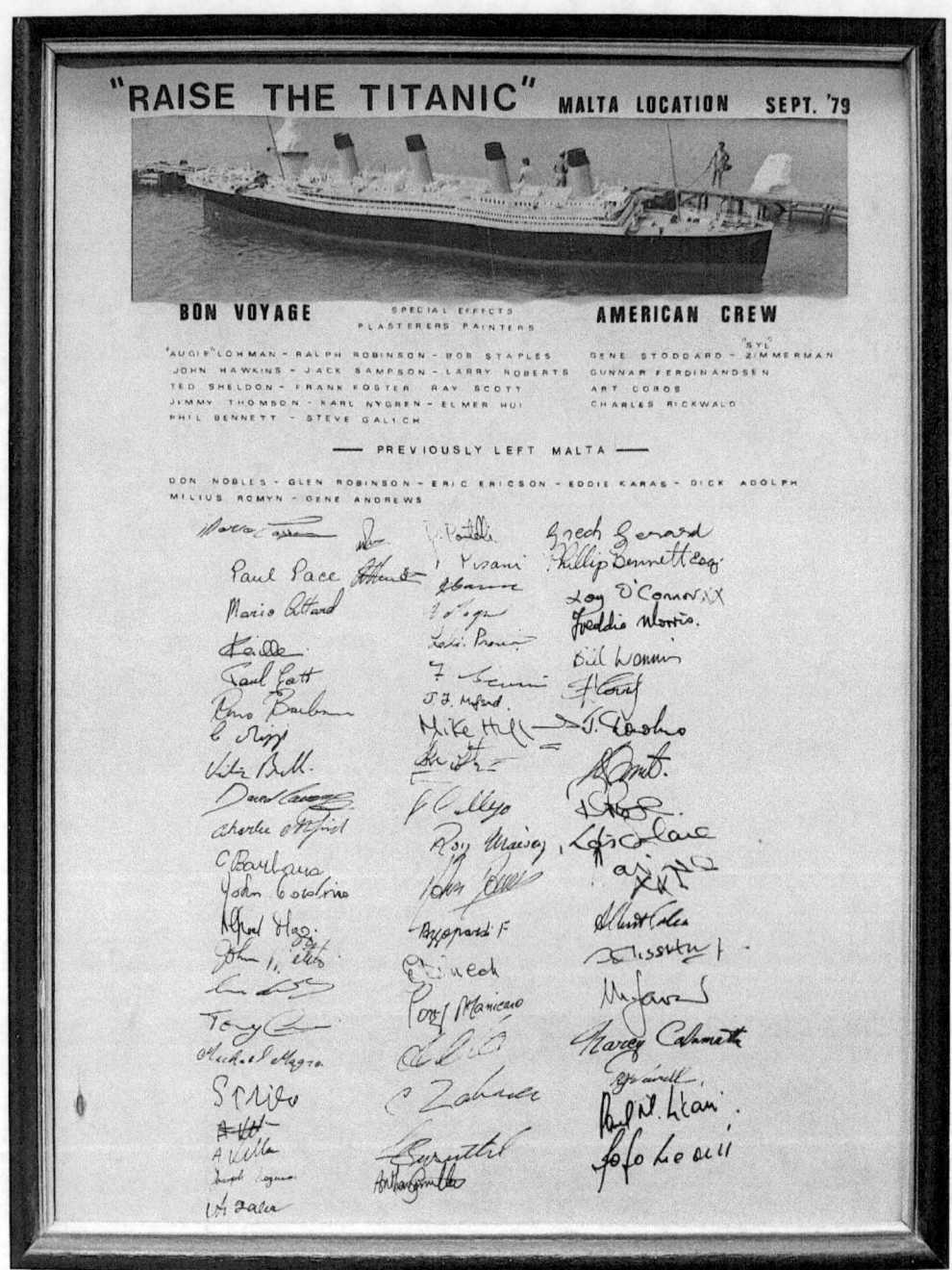

As filming of the sinking *Titanic* came to an end, the parting gift of a mini poster was hand signed by each of the film units on the production and handed out to the American crews before they left the studio to return home in September 1979. *(Jim Thomson collection)*

CHAPTER 12

Cold War Interference

"You want to talk about distress? We've got Navy weather forecasting a Force 12 storm. The Russians are looking down our throats. We're on a ship that never learned how to do anything but sink. That's distress."

Dirk Pitt

Of the many theories that have been circulated over the years regarding the problem with the finished film production of *Raise the Titanic* and to why it was greatly changed from the original Cussler story, the countless screenplay revisions it received has been cited as one main reason. But this was no theory. The screenplay did end up going through several, and at times, gruelling major changes, not only in the story, but also in writers. The Cold War content was to cause many concerns during filming. But that was to be expected given what was happening in the real world during the production of *Raise the Titanic*. As the screenplay came together, Jimmy Carter was serving in office as the 39th President of the United States of America, a position he held from January 20, 1977, to January 20, 1981. During his early days of presidency in February 1977, he urged the Soviet Union to form an alliance with the United States in creating a comprehensive ban on nuclear testing.

The Russians are Coming!

By the end of that year, both the United States and the Soviet Union had made much progress including one important issue, the better control of the deployment of nuclear weapons. But by April 1978 things began to look unsettled as Nur Muhammad Taraki became the president of Afghanistan, forming the Communist Democratic Republic of Afghanistan. Under Takai's new regime, he signed a friendship treaty with the Soviet Union in December. Great political oppression ignited following his efforts to improve education and redistributing land which resulted in mass executions, including those of religious leaders, imprisonment of dissidents, and overseeing the massacre of villages and occupants. And yet during this period, he tried, without any success, to persuade the Soviet Union to offer support in the restoration of civil order. And by April 1979 a general uprising was now in progress. Then on September 11, Amin greeted Taraki at Karbul airport following Taraki's return from Moscow. Taraki forcefully tried to neutralize Armin's power in government by requesting he serve overseas as an ambassador. This led to a conflict between Armin and Taraki and then when Armin refused at first to dine at the presidential palace he was persuaded by the Soviet Ambassador of Afghanistan, Alexander Puzanov, who was a close ally to Taraki, that he must attend the event despite the hostile relationship between the two men. He did so on the 14th of September and was accompanied by the Chief of Police Sayed Daoud Tarun and Intelligence Officer Nawab Ali.

Inside the palace, Taraki's bodyguards opened fire on visitors killing Tarun and injuring Armin, who was able to flee to the Ministry of Defence. Upon arrival, he put the Army on high alert, ordering the arrest and detainment of Taraki, to then telephone Puzanov to inform him of the incident. That evening as tanks for the 4th Armoured Corps entered the city; Armin with a contingent of Army officers marched into the palace and arrested Taraki. Puzanov tried to dissuade Armin from expelling Taraki and his governing associates from their positions, but Armin refused. On September 15 the Soviet battalion from Bagram Air Base along with the embassy, attempted a rescue of Taraki, but withdrew the attempt as they felt Armin's forces had a stronger position. On the 16th of September it was reported over Radio Kabul that Taraki was no longer to continue his duties and that the Politburo of the People's Democratic Party of Afghanistan elected Armin as the new General Secretary. Armin went on to discuss Taraki's arrest with the Soviet Ukrainian politician Leonid Brezhnev asking him what was to be done with Taraki with Brezhnev responding that it was Armin's choice. Armin thinking, he had the full support of the Soviets, ordered the death of Taraki. On October 8, 1979 while in his cell, Taraki was suffocated with pillows by three men sent on Armin's orders with his body being secretly buried at night and the news released he had died of a "serious illness."

When the news reached Brezhnev he was shocked and vowed to protect Taraki. Come December, Armin had lost most of the control of the country, prompting the Soviet Union to commence an invasion of Afghanistan, to culminate with the execution of Armin and put Babrak Karmal in the position of president. What was to follow triggered the Soviet intervention in the Soviet-Afgan war that was to last for over nine years. In America, President Carter had been taken by surprise by the invasion. In response he set vigorous sanctions upon the Soviet Union followed by calling to boycott the 1980 Summer Olympic Games that were to be held in Moscow. That in return raised bitter controversy. President Carter's ultimatum delivered on January 20, 1980, stated that the U.S would boycott the games if Soviet forces did not withdraw from Afghanistan. Many countries were spurred on by the Soviet-Afghan conflict, some 65 countries and regions from the 80 that were invited did not take part in the games. This all brought on a much higher strain on the relationship between the U.S and the Soviet Union resulting in a precarious and highly unstable period for the two countries. The Cold War, which many had hoped was on the rapid decline, was beginning to heat up once again as the media propaganda machines went into overtime.

The Russians are Coming!

At the time of its release in October 1976, Clive Cussler's *Raise the Titanic!* was in book stores as Jimmy Carter's predecessor Gerald Ford sat in the White House. During his time as president between August 1974 to January 1977, he had been continuing on the work previously put in place by the Richard Nixon administration in easing tensions brought about by the Cold War that involved not just America and the Soviet Union but also that of China. But during his time in office, Ford had bigger fish to fry, following his controversial pardon of Nixon after his resignation. With Ford losing to Carter, Carter continued with the work set out by Nixon and Ford to bring relations between the U.S and Russia to a better mutual understanding. That was to change come Carter's term and the fall-out which resulted in the Soviet-Afghan war.

With the screenplay for *Raise the Titanic* now in its early stages, the book-to-screen story was to not only capture the essence of the original story but now required a sympathetic touch reflecting upon the troubles brewing overseas in Central Asia. By late 1979 the script was undertaking yet another metamorphosis as Soviet tanks began rolling into Afghanistan and the media and public turned their attention to the Soviet Union once again. Cussler's novel played out among the pages the battles between America and Russia to great effect. But how were they to transfer those intense conflicts from the pages of a book to that of celluloid without adding concerns to the real-life conflicts happening in Afghanistan and those in government? Higher-ranking officials in both the Navy and at the Pentagon were already scrutinizing the United States Navy's involvement in the film. The changing of sequences, portraying both the Navy and government, Pentagon and CIA, had to be carried out respectfully, with a form of dignity and with a style not making either America or Russia out to be the bad guys.

One interesting aspect of the Cussler novel is that the book's Russian island has the fictional name of Svlardov. But Cussler's island is based on the real cluster of islands known as Novaya Zemlya located in the Arctic Ocean off Northern Russia to the extreme northeast of Europe. Novaya Zemlya is comprised of two main islands, the northern Severny Island and the southern Yuzhny Island, and the waters of the Matochkin Strait that divide them. Cussler's Svlardov, being a fictional place, played no physical part with the Soviet Union but that connection between fiction and non-fiction is all too evident considering that Novaya Zemlya held a series of Nuclear Test programs during the Soviet Union's Cold War periods. Construction of the site began in October 1954 with "Zone A" which was in use between 1955-1962 and again between 1972-1975. The underground "Zone B" followed with tests run between 1964-1990 and "Zone C" operating in 1958-1961 which became the testing site for the 1961 Tsar Bomba , the most powerful nuclear weapon ever to be tested with a yield of 50 megatons, the equivalent of an estimated 1,570 times the combined energy of the bombs which destroyed both Nagasaki and Hiroshima. It becomes clear why Clive Cussler decided to use Novaya Zemlya as the inspiration for Svlardov. The radioactive Byzanium that was robbed from the precise soil on Soviet territory became the focal point of conflict between Russia and America. One has to wonder if the Soviets were that bothered about the Byzanium or were they more fixated with the fact that American boots had trampled their land to conclude this unwelcome invasion as an act of war. With Capt. Andre Prelov coming aboard the raised *Titanic* to confront Pitt, Seagram and Sandecker, he soon made his position and reasons for being there known;

> "We know about the Byzanium, stolen from a mine on Russian territory. You must trust me gentlemen that when I tell you that we are determined to take back what is morally and legally ours. The *Mikhail Kurkov* is a torpedo ship. If her captain has no signal from me… eight minutes from now, he will sink this ship we are standing on."

While viewers of the film, having previously read the book, longed for the ensuing gun battle to begin between the two superpowers, the no-one-is-good-and-no-one-is-bad in this film which was brought about by the heavy editing resulted in an almost tongue and cheek exchange of words, eliminating any potential edge-of-your-seat conflict of ricocheting bullets and explosions. A toddler's school playground misunderstanding would have packed more of a punch than what was used in the end. But while fans wanted such confrontations to take place on-screen, the result of events in the real world forcefully paved the way that *Raise the Titanic*, the movie, needed to appear on the big screen while being acceptable to all involved with the project. Those factors played a crucial part in sinking this *Titanic*.

The U.S. Navy Responds

The sheer production schedule of such a film like that of *Raise the Titanic* is daunting enough to bring to the big screen let alone having to deal with the constant problems that pop up such as camera malfunctions, bad weather during filming, or re-working of actor's lines. But there is no bigger headache than when those in higher authority forcibly get involved and whose involvement reshapes the product beyond its original intended form. It may sound extreme, inappropriate even, but in the case of *Raise the Titanic* nothing was ever going to be that simple. The film's Cold War story was enough to raise concerns when the use of the United States Navy was required for integral parts of the plot not just in the story itself but also on-screen which would warrant closer examination from those in the government. The Navy's crucial part in the film's production with supplying vessels, lighting systems, their latest salvage equipment, and submarines had to deliver positivity to all concerned. A lot would appear to be at stake in portraying the Navy on screen. And so the film had to be run through a process of inspection from start to finish. While the Navy has little to gain during the supporting of a movie project, which may cause some laughter towards their men, the Pentagon on the other hand lacked such relaxed attitudes. Their question was: will this film benefit the services that provided the assistance?

Donald E. Baruch served as the principal liaison at the Pentagon from 1949 to his retirement in 1989. When the Department of Defense was established in 1949 Baruch became the department's special assistant to the assistant secretary of defense for public affairs. Having served as an officer in the Army and Air Force during WWII with previous qualifications of working as a films director's assistant for Paramount Pictures, it was clear he established a position in becoming a consulting federal employee. During his forty-year career, Baruch was associated with many notable films including *The Longest Day* (1962), *From Here to Eternity* (1953), *Stripes* (1981), *The Green Berets* (1968), *Patton* (1970), *The Right Stuff* (1983) and *Top Gun* (1986). Baruch also served as an active member of the Washington Film Council and on to serving as a judge for the U.S. Information Agency's Golden Eagle Awards panel until his passing in April 1997. In June 1977 a copy of Adam Kennedy's script for the Martin Starger production of *Raise the Titanic* landed on Baruch's desk. The script covered 108 single printed pages totaling 299 scenes. After reading that initial script Baruch concluded that the Navy had nothing to gain from supporting such a production;

> "Gives Navy a repeat of Airport '77 - entertaining claptrap of no great significance!! Questionable value, personally sees no reason for Navy wanting to do it."

It was recommended to the Chief of Information that the Navy refuse to offer any help. One would think that even then that harsh judgement would, at least, give the film's production crews time to rethink if the movie was viable. But the huge sums of money already indebted into the project became a point of no turning back. What next? It was decided to approach afresh with a reworking of the script. Lew Grade's Marble Arch Productions on October 12, 1978, would send onto the Navy a newly revised script of which the Navy began to cooperate, albeit by pointing out the numerous technical inaccuracies.

If the prospect of four writers working the script were not enough to make the Navy skeptical to begin with, the revised editions of the story with their inaccuracies had now got the attention of Admiral David Cooney, who, through Bill Graves, the director to the Navy's Los Angeles Public Affairs Office, to deny any support to the film, highlighting to Marble Arch Productions the constant errors and pointing out that consideration would be given if they addressed the story and bring it up to date with the Navy's "current or even possible Navy operations and missions." In May 1979 Admiral Cooney met with Jerry Jameson to discuss the future of the production's story. Cooney made it clear that "very substantive changes" had to be made and that the Navy must enforce Marble Arch Productions to make those changes for the better. The Office of Information instructed Baruch;

> "The Navy cannot assist unless the script is changed to remove that portion that indicates the U.S. Navy might have high seas involvement with the Soviet Navy, and second, that section where the Navy officer is trespassing on Soviet soil without the knowledge of the Russian Government."

And so, Marble Arch Productions and Adam Kennedy went to work, once again, reworking the script to deliver to the Navy on August 27, 1979, a revised final draft consisting of 142 single-sided pages of 411 scenes. Upon receiving the script, it was read by Baruch's department, the Office of Information, and the State Department. The Navy would respond on October 15, 1979, offering their assistance to the movie by saying that the Navy "Interposes no objection to the subject screenplay as presently written." During that time, the Pentagon's Office of International Security Affairs had raised their concerns over the screenplays Cold War aspects. They responded to Baruch that the story "has no relationship to any true historical event, and we find it far-fetched and unrealistic." The idea that an American agent, trespassing on Soviet soil, results in shooting a Soviet soldier would "play into the hands of current Soviet propaganda" making the U.S. on-screen appear to be "provocative" and "militaristic" while the Soviet polices are "peace-loving."

While the Navy on October 15 stated to Marble Arch Productions that *they* had no objections to the script, this was not *their* acceptance of the Pentagon's approval. On October 22 Admiral Cooney had offered to address some areas of the script which the State and Defence Department found problematic. Marble Arch Productions, on the other hand, decided to ignore the request. Then on October 24, the Bureau of European Affairs remarked that;

> "There are aspects of the film which could have an adverse effect on U.S-Soviet relations, if the Department of Defense made its resources available to support the filming, due to the manner in which the U.S-Soviet confrontation is depicted in the film."

But they did conclude that when concerns raised by the Pentagon were to be addressed, that, in turn, would deliver a film within the Department of Defense guidelines. A letter from the International Security Affairs Office to Baruch on October 29 continued, "as written, the film is not particularly helpful to our national interest" but the State Department would require to establish the film does not create any permanent damage to both the U.S. and U.S-Soviet relationships. However, the office still required Baruch to make sure that the film meets, "the established Department of Defense criteria for authenticity and dignity." The reply from Admiral Cooney on October 31 mentions that *Raise the Titanic* had been given approval based on the promises made by Marble Arch Productions on the changes;

> "The Navy position is that providing assistance and will aid in recruiting efforts by showing the public the sophisticated equipment used by the Navy to explore the ocean's depths and give some insight on the expertise required for undersea salvage work."

By November 1979 Marble Arch Productions had still yet to get a done deal. Correspondence to Baruch from the Pentagon outlined that they had authorized the filming of just two scenes in Washington and that Marble Arch Productions had still not yet incorporated the changes to the script as requested. The Pentagon wanted the questionable island off Russia to be changed to one that was under dispute, an island that had no national sovereignty over it. The film had to include some dialogue emphasizing that the Soviet soldier has no right to be on the island. Those delays from Marble Arch Productions were becoming an equal inconvenience to the production as those from the government officials. Without the assistance of the Navy, how were they going to successfully raise the *Titanic*? On November 16, Marble Arch Productions finally saw sense and delivered to the Pentagon their final revised draft of the screenplay with all the requested changes. The approval was completed on November 19 citing that the Navy was giving support to the film on a "non-interference and no additional cost to the government basis" but a screen credit for Navy technical advisor would be welcomed and that the final edit of the film was required to be screened in Washington before Pentagon officials, and before any public release.

Admiral Cooney had previously expressed his dislikes towards the film's intended ending. He expressed that the salvaging of *Titanic* revealing a cargo hold of boxes with nothing but gravel inside as the character of Admiral Sandecker, played by Jason Robards, tries to alleviate Seagram's crushing disappointment by explaining his own concerns over the Byzanium and its potential. Cooney liked Clive Cussler's novel and liked the book's ending of a successful testing of the laser defence system. But Cooney went one step further by re-writing the film's ending and presenting it to Martin Starger. His ending did make it into the August 27, 1979 "Revised Final Draft" of the screenplay from Adam Kennedy. When Pitt and Seagram learn of the true identity of Southby, they arrive at what they presume would be the cemetery which is now long gone; reduced to a memorial playground following a devastating crash during WWII of a German bomber which obliterated the cemetery and those laid to rest, including the grave containing the Byzanium. Admiral Cooney had given permission for his ending to be used and was under the impression that an agreement had come to a positive conclusion on its use. In the end, the finished film was not given a pre-release in Washington while Cooney went on to discover that his ending was never used. Marble Arch Productions explained that they thought it was a suggestion but did intend in using that ending when the scene was sent onto Baruch's office for comment. But it was decided that Adam Kennedy's ending was "creatively the better ending", concluding the unfortunate nature of producer William Frye not notifying Admiral Cooney of the change. Then to add insult to injury a letter from Richard O'Connor, the executive in charge of productions for Marble Arch, addressed in a letter to Cooney that he was not aware of a Pentagon special advanced screening. While the office had clearly stated that such a screening was required, certainly not any form of mistake from Baruch's office since its creation in 1949 to be the studio liaison with the Pentagon, the ignorance from Lew Grade's production companies suggests that the filmmakers had no intentions of delivering any form of the final edit of the movie for Pentagon approval knowing of a backlash before its official world premiere.

Clive Cussler's dislike of the film and how his story had been so poorly adapted for the screen may have been largely down to him not being fully aware of the complications between the studio, Navy, and Pentagon. After all, why would he even be kept in the loop over such dramatics having relinquished his rights over the screenplay before he signed the contract? The politics of the time outweighed the need to be faithful to the source material. It was not something that happened to just *Raise the Titanic* as it is extremely rare that stories adapted for the screen are remotely faithful to the story they were based upon. Cussler had presumed that what he could get away with within the pages of his novel could be recreated to some degree on screen without being questioned; especially at the time that the movie went into production and its contents of two superpowers teetering on possible nuclear war. Meanwhile the real-life events unfolding thousands of miles away resulting in repercussions around the world were largely going unnoticed at the London offices of ITC. They did not care about politics or which countries had a grievance. It was about selling cinema tickets and putting backsides on seats. Lew Grade was probably bewildered by all these constant script changes. The production had quickly and almost quietly changed from that of making a good film to that of a British film studio not understanding American politics while bowing down to the demands of change applied by the U.S government for the sake of not upsetting public relations between the two allies. And yet despite all the ramifications between the films production companies and the Navy, *Raise the Titanic* did go on to show with great advantage the sophisticated salvage and underwater equipment the United States Navy had to hand that fooled the audience into believing that the impossible could be possible.

"The U.S. Navy and CIA join forces to raise the *Titanic*"

That could easily have been a front-page headline given how the subject of searching for the real *Titanic* in 1980 was panning out. The navy certainly had a wealth of technology to hand in such work and in the past had succeeded in the covert operation of raising a wreck. The general public would have taken it more seriously if any of the leading navies in the world had come forward to claim finding the lost liner; more than that of the stories being published of a Texan businessman who previously had failed in finding any evidence of the Loch Ness Monster, the Yeti and Noah's Ark. There is one memorable scene in *Raise the Titanic* where Pitt addresses the U.S. Navy and the CIA when he discloses where the Byzanium is and how he plans to retrieve it. In response to Pitt exclaiming that he intends to raise the *Titanic*, a dumfounded General Dale Busby asks "Can it be done? A ship that big, down that deep?" As the men look to each other for a reaction it is Pitt who breaks the silence; "It's never been done before, no question about that. But we did raise that nuclear sub a couple of years ago." The sub that Pitt speaks of was not a figment of imagination inserted into the screenplay to add depth to the CIA's cooperation in the salvage of deep-water wrecks. The subtle hint of the recovery of a downed nuclear submarine does share an uncanny resemblance to a real-life event that occurred in August 1974 that was carried out by the Central Intelligence Agency.

Code-named "Project Azorian" and under the direction of the CIA, a highly illegal and very controversial deep-sea operation unfolded during the height of the Cold War period and focused on the CIA partially raising the hull of the sunken Soviet nuclear sub K-129 which had sunk in 16,000ft of water in March 1968 during ballistic-missile tests in the Pacific Ocean. Due to the nature of the events, President Nixon authorized the salvage attempt without the assistance of the Soviet Union. In fact, they were totally oblivious to the operation. The U.S Navy declined to have anything to do with the salvage operation and so the role was handed over to the CIA in utter secrecy. The original idea was in the construction of the *Glomar Explorer* that operated under the cover story of a deep-sea mining vessel and kitted with a specially designed crane with a lifting system it would bring the K-129 to the surface for the submarines contents to be extracted. After a number of delays and costs running way over budget, the *Glomar Explorer* recovered only a partial amount of the subs hull at an estimated cost of $800 million ($3.8 billion today). Despite the recovery of two nuclear torpedoes, sonar equipment, and the remains of six crew members, the CIA confirmed it to be a successful exercise regardless of costs and the failed attempt to secure the recovery of the sought-after SS-4 ballistic missiles, code books, and decoding machine. With the CIA and the Navy now involved in the production of *Raise the Titanic*, the questionable Cold War elements were enough to warrant scrutiny in promoting the Navy, their fleet, equipment, and personnel in the correct light. If the studios had thought it through, they may have come up with an alternative solution without the need to turn to the maritime services of the United States Armed Forces, which, in the end, had a serious knock-on effect during the production of *Raise the Titanic*.

Flawed Decision?

The involvement of the navy during the filming of *Raise the Titanic* certainly had a great amount of impact upon the overall look of the movie as their dislikes to the screenplay outnumbered the positives. The heavy editing of the film, done to satisfy the officials at the top, did more damage than any good for the adaptation. The mounting pressure from the re-edits evidentially took its toll on ITC when they decided not to oblige in sending Baruch a copy of the film before its world premiere. When all the issues the navy had with the story are brought to light it begs the question; why did Jerry Jameson, and for that matter the studio, continue to support the needs of having the navy involved when there was no apparent need for their presence? On screen the amount of naval equipment used filled up a lot of transitions between scenes, but all this fodder was mainly for the audience. Jameson had already previously dealt with the navy when they assisted on *Airport '77*. An yet their critical response when approached to work with him again on *Raise the Titanic* should have been the hint that the navy was never that enthusiastic about the production. But Jameson continued with the thinking that the production needed their help. That decision was a foolhardy mistake considering how much of the film's budget had been spent on recreating miniature vessels that could have easily have been repainted and rebranded by removing all decals associated with the navy. After all, ITC had already carried this out with the use of the submersibles by removing all details of them being the products of Lockheed and following through with using the novel's NUMA company logo; something that could have been carried over to the salvage ships.

With the miniatures redressed all onboard scenes could have been completed with the use of studio sets with deck views out to sea utilized using other none-navy vessels dressed accordingly to the scene. The removal of the navy from the screenplay would mean that the story would follow more closely to Cussler's novel with NUMA being behind the salvaging of the *Titanic* allowing for the Russian/American conflict to be better represented on screen. Instead, the use of the navy resulted in pressure being applied to the screenplay as they concentrated on having better on-screen relationships with Russia leaving it neutral for both sides and avoiding any further tensions at a precarious time during the Cold War era. If that decision had been made in restructuring the story, removing the navy's input and changing the fleet brand to keep with the miniatures and the use of sets, *Raise the Titanic* would certainly have been a different film to that finally released. As the film was already using a great number of special effects, the budget set aside and then used for the navy could have been spent on creating set pieces better suited for the style of the film while optimizing rear screen projections and continuing with the miniature work already being filmed in Malta. Potentially the switching out of the real ships of the navy to that of sets would have kept the production more budget-friendly for the studio removing the need to ship tons of equipment over to San Diego and spending 14 days out at sea which could have been accomplished with the use of a sound stage, rear projections and a water tank. If only hindsight had been available to them, things could have been so different.

Jimmy Carter, President of the United States in January 1977. *(Postcard published by Coral-Lee, Cordova, CA – Author's collection)*

Afghanistan president, Nur Muhammad Taraki. *(Kabul New Times, April 1978)*

Politician Hafizullah Amin. *(Kabul Times, 3 November 1979)*

Chapter 12: Cold War Interference • 371

Soviet Ukrainian politician Leonid Brezhnev. *(Associated Press Ltd)*

PEACE poster issued during the 1980 Olympic Games. *(Stefen Moorcroft collection)*

Propaganda poster created during the height of the Soviet Union. *(Ivan Vasilyevich Simakov)*

372 • *Raise The Titanic*

Clive Cussler with his best-selling novel. *(Publicity photograph – Author's collection)*

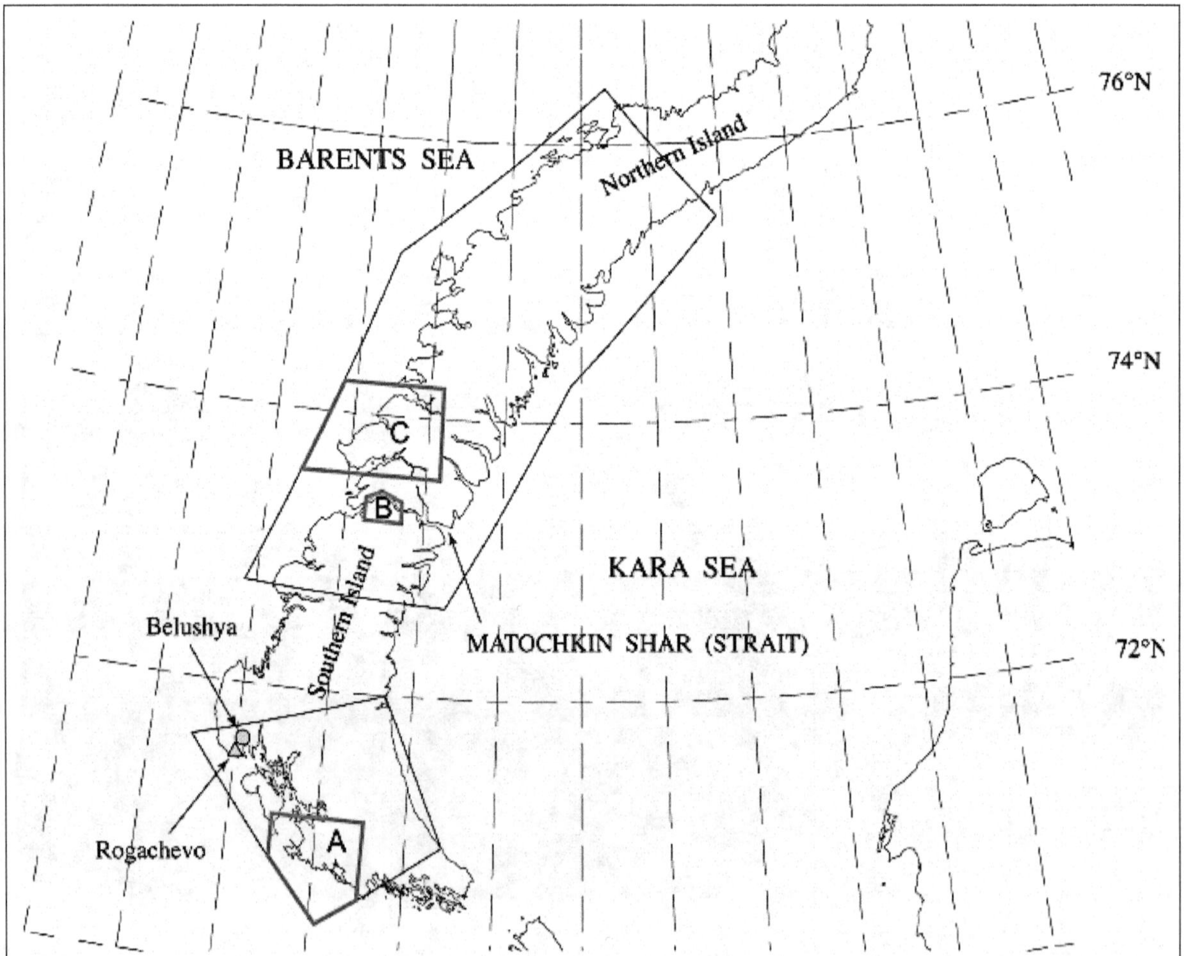

Three of the nuclear testing sites on the island of Novaya Zemlya. *(Paul Richards collection)*

Chapter 12: Cold War Interference • 373

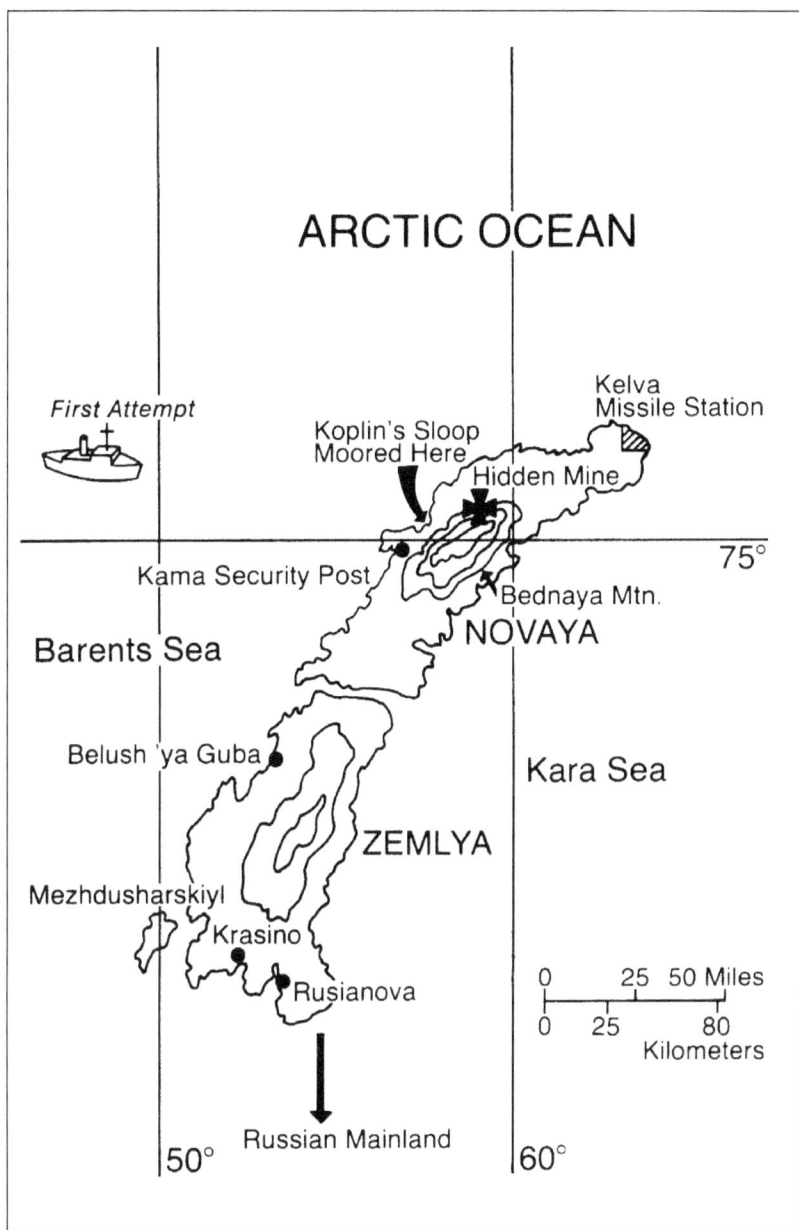

Clive Cussler's fictional island of Svlardov. *(Viking Press Ltd)*

Chief of the Visual Production Branch of the Washington Department of Defence; Donald E. Baruch. *(National Archives - Record Group 330: Records of the Office of the Secretary of Defense, 1921-2008)*

374 • *Raise The Titanic*

Flight 23 is raised with the assistance of the U.S. Navy in Jerry Jameson's *Airport '77*. *(Universal Pictures © 1977)*

c1940 postcard of the Pentagon in Washington, DC. *(Author's collection)*

Chapter 12: Cold War Interference • 375

Marble Arch Productions company logo in 1978. *(Author's collection)*

The use of the Navy was crucial for the production, both in terms of delivering a story for the viewers and portraying the Navy in a positive light. *(Author's collection)*

Executive producer Martin Starger. *(ITC – Author's collection)*

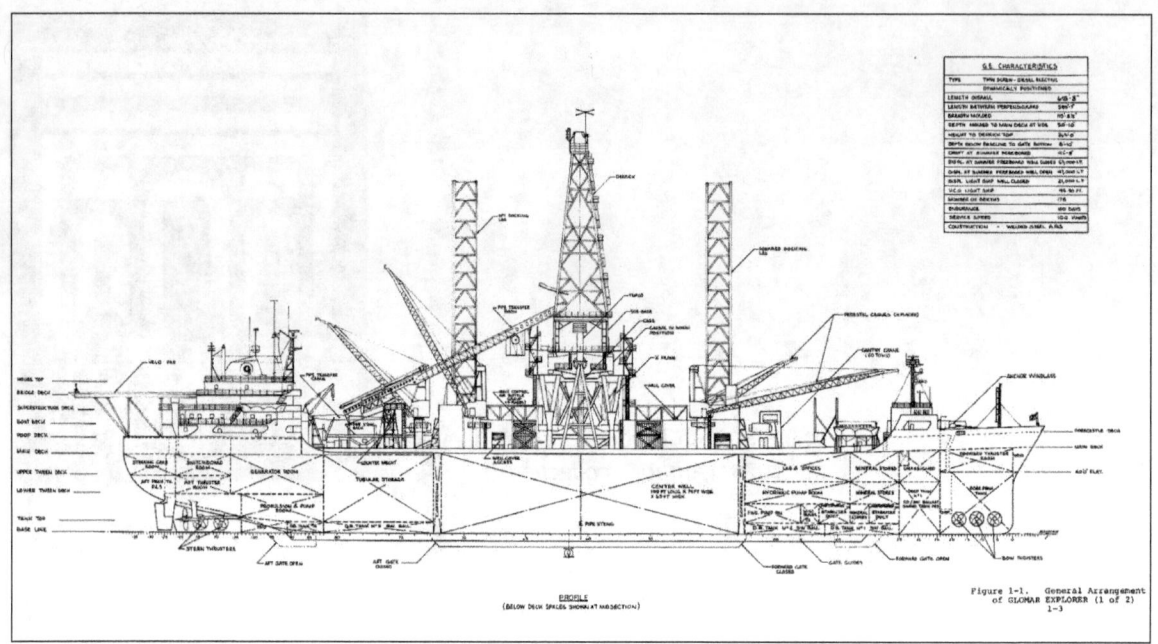

Starboard profile plan of the *Glomar Explorer*. *(Michigan Engineering: University of Michigan Archive)*

Making waves. The news breaks on the successful operation to raise the K-129. *(American Oil & Gas Historical Society)*

Chapter 13

The Mediterranean Caper

"It sounds crazy but you have to be crazy in this business. The offer made financial sense for a picture of this scope."

John DeCuir Sr.

The New Year of 1979 began with *Raise the Titanic* entering a crucial stage of production as chunks of the budget were already wrapped up in the development of the mighty deep tank in Malta, its surrounding buildings, and the ongoing preparations on the models for the next stage of filming. In true Hollywood style, the producers wanted to interject more complications into the movie when they introduced the search for a suitable candidate that would double as the crusty and very rusty *Titanic*. Had no one the forethought in reminding them what year it was? And yet this major film company wanted to track down a vintage ocean liner during a period when ports around the world still berthed many modern-day liners of which none were vintage let alone one being a survivor of the Edwardian era. The advance in shipbuilding over the decades may have resulted in vessels becoming larger and increasing their passenger capacity, but one thing that did not change was the vessel's service life expectancy which was that of no more than 30 years.

The great liners of the early twentieth century were constructed at a time when shipping companies were in tremendous competition with one another. The shipbuilding yards of Harland & Wolff in Belfast had periods where 200,000 to 350,000 tons combined of vessels entered the waters of their yards per annum. *Olympic* and *Titanic*, both 45,000-ton vessels, were major builds for the yard and the shipping line that ordered them. Yet with the increase in new tonnage heading to sea, these giants of the Atlantic were built to have a service expectancy of 20 years before being retired. *Olympic* would go on to have an eventful career that stemmed 24 years from her entry into passenger service in the summer of 1911 to that of her retirement in 1935 when she fell victim to the rota of new ocean liners on the slipways as technology advanced and styles changed leading to her final journey to the breakers yards.

By the early 1930s, the look and feel of crossing the oceans had changed, not only in passenger style but also in ship design as Edwardian life had become almost erased following the events of World War One, the swinging 1920s, and the birth of art deco. Even when Cunard-White Star launched their *Queen Mary* in 1934 she was looking cluttered and outdated in comparison to the equally crafted art deco French goddess *Normandie* of the Compagnie Generale Transatlantique line from 1932. While many Edwardian-built vessels had fallen victim to the cutting torches of the breaker's yards, the new liners now faced an uncertain future as the dark clouds of the great depression and the turmoil of war began to roll in like a tremendous storm.

Insult on a Queen

During pre-production of *Raise the Titanic,* the scouting party was hard at work looking for their other *Titanic*. At one point the production team looked towards the former Cunard liner R.M.S. *Queen Mary* that resides in Long Beach, California following her decommissioning from service in October 1968 and subsequent purchase for £1.2m, an offer that went on to outbid that of the submitted offer for her steel from a Japanese scrap metal merchants. The *Queen* was never shy in being in front of the camera having been used for such films as *Assault on a Queen* (1966), Irwin Allen's disaster classic *The Poseidon Adventure* (1972), and *S.O.S. Titanic* (1979). Art Director John Decuir Sr. saw potential in the *Queen* and envisioned her being the production's newly acquired floating *Titanic* relic. Communications between the studio and the owners at Long Beach proved futile even when the offer of £2m was put on the table to purchase the liner. But when the owners of the vessel were informed that areas of the ship would require redecorating, aging and much reconstruction, the talks went stale and the *Queen* was spared. Speaking in 1980 John DeCuir commented on the efforts behind requiring the ship.

"It sounds crazy but you have to be crazy in this business. The offer made financial sense for a picture of this scope."

And so, the search for the *Titanic* continued.

In February 1979 the production office was in contact with Lloyds of London to increase their search for a floating steel stage they could call *Titanic*. The Lloyds company, originally founded in 1686 by Edward Lloyd in Tower Street in the City of London, operates as a collective of underwriters in a syndicate of a partially-mutualized marketplace for financial backers and powered by a governed corporate body under the Lloyd's Act 1871, which includes maritime and marine insurance. With millions of tons of ships laid-up around the world, it was only a matter of time before a vessel was discovered that could benefit the film studio. Time was now of the essence in tracking down the right vessel for the right price that would fit in the decreasing time frame the studio was already pitted against. Lord Grade's ITC received a copy of the *Lloyd's Monthly List of Laid up Vessels* that February which contained hundreds of ships ranging from cargo vessels to combined passenger and freight ships and former cruise liners, and all with varying constructions periods of the 1950s, 60s, and 70s. The vessels were listed geographically such as those laid up in the United Kingdom, Germany, Asia, Australia, Greece, even Africa, and the Americas. In the course of the search through the Lloyd's booklet, ITC had marked off a total of twenty-three vessels for consideration. Of the vessels underlined in red ink, it was the one on page eleven that would eventually become Captain Grade's *Titanic*.

The Birth and Death of a Shipping Line

Kinosoura, nicknamed "tail of the dog" in Greek, forms part of Salamis Island, Greece, which can be located to the east of the island with ancient Athens laying 14 km away. The area is minimal in terms of residents but is dominated by the port area which caters for both ship repairs and the resting grounds for many decommissioned vessels. Even in February, with the sun at its peak, a cold blanket of air still drifted across the bay causing the rigging cables of the abandoned rusting hulks to rattle like the chains of some ghostly spectral. Dozens of ships of all shapes and sizes and states of repair form an orderly line as they sit at anchor or tied to mooring bitts erected on the shoreline of the island. While the air is filled with the rattle of rigging cables and creaking steelwork, down in the water around one vessel a small convoy of boats sits around the former liner's stern as the occupants communicate with black objects that frequently bob to the surface of the oily water to then vanish in a tumult of bubbles. They are the divers from Medivers Inc as they carry out the hull inspection of the M.V. *Athinai* which had once operated for the Typaldos Lines between the years of 1961 to 1966 before her unexpected decommission in October 1967.

Athinai was built in 1932 and launched under her original name of *Santa Rosa* by the Federal Shipbuilding and Drydock Company, located on the banks of the Hudson in New Jersey. She was one of four liners designed by naval architect William Francis Gibbs, the designer behind America's famous liner *United States* which he went on to design in 1951. The S.S. *Santa Rosa* was owned and operated by the Grace Line for the company's fleet of 'Santa' ships which included the *Santa Paula, Santa Lucia,* and *Santa Elena*. The *Santa Rosa* had a length of 508ft, breadth of 72ft, and 9,135 gross registered tons with accommodation for 209 First Class and 50 Tourist Class passengers. She sailed the popular inter-coastal services between the east and west coast of America via New York, the Caribbean, and the Panama Canal, starting in November 1932. She served as a troop carrier during World War Two before returning to passenger ship duty where she continued her voyages until her retirement in June 1958 where she was taken out of service and laid up at Hoboken, New Jersey until 1961 when she was purchased by her new Greek owners, Aegean Steam Navigation Co otherwise known as the Typaldos Lines where she would once again be fulfilling cruises as passengers were treated to the delights of sailing around the Mediterranean with the 1960s flair in the decorative surroundings of surviving art deco interiors.

The Typaldos Lines was founded in 1949 to operate under the earlier company name of the Typaldos Brothers Steamship Co. Ltd where the brothers operated a fleet of vessels, mainly those previously retired from other shipping lines, in which these ships were refitted and put back into passenger use. Although a Greek company, their headquarters was based in London while their vessels operated from the port of Piraeus in Greece. For a small private company, they did well in running a fleet of twenty-one vessels, two of which were sisters of the Grace Line from 1932, *Santa Paula* and *Santa Rosa*. The two identical vessels once purchased were renamed with the *Paula* becoming the *Akropolis* and *Rosa* as the *Athinai*. Removed from her former Grace Line colours, the newly named *Athinai* now operated in the familiar all-white livery of the Typaldos Lines, customary for many vessels sailing the warmer waters as cruise liners in the days before air conditioning became mandatory. With her sleek clean white hull and superstructure and buff yellow funnels, the *Athinai* still oozed the charms and delight of a vintage liner brought into modern times with her open deck swimming pool, spacious deck areas for sunbathing, and open promenades for those to stroll or take in a book or nap in one of the hundreds of deck chairs put out by deck stewards. Little did these passengers realize that the company they put their trust and faith in as they took in the glorious sights aboard these 10,000-ton steel giants were failing in the basic necessities of vessel maintenance.

Disaster was to strike when the company's 8,922-ton S.S. *Heraklion*, the former *Leicestershire* of the Bibby Line, became caught up in a severe storm in the Aegean Sea on the evening of 8 December, 1966. Her hull was battered by waves and resulted in one of the sets of starboard doors used for loading and offloading of vehicles to give way. Of the 191 passengers and 73 crew onboard, only 46 were rescued. Due to the circumstances of the operating of the vessel as a passenger ferry at the time it became apparent that some passengers were not properly ticketed to travel. The loss of life was that of an estimated 217. Within days of the disaster, an inquiry was launched to investigate the sinking which began to expose the negligence of the Typaldos Lines and the company owners. The Greek government investigations found that the shipping line failed to carry out appropriate lifeboat drills which the crews abandoned their posts the night of the sinking. It was also discovered that the ship's officers not only failed in organizing the abandoning of the vessel but that they delayed in sending out the important call for assistance as the ship sank. Haralambos Typaldos, the Greek owner of the shipping line, and the company's general manager, Panayotis Kokkinos, were both found guilty of manslaughter along with faking legal documents. It was during the investigations that twelve of their ships failed inspections under the international maritime laws. It was concluded that all company vessels were removed immediately from service and sent directly to the breakers yards to the highest bidders leaving just three vessels on the list to be put to one side for either scrap or potential other uses. These three vessels would be the S.S. *Helias*, M.V. *Rodos,* and the M.V. *Athinai*. By 1967 the Typaldos Lines was now defunct while Typaldos and Kokkinos served their prison sentences.

Ghost Ship

Back in Kinosoura bay, the divers from Medivers Inc had completed their inspection of the lower hull of *Athina*i. Reporting back to the inspectors on the boat, a list was compiled outlining what the divers could see. The report for Lew Grade's film company was compiled by marine surveyors Gerald Geddes & Partners of London and Piraeus. It was a simple report of just three pages but it revealed the importance of what the vessel, after a decade laid up, presented to the surveyors through the inspection of the divers. *Athinai* presented a slight list to her starboard side with a heavier draft at her stern compared to the bow. She was termed as being "fully afloat" with external openings being in a "closed up" state. The diver's inspection found the hull to be in good condition with no excessive damage noted. But the submerged area of her hull, keel, rudder, and propellers had an evaluated average of 30cm. thickness of marine growth. Medivers discovered that her starboard anchor was still attached to the chain cable that secured the bow to the sea bed. But the port side anchor had been removed leaving the played-out chain to be caught up in debris that built up around the hull. Onboard, the surveyors from Gerald Geddes & Partners carried out their inspection of the vessel, mainly concentrating on the lower compartments of the hull, holds, engine room spaces, and exterior deck areas such as those exposed to the elements. Both port and starboard prop shaft tunnels were found to be partially flooded but nothing that wasn't repairable. The watertight doors were found to still be in good condition with little work needed to get them operational again. And, surprisingly, her engine rooms were largely intact except for some fittings such as catwalks which had either collapsed over time and some sections of pipework and trunking. *Athinai*'s list to starboard was discovered in areas of accommodation where flooding had taken place from rainwater entering from above through open hatchways, doors, windows, and deteriorating decking. Concerns were made over the large amount of hull shell doors that were all found to be unlocked and open, and more importantly in a very bad state of repair. The report from Geddes was that these doors would require closing and welding shut before any attempt is made to tow the vessel from her present location. Out on deck both the deck equipment, some areas of steel decking, timbered areas of decking, ventilators, and areas of deckhouses were found to be generally in poor condition. Hatches and cargo holds were in reasonable shape but were required to be covered with tarpaulin when the vessel was required to be put to sea during towing.

When members from the film company went on board to catalogue the deck spaces and internal areas of the liner in photographs for the art department, they were surprised at how well preserved some areas were, more so to how some rooms were left. Richard O'Connor, executive in charge of production, recalled the day the film team went on board.

"When we first went on it, I remember we had flashlights and it was really kind of eerie. What had happened was that the crew had just abandoned ship. There were still playing cards and tables set up. There were still pillows and bedding in the bunks."

In most cases, the *Athinai* was a ghost ship with large areas of her interior spaces still complete with furnishings of beds, tables, chairs, display cabinets, curtains, lamps, and even cutlery while shipping line brochures were seen scattered about public areas. Her lavish dining room which would eventually become *Titanic*'s fictional ballroom in the movie was still perfectly preserved with its white painted walls, towering columns, and ornate decorative inlays. And dotted around the room were the dining tables with their chairs sitting atop as if waiting for stewards to appear and make the room ready for diners. In areas where rainwater seepage had not occurred the liner was like a floating museum, a time capsule of a once-proud liner of an era long gone. Deeper down in the confines of the ship were the crew and storage areas that were once busy from the activity of stewards, cabin boys, cleaners, cooks, engineering staff, those from the boiler rooms, cargo holds, and laundry rooms systematically coursed their way around the labyrinth of corridors. They now lay abandoned and deserted of life. Scattered about the corridor floors were discarded equipment, boxes, and varying tools and artefacts. The only sounds to be heard came from the squeals of seagulls, an almost rhythmic clatter of loose fittings tapping against a structure of the vessel to then be lost among the creaks emitting from the materials of the ship as it moved with the swells in the bay. Having been in anchorage for twelve years the *Athinai* showed many signs of deterioration externally with her rust stained hull, crumbling deck vents, and buckled and lifting decking timbers. With over a decade of no maintenance, she was presenting a perfect picture of a long-lost liner that could easily have been found drifting in the middle of some ocean after mysteriously vanishing decades previously during a crossing. She was the perfect stage setting for the film company and their vision of *Titanic*.

One issue at the time of inspection was that documentation drawn up in 1967 by the American Bureau of Shipping when *Athinai* was laid up was not produced for the parties involved in the Geddes inspection. While the surveyors were relatively pleased with the condition of the hull plates in

February 1979 it was in their forethought that some concerns were raised twelve years previous. The report from the surveyors dated 27 February 1979 reached the productions offices of ITC and Marble Arch Productions. In all, despite some concerns outlined in the report, the *Athinai* was deemed to be in an acceptable overall condition and the surveyor's approval was given to proceed to the next level in securing the vessel for the right price. The film production could only hope that the report from Medivers Inc was as positive.

Loose Lips Sink Ships

The *Raise the Titanic* production crew now had their sights firmly set on acquiring *Athinai* as winter passed into spring. Over at the Mediterranean Film Facilities in Malta, the work on getting the huge deep water tank to a point that the tank could be used was proving extremely difficult. With the film production split between the deep tank, the pressure of getting the 55ft *Titanic* model ready to be sunk in the surface tank, more re-writes to the screenplay, and not a single actor on the company payroll, the last thing ITC needed was yet another spanner in the works. But it became less of a spanner and more like the entire toolbox along with its contents. It should have been straightforward. They had finally found the ship they needed. Plans were being drafted up on how to dress her to resemble that of *Titanic*. They had finally decided on a plan of action to tow the *Athinai* out into deeper waters, even a tour around the coast, get scenes in the can and then tow her to the port of Piraeus, berth her up at a quay and film the important New York scenes. What could possibly go wrong? Let's return to that toolbox which has been left precariously teetering on the edge overlooking the production gears.

The letter from Medivers Inc dated 27 February revealed that the marine growth on the lower hull was to such a degree that a full conclusion on the condition of the ship's hull could not be determined unless hydraulic cleaning was carried out. The heavy fouling prevented seeing any damage to hull seams and severely obstructed the liner's rudder and steering gear. It would have been naïve of them to think that vessel could have ever have been brought back to life with a clean and a spark. But while the marine growth had indeed created a dilemma, it was not the end of the production. The Geddes report indicated that the inner hull areas which included the liners ballast tanks were secure and the flooded propeller shaft tunnels were of no concern to the stability of the vessel. Any power required onboard the vessel could be done through portable generators while moving the ship would be done with the assistance of tug boats.

In early March 1979, the marine surveyors Gerald Geddes & Partners were still working for ITC in securing the derelict for the film production and fulfilling their involvement in making sure that the *Athinai* was available for use and that the vessel would be constantly in attendance of specialist marine experts at a cost of $300 per day. A retainer fee was required to be put in place to cover ongoing involvements with the surveyors during the course of the production where *Athinai* was involved. This would mean that from the period of March an advanced retainer fee was required to be paid at a cost of $10,000 in advance that would cover the costs of those involved from Geddes including the period of filming and the return of the vessel back to its owners which was estimated to be in August.

On 26 March an interesting telex came through from the production office to Geddes inquiring about the ship's stability in purposely altering the hulls trim. The question was raised on how much the hull could be listed to port, then starboard, then forwards at the bow. What on earth was the film company planning on doing to *Athinai* that required such drastic actions? Once the money for the loan of the ship had gone through and the paperwork signed and dated the *Athinai* was now the *Titanic*; the famous ocean liner that sank. Through the eyes of the movie's art department they thought it possible that for the film's opening sequence as *Titanic* goes down, they could partially sink *Athinai* for that added realism. The idea was not as ludicrous as it would first seem. After all, Hollywood had done this sort of thing before when in 1960 Metro-Goldwyn-Mayer released *The Last Voyage*. This 91-minute disaster movie weaved around the final voyage of the fictional S.S. *Claridon* which meets her doom when a boiler room explosion tears open the hull and she begins to sink. Even for the time frame that the movie was made, they opted to use a real ship over model effects and actually sink it to achieve the right look. The film production secured the decommissioned liner *Ile de France* which had was built in 1925 and was in service until 1959. As the liner was already heading to the breaker's yards, the movie's director, Andrew L. Stone, seized upon the opportunity to use the liner and wreck it in spectacular fashion for the sake of cinema art. If ITC had any doubts that they could achieve similar results twenty years later for *Raise the Titanic* they were very much mistaken. But it did not stop them inquiring and even getting Geddes to carry out an inspection and report back.

"She can'nae take any more, captain!"

On the 3 April Geddes reported back to ITC on their findings of *Athinai*'s abilities of stability and trim for the proposed and somewhat audacious idea of partially sinking an already derelict vessel. Of course, they were not going to follow it through for the sake of seeing if it could be done. Geddes carried out another three-day inspection of the vessel at a cost of £801. Their findings, theoretical under simulated conditions, were thoroughly calculated and presented but a possibility, albeit an expensive and precarious one. Geddes had mathematically predicted that the vessel could be trimmed, a process of regulating the intake of water into the holds while keeping the vessel on an even keel. But it had drawbacks and limits. The maximum depth they conceived was that of 19ft at the bow by not exceeding that of 3,600 tons of water pumped onboard while 2000 tons of water would drop the vessel's stern by 12ft. This would be relying solely on getting the vessels pre-existing pumping systems which had not been in active service for twelve years and would probably require a costly and time-consuming overhaul. Geddes then put forward their next alternative in omitting water and replacing it with 1,800 tons of sand. The process, less expensive, would be considerably more time-consuming as filming on the bow would require separate filming for the sand to then be transferred to the stern. If the film sequences were not in the can and required reshoots the moving of 1,800 tons of sand from bow to stern and back again numerous times would be troublesome for the production.

Flooding the compartments was looking to be the better solution and one that relied on the onboard aging pumping systems to work. The risk was no less than that of bringing pumping systems to the vessel. While Geddes had calculated the intake to create controlled lists on the hull, this all depended on the fully operational pumps, sealed compartments, and the reliability of crews at hand to carry out such procedures. Another important factor was while Geddes had calculated the possibilities of a controlled partial sinking it was all based on the current condition of the *Athinai* pre-filming phase, stable weather, and without any film constructed sets placed on board that would alter the tonnage of the ship. Their concerns over proposed special effects sequences submitted to be filmed in engine and boiler room areas were enough to warrant Geddes in strongly advising to rethink what ITC wanted to film in those spaces. The art department who were working on storyboarding the movie had put to paper their sequence of the sinking of the *Titanic*. While the *Titanic* miniature was being prepared back in Malta to be sunk in the surface tank the production still required insert scenes with sets and actors to tie the opening prologue together. The *Athinai* was the set that was required to act in both the prologue and the raised *Titanic*.

Art director John DeCuir had worked on a series of storyboards for the sequence that were to be filmed onboard *Athinai* that include an already earmarked location for the story's vault that will contain the remains of Brewster and the crates full of Byzanium. *Athinai*'s engine room and boiler room were also earmarked for several scenes where *Titanic* was going down and crews battle within the confines of the hull. To match the planned scene of *Titanic* losing her funnel as she sinks, it had to be tied in with a sequence filmed in the boiler room of *Athinai* as the cold waters of the Atlantic burst into the boiler room, striking a hot boiler resulting in an explosion which speeds up the rate of the ship's demise and the bringing down of the funnel. It all sounded enthralling, but Geddes saw the problems with pulling off such a sequence using *Athinai*. Regardless of how thorough the production was in cleaning the boiler room spaces and adjacent rooms, there was still a high risk that any simulated explosions could trigger a fire from the amount of accumulated oil that lay around the boiler room and engineering spaces. The combination of the vessel being in a forward trim, down at the bow, areas flooded and explosives, could be a disaster waiting to happen. Geddes advised the studios to evaluate the circumstances for not just the safety of the vessel but for the film units that would have been present.

To Whom it may Concern

By May plans were in action to hire tugs to move *Athinai* out from Kinosoura bay and guide her out into open waters off the coast for the first series of filming to take place. There was one slight problem; several actually. Not for the want of jumping the gun, but the studios not only failed to secure authorization from Coast Ways Towage in securing any tug boat facilities, but crucially, the studios had not secured the hire of the *Athinai*.

But why?

Following the loss of the Typaldos Lines S.S. *Heraklion* in December 1966 and the ensuing investigations, the removal of their ships from service, the collapse of the shipping line, and the ongoing compensations to be awarded to survivors and families of those who were lost in the sinking was still an ongoing process. The complications were that as the *Athinai* was one of three vessels seized by the courts at the time of the inquiry and hearings which resulted in the imprisonment of the shipping lines owners, it meant that *Athinai* was no longer the property of the defunct Typaldos Lines but that of the courts who were in the legal position of the distribution of compensation funds. The studio discussions in obtaining the vessel were constantly ongoing and it would appear that no straightforward action in telling the studio of the complexities created by the aftermath of the Typaldos fiasco was to be acknowledged, that is if the studios had been made fully aware. As far as the courts were concerned, a film studio wanted to hire one of their assets for a fee, and the studios were not in a position to be informed of the legalities of what brought the liner to be where she was laid up, other than *someone* had to inform *some* other that *some* people wanted to pay for *something* that was owned by *someone* that *some* others were not prepared to disclose. Confused? Away from any studio environment, the lawyers started talks in bringing both parties together so a fee could be agreed upon that would benefit both the film studio and the courts. Even though *Athinai* had been laid up for twelve years, one of her cargo holds still contained quantities of illegal tobacco and alcohol which had been impounded by the Greek customs officials at the time. This in turn presented complications in who was fully responsible for the unclaimed and unwanted cargo. For the crucial step of drafting up the paperwork, it was still required for a name to be included on the court papers for the lease of the *Athinai*. It may appear futile considering that the liner was, essentially, waiting on liners' death row, but the vessel had an owner that was not the courts and that owner had to be found for the finalization of completing the proper documentation for the agreement.

The search for the film's *Titanic* that began in early 1979 was finally coming to a close after months of negotiations and searching for the rightful owners of the vessel. On the 10 July, a twenty-page contract had been drawn up by the courts acting on behalf of the selected owners John Kouimanis and Christos Simpoulos the *Time Charter by Demise* for the M.V. *Athinai* to be loaned at a cost of $120,000 for a duration of five months to Marble Arch Productions Inc made payable to Emmanuel Vernikos, the official receiver for the group of creditors on behalf of Typaldos Bros via the courts. Along with the hire charge additional costs were added to the contract including the costs of $70,000 for making the vessel seaworthy in removing her from her current location of Kinosoura and the additional $10,000 in covering the expenses of the vessels return back to the courts once filming had been completed which was estimated around the second week of December. The contract was divided into fourteen clauses of which all had to be agreed upon by both parties and signed by all who had to follow the charter period that included the delivery of the vessel, use and trade of, maintenance of, use of equipment, operating of, risk factors, redelivery of the vessel and the sum of $450,000 which the vessel had been insured for during the period of the contract. In the case of complications arising during the contract between the charters and owners, an additional $200,000 credit was included to last up to and no later than 14 December 1979. As the summer of 79 progressed, the sinking sequence having been filmed back in Malta with the *Titanic* miniatures, the deep tank still not yet finished and no actors signed to contracts, even with the art department working out set pieces to be put on board the *Athinai*, that five-month period was beginning to look like a very expensive gamble in which ITC shareholders, and those in managerial roles at the main offices back in London, must have had grave concerns as the film's budget increased time and time again.

Lloyd's *Titanic* Contenders

The following is the complete list of other vessels that ITC/Marble Arch Productions had underlined in the February 1979 Lloyd's Monthly List of Laid Up Vessels to be considered as the stand-in *Titanic*. The list goes by name of vessel, type, tonnage and where it is laid up.

- *France* (passenger) 66,348 tons (Havre)
- *Niassa* (passenger) 10,742 tons (Lisbon)
- *Uige* (passenger) 10,001 tons (Lisbon)
- *Leonardo da Vinci* (passenger) 33,340 tons (Spezia)
- *Protea* (passenger) 11,334 tons (Trieste)
- *Victoria* (passenger) 11,695 tons (Venice)
- *Patris* (passenger) 16, 259 tons (Patras)
- *Athinai* (passenger) 9,237 tons (Piraeus)
- *City of Athens* (passenger) 9,126 tons (Piraeus)
- *Ellinis* (passenger) 18,564 tons (Piraeus)
- *Mediterranean Sun* (passenger) 13,278 tons (Piraeus)
- *Rodos* (passenger) 2,458 tons (Piraeus)
- *Olympia* (passenger) 17,434 tons (Piraeus)
- *Regina Prima* (passenger) 10,153 tons (Piraeus)
- *Sirius* (passenger) 8,917 tons (Piraeus)
- *Ankara* (passenger) 6179 tons (Istanbul
- *Mei Abeto* (passenger) 12,654 tons (Jakarta)
- *Oceanic Constitution* (passenger) 20,269 tons (Hong Kong
- *Oceanic Independence* (passenger) 20,251 tons (Hong Kong)
- *Oriental Empress* (passenger) 15,337 tons (Hong Kong)
- *Bahama Star* (passenger) 8,312 tons (Mobile)
- *Mariposa* (passenger) 14,812 tons (San Francisco)
- *Monterey* (passenger) 14,799 tons (San Francisco)

The 66,348-ton S.S. *France* during her maiden voyage in February 1962. She operated until October 1974 where she was laid up in Le Havre until mid 1979. The liner was listed down in the February 1979 Lloyds book with her being underscored by ITC as a possible contender. The production company was vastly outbid with the ship being purchased by Norwegian Caribbean Line for a cool $18 million in June that year. She would spend the next ten months being refurbished where she was relaunched in May 1980 under the new name of *Norway*. Her fate would come in 2005 when she was taken out of service and sent to the breaker's yards in Alang; the same yards that scrapped the Athinai. *(Author's collection)*

A titanic task was looming as the scouting teams sent out by ITC had the enormous job of tracking down and securing a vintage vessel that would double as the *Titanic*. It certainly wasn't going to be plain sailing. *(Beken & Son – Author's collection)*

Cunard Line's graceful monarch; *Queen Mary*. *(Author's collection)*

MR.F.C.COCKERILL,
(L/L.REG),
CENTRAL MAIL OFFICE,
LLOYD'S, LONDON.   (L.V.L.U.)

FEBRUARY 1979

LLOYD'S MONTHLY LIST
OF
LAID UP VESSELS

COMPILED BY: Lloyd's of London Press Limited,
Sheepen Place,
Colchester,
Essex, CO3 3LP

Telephone: Colchester (0206) 69222

Telex: 987321 LLOYDS G

EDITOR:
C. J. Fairweather,
Shipping Publications Department
Telephone extension: 249

SUBSCRIPTIONS:
D. J. Petty, Circulation Manager
Telephone extension: 253

£5.50 per copy, £60 per annum, post free

Lloyd's Monthly List of Laid Up Vessels is compiled mainly from information received from Lloyd's world-wide network of Agents.

It comprises only those vessels reported to be laid up through lack of employment, and does not include vessels awaiting orders, awaiting berths, reported in casualty, repairing, etc. Vessels in the U.S. Reserve Fleet are also excluded.

All vessels are general cargo unless otherwise stated; those vessels which are not listed in "Lloyd's Shipping Index" are shown with an asterisk. Vessels which are recorded as having been in casualty since being laid-up are marked +, and brief details of these casualties may be found at the end.

This is the original *Lloyds Monthly List* from February 1979 that was obtained by ITC during their search for vessels. Within the booklet are a number of vessels underscored in ink that had caught the attention of the film company. *(Author's collection)*

ARIANE (ex BON VIVANT) (passenger)	Gr	1951	6725		Jan 10	1978
ARISTIDES	Cy	1935	992	1561	Nov 4	1977
ASPASIA NOMIKOS (tank)	Gr	1953	13415	20972	May 11	1975
ATHENIAN AURORA (tank)	Cy	1956	12447	19206	July 3	1975
ATHENIAN DEMOCRACY (tank)	Cy	1951	8675	13939	May 14	1975
ATHENIAN GLORY (tank)	Gr	1953	11457	17413	Dec 19	1974
ATHENIAN SPIRIT (tank)	Cy	1955	9769	16312	Abt Nov 29	1976
*ATHINAI (passenger)	Gr	1932	9237	7840	Oct 18	1967
ATLANTIC PROGRESS (tank)	Gr	1968	87329	201177	May 16	1977
*ATTICON	Gr	1953	6160	10211	May 3	1978
BABA BAKARE (ex AVGI)	Pa	1956	10312	15692	Apr 22	1975
BALTIC SUN	Cy	1962	959	1651	Sept 2	1978
BESSY K. (tank)	Gr	1958	15895	25722	June 1	1975
BOUBOULINA FAITH	Li	1957	9604	16651	June 15	1978
BRIGHT SUN	Gr	1945	3241	6432	Dec 30	1977
BROTHERS LUCK	Cy	1958	3283	5529	Oct 19	1978
BYRON (tank)	Gr	1963	239	266	Sept 30	1978
CALLIOPE L.	Gr	1955	6216	8580	Aug 23	1977
CAPETAN ALECOS	Cy	1956	9692	11756	Mar 8	1977
CAPETAN NICOLAS	Cy	1954	10905	12369	Oct 23	1977
CAPTAIN B.	Gr	1954	9433	10433	May 6	1977
CASCIOTOS	Cy	1954	1598	2642	Aug 26	1978
*CITY OF ATHENS (passenger)	Gr	1952	9126	2174	Aug 7	1969
CLYTIA (tank)	Gr	1958	22092	43649	May 9	1977
COSMIC	Cy	1953	1598	2743	Mar 14	1976
DAGHILD (tank)	No	1974	125120	260209	Mar 4	1975
DELOS (passenger)	Gr	1950	3921	3043	June 3	1976
DEMIS	Gr	1946	7831	11544	June 5	1975
DESPINA T.	Gr	1951	1575	1880	Sept 3	1978

Page 11 of the list with *Athinai* underscored in ink. *(Author's collection)*

The shipping equivalent of death row. This ITC production scouting party photograph shows a number of vessels laid up in the shallow waters of Kinosoura bay as they wait their fate. *(Author's collection)*

The 9,100-ton *Athinai* laid up in the bay in February 1979. After sitting in this location for over a decade, the vessel was showing many signs of deterioration. *(Author's collection)*

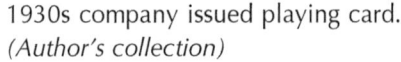

1930s company issued playing card. *(Author's collection)*

Original advertising brochure from the Grace Line advertising their new fleet of liners named the Santa-class. *(Author's collection)*

Athinai in her original days as the *Santa Rosa* operating between New York and Mexico for the Grace Line. *(Author's collection)*

Chapter 13: The Mediterranean Caper • 391

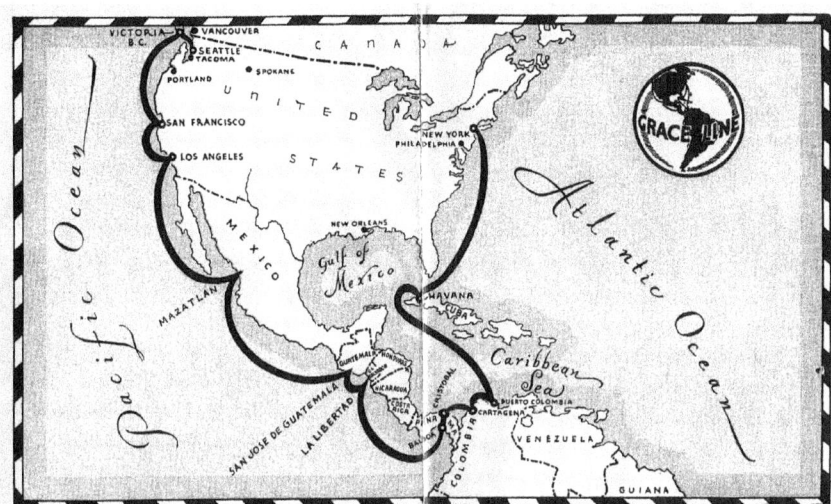

Grace Line map showing the destinations, from port to port, that *Santa Rosa* and her sister vessels operated. *(Author's collection)*

These company issued postcards not only acted as a keep sake for passengers, but also as an advertising tool when the card was mailed from the ship. In the golden age of liners these kinds of interior views would entice future travellers to come and book a cruise on these luxurious ships. With the *Santa Rosa* (right) operating with her sisters *Santa Paula* (entering the dock) and *Santa Lucia* (not pictured) the shipping line cornered a lucrative tourism trade. *(Author's collection)*

Typaldos Lines company logo from one of the ship's bulletin pages that was removed by the ITC crew while on board the *Athinai*. *(Author's collection)*

The former Piraeus offices of the Typaldos Lines. *(Photograph © Henry Brayshaw)*

Chapter 13: The Mediterranean Caper • 393

A new owner; a new cruise livery and a new name; M.V. *Athinai*. *(Author's collection)*

The ill-fated S.S. *Heraklion* pictured here in her days as the *Leicestershire* for the Bibby Line. Her sinking and tragic loss of life would become the downfall for the Typaldos Lines. *(Author's collection)*

Messrs.
Gerald Geddes and Partners,
Akti Miaouli 81,
Piraeus.

RB/LH

27th February, 1979.

Dear Sirs,

SUBJECT: UNDER WATER INSPECTION OF MV "ATHINAI"

Further to your request, our divers have inspected subject vessel lain in Kynossoura, on the 27th February, 1979 and report condition of vessel as follows:

Sides, Bottom, Propeller and Rudder completely encrusted with a variety of marine growth and barnacles. Sides and Bottom's growth is evaluated at an average of 30cm. thickness. The vessel is lying in depths Forward of 20m. and Aft Section in 7m. of water.

No way possible due to heavy fouling to determine any serious damage to the hull or steering gear. It is recommended that for determining the actual condition of the under water part of the vessel, that hydraulic brushing will be necessary.

Yours faithfully,

R. Botsford,
Director.

Medivers Inc letter to Gerald Geddes & Partners, the marine surveyors in Piraeus acting on behalf of Lew Grade's ITC, acknowledging that an inspection had been carried out on the hull of *Athinai*. *(Author's collection)*

Tour of the *Athinai* - The first of a series of photographs taken by the representatives for ITC as they examine and document the *Athinai*. *(Author's collection)*

Tour of the *Athinai* – As the harbour vessel starts its journey alongside the hull, this photograph is taken of the portside bridge wing. What may not be clear to the readers is that the photograph has been doctored during the films production. A blue ink pen was used to highlight where the set designers would remove a section of the wing to form a bridge cab similar to those on *Titanic*. *(Author's collection)*

Tour of the *Athinai* – Looking down the length of the portside hull. *(Author's collection)*

Tour of the *Athinai* – Looking towards the portside bow and the liners played out anchor chain. *(Author's collection)*

396 • *Raise The Titanic*

Tour of the *Athinai* – The weather-beaten portside of the liner. *(Author's collection)*

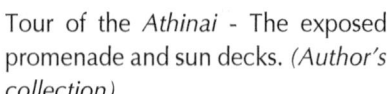

Tour of the *Athinai* - The exposed promenade and sun decks. *(Author's collection)*

Tour of the *Athinai* - The boat has now moved to the starboard side of the *Athinai*. With the liner laid up alongside another derelict, there is not enough room for the harbour boat to pass down the entire side. *(Author's collection)*

Chapter 13: The Mediterranean Caper • 397

Tour of the *Athinai* - One of the ITC representatives boards the *Athinai* via a wooden ladder suspended down from the edge of the liner's foredeck. *(Author's collection)*

Tour of the *Athinai* - The photographer has now moved over to the portside of the foredeck to capture this view overlooking the waters of the bay. *(Author's collection)*

Tour of the *Athinai* – This view is looking from the bow towards the stern on the starboard side of the promenade deck. *(Author's collection)*

Tour of the *Athinai* – Another photograph taken on the starboard promenade deck with this view looking from the stern towards the bow. This area of the promenade would play a key role in the film. The set of doors to the left along with the windows are to the *Athinai*'s dining room that would be turned into *Titanic*'s fictional ballroom with staircase. *(Author's collection)*

Tour of the *Athinai* - Looking from the bow end towards the stern of the portside promenade deck. *(Author's collection)*

Tour of the *Athinai* – The photographer has now arrived at the stern and takes this view looking out over the sundeck with the swimming pool and the aft mast. *(Author's collection)*

Tour of the *Athinai* – Taking to a higher elevation, the photographer captures this view looking over the boat deck towards the ships bridge. *(Author's collection)*

Tour of the *Athinai* – View taken looking across the funnel deckhouse towards the bridge. *(Author's collection)*

Tour of the *Athinai* - The ITC representatives have now ventured inside the vessel with the photographer taking this snap shot on the enclosed bridge. *(Author's collection)*

Tour of the *Athinai* – After heading to the stern the team have now entered into the bar salon. The stairs to the left lead down to upper deck B and the passenger cabins. *(Author's collection)*

GERALD GEDDES & PARTNERS
CONSULTING MARINE SURVEYORS
81, AKTI MIAOULI,
PIRAEUS, GREECE.
C. W. FYANS. B.Sc., M.C.M.S., M.R.I.N.A.
Member of the Society of
Consulting Marine Engineers & Ship Surveyors.

VASILEOS PAVLOU 93,
KASTELLA,
PIRAEUS,
GREECE.

TEL. OFFICE 452 1571
A.O.H. 417 0420

GEDDES & PARTNERS
ENGINEERS, NAVAL ARCHITECTS & MARITIME ARBITRATORS
81 AKTI MIAOULI,
PIRAEUS, GREECE.
TELEPHONE: 452-8842
TELEX: 212753 GEPA

CWF/HS/407G

Reply to:— LONDON / PIRAEUS, 31st March 1979

Supervisor, Marble Arch Productions,
c/o Pimlico Films Ltd., EMI Studios, Shenly Road, Borehamwoods, Herts.

To Gerald Geddes & Partners

"RAISE THE TITANIC"
s.s. "ATHINAI"

To	Attending on board the above vessel at Kynosoura, Piraeus, on 26th February 1979 in order to carry out a preliminary inspection.	
To	Preparing a Report of our preliminary inspection and submitting same to you dated 27th February.	
To	Attending meetings at the offices of Messrs. Halsey Tzalas Marine Limited, Athens on the 26th and 27th February.	
To	Arranging for a diver's inspection of the vessel on 27th February and submitting the Report of Messrs. Medivers Inc. to you the same day.	
To	Proceeding to Malta on 28th February and attending meetings with various interested parties in Malta on 1st and 2nd March, returning to Athens on 3rd March.	
To	Attending on board the above vessel at Kynosoura on 21st, 22nd and 23rd March in company with the Production Team, when various requirements for the vessel's usage were discussed.	
To	Carrying out Stability and Trimming calculations according to your proposed requirements for filming on board the vessel and reporting our conclusions, in writing, dated 3rd April.	
To	Advices and attendances generally up to the end of March 1979.	
	Fees	£ 750.00
	Disbursements, including incidental travelling expenses, boat hire at Kynosoura, photocopies, Telephone and Telex	£ 51.80
	TOTAL	£ 801.80

E & O E

Geddes March 1979 invoice to ITC for the first part of their services towards negotiations in securing the *Athinai*. *(Author's collection)*

Chapter 13: The Mediterranean Caper • 403

The S.S. *Claridon* sinks in the 1960 MGM disaster movie *The Last Voyage*. *(Author's collection)*

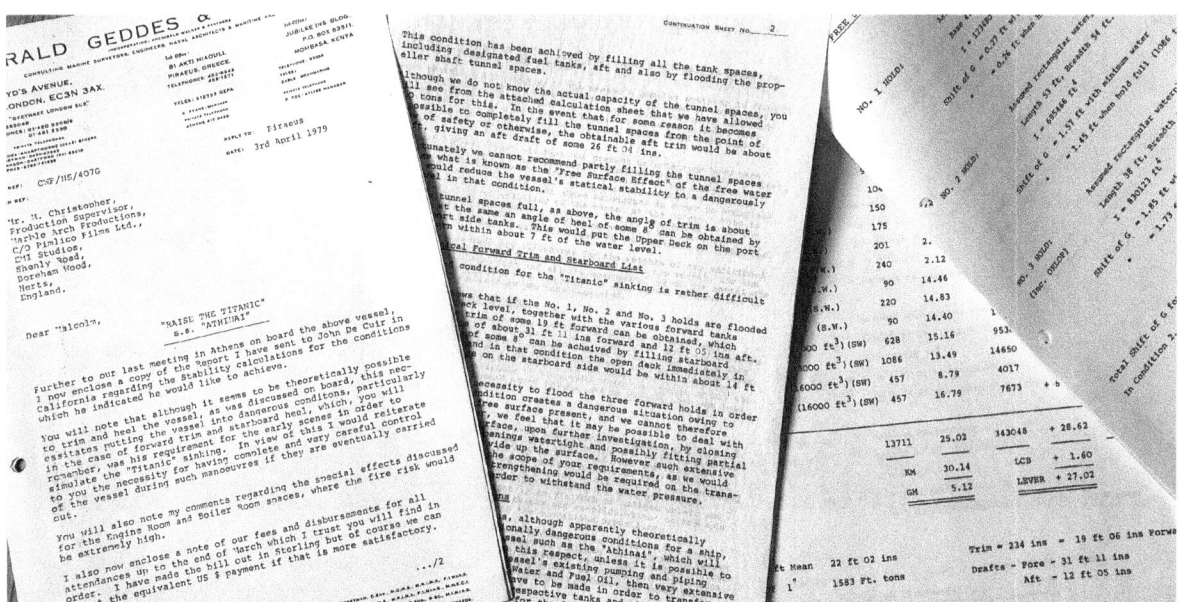

Part of the surveyors reports on the trim and stability of the *Athinai*. The survey was meticulous and extremely thorough. Although they concluded that the ship's hull and compartments were stable enough for regulated flooding, they did advise against going ahead with such a proposal in case anything untoward should occur. *(Author's collection)*

At the request of the film production, part of the survey also covered the possibilities of creating controlled explosions in one of the ships boiler rooms for a sequence storyboarded when a boiler explodes after icy Atlantic water floods the compartment. The explosion would lead to the collapse of the second funnel. *(Author's collection)*

This illustration shows how *Athinai* would have looked if the film studio had gone ahead with flooding a series of forward holds to lower the liners bow into the water while keeping the vessel stabilised enough for filming to be carried out on board. Even though the surveyor's reports were positive, the possible dangers outweighed the need to push forwards with such an adventurous set of film sequences. *(Original Athinai artwork © Henry Brayshaw – Edited by Jonathan Smith)*

Chapter 13: The Mediterranean Caper • 405

After the February surveys on the *Athinai*, the ship was to remain at Kinosoura through the negotiation period and well into the latter quarter of 1979. *(Author's collection)*

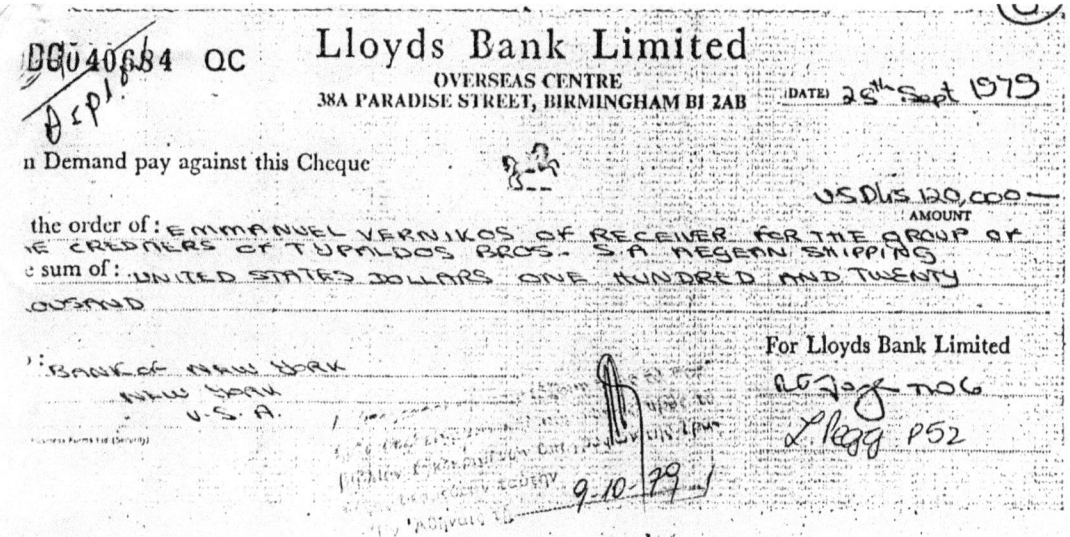

An original proof of payment for $120,000 paid by Lew Grade's company for the hire of the *Athinai* that was kept within the company records on *Raise the Titanic*. *(Author's collection)*

Looking down the starboard side hull of *Athinai's* bow. *(Author's collection)*

DATED 10TH JULY 1979

JOHN KOUIMANIS and
CHRISTOS SIMOPOULOS   (1)

MARBLE ARCH PRODUCTIONS
INC.   (2)

TIME CHARTER BY DEMISE

of

"ATHINAI"

TIME CHARTER BY DEMISE

JOHN KOUIMANIS & CHRISTOS SIMOPOULOS

- and -

MARBLE ARCH PRODUCTIONS INC.

The original signed and dated contract between Lew Grade's Marble Arch Productions and the creditors acting on behalf of the Typaldos brothers. *(Author's collection)*

CHAPTER 14

The Other *Titanic*

"And here lies Arthur Brewster. Sunk with the Titanic."

Dirk Pitt

Lew Grade let out a sigh of relief as he put the receiver down following the telephone call to his office on the successful charter for *Athinai*. The securing of the vessel was a fundamental part of the production as now the next stage could commence in transforming the derelict into yet another derelict which had spent the last 68 years on the bottom of the North Atlantic. Through the haze of his cigar smoke, he pushed ahead the next phase of *Raise the Titanic* in his familiar televisual mogul stance that many in show business had come accustomed to. His *Titanic* was to be the big one for the 1980s, or so he thought. His determination could not be faltered. He was like a child in a sweet shop given the choice of picking anything he wanted. But despite his child-like vigor, this was a child locked in a 73-year-old man's body. Even at that age, he could still do the Charleston. He was confident in his adventure in getting what he wanted and he had a host of people around him who would be at his beck and call, come night and day. Grade's *Titanic* was certainly the talk of the film industry which prompted some to question whether Grade could pull it off. What Grade was not aware of at the time was that some of those who were concerned were within his companies, unfortunately including those in senior managerial roles. Even when the production was being reported to be taking on water, Captain Grade was at the helm and determined to sail his ship to its final destination regardless of the costs. *Raise the Titanic*, he assumed, would live up to its reputation and bring his companies of ITC, ATV, Marble Arch Productions, and Pimlico Films the recognition they deserved in the film industry and put Grade among the big-name studios producing blockbusters for the big screens.

Art Attack

During the process of securing the *Athinai*, art director John DeCuir Sr. had been busy drafting up ideas on how to convert the liner into the *Titanic*. While the *Athinai*, a twin funnel vessel that was over 300ft shorter than *Titanic*, could be made to resemble the ill-fated unsinkable up close, the main issues would be those of the vessel at a distance which had to convince the audience they were looking at the real thing. DeCuir had the advantage of knowing which scene could use the large-scale *Titanic* model in Malta to those where the *Athinai* had to be dressed to fool the audience into believing they were looking at the *Titanic*. By studying the liner, he started to work out set designs which could be constructed and bolted down into place. One key aspect with sets is that they can be achieved to fool the eye when done correctly and working accordingly with the film crews. While the *Athinai* afforded views of enclosed and open promenade decks which were easy to alter by aging the deckhouse walls, windows, doors, and railings, there were open areas out on deck where the main construction was needed to remove the liners original identity and transform her with the use of these specially constructed set pieces into a ship that was recognizable as being *Titanic*. Following on from the documented reports carried out by marine surveyors Gerald Geddes & Partners, who had inspected the liner many times during the late winter into early spring, concluded that *Athinai* was not stable enough for any effects sequences where partially sinking her and even the use of explosives to simulate a boiler explosion were planned. With those ideas now thrown in the dumpster, the costs implemented in bringing those into reality could be put towards the budget for transforming *Athinai* into the wreck of the *Titanic*.

DeCuir's idea for altering *Athinai* was extensive but doable. On request, he surveyed the vessel, both photographically and in person. His tour of the ship meant he could list what was to be left in situ and what was required to be removed to make way for the installation of the *Titanic* sets. From his survey, he could then begin the task of designing the set pieces to sit on and sit around the *Athinai*'s pre-existing main hull and superstructure. The suitable option for the sets was to have cameras locked off at key locations on the vessel or erected from a rig or crane that gave the audience a few seconds of seeing *Titanic*'s rusting hulk even if it was achieved by the simple case of elaborately crafted screens. From bow to stern, DeCuir set out his plans to convert the liner by removing some of the *Athinai*'s deck details such as vents, cargo lifting equipment, constructing bridge wings with cabs to match that of *Titanic*. Even vents positioned around the upper deckhouse where the two funnels were affixed were listed down for removal. *Athinai*'s bridge would serve as that of *Titanic* with her rectangular windows which would have the bridge wings attached to allow filming with actors when the vessel was aged and for the scenes to be filmed on the bridge as the hurricane rolled in.

Of the main sets pieces to be constructed were the funnels and the raised poop deck on the stern. Using the locked-off camera technique and positioned at a high elevation over the bow of the ship, the funnel sets would be made to resemble those of *Titanic* that would be seated around the *Athinai* funnels without the need to remove them. The locked-off camera, positioned at an angle, would film the funnel sets without the need of the audience having to see the *Athinai*/*Titanic* from her profile side. Funnels one, two, and three would be constructed as a single unit piece but only consisting of just three-quarters of each funnel based on the angle they were required to be filmed at. The set-piece would then be dropped in place on the deckhouse, bolted, and welded into place with additional strengthening added beneath to support the extra weight to the deckhouse. This set piece was known as the *bow to stern* section and was estimated to cost $46,800 to construct. The second funnel set-piece, *stern to bow*, was to be constructed to show a lower deck angle with the ascending funnels of four and three. Like the other set, it too would be welded and bolted down in place on the deckhouse and built to an estimated cost of $29,610. Once the stern area of *Athinai* had been cleared away of deck equipment, this would allow for the larger stern set to be built of the raised 3rd class deck space for the poop deck and docking bridge at a cost of $70,000. The set-piece would be sat upon a series of steel frames that would be secured in place to the merchant cruiser stern of *Athinai*. The framework would allow for the area to be built up, forming an overhang that mimics the counter stern of the *Titanic*. From there, a deck with sides, the intended 3rd class entrance, cargo cranes, and docking bridge could be recreated to match with the historical photographs of the *Titanic*.

The contract for this work went to Vernicos Maritime Co of Piraeus, one of the oldest existing maritime enterprises in Greece. Their involvement in the production was to ascertain and carry out the appropriate work onboard the *Athinai* in the removal of deck equipment, machinery, structures, and the strengthening and modifying deck areas for the new set pieces. All that was now required was the approval from the film studio for the laborious work to begin. In a letter from Gerald Geddes & Partners dated 6 October 1979, the marine surveyors produced a four-page document listing the modifications to the *Athinai* following discussions with John DeCuir the day before. The studios had deemed the cost of $70,000 for the poop deck set to be unsatisfactory and wanted something less costly. As the list played out of the work required to be carried out onboard the *Athinai* before sets could be constructed, it is understandable as to why the studio began to count the costs. The 29m tall rear mast cost $3,000 to be removed and stored in the ship's #2 cargo hold while steel blanking plates were welded in place over the hole within the deck. Another $3,000 was charged for the removal and cargo hold storage of the large steel awning canopy that would have once held the canvas screens to shelter passengers from the Mediterranean sun. Some $2,500 was billed for the removal of a pair of stern lifeboats and their davits, while the costs of cleaning out, constructing a framework and steel plating over the stern swimming pool cost a whopping $21,000. While excessive, it was necessary as the deck area was required to take the weight of a landing helicopter down onto the structure when the film's villain, Captain Prevlov, boards the raised *Titanic*. The costs of the promenade deck extensions came to $30,000 while $4,000 was billed for the removal of equipment from the forecastle on the bow. The costs did not stop there. As crews went about cutting and removing various sections from the vessel, adequate fire precautions had to be put in place at a cost of $15,000, even though an additional $5,000 was required for the supply of a fire pump. Next came the cost of hiring a floating crane which took another $10,000 from the budget followed by $20,000 for workers staging and $12,000 for the hire of a supervisor.

A compromise was made on the stern set for the *Athinai* with a more modest piece consisting of the forward wall of the 3rd class entrance with the stairs on either side leading up to the poop deck. A small section of deck was crafted and shored up in place to allow Richard Jordan to step upon once he had ascended the stairs from the well deck. From there aft would be nothing but a safety rail for the actors and camera crews' purpose. It was decided that the actual poop deck space could be built in the now cleared open area of the ship's stern in the location built over the swimming pool that was plated off and covered in decking. Sections of railings that had previously been removed were reassembled, forming *Titanic*'s rounded stern deck with its 26ft tall flag pole in which Pitt hoists up the White Star Line flag. A makeshift stage area was constructed at the stern of *Athinai* and erected behind the simplified 3rd class entrance. The stage was fitted with another stern flag pole in which a flag could be flown. Its purpose was to tie in with one of John DeCuir's matte paintings that would be fixed to a frame and shot via a locked-off camera. The view would be looking from the port side aft end of the enclosed promenade overlooking the stern. And with the matte backdrop in place and the camera locked off, the view would be that overlooking the stern of *Titanic* with its cargo cranes, vents, and docking bridge, while behind it the makeshift raised stage area with its flag pole and flag would be apparent. DeCuir's matte stern painting was completed at a cost of $10,000 and even installed onboard the *Athinai* for the stern views. Whatever the reason was, the matte painting and the filmed scenes never ended up in the final edit of the movie. One last stern set was created and used for the scene as Pitt raises the White Star Line pennant over the stern of the *Titanic*. Once any scenes with the makeshift staging with flag pole had been filmed the stage area was taken down and replaced with a full-scale set piece of the round stern plates of *Titanic* showing the portholes to the steering gear room for the rudder and her distinctive **TITANIC LIVERPOOL** nameplate. The set-piece was suspended from the curvature of *Athinai*'s stern. With a camera positioned in a smaller craft on the water looking directly up, the angle was perfect in that it not only captured the scene they storyboarded but the other stern set-piece could not be seen due to the camera angle. But to catch such an angle with such sets required the vessel to be moved from her current laid-up position at Kinosoura bay.

The Mediterranean Caper Resumes

Filming on board the *Athinai* was to take place at two locations; out at sea and in port, as the filming stages had to be divided between the works required aboard the liner in the removal of equipment, construction, and painting of sets before actors and filming crews carried out the next step of the production. As the works began on board, the next stage was to get the *Athinai* tugged out from her present location and the journey around the coast to film in the open sea and then tugged again to the port of Piraeus for berthing in dock for the New York scenes. But on dry land problems began to surface as some areas of the signed contract were brought into question. The court-selected owners of John Kouimanis and Christos Simopoulos found a loophole in the contract that was signed on 10 July, 1979. Through their lawyers, they wanted the terms of the charter revaluated and revised as the printed contract was amended in ink by hand during the official handover on several clauses. This apparent lack of elegance was now being used as a way of adding further delays to an already delayed production. By the end of September, the disagreement between the owner, their lawyers, and those acting on behalf of Lew Grade's film company had still not been resolved, even following amendments to the contract put in place that same month. By 12 October the problems were still escalating as the lawyers acting for the film company spoke of Kouimanis and Christos acting the roles, with intent, in causing problems. And what were these issues that were causing so much upheaval?

The original July *Charter by Demise* contract outlined that the charter party, Lew Grade and Martin Starger's joint film company of Marble Arch Productions, were to be held accountable for changing the clause on purchasing the vessel. The film company wanted to hire the derelict while the court-appointed owners wanted the studios to buy it. The charter party was given no more than 30 days to complete the transaction. But the signed agreement of 10 July by the owners and the representative for the film studios was not void when the hand alterations to the agreement were carried out. This change in the agreement, so the owners thought, meant that the vessel would not be purchased to become the property of Marble Arch Production but remain in the hands of the selected owners. It became apparent that Kouimanis and Christos wanted more than just the hire costs and not wanting to deal with the charges that would be charged to them once the film company contract ended in December. By the end of October, an agreement had finally been settled by both parties. The charges for the hire of *Athinai* would still be met by Marble Arch Productions, as originally contracted, but the amendments now meant that once the studios had finished with the vessel they would cover the costs of its return and the *Athinai* would be put back into the hands of the courts to await her fate.

Port of Piraeus

October was proving to be a rather trying time for the production as anything that could go wrong, did. The ongoing process of converting the *Athinai* was forever changing which reflected the budget set aside for her conversion to the *Titanic*. The fluctuating costs were taking their toll not only on the studio but those hired by the studio to bring the film to fruition as restrictions from the top rained down. The official documents for the work were signed on October 17 for Vernicos Maritime Co on board the *Athinai*, followed by an appointed photographer who, at the request of the film company, went on to photograph various areas of the vessel and the suggested areas for changing, dressing, and filming of. As workers busied themselves about the vessel, another series of obstacles was looming upon the horizon.

As the expenditures for the production were being changed in London, the news of such was not being forwarded on to John DeCuir. The cost of the original sets that had already raised concerns for the studio meant that the larger set pieces, such as the funnels, had now been changed. The decision was to switch out the larger sets pieces, with the exception of the simplified 3rd class stern area and the deckhouse of the 2nd class boat deck entrance, and replace the stern deck, the rear of the aft superstructure, and *Titanic*'s bridge front with those of three matte paintings at a combined cost of $30,000 that would be locked off in place and filmed from a single advantage point. This decision was late in reaching John DeCuir back in America creating tension between the art director and Dick O'Conner, the executive in charge of production, with Dick insisting that he was personally informed of any changes in art direction brought about by John DeCuir. This breakdown between departments was not good for morale in an already turbulent feature film. As cracks brought about by budget restraints began to emerge a bigger problem was now becoming apparent. Previous weeks of discussions for the moving of *Athinai* and towing her out into open waters and over to Piraeus was becoming heated. The prospect of moving a derelict such a distance and then getting port authorization to have her berthed in dock was proving to be a major problem for all involved. It did not help when the studios asked if they could berth the vessel up for free.

Piraeus is located on the Saronic Gulf of the western coast of the Aegean Sea and is not only the largest port in Greece but also in Europe. The port can be dated back to 493 BC when the low-lying areas of the island would flood with seawater. Since then the port has grown into a highly economical business with an estimated 5.6 million tons of freight and an impressive 17.4 million in passenger traffic passing through the port each year. The cruise ship terminals that are still in use today were originally built in 1966 with newer extensions expanding the port during the 1970s. One such building, Pagoda of Piraeus, became the focal point for the movie to become the setting of the Brooklyn shipyards in New York where *Titanic* would be towed into for the film's crucial opening of the vault. Designed by Ioannis Liapis and Elias Skroubelou, it was constructed in 1967 as the Passenger Station of Agios Nikolaos to serve the port when the large passenger liners *Queen Elizabeth II* and the *France* came to Athens. The building measures 606 feet in length and 167 feet in width and sits parallel with the quay of Dock 12. The ground floor of the building contained the customs services for the dock along with the goods facilities. The first floor consisted of the passenger waiting areas, tourist offices, small shops, a post office, restaurants, and an open viewing gallery. The second floor contained the refreshments room for passengers and the point of embarking and disembarking with easy access to the building's outdoor carpark. Facing the waters of the dock was the balcony which gave well-wishers the chance to say bon voyage to family and friends as the liners left the quayside.

When the film studios arrived at the port the building was dressed to disguise the fact that the location was filmed in the Mediterranean while being passed off on camera as the dockyards of New York. A simple method was used in dressing the terminal in banner flag bunting and the Stars and Stripes of the United States. One last final touch was that of a 1965 Buick Special which had been found, repainted, and dressed to represent an NYPD police car; a vehicle that was not in use by the city's police departments. Even after all the building dressing, the position of a mock-up police vehicle, and the addition of several extras in NYPD uniforms, the quayside, and surrounding roads were still cluttered with many European vehicles which would have been rarely imported into the United States at the time in such a wide range of makes and models. It was the inclusion of matte FX work by Wally Veevers using the optical matte technique of hand-coloured photo cuts outs such as the closing shot of *Titanic* tied to the quayside with the New York backdrop and fluttering flags on her rigging as spectators look on from the dock building. To fill out the quay and building the production team made a call through Armed Forces Radio requesting help from military personnel by inviting them and their families to be used as extras.

With the *Athinai* being prepared to be towed into Piraeus it was done so under the displeasure of the port's harbourmaster. Piraeus Port Authority was not entirely satisfied with the plans set out by the studio for the use of the quay and the docking of the *Athinai*. It was a procedure that was not likened by those in senior management who believed that the studio's request of wanting the berth free of charge to be unprofessional and that of an unorthodox move. As the discussions between the ITC/Marble Arch Productions and the port authority stumbled it brought about unnecessary delays that began to slowly affect the time frames of the agreement on the hire of *Athinai*, the tugs, and those hired on the production. By 26 October 1979, there was still no confirmation from the Piraeus Port Authority on the berthing of the ship. And to make matters more complicated the Greek tourist board were now involved and making their concerns known. All these delays were becoming costly and more importantly for the film production reducing the timeframe of the works required to take place in making *Athinai* ready for lensing. Then during the first week of November, the all-clear from the Greek tourist board and the port authority was given. The time had finally come to take *Athinai* out on her delayed voyage.

Her arrival into the port and docking at the quay was going to be an unusual sight and one that raised eyebrows among port officials from the Ministry of Commercial Navigation. As a working passenger terminal that processed thousands of passengers each week through the port, the thought of a rust-covered decrepit liner from the 1930s berthed up just meters away from new cruise liners was not good for business. The joke of *Titanic* being brought into Piraeus was the least of the harbourmaster's concerns when the day came to finally tow the liner from the surrounding waters of Kinosoura, through the bay, and into the port. Once the *Athinai* had been approved for removal the three tugs, *Evagelistria*, *Titan*, and the *Bepnikoi Nikoi* hired for the job at a cost of $2,000 per vessel per hour could begin the process of dragging the hull from her slumber of twelve years and out into open waters. For the 7-kilometre journey ahead of the crew the *Athinai* was put under the master of Captain Kapthreptis and his two assisting officers, Costas Dafereras and Yannis Sorotos. The moving of derelict vessels laid up along the shoreline of Kinosoura would have been part of a parcel of crews operating in those waters of the adjacent docks. What was unique about this adventure was that their vessel was no derelict being sent off to the breakers yards but one to be moved about and treated almost like that of a celebrity at the beck and call of a film studio. As the liner with tugs crossed the bay and entered the mouth of the harbour where she would be swung about to align with the docks and breakwaters, a small incident occurred when during being turned about it was done in the direct path of the outgoing American Sixth Fleet's Mediterranean forces of aircraft carriers and destroyers which operated out from Eleusis and were departing from Athens for the voyage to the Gulf following the outbreak of the Iran/Iraq war. With a hasty change of tug positions, it prevented any mishaps from occurring that could have resulted in embarrassment for both the film company and the Navy. Having completed her maiden voyage into cinematic history the *Athinai* was successfully berthed and secured to the quay of Dock 12 alongside the Passenger Station of Agios Nikolaos for the next stage of her conversion.

Titanic Reborn

The logistics of using such an old liner which had been laid up for over a decade was that the vessel could not rely on her own power. The supplying of the proper amenities before substantial works could commence meant that the production company was faced with providing fresh running water, toilets and washrooms, electricity via generators, resting quarters, and cooking facilities before a single person was allowed on board to work. Even as a derelict, the *Athinai* still maintained much of her cabin spaces with former passenger staterooms still with beds, furniture, and even curtains. Some of these compartments were cleaned up and put back into use for those working onboard the vessel during the production. While the vessel was not of a condition where larger groups could be catered to sleep on board for long periods of time, there were staterooms where some of the leading crew and actors could escape between takes and rest up in comfort before being taken back to the surroundings of the Chandris Hotel in Athens.

For the weeks to follow, set designer John DeCuir and his team worked tirelessly on turning both exterior and interior of the *Athinai* into the ravaged interior of the *Titanic*. With the sounds of hammering, cutting tools filling the air, dust, and debris piling up around the quay, regardless of the concerns of the port's harbourmaster, the rather bizarre transformation taking place in full sight of passengers who had invested their life earnings in taking in the views around the Mediterranean while onboard gleaming white cruise liners that were being tugged back and forth from the cruise terminus just meters away, it may not have been picture-perfect for those, but it must have been a topic of conversation over lunch and dinner for the many who came into the port and those who started their voyages into the sun. But the life of luxury at sea was far from the mind of ITC as they kept up the correspondence between the art department and the studio on the changes being incorporated to the *Athinai*. As set-pieces took shape the vessels existing decks and structures underwent their aging transformation as tons of concrete was applied in layers through spraying equipment. Everything that was listed out by the art department was targeted for the application of the concrete. At first, it would seem that concrete was an unusual material to use. But from the advice of marine experts, it became apparent that the use of the material would mimic layers of growth that would adhere to *Titanic*'s steel skin over the next seven decades following her sinking into the black abyss. With the stern sets complete and the area that once contained the *Athinai*'s open swimming pool covered over with wooden decking, tons of sand and soil were brought on board, piled up, compacted down, and then wetted to give the appearance of washed-out sediment. From here the actors and their scenes could be lensed before the film crew shifted to another location onboard the vessel. With the work underway on the interior areas of the ship, the remaining exterior deck scenes could be finished off.

Sporting a new livery of badly stained and rusted black hull and white superstructure the *Athinai* was tugged back out to the open waters of Faliron Bay located off the coast of Palaio Faliro to the east of

Piraeus. Here a number of sequences would be filmed that included the arrival of Prevlov via helicopter and his subsequent and somewhat ill attempt of sabotage; the full-sized pair of converted V class United States Navy tug boats that would secure their towing cables to *Titanic* for the journey to New York; the scenes of Dirk Pitt as he drops down onto the stern of *Titanic* following her raising and his brief tour of the liners decayed ballroom with staircase; several scenes of on-board activity as the hurricane passes through, and the raising of the White Star Line pennant from her stern jack staff. The clearing off of *Athinai*'s once built-up stern decking allowed a larger deck space for the assembly of several deck sets to be utilized including that of dressing the area for when Dirk Pitt is lowered on board moments after the raised *Titanic* stabilizes herself. As Pitt clambers over the overturned deck benches he makes his way to the ship's main superstructure to gain access to the ship's iconic and once ornate staircase for the movie's most poignant and magical trip back in time.

"We went dancing in the ballroom!"

Following his return dive from the wreck of the real *Titanic* in July 1986 her discoverer, Dr. Robert D. Ballard, exited the deep-sea vehicle *Alvin* in a joyous report of cheering from his fellow explorers. Speaking of the sights that his robot camera *Jason Junior* had caught on tape as the remote vehicle ventured into the shattered remains of the liners grand staircase to illuminate a preserved cut-glass and gilded chandelier, Ballard exclaimed excitedly "we went dancing in the ballroom." Jubilant as it may seem, the reality was that no such ballroom ever graced the interior decks of the *Titanic*. Six years previously the idea of passengers as they took to the polished floor of such a room did not deter the filmmakers who wanted to bring some form of romance to an otherwise waterlogged and rotting interior of the world's most famous ocean liner.

The location for the filming of the ballroom with its sweeping staircase was that of the former dining room that was located midships on the Promenade Deck of *Athinai*. When the film studios recce party boarded the liner earlier in the year, they documented the vessel in photographic detail in which the art department could judge, from the images, what was required in changing the room into that of the *Titanic*'s fictional ballroom. The large dining room that once could seat 148 passengers in comfort had hardly changed since the heyday of its creation nearly fifty years ago. Around the room, the huge columns continued to dominate as natural sunlight bathed the interior through the fourteen sets of panelled windows. Deserted as it was, it still retained much of the grandeur of an ocean liner from an era long gone. But this time capsule would soon enter a new phase of life as the FX department arrived to erase the *Athinai*'s identity. Under the supervision of art director John DeCuir, fx supervisor John Richardson and set decorator Mickey S. Michaels, the transformation could begin starting with the clearing of the room of all its furniture to free up the entire floor space. The first major alteration made was the installation of water pipes that would be connected to pumps that took water in from Faliron Bay and circulated it around the room through tubing that ran up through the walls and around the edge of the roofline that would allow the water to trickle down from the high advantage points where cameras could not easily pick them up. This simple trick would give the effect of access water streaming down from the upper decks of the liner in the minutes following her successful raising.

At the base of the aft wall of the room, a full-scale staircase set-piece was created featuring seven steps with three newel posts, with the center post adorned with the cherub light fixture. The three sets of handrails even included the decorative wrought iron-type details mimicking those on the original grand staircase of *Titanic*. It was unfortunate that the set-piece did not receive the care and attention through the lens of the camera like that of its creators in its all-too-brief screen time as Pitt ascends two steps to gaze up at the damaged glass dome above the staircase. This set piece was one of three suggested by DeCuir. As the changes to the vessel came about DeCuir wrote to Jerry Jameson on 20 November expressing the use of a glass matte painted backdrop that would work with the set-piece. Five days later the glass matte was dropped in favour of a more conventional 1:12 scale model of the entire A-Deck staircase with dome and walls that would blend in with those in full scale in the dining room of *Athinai*. The turnaround with the model was incredibly quick with the piece designed and crafted during December for use in filming before the festive season dropped. The miniature was incredibly detailed with its sweeping staircase, intricate balustrades, cherub light fixture, ornate glass dome, and even the illustrious clock centerpiece of Honour and Glory Crowning Time. With the model aged and littered with debris, it would be suspended from a wooden framed rig that was secured to the edge of the *Athinai*'s dining room ceiling that formed the sliding roof to the room. From there a locked-off camera unit was placed on the balcony of the forward-facing wall and adjusted, known technically as a nodal point, to bring the model and the background of the actual room together giving the illusion that the staircase was full size.

    The next stage in the room's transformation was to tank out the floor to allow the room to be flooded without allowing further water to penetrate the compartments below the liners Promenade Deck. The circumference of the interior side of the dining room was fitted with timbered boards at floor level to create a lip that allowed for a black polythene membrane to be laid across the room's floor and up the sides of the lip creating a shallow surface pool that could be filled with water and controlled by pumps. With the dining room floor tanked and the boards covered over with debris to hide the edges of the tank, the purposely destroyed furniture, window frames, doors, walls, pillars, and ceiling was coated in sprayable concrete to match with the exterior locations. The final touch was the addition of a slimy growth trailing down the walls that represented the fictional salvage lifting foam Syntathic. With a combination of mixed soil and sand laid around the floor and banked up in certain areas, the room was ready to be partially flooded for the camera crews and the lensing of scenes with Richard Jordan. Once the footage was in the can of Jordan's walk around the fictionalized ballroom, the set was then dried off, none slip mats laid down and the room dressed with portable lights, tables, charts, and electronic equipment. The full-size staircase set that sat against the aft wall of the dining room had been disassembled and removed to allow for the 1:12 scale miniature to be repositioned for a new camera angle of the room leading up to the arrival of Prevlov and Pitt's deliverance of the "surprise package".

Brewster's Vault

With the completion of scenes that required the location lensing in Faliron Bay, the *Athinai* was tugged back to the Port of Piraeus and berthed again alongside the Passenger Station of Agios Nikolaos building for the remaining New York sequences and the onboard scenes to be completed. By early December John DeCuir's illustrations had now been approved for the work to commence in constructing the eight-foot-square vault that would be opened up to reveal its grisly contents. Early drafts for the filming of the opening of the vault were to take place out on deck using the transformed foredeck of the *Athinai* following the opening up of the cargo hatch and the vault lifted up and out of the hold and dropped onto the deck. The scene was to utilize a matte view of the *Titanic* in New York at night, filmed as a "day-for-night" shot, that would see the vault prized open out on the open deck. As budget restraints took hold the sequence was changed and relocated to the interior of the *Athinai*. The cargo hold was in the most unlikely of places on the vessel; the ship's laundry room located on the starboard side of the liner's main deck. Its position was adjacent to the crew's corridor and a pair of hull shell doors which could be opened up to allow for the flat-packed vault to be brought through the doors and down the short crew corridor into the laundry room for assembly. Very little of the facilities equipment remained and what was left was thrown to one side of the room as the vault was bolted together in its new location. Now the FX department could dress the room and the adjacent corridor with layers of sprayed-on concrete and paint depicting rust and traces of the salvage foam. Even though the setting would be relatively dark, the room and corridor was transferred fully with floors, walls, ceiling, and meters of ships pipework and air ducting being treated with fx paint. Actors Jason Robards, Richard Jordan, David Selby, Paul Carr, Norman Bartold, and Charles Macaulay were filmed in character as two members of the films crew cut through the lock to the vault door, to open it and reveal the seven wooden crates and the prosthetic body crafted by the Burman Studios. "And here lies the body of Arthur Brewster. Sunk with the *Titanic*", chillingly delivered by Jordan as he pulls back on the arm of Selby. The filming of the scene was daunting for the actors who had to endure the toxic smells coming from the chemicals used to mimic the salvage foam. The narrow spaces that both actors and crew had to work in soon began to take its toll. Filming kept being paused so actors and crew could exit the ship for fresh air, as the unwanted inhaling of the chemical smell from the fx materials made them continuously nauseous in such confined spaces.

The fifteen-day filming in the port did encounter some mishaps when during the night a fire broke out onboard the *Athinai* just before 2 am. The fire was thought to have been smoldering from work carried out on board with cutting equipment. Luckily the damage was kept to a minimum and it was not considered sufficient enough to postpone filming. Unlike the next incident. During a very stormy night in port, and as winter gales swept across Piraeus, a number of the production storage units and caravans were blown along the quayside and into the hull of *Athinai,* to then finally be ditched into the choppy waters of the port. With Christmas and New Year over, the beginning of January 1980 was to have an all too familiar pattern to it as old and new problems began to appear. Filming had now come to a close in Greece and with attention now diverted to the main miniature work back in Malta and the return to St Ives for reshoots, the *Athinai* was being made ready for her return back to the courts as instructed by the Time Charter by Demise agreement.

Bumping up the Costs

The last week of January 1980 was proving to be tiresome and a bad start to the year for ITC when the company, Dimitri Dimitriadis Motion Picture and Television Enterprises in Athens who were acting as the representatives of the studio during their stay in Greece, received a letter from the President of the Council to the Greek Tourist Board concerning the arrangements over the fees for the berthing of the *Athinai*. Despite the studio's hopes of wanting to have the quay for nothing because they saw the opportunity of a major motion picture studio filming on location as being positive for Greece and the country's economy, their request was being ignored and costs were being accumulated. The studio could only wait to see if the Tourist Board had a change of heart. They did not. The new General Secretary of the Tourist Board had examined the agreements between the studio and their predecessor, Takis Lambrias, and concluded that while some amenities were agreed upon without any fees, the permit for berthing the *Athinai* at the quay was not one of these amenities and did come at a cost. And then to add insult to further injury the news arrived at the studio of an incident that occurred during the return of the *Athinai* back to the courts and her unexpected anchorage point in the waters off Eleusis.

The port of Eleusis is located 18 kilometres northwest of Athens and along with its busy port and tourism destination, the waters in the bay were also the dumping ground for a number of decommissioned shipping. The waters of the bay were not to be the final destination for the liner but the vessel's final voyage was to become short-lived. With the terms of agreement for the return of the *Athinai* set in stone and the arrangements to be fulfilled by the film company in the delivery of the vessel, these arrangements constituted all essential costs billed to the studio including the use of the hired tugboats. As the liner was tugged through the waters off Eleusis coast on the afternoon of 19 January, the towing cable connecting the leading tug *Perseus* to the *Athinai* snapped with the cable springing back into the water and wrapping itself around the propeller of the tug causing substantial damage to the propeller and partial damage to the propeller housing. The tug's master decided for the remaining towing cables to be dropped and the *Athinai* to drop anchor in the waters short of Eleusis Bay in sight of the other laid up shipping before the *Perseus* limped back to port for inspection. The quick disposal of the *Athinai* was unexpected and was not part of the agreement for the redelivery of the vessel. But the damage sustained to *Perseus* took precedence over the circumstances. The *Perseus* was immediately drydocked for assessment where it was discovered that a propeller blade had been completely ripped away from the main hub. Thankfully such vessels have spars kept in storage and so the insurance claim was reduced but the costs of being removed from service, drydocking and repairs carried out still required submitting an insurance claim. But under the towage conditions set out by the contract between the courts and the film studio, the *Perseus* was damaged before the end of the served contract meaning that the costs would go directly to ITC. Adding to this dilemma those acting as the representatives of the selected owners of

Athinai were now playing on the unfortunate circumstances of this incident by passing judgment on the film studios and holding them negligent in failing to properly redeliver the vessel. They concluded that the film studio was responsible for the delay, the expenses that were to follow, and demanded that *Athinai* be delivered to them within 24 hours. Little did both parties know of the events unfolding out in the waters of the bay.

By the 4 February, while the *Perseus* was out of the drydock facility and back in service, on dry land the blame-game had now begun between the film company and the tugs owners Vernicos as they argued their position of not being held accountable for the £3,500 in costs for drydocking, replacement propeller and labour charges brought about by the incident out in the bay. As both parties ironed out their grievances over the insurance claim the matter would not be settled until 21 April upon the receipt of payment from the film company as they came to an amicable agreement. But this would not be the end of the matter where the *Athinai* was concerned. As the liner sat out in Eleusis Bay the authorities came onboard to inspect the vessel following the redelivery from the studios. They discovered that the vessel was listing from flooding and with a list that was so obvious that the salvage team from The Salvage Association were required to board. Water was found entering the hull from the location of the stern frame, and, according to the vessel's owners, it was so severe that the vessel was in imminent danger of sinking forcing them to submit a $40,000 bill for the salvage claim to ITC. The studio was dumbfounded by the unexpected turn of events and instructed their legal team to investigate the claim of any liability upon the company. As the lawyers acting for ITC/Marble Arch Productions began their investigation another picture began to emerge. The report that was finally sent from The Salvage Association indicated that at 1400 hours on the 2 February the salvage tug *Vernicos Dimitrios* attended the *Athinai* out in the waters of Eleusis Bay to find that the seal around the rudder on the stern frame had perished allowing water to enter the stern of the vessel. The salvage team rigged up a portable pump to remove 30cm depth of water from the rudders steering box. The issue was rectified with the fitting of a cement box over the gland. What could not be ignored was that concerns over the rudder seal first came to light in January 1979 during the initial inspection of the vessel when she sat at Kinosoura and before the agreements were drafted up and signed. This alone would indicate that any future issues would be the responsibility of the vessel's owners if the seal had not been fixed before the signing of the contract and the handover to the film company. But the issue was that the seals were not rectified before the handover as this would require drydocking. The leakage was maintained with the use of pumping units purchased by the production office and operated during the timescale of the film's production onboard the vessel. Once the production had finished with the vessel and she was made ready for the return back to the owners the pumps were turned off.

But it was not all bad news as the area around the rudder assembly on the stern frame was part of the vessel's watertight compartments. It was the timing that resulted in the owners going overboard and they pushed for an answer as the *Athinai* was still under the charter and responsibility of the studio until 25 February 1980. The Salvage Association did agree that the sum of $40,000 was excessive and concluded that the leak was not of any concern in the overall stability of the vessel. They also concluded that the time charter of the vessel had been executed upon the vessel being laid up in the bay and that no lay-up survey would have been necessary. The matter finally came to a close in early April when it was passed onto the international insurance brokers of Wrightson Marine Ltd established that the *Athinai* was in no way in any threat and that the apparent claim was legally binding, citing that "no insured peril had been operated." The *Athinai* remained at the anchorage point of Eleusis Bay for the next nine years, through storms and tempest, and becoming just another abandoned derelict for sightseers. But for the film enthusiasts who holidayed in Athens and who ventured to the bay to see the other *Titanic*, they would have been surprised to see that much of the sets built for *Raise the Titanic* still existed; the stern section, the 2nd class entrance, the camera stages that were suspended over the side of the hull and even the rusty steel letters of T I T A N I C still welded onto the hull. Even in her distressed state she still maintained a sense of beauty with her hull lines from the 1930s proved to be still photogenic in her demise. Her final voyage would come in 1989 when after nearly a decade moored up, she was towed to the breaker's yards of Aliağa in Turkey where cutting torches got to work in reducing this once great ocean liner to heaps of scrap metal.

Chapter 14: The Other *Titanic* • 419

Lew Grade who thought big, started big but always prepared to be knocked down a rung or two of the entertainment ladder. *(Author's collection)*

ITC resumes its publicity for *Raise the Titanic* releasing this teaser in their 1979 company magazine. *(Author's collection)*

Art director John DeCuir Sr in 1984 during working on *Ghostbusters*. *(Author's collection)*

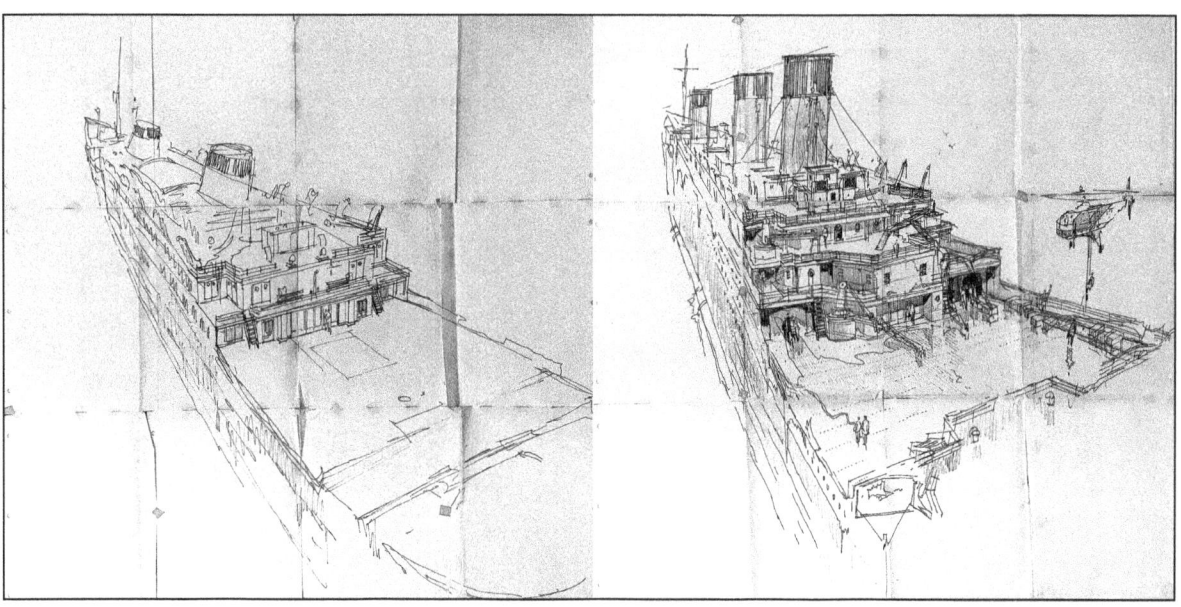

Creating the impossible. These two large scale ink and pencil drawings by DeCuir show how he had worked out how he planned to convert the *Athinai* (left) into the raised *Titanic*. The idea looked good and promising on paper. But in reality, it would never work. The extent of the conversion depended on two main factors; one being the owners allowing such work in the removal of large structures while the other being the studios budget to create huge new sets. It was adventurous and somehow amusing that the studio thought that a complete deck area with deckhouses and funnels could have been built while budget constraints stifled the production. *(Author's collection)*

This crude production sketch was done to show an example how the sets working with locked off cameras could achieve a basic view of the *Titanic*. *(Author's collection)*

Athinai's main bridge would undergo a makeover with aging the interior and exterior areas to represent that of the *Titanic*'s rusted and silt covered navigational area. *(Author's collection)*

```
                                                    Malcolm
    15/05 14.56
    212 FFACIL MW

    212753 GEPA GRGA
    212 FFACIL MW                              18 MAY 1979
    15TH MAY 1979

    ATTN  FRED MULLER  -  'RAISE THE TITANIC'

    RE MTGS LAST WEEK WOULD ADVISE AS FOLLOWS AFTER SURVEY ON THE SHIP:

    AA. ITEM 11 OF MALTA DRYDOCK QUOTE 30/4/79.
        DECK PREPERATION FOR FUNNELS.
        REMOVALS IN WAY OF AFT FUNNEL PROBABLY INVOLVE:
        - STEEL DECKHOUSE LENGTH 4.0 M WIDTH 4.7 M HEIGHT 2.7 M
          ENCLOSING SERVICE ELEVATOR WINCH GEAR, BATTERY LOCKER, AND
          SMALL DECK STORE.
        - ATTACHED WOOD AND WIRE MESH FRAME DECK WORKSHOP LENGTH
          3.0M WIDTH 4.7M ENCLOSING WOOD SHELVES AND WORKBENCH.
        - TWO COWL VENTS ON FIDLEY DECK CLOSE TO EXISTING FUNNEL.
        - POSSIBLY ONE MUSHROOM VENT HEAD AND ONE VENT FAN UNIT
          LOCATED AT ABOUT FRAME 130/131.

        FORWARD FUNNEL FITTING SHOULD NOT BE APROBLEM PROVIDED BASE
        ADJUSTED TO SIT OVER EXISTING RESTAURANT DOME IF NECESSARY.


    BB. ITEM 27 OF MALTA DRYDOCK QUOTE 30/4/79.
        REMOVALS FOR INSTALLATION OF GRAND STAIRCASE.
        INSIDE ENGINE CASING THERE IS:
        AT FUNNEL DECK - HORIZONTAL STEEL GRATINGS.
                       - STEEL LADDER TO BOAT DECK.
                       - FOUR VENT TRUNKS PASSING UP INTO FUNNEL.
                       - ONE SMALL EXHAUST VENT FAN AND ONE SMALL
                         HEADER TANK MOUNTED ON END OF RESTAURANT DOME.
        AT BOAT DECK   - STEEL GRATINGS.
                       - STEEL LADDER TO PROM DECK.
                       - TWO ENGINE ROOM EXHAUST VENT FAN UNITS AT FRAME
                         117/120 PLUS TRUNKS.
                       - AT FRAMES 121 - 124 SERVICE ELEVATOR SHAFT, SPIRAL
                         STAIRCASE AND STORE CUPBOARD.
                  NOTE: ENGINE CASING AFT TRANSVERSE BULKHEAD AT FRAME 121.
        AT PROM DECK   - STEEL GRATINGS.
                       - FOUR VERTICAL VENT TRUNKS.
                       - LAGGED HEADER TANK MOUNTED HORIZONTALLY AT FRAME
                         112/114 DIAMETER 7FT LENGTH 12FT PLUS ASSOCIATED
                         CONNECTING PIPES WHICH TO BE CROPPED AS NECESS.
                       - AFT OF FRAME 121 AS AT BOAT DECK.

    DETAILS OF SPACES OUTSIDE ENGINE CASING AS PER THE VESSEL'S ORIGINAL
    GENERAL PLAN WHICH YOU HAVE.

    TRUST THIS SATISFACTORY FOR TIME BEING, AM SENDING BY EXPRESS POST
    COPIES OF DETAILED DRAWINGS OF THE ABOVE FOR INFO.

    CORRECTION:
    BB. AT BOAT DECK - TWO ENGINE ROOM EXHAUST VENT FAN UNITS AT
        FRAME 112/113
                    - TWO ENGINE ROOM VENT FAN UNITS AT FRAME 117/120
        PLUS TRUNKS.



    BEST REGARDS
    CHRIS FYANS
```

This early survey report was drafted up while the *Athinai* still sat in Kinosoura bay. The report lists potential deck structures and fitting earmarked for removal to allow for new sets to be incorporated into the liner's existing structure. *(Author's collection)*

422 • *Raise The Titanic*

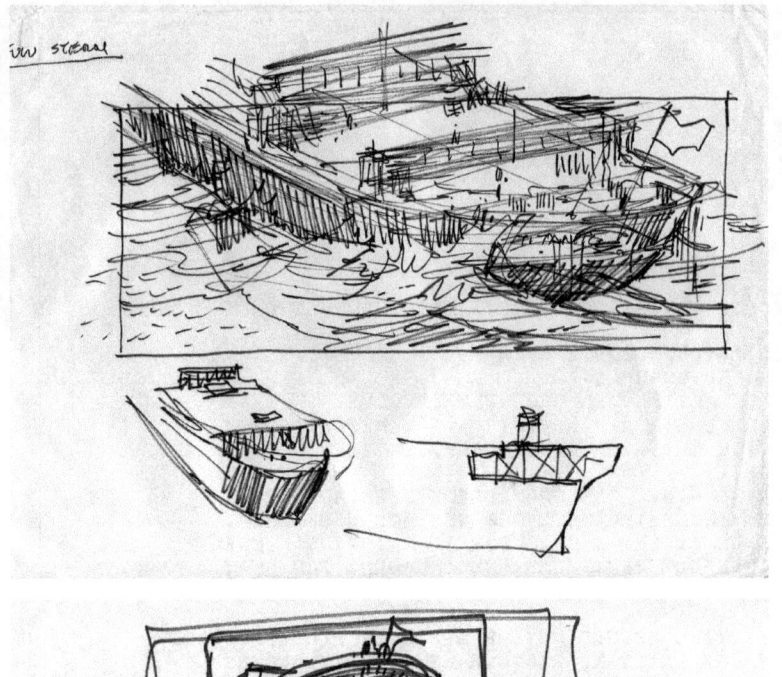

These two crudely drawn production sketches show how DeCuir wanted to create a completely new stern for the *Athinai* that had some resemblance to the counter stern and poop deck of the *Titanic*. With the use of scaffolding to hold up the set deck, the art department could create a replica of the deck area with cargo cranes, vents and docking bridge. *(Author's collection & ITC/ITV Studios)*

Chapter 14: The Other *Titanic* • 423

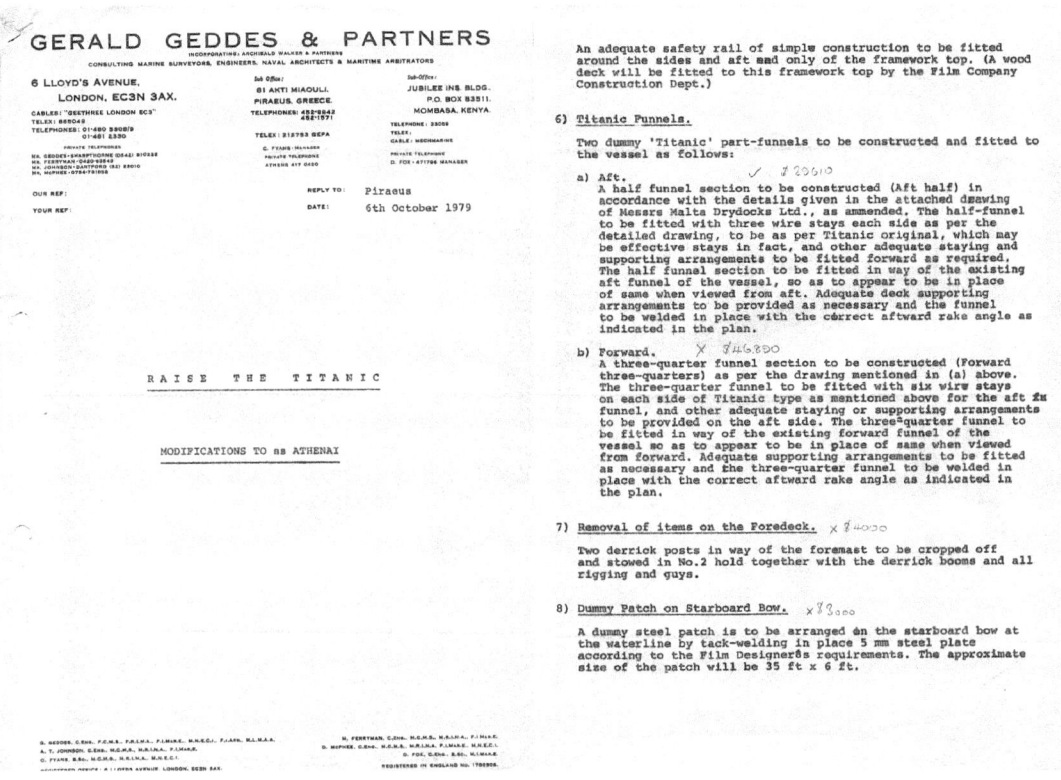

Even though ITC could build the sets using their own constructions crews, the removal of fittings and structures on *Athinai* was to be appointed by the marine surveyors at cost to the film studio. This also included the heavy-duty construction where steelwork was required. This sample of costs from Geddes highlights the staggering fee's for work such as the building of one of the *Titanic* funnels at a cost of $46,800. *(Author's collection)*

This view looking aft over the funnel deckhouse of the *Athinai* while she was laid up in Kinosoura bay in February 1979 reveals the cluttered deck space that the set creators had to work with. *(Author's collection)*

TOP: Anchor gear on the foredeck of *Athinai* in February 1979. ABOVE: This view is looking directly towards the front of *Titanic's* superstructure and the liner's bridge and starboard bridge wing in April 1912. OPPOSITE BOTTOM RIGHT: This area of the bridge of *Athinai* with the railings is part of the flying bridge which was due to be cut away and include a new set piece to mimic the bridge cabs on the *Titanic*. *(Author's collection)*

The sun deck on the open area of the stern with the open swimming pool and steel awning that would have held sun screens for those wanting the breeze but not the direct heat of the sun. As work began to convert Athinai into the Titanic, this area of the ship would be cleared away. The awning frame would be cut apart. The swimming pool would be plated over, the deck levelled off and re-planked and a newly constructed set piece made of the Titanic's stern deck. (Author's collection)

Photographed from the aft end of the boat deck and looking directly over the stern. *(Author's collection)*

```
NP


218500 DDFP GR

847505 PINEWD G
23 10 79

ATTN: RAY FRIFT C/O DIMITRI DIMITRIADES

TO CONFIRM OUR TELEPHONE CONVERSATION THIS MORNING.  I HAVE NOW
BEEN INSTRUCTED BY DICK O'CONNOR (I IMAGINE WITH PRIOR CONSULTATION
WITH THE DIRECTOR AND PRODUCTION DESIGNER) THAT YOU MAY PROCEED
WITH THE FOLLOWING METALWORK ON THE SHIP:-

1)  CUT OFF REAR MAST AT DECK LEVEL
2)  CUT OFF AWNING STANCHIONS ON REAR DECK
3)  CUT OFF EXISTING CANOPY OVER BAR ENTRANCE
4)  SWIMMING POOL COVER TO BE CONSTRUCTED OUT OF TIMBER
    AS CHEAPLY AS POSSIBLE.
    NOTE:   THE HELICOPTER DOES NOT LAND BUT HOVERS OVER THE REAR DECK
------------------------------------------------------------------------
5)  CONSTRUCT 3/4 ROUND REAR FUNNEL (AROUND EXISTING FUNNEL)
6)  REMOVE TWO REAR STARICASES AND REFIT FROM PROMENADE DECK TO
    BOAT DECK.
7)  REMOVE DAVIT POSTS AND DAVITS NEAREST TO BOAT DECK.

REMAINING COSTS - FLOATING CRANE, STAGING, FIRE GANG, SUPERVISING
AND UNFORESEEN EXPENSES (10 PERCENT) - I IMAGINE WILL BE REDUCED
IN PROPORTION.
```

TOP AND RIGHT: Part of the revised work list from October 1979 with accompanying costs. *(Author's collection)*

Athinai

19.10.1979

FROM: RAY FRIFT

TO: DICK O'CONNOR
    BERNARD KINGHAM
    MALCOLM CHRISTOPHER
    RON COOK

THE FOLLOWING IS THE REAPPRAISAL FROM VERNIKOS MARITIME S.A.
FOR THE MODIFICATIONS TO THE 'ATHINAI'.

REF.: RAISE THE TITANIC

QUOTE
REMOVAL OF ITEMS ON THE PROMENADE DECK
A. LABOUR INCLUDING MATERIAL+ OXYCETYLENE   U.S. DOL. 3,000
B.+C LABOUR INCLUDING MATERIAL   ,,,   2,000
D. INDICATIVE PRICE   ,,,,   2,000
E. INDICATIVE PRICE   ,,,,   3,000

REMOVAL OF ITEMS ON THE BOAT DECK

A. LABOUR INCLUDING MATERIAL   ,,,,   2,500
B. LABOUR INCLUDING MATERIAL   ,,,   1,000

SWIMMING POOL COVER

X PREPARATION OF AREA TO BE COVERED   ,,,   1,000
   STEEL COVER INCLUDING STIFFS 8,000 KGS X2.5   ,,,   20,000

   TITANIC FUNNELS

A. STEEL STRUCTURE 15630 KGS X U.S. DOL 3   ,,,,, 46,890

REMOVAL OF ITEMS ON THE FORW DECK

X INDICATIVE PRICE   £ 4,000   LBBDWL LRVFPP.

FLOATING CRANE, TUG BOATS ETC.   ,,,,   -10,000 — ? Poss Plus.
STAGING   AT COST ,,, 20,000 — ?
FIRE GANG 3X3X30 DAYS   ,,,   7,500
HIRE OF FIRE PUMP DRIVEN BY DIESEL ENGINE ,,, 5,000
SUPERVISING   AT COST. 12,000 — ?
UNFORSEEN EXPENSES 20%   ,,,, AT COST. 28,500 — ?

THE TOTAL IS U S DOLLARS   168,390.   Could...

R A I S E   T H E   T I T A N I C

MODIFICATION TO S/S ATHENAI

1. REMOVAL OF ITEMS ON THE PROMENADE DK

a) Labour including material+
   + (oxycetylene) $ 3.000
b+c) Labour including material $ 2.000
d) Indicative price $ 2.000
e) Indicative price $ 3.000

2. REMOVAL OF ITEMS ON THE BOAT DK

a) Labour including material $ 2.500
b) Labour including material $ 1.000

3. SWIMMING POOL COVER

   Preparation of area to be covered $ 1.000
   Steel cover incl stiffs 8000 kgs x 2,5 $ 20.000

4. TITANIC FUNNELS

a) Steel structure 15630 kgs x $3 $ 46.890

5. REMOVAL OD ITEMS ON THE FORW DK

Indicative price $ 4.000

   Floating crane tug boats etc $ 10.000
   Staging $ 20.000
   Fire gang 3x3x30 days $ 7.500
   Hire of fire pump driven by diesel engine $ 5.000
   Supervising $ 12.000
   Unforseen expenses   10% (20%) $ 28.500

              T O T A L $168.390

428 • *Raise The Titanic*

John DeCuir takes a walk around the cleared off stern deck of the *Athinai*. *(Author's collection)*

The adapted stern of the *Athinai* with the *Titanic* sets in place in November 1980 and another view taken around 1985. *(ITC – Author's collection)*

Chapter 14: The Other *Titanic* • 429

Titanic's starboard area of the stern taken while the liner sat at anchor off Roches Point, Queenstown, 11 April 1912. This area of the ship was deck space for 3rd class passengers. Just behind the stairs is the 3rd class entrance that led into an enclosed section of the ship with a staircase and designated recreational areas for passengers. *(Cork Examiner)*

The same area recreated on the stern of the *Athinai*. *(Author's collection)*

RIGHT: Some of the production crew are seen on *Athinai*'s stern in front of the portside of the set piece. Note that the set differs here to that of the starboard as the steel wall is incorrectly too narrow. *(Author's collection)*

One of two pairs of mooring bitts that were made from wood and fibreglass and spray coated with concrete. *(Author's collection)*

John DeCuir's foreground matte of *Titanic*'s poop deck that was painted to a cut section of hardboard wood known in the industry as Masonite Board. *(Author's collection)*

This candid photo of David Selby and Richard Jordan on the portside of *Athinai*'s promenade deck shows the foreground matte attached to a makeshift frame and hung up off the deck. The matte is actually directly above the actors heads and when a locked off camera was placed on the next deck above (boat deck) the camera angle would film people on the deck below while all the time the matte foreground would be in frame and matched to scale with the set pieces. *(Author's collection)*

Chapter 14: The Other *Titanic* • **431**

LEFT AND BOTTOM: Once shots of Richard Jordan ascending the stairs to the poop deck had been filmed, the deck area was cleared away for the next set piece of the stern railing, flag pole and the deck benches. *(First image: ITC/ITV Studios. All behind the scenes photographs: Author's collection)*

Dirk Pitt attaches the White Star Line pennant to the stern jack staff of the *Titanic*. The scene was filmed on a small set piece that was constructed on the cleared off stern of the *Athinai* and attached to the outer edge of the curve of the stern. With a camera unit positioned at water level, and with the camera pointing upwards, the sharp angle would cut-off the *Athinai*'s stern deckhouse to show only the set with Richard Jordan. The photograph of *Athinai* during her transformation to *Titanic* shows the liner's curved stern before the set piece was built and put in place. *(ITC/ITV Studios – Author's collection)*

shall be borne by the Charterers and it is agreed that the said costs shall be ~~not less than U.S.$30,000 and not~~ [No] more than U.S.$70,000. Payment of U.S.$ ~~30,000~~ [20,000] on account of such costs shall be made by the Charterers to the Owners upon production by the Owners to the Charterers of the documents referred to in clause 2 (h) and confirmation that the Owners will commence the agreed works forthwith. In the event that the Owners fail to comply with the conditions for delivery as specified in clause 2, then the sum paid in respect of the said costs shall be refunded at the cancellation date referred to in

OUR REF 8 DM/FM   12th October 1979
YOUR REF

Pimlico Films Ltd.,
Pinewood Studios,
Iver Heath,
Bucks.

Attention Mr. Malcolm Christopher

Dear Sirs,

Raise the Titanic
Demise charter of "ATHENAI"

We thank you for your memorandum of the 10th October together with the enclosures thereto. The translation of the charter which has been executed on behalf of the party does indeed lack the legal elegance which we would have hoped to see however, it appears that Mr. Skoufis has managed to negotiate most of the points set out in our lengthy telex of the 1st October 1979 to his partner Mr. Avrameas.

As the contract is governed by Greek Law we must of course accept the advice of Mr. Skoufis and whilst certain of the clauses seem somewhat unclear to us it may well be that they have lost much in translation.

In any event we are pleased to note that you now have a concluded agreement and that the vessel will shortly be at your disposal.

We understand that Messrs. Simopoulos and Kouimanis are intent upon making trouble in Piraes and we spoke with Mr. Avrameas on this matter when he was in London recently.

We would refer you in particular to clause 13 of the original charterparty which provided, that the charterparty is subject to and shall only take effect if the owners complete the purchase and take possession of the vessel within thirty days of the signing of the charter agreement.

Part of the July 1979 signed contract between Lew Grade's company and the owners of the *Athinai*. The lawyers, acting on behalf of the owners, raised objections to the number of alterations carried out by hand. Even though amendments were carried out, fee's paid, and hands shakes across the table, the owners still caused ITC concerns. *(Author's collection)*

The Port of Piraeus. The image has been edited to show the route the *Athinai* took from Kinosoura bay, where she had been laid up for over a decade, to Dock 12 of Piraeus. *(Diari Arbat)*

John DeCuir working on the superstructure foreground matte while it sits attached to a makeshift frame on the deck of the *Athinai*. *(Author's collection)*

It is not until you take a closer look that this view of the raised *Titanic* reveals it is nothing more than matte with the superstructure of the *Athinai* behind it. *(ITC/ITV Studios)*

The third and final foreground matte; the bridge and superstructure. Note the additions of mast rigging, deck mushroom vents and the lower sections of the cargo derricks to match in with *Athinai*. *(ITC – Author's collection)*

```
847505 PIMEWD G
26.10.1979

FROM:  RAY FRIFT

TO:    MALCOLM CHRISTOPHER

RE:    RAISE THE TITANIC

WE ARE STILL HAVING PROBLEMS WITH THE PORT AUTHORITY FOR THE
BERTHING OF THE 'ATHINAI' AT PERAMA. LAST NIGHT I HAD A
MEETING WITH NICOS VERNICOS AND CHRIS FYANS TO DISCUSS THE
POSSIBILITY OF EITHER DOING THE WORK ON THE 'ATHINAI' ON ITS
PRESENT POSITION. OR MOVING IT TO FALIRON IF WE CAN GET
PERMISSION FROM THE TOURIST BOARD. BECAUSE OF THIS HOLD UP I
HAVE NOT BEEN ABLE TO GIVE NICOS VERNICOS THE GO AHEAD TO
START WORK AS HE REQUIRES THIRTY DAYS FROM THE DATE THAT THE
BOAT IS BERTHED. I ALSO GAVE HIM PERMISSION TO RE-MOOR OR
SECURE THE 'RODOS' WHICH HE WILL DO AT COST.
```

The telex sent to ITC about the ongoing dispute over the docking of *Athinai* in Piraeus. *(Author's collection)*

This early 1960s postcard view of the port shows Dock 12 to the right in the years before the iconic Pagoda of Piraeus was constructed. *(Author's collection)*

Chapter 14: The Other *Titanic* • **437**

Piraeus Port Authority Passenger Station, otherwise known as the Pagoda of Piraeus. *(Photograph © Dimitris Kalapodas)*

Dock 12 doubles as the U.S. Naval base in Brooklyn, New York, with the docked *Titanic* attracting the crowds. *(ITC/ITV Studios)*

Breakdown of the New York FX: The first part of creating the illusion of the *Titanic* in New York began with capturing on film the *Athinai* berthed at Dock 12 in Piraeus. (1) The live action plate was captured first with a dressed set and extras. (2) Over in Malta a still photograph was taken of the 55ft *Titanic* model in the surface tank. (3) A matte plate was created of the New York skyline. (4) The flags on the *Titanic* were created by a plate with the shape of each flag cut out and a multi-coloured roller being cranked at the rear of the plate to give the impression that the flags are fluttering. (5) All the elements are brought together for the final scene. While the scene is interesting it is without fault. What fans of the film may not realise is that the photographic still of the *Titanic* taken in Malta has been flipped as the vent locations around the forward funnel are not right. As the scene came together the ships bow name was then painted in. *(ITC/Author's collection)*

Optical matte artist extraordinaire Wally Veevers on the set of *Raise the Titanic* in November 1979. *(ITC - Author's collection)*

Chapter 14: The Other *Titanic* • 439

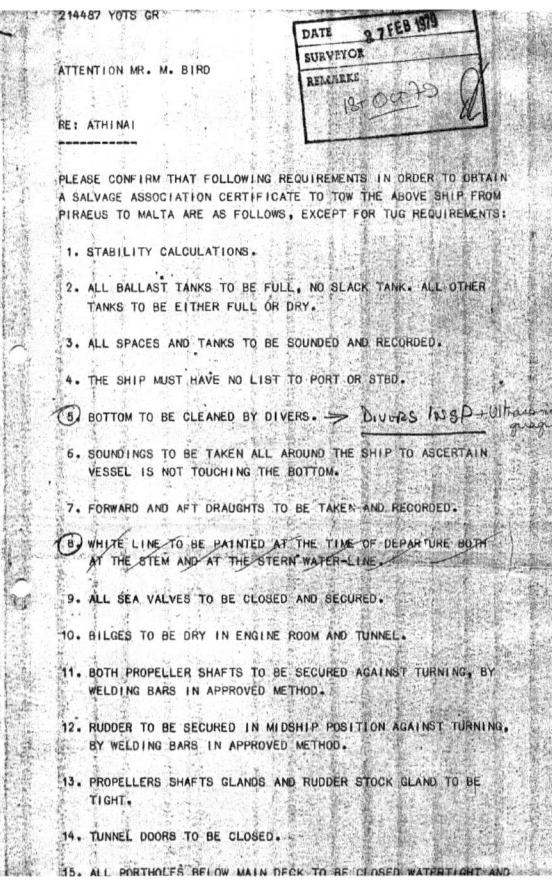

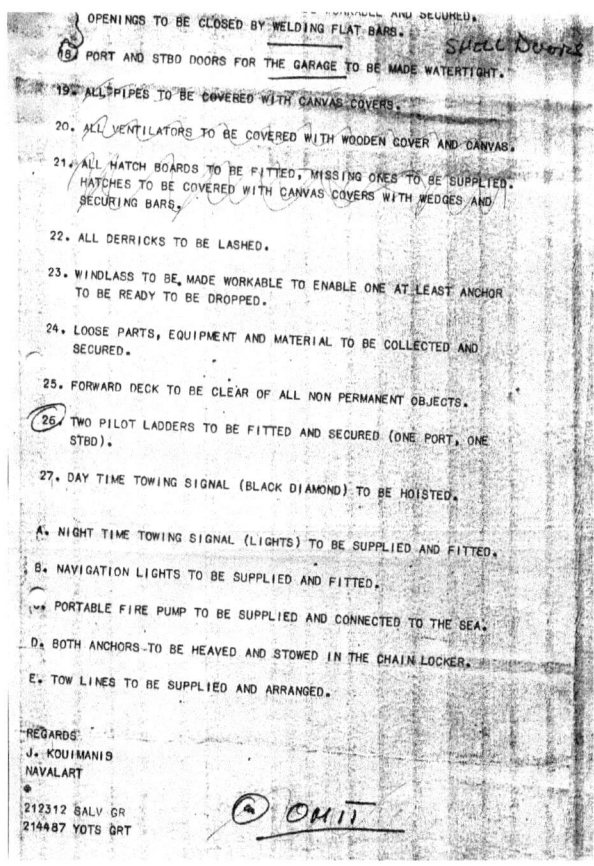

Telex sent from the surveyors to the towage company on the 27 February 1979. The report outlines what is required by marine law in preparation to move the *Athinai* from her moored location at Kinosoura bay to the Port of Piraeus, 7 kilometres away. *(Author's collection)*

Back to Sea

The following four pages chronicle the voyage of the *Athinai* as tugs pull her away from the shallow waters of Kinosoura bay for the journey to the port of Piraeus. At her starboard stern the tub boat *Evagelistria* gets into position to push the liner out into the clearer waters. After a couple of hours of towage, the *Athinai* arrives at Piraeus and is pushed into Dock 12 for work to continue in converting her into the legendary *Titanic*. *(All photographs - Author's collection)*

Chapter 14: The Other *Titanic* • **441**

Chapter 14: The Other *Titanic* • 443

```
TRANSLATION OF THE ABOVE LETTER

FROM: TOURIST BOARD
TO  : DIMITRI DIMITRIADIS            DATE: 25.1.1980

Dear Sir,
In answer to your letter dated 16.1.1980 re facilities at the quay of Faliron,
please be advised that without ignoring that foreign film productions like yours
help a lot the publicity of Greeece abroad, however we aknowledge to you that you
are charged and you have to pay  the costs of berthing at Faliron quay. Mr. Labrias
has informed me that he never promised you that the berthing of the vessel at the
quay was to be completely free. Therefore, the subject was discussed by the Counsil
of Greek Tourist Board  and we found out that the permit of berthing was given to
you only without any further  facilities as free berthing or discound of the fees.
Sincerely Yours
G. D. DASKALADIS  -  President of the Counsil of the GREEK TOURIST BOARD
```

After the actors and crew had moved on, the debate over berthing *Athinai* continued to antagonise the production well into January 1980. *(Author's collection)*

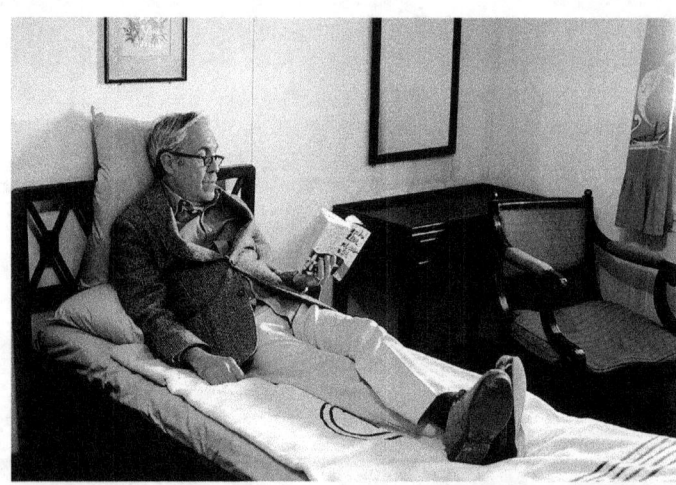

Jason Robards takes a break in one of the staterooms during filming on board *Athinai* while the liner sat at Dock 12. The room still maintained some of its original furniture including the bed, dressing table, drapes and even linen. *(ITC – Author's collection)*

The Chandris Hotel, Athens. *(New York: Greek-American Monthly Review Magazine, November 1982)*

The reduced *Titanic* set taking shape on the aft end of *Athinai*'s superstructure. The set piece is not historically accurate to *Titanic*. But it gave a basic representation of the 2nd class boat deck entrance with A-Deck promenade deckhouse below it. *(Author's collection)*

Another newly fabricated set section that mimics the curvature of the steelwork from the enclosed portion of the promenade deck to that of the more open spaces. The sets of stairs used came from the ships promenade deck. Once removed, the deck area above the opening was closed off and the promenade converted to a derelict. *(Author's collection / ITC/ ITV Studios)*

Chapter 14: The Other *Titanic* • **447**

Athinai sports a new and very familiar name. *(Author's collection)*

Close-up of the artificially aged hull of the *Athinai*. *(ITC – Author's collection)*

ABOVE: Crews at work on one of the cargo derricks laying over hatch #1. *(Author's collection)*

LEFT: While *Athinai* sat in dock it gave the film company the opportunity to have a number of publicity shots taken with the actors. Anne Archer poses for the camera in this shot taken on the stern of the liner while the *Titanic* deck set was still under construction. *(ITC – Author's collection)*

Chapter 14: The Other *Titanic* • **449**

Anne provides a startling contrast between beauty and the harsh surroundings of the wrecked *Titanic*. *(ITC – Author's collection)*

David Selby relaxes on a pair of ship's chairs outside the doors that once led to the *Athinai*'s dance hall. *(ITC – Author's collection)*

Anne touches up her lip gloss before a joint publicity photo shoot with co-star David Selby. The area of the *Athinai* where they are photographed is the built-up area of the set which has been constructed directly over the top of the empty swimming pool and which was used as the open deck of *Titanic*'s stern. *(ITC – Author's collection)*

450 • *Raise The Titanic*

(ITC – Author's collection)

Richard Jordan on the portside of *Athinai*'s promenade deck. *(ITC – Author's collection)*

Jordan poses for the photographer on the walkway between the *Athinai* and the Passenger Terminal of Dock 12. *(ITC – Author's collection)*

Jordan and Archer joke around during a break in filming. There was a reason as to why Anne was in Piraeus during this stage of the production. With the *Athinai* doubling as *Titanic* and the Greek dock at New York, a short sequence was filmed with Archer, Jordan and Selby as the characters of Seagram and Dana finally repair their strained relationship. *(ITC – Author's collection)*

Dock 12 in Piraeus is dressed to represent the Brooklyn naval docks in New York as crowds gather to see the *Titanic* (*Athinai*) completing her maiden voyage after nearly 70 years. *(Author's collection)*

The ghost ship of Piraeus. What an unusual but memorable sight it must have been for passengers arriving in the port aboard new cruise liners to see this rusting relic from the past. *(ITC – Author's collection)*

Athinai is tugged out to the waters off Palaio Faliro for a several days of filming out at sea. This starboard view of the liner shows how only the first quarter of the bow had been aged for some close-up scenes including a planned sequence of the iceberg damaged hull with the salvage plates being inspected after the ship had been raised. The plates were to be cut from steel and welded to the hull as part of the production set designs. *(ITC – Author's collection)*

This portside profile demonstrates the extent of the aging process applied to the ship by the set department. At a distance the *Athinai* looks nothing like the *Titanic*. But with the aid of movie magic, certain scenes filmed at certain angles would fool the audience into thinking that the ship was indeed the salvaged *Titanic*. Note the sets in place on the stern along with the stern jack staff with the White Star Line pennant flying in the breeze. *(ITC – Author's collection)*

Behind the scenes of the filming with the converted V class tugs arriving around the bow of the *Athinai*. (ITC / The Last Great Human Adventure promotional film – Author's collection – ITV Studios)

Chapter 14: The Other *Titanic* • 457

The filming of the salvage crews as they try to lift the mast cargo derricks blocking the entrance to the cargo hold that contains Brewster's vault and the Byzanium. (ITC – *Author's collection*)

Richard Jordan waits to be filmed for a scene with David Selby on the foredeck of the *Athinai*. *(ITC – Author's collection)*

Jordan and Selby take a quick break during filming. As soon as the camera unit is ready to roll, the two actors are filmed for a sequence on the bow of the *Titanic* (*Athinai*) as Pitt and Seagram finally see eye to eye and celebrate the raising of the wreck. *(ITC / The Last Great Human Adventure promotional film - Author's collection)*

Executive Producer William Frye gives an interview on the progress of filming on *Raise the Titanic*. *(ITC / The Last Great Human Adventure promotional film – Author's collection)*

Chapter 14: The Other *Titanic* • 459

To create the illusion of the bridge and front of the superstructure of the *Titanic*, art director John DeCuir created a matte foreground painting that would be positioned in such a way that a locked off camera could capture footage with the matte while actors and extras were in shot. First, a camera platform was built and attached to the starboard side of the foredeck of the *Athinai* where a camera unit could be positioned. Next came the steel framework that was measured and positioned on the deck of the *Athinai* in line with the camera unit platform. With the *Athinai* in Dock 12, the matte foreground painting is attached to the framework and adjusted until it matches up near as perfect with the lines of the *Athinai*'s own bridge front. Now positioned just a matter of feet from the camera lens, aligned perfectly, filming can begin as actors walk into shot while all the time remaining in frame beneath the suspended matte painting. It is only on a closer inspection that the steel frame holding the matte can be seen. *(Images: ITC / Selim San / Author's collection / ITC – Author's collection)*

Dirk Pitt walks through the sodden and rotten remains of *Titanic*'s once lavish ballroom. *(ITC – Author's collection)*

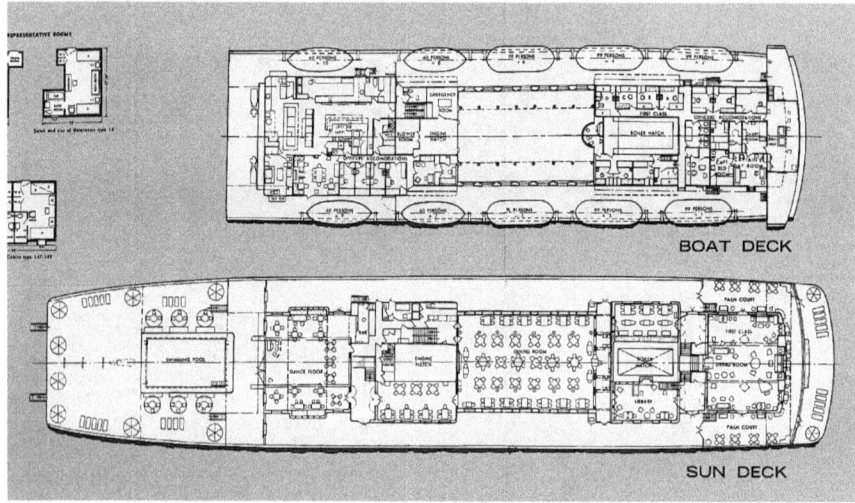

Part of a passenger's deck plan issued by the Typaldos Lines for the *Athinai* showing the sun deck, otherwise known as the promenade deck, and the location of the large dining room that would be turned into *Titanic*'s fictional ballroom. *(Author's collection)*

The elegant surroundings of the 1st class dining room when the liner originally operated as the S.S. *Santa Rosa* for the Grace Line. Seating 149 passengers, the one special feature was that a section of the dining room roof could be slid backwards to allow passengers to dine under the stars. *(Author's collection)*

Chapter 14: The Other *Titanic* • **461**

This period postcard shows the beautiful architecture of the dining room that made it such a focal point for elegant dining during a voyage. *(Author's collection)*

The aft wall of the dining room featured a large painting of the sailing vessel *W.R. Grace*, the first ship registered to sail under the Grace Line & Co and named after the owner, William Russel. *(Author's collection)*

The dining room in the early 1960s when the liner was operating as the *Athinai*. Note the addition of a balcony where musicians have assembled to play to the dining passengers below. *(Author's collection)*

These slightly blurred photographs were taken when *Athinai* was finally obtained by ITC for the production of *Raise the Titanic*. Even after twelve-years of being abandoned, the dining room was still in a useable state as if it were waiting for ships stewards to arrive and lay the tables for dinner. Just a few weeks later as the *Athinai* sat at Dock 12 this room would undergo a major transformation at the hands of the special effect's artists into something haunting yet strangely beautiful. *(Author's collection)*

```
TO:   JERRY JAMESON, DIRECTOR
      BILL FRYE, PRODUCER
      DICK O'CONNOR, EXECUTIVE PRODUCER

FROM: JOHN DE CUIR, PRODUCTION DESIGN
                   CONSULTANT

      AS PER OUR DISCUSSION ABOUT THE SHOOTING OF THE TITANIC SEQUENCES
IN ATHENS ON THE SHIP "ATHENA", IT BECAME EVIDENT THAT CERTAIN ITEMS
WERE ESSENTIAL.  THEY ARE LISTED BELOW, AS ADDITIONS TO PREVIOUS TWO TELEXES:
   A. FORTY FOOT VERTICAL BULK HEAD SECTION OF VERTICAL WALL
      AFT OF THE WELL DECK WITH LADDERS FOR FOURTH WALL FRAMING
      OF ALL SHOTS ON THE WELL DECK, AND TO ACCOMODATE PITT'S
      WALK TO THE JACK STAFF WHERE HE HANGS THE PENNANT.

   B. EIGHT FOOT STRIP OF HULL PAINTED AND AGED SHOULD BE PLACED
      FROM THE TOP RAIL DOWN ALONG THE WELL DECK.

   C. FOR THE HANGING OF THE PENNANT, A TWENTY FOOT SECTION OF
      THE EXTREME STERN DECK SHOULD BE PAINTED AND DRESSED.

   D. THERE SHOULD BE TEMPORARY SHORING UNDER FILLED-IN DECK OF THE
      SWIMMING POOL TO ACCOMODATE THE HELICOPTER'S LANDINGS AND
      TAKE-OFFS.

   E. THE AFT DOORS ADJOINING THE WELL DECK SHOULD BE PREPARED SO
      THAT ENTRANCES AND EXITS FROM THE WELL DECK CAN BE TIED TO
      THE LARGE SALON.  THESE SAME DOOR UNITS WILL DOUBLE AS THE
      FOURTH WALL OF THE GRAND SALON SO THAT ENTRANCES AND EXITS
      CAN BE MADE INTO THIS AREA.

   F. PAINTING AND DRESSING OF THREE INTERIOR ROOMS: FORWARD PALM COURT
      ROOM, LIBRARY AND WRITING ROOM, GRAND SALON.
```

This John DeCuir letter was sent to Jerry Jameson and covered what was needed to be done with interior areas and set pieces, including the building of the stern hull piece and the aging and dressing of the *Athinai's* living room, library and dining room. *(Author's collection)*

Chapter 14: The Other *Titanic* • 463

Pitt gazes into the wrecked interior of the *Titanic* as he becomes the first man to step foot on board the legendary liner after 68 years. However, contrary to popular belief, this room is not the liner's fictional ballroom but that of the lounge which was the aged living room of the *Athinai* before moving aft into the ballroom with staircase. *(ITC – Author's collection)*

The stately 1st class living room on *Athinai* as photographed in February 1979. *(Author's collection)*

The living room after its transformation into the *Titanic*. The large windows look out onto the palm court deck that faces directly out over the bow. The window to the far left of the photograph looked out onto the portside area of the palm court. *(Author's collection)*

This wide view of the living room is looking directly towards the portside with the open doors revealing the concrete covered palm court deck. The fireplace was still present including the painting on the wall that the FX department have covered in concrete and paint. *(Author's collection)*

The starboard enclosed section of the palm court deck in February 1979. Note the rectangular windows to the right that would later be aged and caught on camera as Pitt prepares to walk into the room. *(Author's collection)*

In this shot of Pitt entering the lounge, the windows to the enclosed section of the starboard palm court deck is clearly visible. *(ITC/ITV Studios)*

In this close-up can be seen a section of wooden trellis that was used on the promenade deck of the *Athinai* to disguise a number of exposed pipes that were fixed to the underside of the boat deck. *(ITC – Author's collection)*

BELOW: The ballroom of the *Titanic*. This view is looking from the portside over towards the starboard side of the vessel and forwards towards the bow. Behind the wall with the balcony was the boiler uptake, a large open shaft where the first funnel sat and passed down to the boiler rooms below. *(Author's collection)*

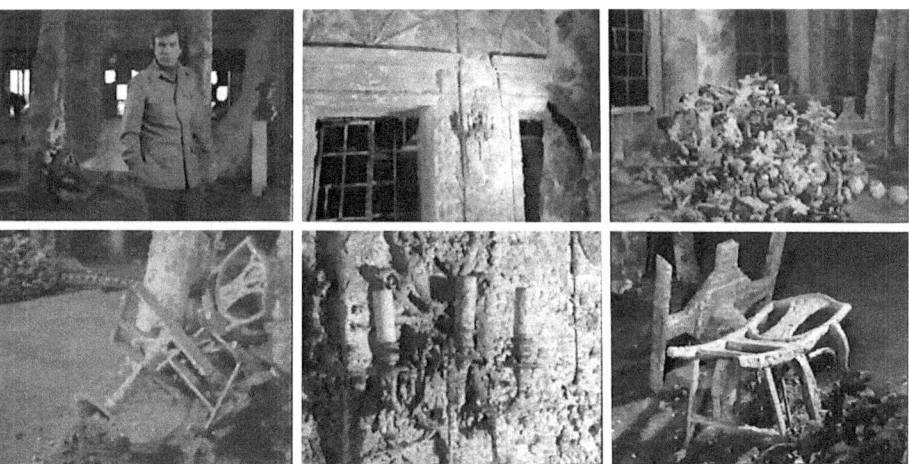

Television presenter and producer Doug Llewelyn takes a small tour around the converted dining room for the ITC promotional film. *(ITC / The Last Great Human Adventure promotional film – Author's collection)*

466 • *Raise The Titanic*

This still from the production reveals one of the water drainage pipes that rained water down from above. A hose connected to a water pump out on deck was passed through a removed pane of glass in the circular window and fixed to a stationary pipe with holes drilled into the metal. The set-up was duplicated in varying locations around the dining room. *(Author's collection)*

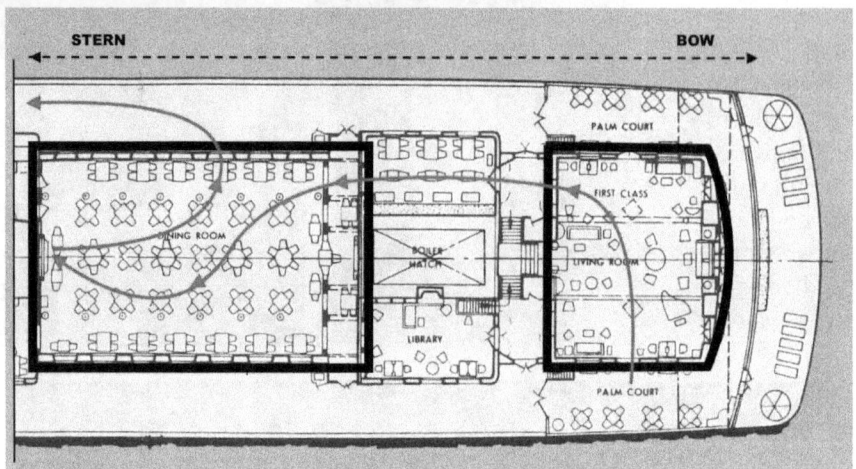

This plan of the *Athinai* has been edited to show the route that Richard Jordan (Pitt) took as he travelled back in time to marvel at the long-lost beauty of the *Titanic*. *(Edited by Jonathan Smith)*

```
THIS APPROACH HAS BEEN DEVELOPED TO REGAIN THE SCALE AND THE
MAGNITUDE OF THE TITANIC WHICH WE FELT HAD BEEN LOST THROUGH CERTAIN
SET CONSTRUCTION ELIMINATIONS.  IN THE FOLLOWING WE ARE LISTING THOSE
SHOTS AND THE SCENE NUMBERS WHICH WILL BE INVOLVED.

    A.  A GLASS SHOT POSITIONED ON THE PORT SIDE OF THE AFTER
        WELL DECK SHOOTING FORWARD.  THIS SHOT WILL GIVE US FULL
        SUPER STRUCTURE FOUR DECKS HIGH PLUS THE THREE REMAINING
        FUNNELS, AND WILL BE ON A NODAL MOUNT GIVING US THE OPPORTUNITY
        OF PANNING AND TILTING.    (Sc: 319, 322A, 367)

    B.  A GLASS SHOT POSITIONED ON THE STARBOARD SIDE OF THE BOW
        DECK SHOOTING AFT.  THIS WILL GIVE US THE FULL FACE OF THE
        BRIDGE, PLUS THE THREE FUNNELS.  (Sc: 323, 338, 362, lead in 382)

    C.  A GLASS SHOT HIGH ON THE PORT SIDE OF THE GRAND SALON GIVING
                                                       Sc:
        US THE FOURTH WALL WHICH WOULD BE THE GRAND STAIR CASE.  (319, 328,345, 391)

    D.  A GLASS SHOT REPRESENTING NEW YORK HARBOUR WITH THE TITANIC
        AT THE DOCK...SKYSCRAPERS IN THE BACKGROUND...GENERAL DRESSING
        AND EXCITEMENT IN THE SURROUNDINGS.   (Sc: 384, 385, 386)
```

Part of a telex sent from John DeCuir in Piraeus to Jerry Jameson and dated 20 November, 1979. The correspondence covers matte works that would replace the rejected and expensive full-scale sets. What is of particular interest is item "C" that indicates *Titanic*'s grand staircase was originally to be created as a large glass matte. *(Author's collection)*

Pimlico Films Limited

a subsidiary of Associated TeleVision Corporation Limited

ATV House
17 Great Cumberland Place
London W1A 1AG
telephone 01-262 8040

Directors
Lord Grade
B J Kingham

M E M O

TO: MALCOLM CHRISTOPHER

FROM: RAY FRIFT

DATE: 25th November 1979

RE: JOHN DE CUIR'S VISIT TO ATHENS FRIDAY 23RD NOVEMBER - SUNDAY 25TH NOVEMBER

1. MATTE OR GLASS SHOTS

    6 - 8 will be required.

2. To get the matte shots two 8' overhangs which will involve metal work to be built on the boat. One of these will be from the well deck aft-portside. The other one will be starboard side, bow end. Also, the port side aft end, we will require to remove the railing approximately 30' and it will have to bent out behind the 8' overhang.

3. The hanging miniature for the Grand Staircase for the Grand Salon.

    For this we will require a draughtsman and two model makers.

4. NEW YORK SEQUENCES

    They are still as they are in the script but not according to the schedule. The major sequence, according to the schedule, was to be played in the Salon. John de Cuir now tells me that it will be as per the script which means to say we will require to take the boat into the Customs area at Piraeus. This will involve quite a lot of dressing and probably 200 or 300 extras.

5. For all the exterior shots we will require the American type tugs plus various other fire boats etc.

Three days later the response from the film studio was to go ahead with building a large-scale miniature of the grand staircase and the continuation of other works on board. *(Author's collection)*

SFX PRODUCTION SHOTS ON THE ATHINAI

1. **EXT. STERN SHOOTING FORWARD TOWARDS BOW (CHOPPER SHOTS)**

    a) Pitt's walk across deck with or without Chopper

    b) Prevlov's arrival and departure (already shot)

    c) Pitt meets Seagram after hanging pennant.

2. **STERN SHOOTING AFT**

    a) After pennant has been hung Pitt meets Seagram and has dialogue.

3. **BOW SHOT LOOKING AFT TOWARDS THE BRIDGE INCLUDING HATCH COVER**

    a) Off left side - water up ?

    b) Chopper down to hatch   ?

4) **HANGING MINIATURE IN GRAND SALON**

    a) Pitt's walk through water and slush (already shot)

    b) Cleaned up and dressed version with the Navy equipment set up in the room.

    c) Miniature model moved to new position on the floor (Night ?) Discussion at table - Postcard (Low Set Up)

    d) Shooting P.O.V. Pitt from third step looking up at dome (Possible matte work)

These shots are to be completed shots on the Athinai with no further studio optical work necessary except for possibly 4 (d).

Athinai

NP

218500 DDFP GR

847505 PINEWD G
23 10 79

ATTN: RAY FRIFT C/O DIMITRI DIMITRIADES

TO CONFIRM OUR TELEPHONE CONVERSATION THIS MORNING. I HAVE NOW BEEN INSTRUCTED BY DICK O'CONNOR (I IMAGINE WITH PRIOR CONSULTATION WITH THE DIRECTOR AND PRODUCTION DESIGNER) THAT YOU MAY PROCEED WITH THE FOLLOWING METALWORK ON THE SHIP:-

1) CUT OFF REAR MAST AT DECK LEVEL
2) CUT OFF AWNING STANCHIONS ON REAR DECK
3) CUT OFF EXISTING CANOPY OVER BAR ENTRANCE
4) SWIMMING POOL COVER TO BE CONSTRUCTED OUT OF TIMBER
   AS CHEAPLY AS POSSIBLE.
   NOTE: THE HELICOPTER DOES NOT LAND BUT HOVERS OVER THE REAR DECK
----
5) CONSTRUCT 3/4 ROUND REAR FUNNEL (AROUND EXISTING FUNNEL)
6) REMOVE TWO REAR STARICASES AND REFIT FROM PROMENADE DECK TO
   BOAT DECK.
7) REMOVE DAVIT POSTS AND DAVITS NEAREST TO BOAT DECK.

REMAINING COSTS - FLOATING CRANE, STAGING, FIRE GANG, SUPERVISING AND UNFORESEEN EXPENSES (10 PERCENT) - I IMAGINE WILL BE REDUCED IN PROPORTION.

THIS IS NOW THE PROPOSED SHOOTING SCHEDULE (AS OF 22.10.79):-

```
FLY FROM USA AND/OR UK TO ATHENS      12/13 DECEMBER
PREPARATION DAY                          14 DECEMBER
SHOOT (ATHENS)                        15/21 DECEMBER (INC)
FLY UK                                   22 DECEMBER
XMAS HOLIDAY                          23/26 DECEMBER (INC)
FLY UK - ATHENS                          27 DECEMBER
SHOOT ATHENS                          28/29 DECEMBER
REST DAY                                 30 DECEMBER
TRAVEL UK                                31 DECEMBER
REST DAY                                  1 JANUARY
FLY CORNWALL                              2 JANUARY
SHOOT CORNWALL                          3/6 JANUARY (INC)
TRAVEL CORNWALL/LONDON                    7 JANUARY
```

(HOW MUCH DO YOU BET THAT CHANGES BY TONIGHT - PENNY)

LOVE TO ALL,

MALCOLM.

847505 PINEWD G

218500 DDFP GR

470 • *Raise The Titanic*

The large scale model of the grand staircase. *(ITC – Author's collection)*

Another comparison, this time the bronze cherub holding the light fitting atop of the staircase newel post. *(Author's collection)*

BELOW: Close up of the *Honour & Glory Crowning Time* carving on the miniature in comparison with the original. *(Author's collection)*

Two cleaned up stills from the production that show the fine detail incorporated into the grand staircase miniature. *(ITC/ITV Studios)*

The grand staircase model photographed from the nodal point where the foreground miniature and the background align. *(ITC – Author's collection)*

The staircase miniature fixed to the wooden framework that was then anchored in place and suspended from the barrel ceiling of the dining room on board the *Athinai*. *(ITC – Author's collection & Ken Marschall collection)*

The only known photograph that shows the partial full-scale staircase set built against the rear wall of the dining room; the same wall that once displayed the large painting of the sailing vessel *W.R. Grace*. The camera angle was tight as little room was to spare for the camera unit that set up the rig to the right of the set piece. *(ITC – Author's collection)*

Dirk Pitt pauses at the bottom of the grand staircase to look up at the damaged but still ornate wrought iron and glass dome. In reality Richard Jordan was looking at the blank wall of the dining room that was just a couple of feet in front of him. *(ITC/ITV Studios)*

This still from the ITC publicity film features presenter and producer Doug Llewelyn in front of the staircase set. Note that this area of the dining room had not been aged as the walls still maintain clean paint. *(ITC / The Last Great Human Adventure promotional film – Author's collection)*

Chapter 14: The Other *Titanic* • **473**

Doug Llewelyn stands at the foot of the staircase set. *(ITC / The Last Great Human Adventure promotional film – Author's collection)*

Prevlov (Bo Brundin) delivers his threats to Sandecker, Pitt and Seagram after revealing that he is aware that American agents stole materials from a Russian island and that the consequences, nearly 70 years later, come with punishment. *(ITC – Author's collection)*

Sandecker delivers the shocking truth to Seagram about the governments *other* plans in using the Byzanium. *(ITC – Author's collection)*

"A dead man and seven boxes of gravel." After all the lives lost; the money involved and the efforts to achieve what was deemed the impossible, the vault in *Titanic*'s cargo hold reveals such a tragic irony. *(ITC – Author's collection)*

Chapter 14: The Other *Titanic* • 475

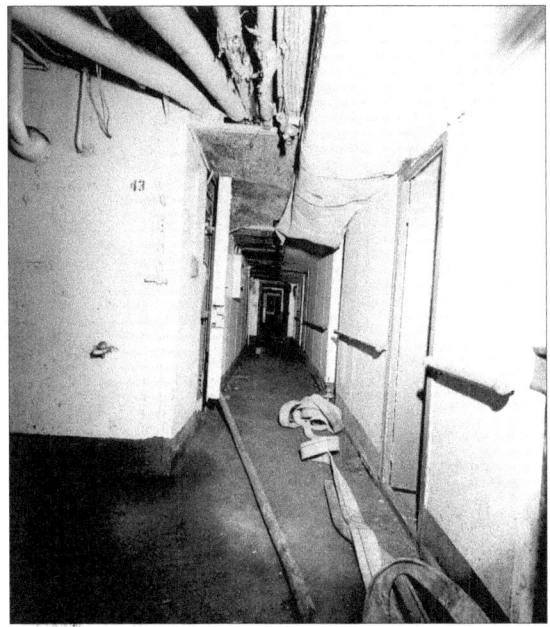

During the tour of the *Athinai* in February 1979, representatives for ITC started photographing areas of the liner for consideration for the production. From those interior photographs taken were crew areas that could be repainted and dressed. This corridor down on C deck was part of the berthing quarters for crew members. *(Author's collection)*

The search has come to an end. Just forwards on the starboard side of C deck, in the crew area, a large room is found that can double as part of the cargo hold. *(Author's collection)*

What is lying in wait behind those large sliding wooden doors? *(Author's collection)*

The location of *Titanic*'s cargo hold containing Brewster's vault was the *Athinai*'s former laundry room. Much of the items left within the room ended up being sprayed over with concrete and gallons of paint. *(Author's collection)*

476 • Raise The Titanic

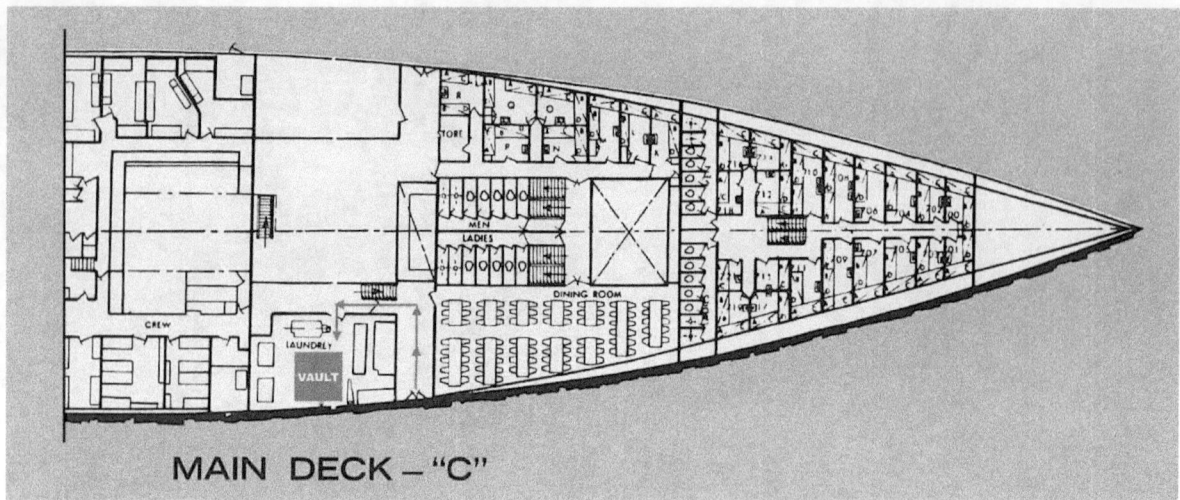

This original plan of the *Athinai* from the 1960s shows the location of the laundry room and edited to include Brewster's vault. *(Author's collection)*

Looking from inside the cargo hold (laundry room) out towards the crew corridor. The area has been heavily dressed in concrete, FX paint and, more noticeably, vast amounts of construction foam that was to represent the salvage foam pumped down into the lower holds of the *Titanic*. The foam used was toxic, causing headaches and nausea. Filming in such confined areas had to be kept short so that the actors and crew could escape to the exterior to get some fresh air before returning back inside again. *(ITC/ITV Studios)*

Behind the scenes on filming the opening up of Brewster's vault. With the door now open, the actors get back into character with David Selby heading first into the vault. The vault itself measured 8-feet-square and was made of metal and wood. The set piece was made in sections, like a flat-pack, that was brought aboard the *Athinai* and bolted together inside the laundry room. *(Author's collection)*

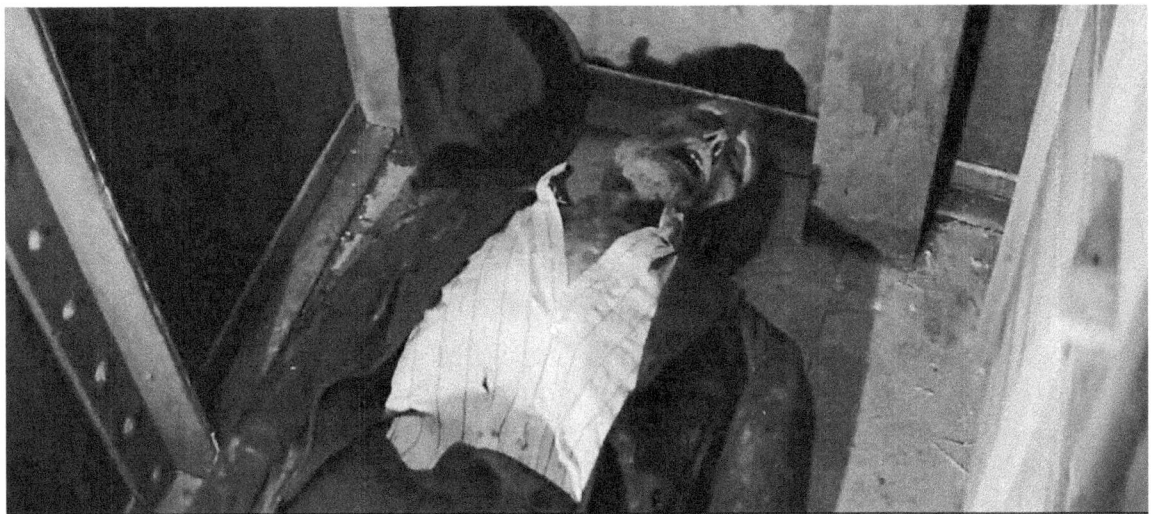
"And here lies Arthur Brewster. Sunk with the *Titanic*!" *(ITC/ITV Studios)*

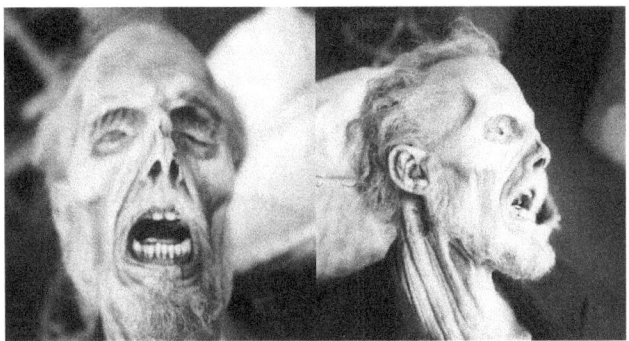
Only a face that a sculptor could love. The amazing work of The Burman's Studio of California on the life size mannequin of Brewster. *(Original Polaroids – Author's collection)*

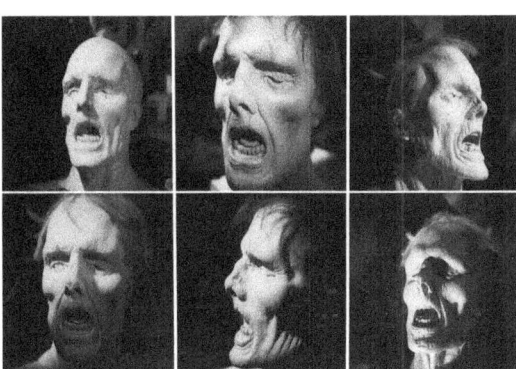
Early version of Brewster during stages of sculpt at The Burman's Studio. *(Original Polaroids – Author's collection)*

After recovering the personal artefacts from Brewster's body, Pitt goes through the relics and stumbles upon a familiar name within the fine print on the back of a picture postcard. *(ITC/ITV Studios)*

> FROM RAY FRIFT   Athinai
>
> FURTHER TO OUR CONVERSATION LAST EVENING THE FOLLOWING IS THE TELEX RECEIVED FROM DIMITRI:
>
> QUOTE:
>
> 30.1.80
>
> FROM: DIMITRI DIMITRIADIS
> TO: MALCOLM CHRISTOPHER/RAY FRIFT
>
> PLEASE BE ADVISED THAT WE RECEIVED THE FOLLOWING TLXES FROM VERNICOS TSAVLIRIS CONSORTIUM PIRAEUS:
>
> QUOTE
>
> NO 62/FC/MK   28.1.80   12.35HRS
>
> THIS IS VERNICOS TSAVLIRIS CONSORTIUM PIRAEUS
>
> M/V 'ATHINAI' (TITANICOS)
>
> THIS IS TO ADVISE YOU THAT OUR T/B PERSEUS SUSTAINED DAMAGE TO HER PROPELLOR DURING THE TOWAGE OF YOUR ABOVE VESSEL FROM KALAMAKI TO ELEUSIS BAY, ON THE 19TH OF JAN 1980 AT 17.30HRS. AS PER THE TOWAGE CONDITIONS WE REGRETFULLY HOLD YOU RESPONSIBLE AND WILL ADVISE YOU TO APPOINT YOUR SURVEYOR TO ATTEND THE NECESSARY REPAIRS IN DUE COURSES
>
> REGARDS
> VERNICOS/TSAVLIRIS
>
> UNQUOTE

The telex that ITC really didn't need. As disputes continued over the charter of the *Athinai*, news comes in that during the transfer of the vessel from ITC back to the owners, the towage from the Port of Piraeus to her final drop-off point resulted in an accident between the *Athinai* and the tug *Perseus* out in the waters of Eleusis Bay ending with damage sustained to the tugs propeller. *(Author's collection)*

Marbarch Insurance Services Limited
a subsidiary of
Associated Communications Corporation Limited

ACC House
17 Great Cumberland Place
London W1A 1AG
telephone 01-262 8040

cables and telegrams
Ayteevee London W1
telex 23762

Directors
J F Gill CBE
D S Williams
R A Muckleston

M Christopher
Pimlico Films
Pinewood Studios

7th February 1980

Dear Malcolm,

M/V ATHENAI

Following our various conversations with yourself and Ray ~~Thrift~~ FRIFT, I confirm that although there is cover under the marine policy we effected for Athenai, in respect of any liability arising under a towage contract it will be necessary to satisfy underwriters that a contract existed and if this claim is pressed by Vernicos you will then have to invite him without comment on your part to state in writing under what contract conditions he was towing.

I am hoping that, however, between the marine surveyor and yourself this claim will not be pressed home.

It would however be helpful for you to let me know what might be involved in cash terms.

Yours sincerely,

PHILIP BLOY
Manager

Correspondence from the insurance company to ITC, 7 February, 1980, with the company manager Philip Bloy expressing that regardless of what the towing company states, the film company is not liable for any claims; but be prepared just in case. *(Author's collection)*

```
847505 PINEWD G
212753 GEPA GR

27TH FEB 1980

ATTN MALCOM CHRISTOPHER - RAISE THE TITANIC

TUG 'PERSEUS'
-------------

FURTHER OUR TX 15/2/80 AND TELCONS HAVE NOW SIGHTED A DAMAGED
PROPELLER STATED TO HAVE BEEN REMOVED FROM THE ABOVE VESSEL, AND
HAVING ONE BLADE COMPLETELY MISSING. THIS PROPELLER CAN ONLY
BE SCRAPPED THEREFORE AND A NEW ONE SUPPLIED. A SPARE HAS BEEN
FITTED TO THE TUG AND IT IS BACK IN SERVICE.
AM NOW AWAITING FULL DETAILS OF THE INCIDENT I.E. TUGMASTER'S
REPORT ETC. AND WILL REPORT IN FULL IN DUE COURSE. FOR INFO
THE COSTS OF REPLACING THE TUGS PROPELLER BY SPARE (DRYDOCKING)
WAS ABOUT US DOLLARS 2000. QUOTATION FOR REPLACEMENT PROPELLER
BEING OBTAINED.

BEST REGARDS
CHRIS FYANS
GERALD GEDDES AND PARTNERS, PIRAEUS.

212753 GEPA GR
847505 PINEWD GT
```

Another telex sent to ITC that mentions that the damage sustained to the tug's propeller was severe enough that a complete blade had been lost. The tug would then be required for dry docking and a completely new replacement propeller. *(Author's collection)*

Pimlico Films Limited
a subsidiary of Associated TeleVision Corporation Limited

ATV House
17 Great Cumberland Place
London W1A 1AG
telephone 01-262 8040

Directors
Lord Grade
B J Kingham

Agents for:
MARBLE ARCH PRODUCTIONS INC.   29th February, 1980

                         FROM: MALCOLM CHRISTOPHER

TO: PHILIP BLOY
    BERNARD KINGHAM
    RON COOK
    copy retained for file

I am enclosing herewith the following relevant documents regarding the various claims received from Greece, subsequent to our shooting on location with the ship "Athinai":-

(1) Insurance Claim for damage to the tug "Perseus" with relevant telexes and replies.

(2) Decision of the Hellenic Court re. charter of the ship "Athinai".

(3) Judgement of the Piraeus Distric Court re. the charter of the ship "Athinai".

(4) Contract in Greek duly signed by Malcolm Christopher and Emmanuel Vernicos.

(4)A English translation of the above (3) duly notarised.

   Note: Page one of the contract is for five <u>years</u> and not five <u>months</u> - one wonders whether this is a true translation?

(5) Insurance claim dated 25th February for £40,000 and the telex of redelivery. (5A)

(6) Cheque for the £120,000 for the charter period and the Greek acceptance of same. Please note that Emmanuel Vernicos, the Receiver for the Typaldos Brothers also received a £30,000 "kick-back" that was paid to his nephew's Company who are owners of the tug "Perseus" in question.

MALCOLM CHRISTOPHER

Registered Office: ATV House 17 Great Cumberland Place London W1A 1AG
Registered in England No. 482139

29 February 1980, and the problems keep mounting up for ITC as the Athens fiasco continues. *(Author's collection)*

Halsey Marine International Charters Limited

22 Boston Place, Dorset Square, London NW1 6HZ.
Telephone: 01-724 1303.
TELEX: 265131 HALSEY G.   CABLES: HALSEYOT LONDON NW1.

21st April 1980   HDH/CJ/CH

Malcolm Christopher, Esq.,
"Raise the Titanic",
c#o Pinewood Studios,
Elstree,
Herts.

Dear Malcolm,

Following our meeting last week, I gather that Harry has received the relevant letters. I am accordingly returning a cheque for Pds.1,500 together with our invoice for Pds.3,500 which has been paid, which now balances the accounts between us.

I am very glad that Harry has offered to try and sort out the problems you are left with in Athens as this hopefully will prove beyond any shadow of a doubt the importance of professional brokers assistance in negotiating the hire of ships and yachts.

Hoping that you are feeling better.

Yours sincerely,

David Halsey
Managing Director

Director: David Halsey, Registered in London. Regd. Office: 18 Charing Cross Road, London, W.C.2. No. 1387744

21 April 1980, and a light is finally seen at the end of the tunnel. *(Author's collection)*

The year is 1985 and the *Athinai* still sits in the spot where she was ditched following the collision with the tugboat *Perseus* on the 28 January 1980. After five years, the ship still retains some of the sets built for *Raise the Titanic*. *(Author's collection)*

The *Athinai* shortly after being abandoned. *(Author's collection)*

LEFT AND ABOVE: The *Athinai* makes her final journey to the breaker's yards in Aliağa in Turkey. *(Photographs © Selim San)*

RAISE THE TITANIC
Piraeus harbour
Greece
Dec 1979 - Jan 1980

Pic. 1

Pic. 2

Pic. 3

Pic. 4

Pic. 5

Pic. 6

Pic. 7

New York comes to Greece

The next few pages are a rare glimpse into the filming at the port of Piraeus when the *Raise the Titanic* film production came to Greece for a couple of weeks shooting between late December 1979 into early January 1980. The images, actually stills taken from a rare private Super8 reel, was filmed by Nicolas A. Vernicos whose father was the owner of the tug haulage company Vernicos that towed the *Athinai* in and out of the waters of Piraeus during filming on the production. Probably thought not of much importance back in 1980, today the footage reveals a part of the production that is not so widely available to the public as no official making of documentary or published behind the scenes books or magazines covered the subject until recent times. The following stills provide a brief glimpse to what was happening behind the cameras and the efforts the film crews undertook to recreate the wreck of the *Titanic*. The complete 6-minute silent film is available to watch on the official website of Aylon Film Archives at *www.aylonfilmarchives.com*.

(1) The port side bow of the *Athinai* as the former liner rests at Dock 12. Off to the ships starboard side is the tug boat *Vernicos 1*. (2) This view looking up at the distressed port side superstructure has the gangway in view that was used for crew to pass between ship and the Passenger Station. It was from this spot where the scene of Pitt (Richard Jordan) complains about being in "distress" as the hurricane approaches. (3) The Buick that belonged to Vernicos family that underwent a transformation into a New York police car. (4) Looking towards the stern of the *Athinai/Titanic* from the quay side of Dock 12. Here can be seen the full scale (in width) set of the stern set of the *Titanic* that is secured in place. (5) The Passenger Station viewing gallery as seen from the promenade deck of the *Athinai/Titanic*. (6) After handing the film camera over to someone else, Nicolas A. Vernicos poses with family members and crew on the stern set of *Titanic*. (7) Now back in charge of the camera, Nicolas captures this view of the stern set. The cowl vent was one of the units that was removed from the ships bow and brought over to the stern to replicate some of the *Titanic's* features. The reader may be interested to know that directly beneath the feet of the men is the false steel and timbered deck that covers the ships former swimming pool. *(All images © Nicolas A. Vernicos / Aylon Film Archives)*

486 • *Raise The Titanic*

Pic. 8

Pic. 9

Pic. 10

Pic. 11

Pic. 12

Pic. 13

Chapter 14: The Other *Titanic* • 487

Pic. 14

Pic. 15

Pic. 16

Pic. 17

(8) Director Jerry Jameson (right) with Jason Robards on the stern set of *Titanic*. Behind them is the starboards stairs up to the 3rd class poop deck. Just visible under the cover is one of the wind machines that was used for scenes depicting the hurricane. (9) Looking over to the starboard side of the stern *Titanic* set as a press helicopter comes into view. (10) Viewed from the roof of the Passenger Station, this stern view of the *Athinai* reveals the raised *Titanic* set and the scaffolding tower that contained a stern flag pole. (11) Nicolas has turned the camera towards the *Titanic* stern set built up around the aft end of the *Athinai*'s superstructure. (12) A rare view looking towards the aft wall of the dining room of the *Athinai* with the lower section of *Titanic*'s Grand Staircase with cherub. (13) The concrete covered interior of the dining room. The peculiar object to the left is a light diffuser. (14) This shot looking directly up at the wall and ceiling of the dining room reveals a set prop that was never filmed in use; a section of damaged and collapsed staircase dome metal frame. (15) Hidden beneath all those layers of concrete and FX paint was the once gleaming white paint of the dining room. (16) and (17) the sediment covered remains of furniture in the living room of the *Athinai/Titanic*. *(All images © Nicolas A. Vernicos / Aylon Film Archives)*

Pic. 18

Pic. 19

Pic. 20

(18) and (19) With tugs at her side, the *Athinai/Titanic* is pulled out backwards into the open waters of Piraeus port as the ship is made ready to be towed out to the shallow coastal waters for a number of scenes that were to represent the raised *Titanic* moments after salvage as Pitt boards the wreck, the arrival by helicopter of Prevlov and views of *Titanic* as she is towed towards New York with tugs. (20) A rare uninterrupted view into the production-built Arthur Brewster's vault and the seven wooden crates that contain Brewster's deadly and costly secret. *(All images © Nicolas A. Vernicos / Aylon Film Archives)*

First they said God Himself couldn't sink her.

Then they said no man on earth could reach her.

Now – Go to Volume Two to see how they will...

Bibliography

Ballard, Robert D., *The Discovery of the Titanic*, Madison Press Books, Canada, 1987

Bottomore, Stephen, *The Titanic and Silent Cinema*, The Projection Box, UK, 2000

Chester, Lewis, *All My Shows Are Great: The Life of Lew Grade*, Aurum Press Ltd, London, 2010

Cussler, Clive, *Raise the Titanic*, The Viking Press, New York, 1976

Davis, Clifford, *How I Made Lew Grade a Millionaire and Other Fables*, Mirror Books, London, 1981

Delfont, Bernard, *Bernard Delfont Presents East End, West End*, Macmillian Publishers, London, 1990

Falk, Quentin & Prince, Dominic, *Last of a Kind: The Sinking of Lew Grade*, Quartet Books Ltd, London, 1987

Grade, Lew, *Still Dancing*, William Collins Sons & Co, London, 1987

Grimm, Jack & Hoffman, William, *Beyond Reach: The Search for The Titanic*, Paul Harris Publishing, Edinburgh, 1981

Kramer, Stanley, *A Mad, Mad, Mad, Mad World: A Life in Hollywood*, Aurum Press Ltd, London, 1998

Leonard, Geoff, *John Barry: The Man with the Midas Touch*, Redcliffe Press Ltd, Bristol, UK, 2008

Mills, Simon, *The Titanic in Pictures*, Wordsmith Publications, Buckinghamshire, UK, 1995

Parks, James, *A Day at the Bottom of the Sea*, Crane, Russel & Company, New York, 1977

Read, Piers Paul, *Alec Guinness: The Authorised Biography*, Simon & Schuster UK Ltd, London, 2003

Richardson, John, *Making Movie Magic: A Lifetime Creating Special Effects for James Bond, Harry Potter, Superman & More*, The History Press, Gloucestershire, UK, 2019

Suid, Lawrence H, *Guts & Glory: The Making of the American Military Image in Film*, The University Press of Kentucky, 2002

Suid, Lawrence H, *Sailing on the Silver Screen: Hollywood and the U.S. Navy*, Naval Institute Press, Maryland, 1996

Nesmeyanov, Eugene, *The Titanic Expeditions: Diving to the Queen of the Deep 1985 – 2010*, The History Press, Gloucestershire, UK, 2018

Websites & Organisations

www.raisethetitanic.co.uk
www.maltafilmcommission.com
www.cusslersociety.com
www.cusslermuseum.com
www.hunley.org
www.kenmarschall.com
www.drewstruzan.com
www.titanichistoricalsociety.org

www.britishtitanicsociety.com
www.titanicverein.ch
www.titanicinternationalsociety.org
www.seacitymuseum.co.uk
www.titanicbelfast.com
www.nmni.com
www.pcpmalta.com
www.aylonfilmarchives.com

LIMITED EDITION  **COLLECTOR'S PACK**

THE MAKING OF THE MOVIE
RAISE THE TITANIC

Once they said God himself couldn't sink her. Then they said no man on earth could reach her. Now --- you are finally here to see the raising of the legendary ocean liner. To accompany the release of RAISE THE TITANIC: The Making of the Movie, Titanic historian and author Jonathan Smith has selected a number of rare items from his personal archive and reproduced them for film fans, collector's and Titanic enthusiasts. This deluxe collector's set features a number of reproductions taken from the original ephemera in the authors collection and highlights a part of the movies production from 1976 to 1980 that was not widely available to the public.

RAISE THE TITANIC: The Making of the Movie Collector's Edition is strictly limited to only 500 sets world-wide, making it a cherished collectible with an interest in the old days of movie making, special effects and Titanic on film that fans can enjoy for years to come.

CONTENTS

- Specialty bookplate signed by the author, numbered, embossed and ink stamped
- Collector's Edition sticker that can be attached to the cover of the book
- Set of 10 behind the scenes images from the production of Raise the Titanic
- National Underwater Marine Agency (NUMA) salvage operations identification card
- Letter sent from the book publisher Viking Press to Raise the Titanic author Clive Cussler announcing that his novel is going to be published
- Colour publicity card from 1980 of the raising of the Titanic
- 1979/80 ITC film crew equipment tie-on tag
- Film logo vinyl sticker
- Arthur Brewster's 1912 "Thank God for Southby" postcard
- UK cinema front-of-house promotional poster art card
- Viking Press Raise the Titanic book publishers trade information card from 1976
- U.S insert poster design collector's card # 1 (raising Titanic)
- U.S insert poster design collector's card # 2 (seabed Titanic)
- 1977 Raise the Titanic bookmarker design collector's card # 3
- 1980 Bantam Books Clive Cussler novels bookmarker design collector's card # 4
- 2021 Raise the Titanic raising wreck collector's card # 5
- 1978 "A PROJECT TO STAGGER THE IMAGINATION" advanced ITC promotional print
- 1980 storyboard depicting the discovery of the Titanic in the movie
- Deleted sinking scene from the film's intended 1912 prologue
- Hydrozene salvage tank schematic
- Admiral Sandecker's press conference Titanic profile plan
- July 30, 1980 World Premiere ticket for Raise the Titanic

ORDER YOURS TODAY AT

www.raisethetitanic.co.uk

www.ingramcontent.com/pod-product-compliance
Lightning Source LLC
Chambersburg PA
CBHW060502300426
44112CB00017B/2526